Cutting-Edge
Social Media Approaches
to Business Education

Teaching With LinkedIn, Facebook, Twitter, Second Life, and Blogs

A volume in
Research in Management Education and Development

Series Editor:
Charles Wankel, *St. John's University*

Research in Management Education and Development

Charles Wankel, Series Editor

Rethinking Management Education for the 21st Century (2002)
edited by Charles Wankel and Robert DeFillippi

Educating Managers With Tomorrow's Technologies (2003)
edited by Charles Wankel and Robert DeFillippi

Educating Managers Through Real World Projects (2005)
edited by Charles Wankel and Robert DeFillippi

The Cutting Edge of International Management Education (2006)
edited by Charles Wankel and Robert DeFillippi

New Visions of Graduate Management Education (2006)
edited by Charles Wankel and Robert DeFillippi

University and Corporate Innovations in Lifelong Learning (2008)
edited by Charles Wankel and Robert DeFillippi

Management Education for Global Sustainability (2009)
edited by Charles Wankel and James A.F. Stoner

Emerging Ethical Issues of Life in Virtual Worlds (2010)
edited by Charles Wankel and Shaun Malleck

Being and Becoming a Management Education Scholar (2010)
edited by Charles Wankel and Robert DeFillippi

Cutting-Edge Social Media Approaches to Business Education

Teaching With LinkedIn, Facebook, Twitter, Second Life, and Blogs

edited by

Charles Wankel
St. John's University

in collaboration with
Matthew Marovich and Jurate Stanaityte

Information Age Publishing, Inc.
Charlotte, North Carolina • www.infoagepub.com

Library of Congress Cataloging-in-Publication Data

ISBNs:
  Paperback: 978-1-61735-116-7
  Hardcover: 978-1-61735-117-4
  eBook: 978-1-61735-118-1

Printed in the United States of America

CONTENTS

1. Technologies That Bring Learners Collaboratively
   Together With the World
   Charles Wankel *1*

2. Defining Interactive Social Media
   in an Educational Context
   Aditi Grover and David W. Stewart 7

3. Teaching and Learning With Skype
   Alanah Mitchell, Charlie Chen, and B. Dawn Medlin *39*

4. Social Media for the MBA Professor: A Strategy for
   Increasing Teacher-Student Communication
   and the Tactics for Implementation
   Allen H. Kupetz *57*

5. Applications of Social Networking in Students' Life Cycle
   Vladlena Benson, Fragkiskos Filippaios, and Stephanie Morgan *73*

6. User-Generated Content in Business Education
   Domen Bajde *95*

7. Facebook "Friendship" as Educational Practice
   Eva Ossiansson *117*

8. Using Second Life for Teaching Management
   of Creativity and Innovation
   Gary Coombs *141*

9. Social Media Engages Online Entrepreneurship Students
   Geoffrey R. Archer and Jo Axe *159*

10. Intersection of Regulations, Faculty Development, and Social Media: Limitations of Social Media in For-Profit Online Classes
Hamid H. Kazeroony *179*

11. Real Lessons in Virtual Worlds: Using Virtual World Technology to Educate and Train Business Students
Natalie T. Wood *195*

12. Uses, Challenges, and Potential of Social Media in Higher Education: Evidence From a Case Study
Suling Zhang, Caroline Flammer, and Xiaolong Yang *217*

13. The Use of Social Media and Networks in Teaching Public Administration: Perceptions, Practices, and Concerns
Thomas A. Bryer and Baiyun Chen *241*

14. Social Media Strategies for the Academic Department: A Three-Phase Framework
Irvine Clarke III and Theresa B. Flaherty *269*

15. Social Media Overload: What Works Best?
Walkyria Goode and Guido Caicedo *289*

16. Curriculum Redesign: Engaging Net Generation Students Through Integration of Social Media in Business Education
Jeanny Liu and Deborah Olson *315*

About the Contributors *337*

CHAPTER 1

TECHNOLOGIES THAT BRING LEARNERS COLLABORATIVELY TOGETHER WITH THE WORLD

Charles Wankel

The Millennial Generation of business students are digital natives, coming into our programs with great sophistication in social media uses and possibilities (Wankel, 2009). Businesses and other organizations are expecting our graduates to be highly proficient in these technologies. This book provides an overview of a diversity of uses of the main social media in teaching business.

Chapter 2, "Defining Interactive Social Media in an Educational Context" (Aditi Grover and David W. Stewart), frames social media tools as disruptive technologies that have radically changed the way people envision communication. Transformation is happening in many aspects of everyday life, including education. Knowledge construction is now a shared task among instructors, learners, and other individuals who sometimes bring passion into the mix. Grover and Stewart explain how creating an efficient relationship among these participants first and foremost necessitates a clear and concise understanding of the construct "social media." They define the salient dimensions of the social media construct as modality, learner dimensions, and instructor dimensions. They provide

Cutting-Edge Social Media Approaches to Business Education:
Teaching With LinkedIn, Facebook, Twitter, Second Life, and Blogs, pp. 1–5
Copyright © 2010 by Information Age Publishing
All rights of reproduction in any form reserved.

an overview of the characteristics of each of these dimensions and their constituent dimensions.

Chapter 3, "Teaching and Learning With Skype" (Alanah Mitchell, Charlie Chen, and B. Dawn Medlin), discusses the benefits and challenges of e-learning with a focus on Skype and VoIP (voice over internet protocol) technology. They discuss the background of e-learning systems and present a collaborative process for teaching and learning with Skype. The special issues associated with applying the process to intercultural communication are considered. As educational organizations become ever-more global, being able to work with diverse cultures becomes increasingly important. The chapter presents how Skype has been used successfully for learning intercultural communication between U.S. and Taiwanese students. The processes described in detail and the research results from this experience suggest that VoIP technology provides a good fit for one-on-one e-learning in addressing each culture.

Chapter 4, "Social Media for the MBA Professor: A Strategy for Increasing Teacher-Student Communication and the Tactics for Implementation" (Allen H. Kupetz), discusses social media as a strategy for increasing student-teacher communication and shares tactics for implementing them. Of the thousands of social media applications, he focuses on five: blogging, Twitter, wikis, Ning, and Hotseat. He contrasts course management tools like Blackboard with externally hosted blogs, which he believes have better functionality for integrating text and video into single messages. He discusses Twitter as a networking tool and the basics of using it. He suggests having students collaborate in documents and reports to create better products. He discusses the benefits of Facebook groups which, unlike Ning, are free. He suggests Hotseat to create collaborative microdiscussion in and out of the classroom. He concludes with an overview on social media mistakes to avoid and advises the instructor to be an equal with students in the doings of the class rather than dominating the technology.

Chapter 5, "Applications of Social Networking in Students' Lifecycle" (Vladlena Benson, Fragkiskos Filippaios, and Stephanie Morgan), addresses the issues of graduates to create social capital through social networking, share knowledge, and enhance employability. They summarize the results of alumni of several European universities. They found international differences in the appreciation of benefits of online social networking.

Chapter 6, "User-Generated Content in Business Education" (Domen Bajde), examines the possibilities opened up by using mediated communication to create and share user-generated content (UGC). Bajde defines and categorizes UGC, sketches out its vital role in social media, and addresses its implications and challenges for business education.

Chapter 7, "Facebook 'Friendship' as Educational Practice" (Eva Ossiansson), shares her experiences of using Facebook in teaching and how it affected her students, interaction in the course, course norms, and the way the course was collaboratively created. This autoethnography reveals the shifting roles of university faculty to more mentoring and facilitating. She found that Facebook fosters a more collegial atmosphere among faculty and students.

Chapter 8, "Using Second Life for Teaching Management of Creativity and Innovation" (Gary Coombs), discusses the unique opportunity for teaching the management of creativity and innovation in organizations through the medium of Second Life. The learning curve for both the instructor and students engaging in rich 3-D immersive environments like Second Life can be steep, although many students come with interactive gaming, and even massively multiplayer online game (MMOG) experience to leverage. Coombs offers an overview of his student cadre, whose experience and reactions are unique rather than typical.

Chapter 9, "Social Media Engages Online Entrepreneurship Students" (Geoffrey R. Archer and Jo Axe), discusses their experience at a Canadian university in which students recorded a 2-minute elevator pitch that they posted to YouTube. They also utilized social media in a team-based exercise called "The Online Venture Challenge." Using a wiki such as Wetpaint, four-person teams designed and created a mission-driven e-commerce website. This assignment helped students dispersed in far-flung places form bonds. The Video Elevator Pitch assignment encouraged creativity which was seen as a critical skill for entrepreneurs.

Chapter 10, "Intersection of Regulations, Faculty Development, and Social Media: Limitations of Social Media in For-Profit Online Classes" (Hamid Kazeroony), discusses for-profit higher education institutions and the utility of social media for creating and transferring knowledge in alignment with accreditation agency expectations. He discusses the measurement of learning outcomes associated with student use of social media in a regulatory context where radical innovation is frowned upon.

Chapter 11, "Real Lessons in Virtual Worlds: Using Virtual World Technology to Educate and Train Business Students" (Natalie T. Wood), discusses the promise that virtual worlds such as Second Life hold for higher education. She explores the characteristics of virtual worlds that make them usefully different from other social media, and the potential hurdles that instructors introducing virtual world educational endeavors must overcome.

Chapter 12, "Uses, Challenges, and Potential of Social Media in Higher Education: Evidence From a Case Study" (Suling Zhang, Caroline Flammer, and Xiaolong Yang), addresses emerging social media phenomena and their challenges and opportunities in higher education. They present a case study at a medium-sized public university in the United States, taking a comprehensive approach, incorporating the perspectives of the key stakeholders. They investigate official and unofficial social media use at the university and differences between the adopters and nonadopters. They found that professors need to be creative and innovative in using social media for teaching. Particularly, they recommend experimentation. They discuss the usefulness of partnering with IT people at the university, particularly in integrating social media with existing course technologies.

Chapter 13, "The Use of Social Media and Networks in Teaching Public Administration: Perceptions, Practices, and Concerns" (Thomas A. Bryer and Baiyun Chen), presents an exploratory study on the use of social media in teaching public administration. They present findings from a survey and interviews, and also analyze one of the author's uses of social media in teaching an undergraduate course in civic engagement. They discuss new directions in social learning assessment, distinct cultural orientations, defining the relationship of personal/private and public identities, cyber-bullying, student-faculty relations outside of the traditional classroom environment, institutional policies, and innovation diffusion in academia.

Chapter 14, "Social Media Strategies for the Academic Department: A Three-Phase Framework" (Irvine Clarke III and Theresa B. Flaherty), is aimed at academic departmental leaders to sensitize them to the issues associated with implementing departmental-level strategies. Social media approaches by departments to reach students and other departmental stakeholders, such as alumni, parents, and employers are considered. They present a three-phase framework to assist readers in the creation, implementation, and management of social media strategic plans.

Chapter 15, "Social Media Overload: What Works Best?" (Walkyria Goode & Guido Caicedo), presents a critical analysis of social media tools in the context of MBA education. They discuss the use of social media for content delivery, discussions, content creation, and collaboration. The online services used include a range of content-creation and sharing sites like Wordpress, YouTube, and MixedInk; group-oriented sites like Google Groups and Wiggio; and the increasingly ubiquitous social networking website Facebook.

Chapter 16, "Curriculum Redesign: Engaging Net Generation Students through Integration of Social Media in Business Education" (Jeanny Liu & Deborah Olson), discusses the integration of social media into class assignments and the engagement of students in the learning process. They focus on understanding behavioral patterns and learning preferences of Net Generation students and redesigning curricula to engage them in learning and in the knowledge-creation process. They start with an overview of the impact of social media in business education, then discuss the social learning paradigm of Net Generation students, offering four behavioral themes impacting course design and assignment development. They conclude with examples of how they have used social technologies in business courses to create empowered learning.

Currently Web 2.0 is characterized by its mobile and virtual world collaborative platforms. Social media is continuing to evolve. Indeed, over the next decade, Web 3.0 will emerge with its facilitation of deeper and easier retrieval of connected and related information. This book has shown how social media can enable learners to interact using their mobile devices wherever they happen to be. Class assignments can now involve collaborations of a huge number of learners in disparate locations. We expect that learners developing increased wherewithal in business uses of social media will be advantaged over their peers whose programs emphasize antiquated media for collaboration.

REFERENCES

Wankel, C. (2009) Management education using social media. *Organization Management Journal, 6,* 251-262.

CHAPTER 2

DEFINING INTERACTIVE SOCIAL MEDIA IN AN EDUCATIONAL CONTEXT

Aditi Grover and David W. Stewart

Social media tools are disruptive technologies that have radically altered the way people view and use communication. This transformation is occurring in many ways and in many places that influence lifestyle and social interaction. Education is no exception and the impact of these media in education is likely to be large. Numerous new participants will enter the traditional educational relationship and revolutionize the learning process. The task of knowledge construction will now be shared among the instructor, student and other individuals who find passion for the subject at hand. Creating an efficient relationship among these participants, first and foremost necessitates a clear understanding of the construct of social media. This chapter is an effort in this direction. It defines the salient dimensions of the social media construct—modality, learner and instructor dimensions. Characteristics of each are delineated and are further exemplified by their constituent dimensions.

From its earliest origins teaching has been a social and interactive activity. For much of history the sharing of information has involved face-to-face

Cutting-Edge Social Media Approaches to Business Education:
Teaching With LinkedIn, Facebook, Twitter, Second Life, and Blogs, pp. 7–38
Copyright © 2010 by Information Age Publishing
All rights of reproduction in any form reserved.

interaction using the spoken word, demonstrations, questions and answers, and group activities. In the context of formal education, classroom teaching was and remains the primary social and interactive medium for information transfer. It was only with the advent of new, disruptive technologies that the link between social and interactive activities and learning was altered. The advent of the written language created new ways to share information that removed the interactive and social elements of such sharing. The printing press moved the transfer of knowledge to a mass audience through production of relatively inexpensive books and further diminished the need for the social and interactive elements of learning. Radio and television provided new technologies for information sharing, but use of these technologies in a truly interactive context has been the exception. The emergence of the computer, which has become an important tool for sharing information, was originally more of an extension of the book than the classroom. Thus, there has emerged a dichotomy in teaching and learning characterized by the social and interactive elements of classroom instruction on the one hand and the relatively solitary pursuit of knowledge though reading, watching broadcasts, listening to books, and similar pursuits that involve little social interaction. This dichotomy is fast coming to an end.

The emergence of technologies facilitated by increases in bandwidth has provided opportunities to add the dimensions of interactivity, social interaction and collaboration to computer mediated media (Cavazza, 2008; Solis, 2008a, 2008b). These new computer mediated interactive and social tools include Facebook, Myspace, Twitter, Google Groups, Windows Online, blogs, and Wiki's among many others. These interactive social tools have created new opportunities for the dissemination of information, collaborative learning and interaction.

The purpose of this chapter is to explore the opportunities for the use of computer mediated social and interactive tools for information dissemination, teaching, and learning. This chapter is organized as follows. First, we present a brief introduction to social media. Next, we discuss the importance of social media in education and learning. The third section introduces and briefly discusses the characteristics of the dimensions of computer mediated, interactive social media, and then explores implications of these dimensions for dissemination of information in an instructional context. Finally, in the fourth section, concluding remarks and comments are presented along with areas for future research.

ON DEFINING SOCIAL MEDIA

Social media have been defined as "a group of Internet-based applications that build on the ideological and technological foundations of Web

2.0, and that allow the creation and exchange of user-generated content" (Kaplan & Haenlien, 2010). Both social media and more traditional media convey information content. The key difference between the two is that social media allow the user to engage in the creation and development of content and to gather online to share knowledge, information, and opinions using web-based applications and tools. Though Web-based, social media may involve numerous technologies such as telephone phone, computer, and interactive television. These social media are changing rapidly and are characterized by a variety of dimensions. Social media vary along these dimensions and are differentiated by them. Thus, any discussion of social media should include identification of the dimensions and elements of social media that define such media and facilitate classification.

Social media are usually synonymously used with Web 2.0, although the two terms are not identical. Web 2.0 is an umbrella term coined by O'Reilley (2005) that is used to refer to the read-write web that represents the "second phase of evolution of the online world." Web 2.0 uses the Web as a "participation platform" and develops software applications on the web (O'Reilly & Battelle, 2004). That is, Web 2.0 is the means by which media are made social and has transformed the way social media was originally conceptualized. Another step in the development of the Web, which is expected in the future, is Web 3.0 or the Semantic Web, a term coined by Tim Berners-Lee. Web 3.0 is where artificial intelligence and the Web converge. The computer is proposed to understand, categorize and use information like humans do. Some experts believe that Web 3.0 will act as a user's personal assistant—that is, remember the preferences of the user as he or she navigates the web. The development and future of Web 3.0 is yet to come, but what is Web 2.0 and how does it differ from Web 1.0?

Unlike Web 1.0, the "first generation of commercial Internet," where information is published with little or no interaction among users, Web 2.0 allows knowledge to be created, shared and reorganized. Web 2.0 enables numerous applications such as wikis, blogs, podcasts, and social networking sites that allow and even encourage user-generated content. (Table 2.1 lists characteristics that differentiate Web 1.0 from Web 2.0). Web 2.0 represents a user-generated system, whereas Web 1.0 consists of websites published primarily by experts in their specific fields. Furthermore, Web 2.0 allows users to label content, generating what are referred to as "folksonomies" in contrast to the taxonomical system generated by Web 1.0.

The social interactivity that Web 2.0 promotes can take place via a desktop computer, laptop, mobile phone, personal digital assistant or the iPod. Farnsworth and Austin (2005) characterized the iPod as "miniaturized hybrid assemblages" that bring together audio, video, and text tech-

Table 2.1.   Comparing Web 1.0 and Web 2.0

Web 1.0	Web 2.0
Publishing	Participation
Content management system	Wiki
Directories (taxonomy)	Tagging (Folksonomy)
Personal websites	Blogging

Source: Adapted from O'Reilley (2005).

nologies and allow interaction among other media. The iPod technology is a creative enabler for acquiring educational material. Users can simultaneously listen to and watch videos, record audio, and "read" a text while walking or driving. Researchers have termed pedagogy via podcast as "podagogy" (Anon, 2007).

Social media take many forms and continue to evolve. There have been numerous efforts to classify social media. Some classification schemes have focused on the primary use of a particular medium, such as communication, collaboration, relationship maintenance, transaction, entertainment, and sharing opinions (Vermaas & Van de Wijngaert, 2004). Other classification systems have focused on the degree of self-presentation/self disclosure and the degree of social presence and media richness (Kaplan & Haenlein, 2010). Still other classifications have been based on the content of a medium, such as, text, pictures, video, documents, et cetera (Safko & Brake, 2009). Finally, there are various hybrid classifications that mix content, uses, types of media and other characteristics. For example, Solis (2008a, 2008b) has suggested a "conversation prism" that lists many different types of social media though the basis for this classification is unclear.

ON THE ROLE OF SOCIAL MEDIA IN LEARNING

Web technology is rapidly becoming commonplace in educational institutions (Arbaugh, 2005; Boulos, Maramba, & Wheeler, 2006). Social media afford learners the opportunity to interact virtually in ways that could not have been imagined even a few years ago. Before societies fully capitalize on the benefits of social media, there is a need to understand the ways in which social media-driven change are altering the traditional instructional relationship between the learner and educator.

The emerging practices of delivering education and of learning via a multidirectional flow of information define "Learning 2.0," which is inextricably linked to the concept of participatory social learning. Social media are, therefore, beginning to transform learner-instructor-knowledge relationship(s). Social media provide access to new sources of knowledge and new opportunities for learning both within the traditional model of learning between the learner and the instructor and in new and evolving ways. Under the traditional learning paradigm instructor is the primary source of disseminating information to the student. In this model, the instructor is an expert and the primary source of information for the learner. However, social media are changing this relationship as the learner becomes an active coproducer of content and meaning, along with the instructor and the rest of the world. Moreover, other learners and individuals interested in the subject at hand may enter this relationship, thereby changing the flow of information from unidirectional to multidirectional.

Learning 2.0 is a complex holistic phenomenon in which the student and the locus of knowledge come together and learners interact with networks of other learners. Engeström posited activity theory which focuses on understanding learners' perspectives as a part of a larger community and emphasizes the importance of interactions among the "players" (Engeström, 1987) (refer to Figure 2.1) just like social media emphasizes the need of multiple players. Community is defined to include all individuals who are interested in the matter being "discussed." Object is defined as the subject of interest. Division of labor signifies the shared effort made by learners to understand the object. When all the factors, tools and signs, rules, community, the subject and the division of labor intersect, sense and meaning are developed with respect to the object of interest.

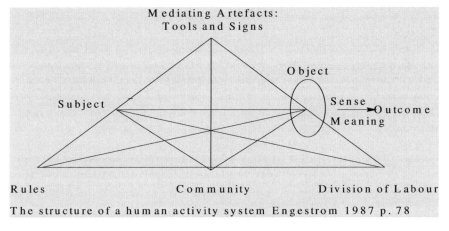

Figure 2.1.   Engeström's representation of activity theory.

Social media are poised to change the landscape of teaching and learning, and redefine the basic tenets of familiar learning theories (e.g., behaviorism, cognitivism, and constructivism) that describe learning as a process that occurs within an individual. Two new approaches to learning theory are warranted given the development of social media. First, "social constructivism," or communal constructivism, refers to students actively engaging in the construction of knowledge for themselves and for the edification of others (Duffy & Cunningham, 1996). What emerges under communal constructivism is an interweaving of relationships between teachers, students, experts, and community members. Another emerging concept is "connectivism" which reflects learning that occurs in a networked society. Connectivism focuses on the generation of ideas and interaction within a social network. The role of the "instructor" changes within this paradigm and perhaps becomes even more important than before. However, the instructor is no longer the sole source of knowledge. Rather, (s)he now acts as a facilitator and mediator of knowledge. Further, the instructor ideally is now responsible for ensuring that the learner indeed has mastered the course content through the learner's immersion in the learning process. Despite its many benefits social media could encourage social loafing, where individuals make less effort to achieve a goal due to diffusion of responsibility within the group activity. Moreover, learners might have to waste time and effort on websites that do not provide any incremental knowledge to them before identifying the more effective or beneficial source(s) of knowledge. This could hamper overall concentration and the "immersion" in learning. Directions from the instructor or "chaperoning" is thus crucial to assist the learner in effectively utilizing time.

In summary, Web 2.0 facilitates dynamic multidirectional relationships among and between learners, instructors and the rest of the world. While the technology and social media that it enables is new, the notions of learning suggested by connectivism and social constructivism are not conceptually novel or revolutionary. Dewey (1938) introduced the notion of "educational transaction," wherein learners' interpretations are actively considered in achieving the knowledge potential. Dewey's concept of educational transaction remains surprisingly valid even in the early twenty-first century, a time when the field of education has assumed new meanings as a result of growth and development of social media (Mason & Rennie, 2008). Yet, unless these newly assumed meanings are well understood, the relationship between students and instructors could fracture. Social media are not uniform nor are they equally likely to find their way into mainstream educational environments.

In the remainder of this chapter we seek to better comprehend the role and implications of social media in the domain of education. The section to follow identifies certain dimensions that can be used to characterize and differentiate social media.

DIMENSIONS OF THE SOCIAL MEDIA CONSTRUCT

With the ever evolving capabilities of social media, it is becoming increasingly important to define this theoretical construct and appreciate fully its fundamental offerings. Once the dimensions of social media are delineated and linked to potential learning outcomes, educational programs can be tailored to the unique needs of an individual to serve as a well-meshed and integrated curricular platform. Most educators recognize the need for pedagogical pluralism so that the learning needs for all students are effectively met. Therefore, a framework that identifies the salient dimensions of social media can offer instructors and researchers a guide for facilitating interaction among users in an education context.

Stewart and Pavlou (2007, 2008) have argued that interactive communications are best examined by treating the interaction as the primary unit of analysis. They suggest that neither the characteristics of the medium nor the characteristics of the actor are sufficient for an understanding of the behavior and outcomes associated with interaction. Rather, such characteristics of the medium and actors must be placed within a context that also includes the goals of the actors and the purpose(s) of the interaction. People use interactive social media for many reasons and in a multitude of ways. They choose and use different media based on their specific goals at a particular point in time, their prior experiences, and their expertise (Hutchinson & Eisenstein, 2008).

Because various media provide consumers with unique affordances and constraints (Norman, 1999), they vary in terms of how much they can facilitate or hinder goals, both individually and in combination with other media. For example, when the goal of a learner is to quickly share information with many others the learner may prefer to post to a website rather than directly interact in real time. On the other hand, if the goal is to complete a collaborative group project, the learners may prefer to use a real time collaborative tool. Thus, learners' goals, expertise, and specific media characteristics influence their construction, integration and personalization of interactive social media.

Indeed, learning is a personally reflective process (Garrison & Anderson, 2003) characterized by learner goals which might be uniquely satisfied depending on individual learning styles (LS). Education researchers have long discussed the importance of learning styles known to influence the effectiveness with which learners learn, although there is much disagreement in terms of how to measure and apply LS. Social media provide a palette of tools that can be mixed and matched to serve the specific learning style of learners and to enhance academic performance. Given the diversity of students' learning styles, careful attention and planning is necessary before social technology tools are deployed in the classroom to appropriately address needs, familiarity with, and expectations about social media tools.

A learning style (LS) may be said to be a composite of cognitive, affective and psychological factors that serves as an indicator of how an individual interacts with and responds to the learning environment (Duff, 2000). Keefe (1979) defined learning styles as an indicator of how students perceive, interact and respond to learning environments. That is, every individual has his or her own method or strategies by which he or she understands and assimilates course materials. Such methods are usually specific for each individual learner and their distinct 'habitual' manner of acquiring knowledge. For example, some students respond better to verbal content, others are more successful in learning in response to visual information such as pictures, diagrams and pictorials, and still others may prefer various combinations of text and visual information.

The literature on learning theory describes several classifications of learning styles, including Kolb's (1976), Dunn and Dunn's (1978), and Felder and Silverman's learning styles. Kolb (1976) and Dunn and Dunn (1978) posit that LS are stable aspects of personality. Furthermore, Felder and Brent (2005) suggest that instructors attempt to better understand different learning styles in order to improve students' chances of success: instructional methods and environments should be provided accordingly (Carver, Howard, & Lane, 1999). This will benefit both the learner and the instructor.

Individuals' unique learning styles are influenced by culture and life experiences (Dunn et al. 1990). Since experiences and expectations can vary by generations, Cambiano, De Vore, and Harvey in their 2001 paper offer recommendations for lifelong learning depending on different generational cohorts. For example, baby boomers (born between 1946-1964) prefer hands-on learning. Television is the dominant medium that shaped their lives. On the other hand, for Generation Y (born between 1978-1994), given their love of technology, consider the Internet and computers as an infrastructure basic to their education. Discussion boards, instant messaging, and blogging therefore become an important part of their educational design. Internet-generation learners in contrast to the television-generation learners are considered to be more independent, active, open, innovative, curious, and self-reliant. Some of the emerging learning styles for Generation Y and the evolving Generation Z (born after 1995), therefore include adeptness in multiple technological media, virtual settings, and collaborated learning involving interaction across a community. Note however that the generational learning styles cohorts are not rigid boundaries. For example, many baby boomers exhibit characteristics of the later generations and vice versa.

Adapting teaching to the unique learning styles (LS) of students has been shown to produce greater academic success, although not without reservation. Felder and Silverman (1988), Boles, Pillay, and Raj (1999) and other researchers have demonstrated that students whose LS have been taken into account retain information longer, apply information more effectively, and have a positive attitude towards their courses. The diversity of social media provide new opportunities for tailoring context to individual learning styles through the coordinated use of both traditional classroom instruction and use of social media.

Little research has examined these types of media coordination issues. It is also possible that instead of viewing alternative media in the same way, different learners may have different evaluations and preferences for different media. For example, one learner may prefer reading text, while another learner may prefer voice communication. While an instructor may steer the learning of individuals in a direction that matches his or her learning needs, the student is also capable of crafting for himself or herself a Personalized Learning Environment (PLE). In terms of the key dimensions identified in the section below, a PLE might be created with varying levels of visual-verbal components, size of the network and nature of the relationships within the network. PLE is defined as a personalized aggregation of tools, network and content from a pool of available choices. The creation of PLEs would define paths for individuals to express themselves, differentiated according to their specific needs. In contrast to a traditional learning approach in which content is organized and prepackaged for the learner, in PLE the learner plays a seminal role in creating, constructing, and organizing content based on his or her affinities and interests. Learners are thereby likely to experience feelings of self-mastery and self-empowerment and experience a sense of fulfillment or accomplishment.

A more nuanced characterization of the dimensions of interactive social media is needed in order to stimulate research that adequately recognizes, analyzes, and explains the complexity of behavior and learning outcomes. Prior research in communications and internet behavior provides a starting point for such a nuanced characterization. For example Stewart and Pavlou (2002, 2007, 2008) have proposed various dimensions of the interactive media environment. Similarly, Dholakia et al. (in press) have proposed a framework for characterizing the interaction of media and actors that explicitly accounts for: (a) what actors *bring*, (b) what they *encounter*, and (c) what they *do* during their interactions. In addition, because media-actor interactions may occur within the domain of another actor's control, such as a teacher, they consider the ways in which such an actor can influence actor-media interactions. Dholakia et al. (in press) focus on interactions among consumers and marketers, but their framework can be readily adapted to a learning context. An adaptation of this framework with an education context is summarized in Table 2.2 and described in greater detail in the next portions of this chapter.

Social media are multidimensional constructs. To better appreciate the nuances of social media tools it is important to consider them in terms of the following core dimensions: (1) modality, (2) learners and (3) instructors. The following section delineates each of the identified dimensions that in turn are defined in terms of dimensions that comprise and qualify or describe it.

Modality

It is useful to consider the dimensions along which interactive social media may vary in order to understand their constraints and advantages. Perhaps the most basic distinction is whether a medium is used for the dissemination of information or for the evaluation of some behavior or measure of performance. In other words, is the medium used for acquiring information or for demonstrating mastery involving some performance metric. Another characteristic by which media may vary is whether they are *physical* or *virtual*. This dimension is interesting not only because many learners seek sensory information, but also because technological advances are constantly increasing the physicality of channels that were previously virtual (Riva, 2007). Third, channels vary in their *degree of accessibility*. With the widespread adoption of wireless Internet and mobile phones, some media can be accessed by virtually anyone at any time across the globe, whereas others, such as proprietary courseware permit more limited access and may require specific technologies, permission or equipment for access.

A fourth dimension is the *type of communication* that a channel permits. For example, some online media such as email lists or bulletin boards allow only asynchronous communications. In contrast, other media such as telephones (or Skype) or chat-rooms permit real-time synchronous communication among actors. Fifth, media can also vary in the *nature of their interface*. For example some media can be personalized and customized by an individual user while the interface of other media is fixed and the user has no control over the interface. A sixth dimension is the *level of convenience* a medium provides to actors. Some media, or more often the content delivered by a particular medium, may be available around the clock, while other content or opportunities for interaction may be limited by the availability of the medium itself or of other actors.

Table 2.2. Relevant Dimensions and Variables Relevant to Interactive Social Media in Education

		Learner		
Modality	*Instructor*	*What They Bring*	*What They Encounter*	*What They Strive for and/or Do*
• Dissemination versus evaluation	• Filtered versus unfiltered	• Goals	• Priming	• Knowledge
• Physical versus virtual	• Instructor controlled versus learner controlled	• Values	• Potential for collaboration	• Skill
• Accessibility		• Memory	• Ability to customize	• Mastery certification
• Synchronous versus synchronous	• Niche content versus breadth of content	• Perceptual bias	• Ease of processing	• Personal enrichment
• Fixed versus customizable		• Categorization	• Variety perceptions	
• Convenience		• Traits	• Stimulation/arousal	
• Flexible versus static		• Learning style	• Sensory and haptic factors	
• Learner history		• Emotion	• Design factors	
		• Self-efficacy	• Social influences	
		• Affiliations		

Source: Dhoakia et al. (in press).

Seventh, media may vary in terms of the flexibility in the organization and portrayal of their information content. For example some media allow actors the option to self-organize information so that it aligns with their cognitive structure. Finally, media may vary in the extent to which they store an actor's *behavioral history*. Whereas some media (i.e., online shopping such as Amazon) maintain a permanent or historical record of a customer's transactions, others (i.e., Wiki's) retain little or no memory.

Learner Dimensions

Users of interactive social media, including those who use such media in an educational context can be characterized by three broad dimensions: (1) what they bring to the encounter; (2) what they encounter themselves; and (3) what they strive for or do, during their choice of, and use of a particular medium.

What Learners Bring

Users of interactive social media possess a number of characteristics that influence their choice and use of a particular medium. Thus, they "bring" these factors to their interactions. First, actors may have a variety of superordinate and specific goals that influence their use of a given media, some of which may be enduring and others generated by immediate situational conditions. In addition, users also possess a broad set of functional and terminal values that may favor certain types of media and disfavor or even eliminate others. Interactions are also influenced by a user's level of prior experiences with and memory of prior use of a particular medium. For example, a positive experience with a particular collaborative tool may predispose a learner to favor it over other tools. The choice and use of a particular medium is also susceptible to a host of possible perceptual biases. These biases may favor certain media characteristics at a particular time, or affect the manner in which content or interactions are framed or categorized. Actors also bring a host of individual differences to interactive social media. These include personality traits, learning styles, moods and emotions, a sense of self efficacy (or lack thereof) and various affiliations.

What Learners Encounter

When interacting with a particular medium, an actor is likely to be influenced by various features of the medium "encountered" during an interaction. For example, the layout of information, the colors, backgrounds, and fonts used for an online shopping website may prime particular aspects of consumer memory (e.g., Mandel & Johnson, 2002) and also affect perceived ease of processing, perceptions of variety, and level of stimulation and arousal (Balasubramanian, Raghunathan, & Mahajan, 2005). Other important media elements that actors may encounter include sensory and haptic factors, design factors, and various social influences including the number and characteristics of other actors involved in an interaction. These elements are likely to influence how a learner experiences the interaction, how the medium is evaluated subsequently and various outcomes. For example, differences in the verbal and visual content in an encounter interact with specific learner characteristics and influence learning outcomes.

The Verbal-Visual Dimension

The verbal-visual dimension is related to the form of content the learner encounters. Some learners have a preferred format for apprehending, creating, and contributing information to the course or the subject of interest. Thus, there may be an interaction between what the learner encounters and the specific characteristics of learner. The verbal/visual dimension may be conceptualized as a continuum defined by two poles. At one end lies verbal content in form of text and audio, while at the other lies visual content in the form of video, diagrams, graphs, demonstrations and images. Each learner in collaboration with the instructor and based on his or her preferred format of receiving and apprehending information, can choose a personalized mix of verbal and visual content. The position on the spectrum reflects the learner's preference for a unique mix in order to achieve a learning objective.

It is widely believed that the left and right sides of the brain are specialized and perform differentiated functions. While the left side of the brain is analytical and processes verbal and logical forms of information, the right side of the brain is creative and processes sensory stimuli. Individuals tend to respond more favorably to information either in verbal or visual form and, are sometimes referred to as predominantly "left brained" or "right brained" respectively. Both verbal and visual forms of representation are means by which one stores memory, processes information and expresses the self. While the verbal system is associated with linear and conceptual thinking, and is consciously controlled, the visual system is holistic, emotional, and imaginative.

The combination of visual and verbal input can produce an impact that is much more powerful than either form alone. Text accompanying the visuals may add a layer of meaning that might not otherwise be accessible to the observer. For example, a caption added to an image uploaded from Flickr orients viewers toward different or varied interpretations of the possible meanings attached to the picture.

Along the visual-verbal spectrum, social media technology provides several options for the learner—Podcasts and vodcasts on a device—mobile (e.g., i-Pod, mobile phone, laptops) and nonmobile (e.g., desk top computer). Podcasts and vodcasts or vidcasts are digital files, in audio or video format that enable users to engage in or watch content. Coupling pictures with the spoken word rather than relying on one presentation medium enhances learning (Mayer, 2001). Those whose LS favor a visual style of content might prefer games and slide share presentations. On the other hand, those who respond best to verbal content might receive the similar content in the form of podcasts and online discussion groups. Table 2.3 presents the different software tools that are salient to the different learning traditions.

In the traditional education model between learner and instructor, learning is primarily verbal and spontaneous, and limited to the learner and educator. The proposed verbal end of the spectrum described above in the social media ecosystem is not identical to a traditional education model where the instructor provides information to the student. (For a comparison between Learning 2.0 and Learning 1.0, refer to Table 2.3.) The ability of social media to store and replay lectures in form of podcasts and vodcasts or vidcasts enables learners to reflect on, comment and elaborate on the material given during class sessions. In fact, podcasts offer superior support for auditory learners, who comprise at least 30% of an average population (Garrison, Anderson, & Archer 1999). Podcasts or vodcasts may be downloaded on portable devices such as Apple iPod, MP3/MP4, laptops, or desktop computers which allow the digital files to play back later, allowing for flexibility of usage or "learning on-the-go" (Chan & Lee, 2005). The iPod today is a popular cultural icon (Dale &

Table 2.3.   Comparing Use of Social Media in Learning 1.0 and Learning 2.0

	Learning 1.0	*Learning 2.0*
Verbal		
• Text	Print, e-mail, webpages	Blogs, Wiki, Wiki blogs, online discussion groups
• Audio	Audio clips, telephone support	Podcasts
Visual		
• Video	Video clips, webcasts TV	Vodcasts
• Images	Photographs	Share and edit, such as, Flickr, simulated animations, simulations games

Source: Adapted from Mason and Rennie (2008).

Pymm, 2009). While podcasts have advantages in terms of mobility, a major disadvantage is that browsing for information in an audio format is difficult.

Flickr is an online system that allows users to store, organize, and share pictures, and also serves as a medium of self-expression, and learning about other members' lives. The images aid in expressing ideas, aspects of relationships, and emotions that may not be easily verbalized and are stored as personally powerful memories. Working with images, individuals might express and represent not only their actual self but also elements of their imaginary or ideal self (Suler, 2008). Sharing is the most important feature of Flickr because individuals can "congregate" and share pictures; sharing extends the traditional boundaries of private and personal life. Users can add descriptions, notes and tags to their pictures. The type of learning that takes place via Flickr may be described in terms of the theory of self-identity and affinity spaces (Gee, 2004). Individuals build a sense of identity in relation to the pictures they upload, develop a way of seeing others in terms of the pictures they have uploaded, and by developing shared ways of "talking" about the images they share.

A powerful social media tool for learning in either the verbal or visual format are discussion groups. Online discussion groups might assume two basic forms—asynchronous, which do not occur in real time, or synchronous, which occur in real time. Synchronous discussions such as video conferencing and online chat closely resemble face-to-face conversations. Like live face-to-face conversations, synchronous discussions might present fragmented ideas and a deep understanding of the material might not emerge. Some researchers argue that asynchronous discussions are more suitable for knowledge construction because participants can spend time and reflect on other members' comments, then respond to their comments or an element of the topic of discussion. However, synchronous discussions might not always lead to a spearheaded discussion of the topic because the potential time lapse between comments might detract people from mutually focused discussion (Bober & Dennen, 2001).

What Learners Do

When interacting within a particular medium, an actor can engage in a variety of behaviors such as searching for information, directly interacting with others, reading, listening and viewing content, solving problems, and asking and/or answering questions, among others. In addition, actors can also engage in activities and behaviors that arise from an interaction such as complaining or spreading positive word of mouth. These behaviors may be influenced by the nature of a particular medium and vice versa. What learners do is also influenced by what they are attempting to achieve, such as, obtain knowledge, acquire a skill, obtain certification of mastery of a domain of knowledge, or engage in personal enrichment. Two dimensions are defined to broadly represent what learners do namely, social-solitary and collaborator versus observer dimensions.

Social-Solitary Dimension

The social-solitary (S-S) dimension, critically important to learning, relates to the extent of social interaction that the learner selects when he or she endeavors to understand course materials or a topic of interest. This dimension underscores the role of social relationships in determining the extent of interaction and is defined by poles. On one end of the polar dimension lies the social dimension in which the learner interacts with other users of social media; on other end lies a learner who chooses to work independently. Just like the visual-verbal dimension, each learner, based on his or her preferred extent of social interaction, displays a particular level of connectedness. The level of connectedness preferred by a learner and its' association with an optimal learning outcome may vary by the specified task, type of learning and content, and stage in the learning process.

According to Engeström's activity theory and the sociocultural learning theory, the personal background (e.g., culture, religion) that each learner brings to the group process or experience is important to the fundamental learning environment. Vygotsky (1962) proposed a social development theory that highlights the significance of social interaction in the process of learning. When learners exchange information and ideas, they help create a "new" culture that is a function of their own unique individual characteristics interacting with the characteristics of the other learners. In other words, the learners create a community. This community will be further defined by its own culture, which in turn is an outcome of the interplay of the cultures of the members that comprise the community, thus contributing to group dynamism in an online format that is distinct from that of traditional small group activities.

The network of social relationships created utilizing social media differs from small group formation that traditional learning produces. While small groups play an important role in inculcating team-building skills and joint production, social networking transforms the dynamics of group formation. Social media can create networks of individuals similar in terms of interest in content, motivation to learn, and passion for the material such that they can convene and participate in the formation of communities. The relationship among the members of the community in a learning framework can be best represented by Laurillard's (1995) three-dimensional conversational framework that represents learning as a complex phenomenon that could potentially be an outcome of interaction among three-distinct identities (Figure 2.2). Each of the three dimen-

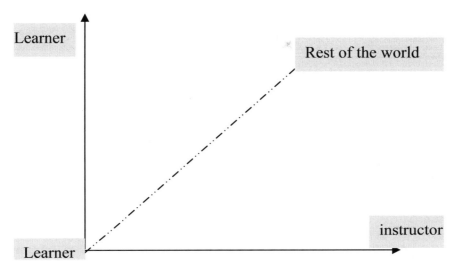

Figure 2.2.   Representing the multidirectional relationship in the domain of social media.

sions can moderate and impact the social process of learning in a significant way. This framework suggests that learners are now developing more relationships than they would otherwise have.

Learner-Instructor

The learner-instructor dimension still remains a critical relationship because the instructor is responsible for defining learning objectives such that pedagogical goals are met in the most effective manner. Although Web 2.0 facilitates an increase in the number of types of relationships (Garrison, 1990), the teacher or instructor no longer presides in what heretofore has been an ontologically advantaged position, but engages with the student in the task of explanation, understanding and knowledge creation (Lee, Miller, & Newnham, 2008). The instructor now becomes a facilitator of online interaction and a partner in learning (Beldarrain 2006).

Learner-Learner

The learner-learner dimension of Laurillard's three-dimensional conversational framework is of significant importance. The learner-learner dimension may manifest as either a weak or a strong tie; a strong tie is a relationship in which one individual is directly connected to another on the same network, while a weak tie is a relationship in which two individuals are connected via a third person. In this framework, people are not limited to a circle of friends; they traverse the network to form a border-less community of like-minded individuals. Note that these boundaries are permeable, allowing members to move in and out of the "relation-ship" without formalization. The greater the human interaction the greater is the likelihood of learners to develop people management and negotiation skills.

Learning without boundaries is likely to have a tremendous advantage within diverse populations of learners. Research has demonstrated that multiplicity of class, language, gender, nationality, ability, and religion influences communication within real-world networks; however, the appli-cation of social media tools transcends these differences because conver-sations and groups are randomly formed to produce a cohesive and productive unit geared towards a singular, common goal of understand-ing. Furthermore, as classrooms steadily become culturally diverse (Mason & Rennie, 2008), courses need to be designed to take into account the huge variety in learners' background knowledge.

Individual differences can account for some of the variation in the use of online tools among users. Orr et al. (2009) report that shyness is signif-icantly related to the time spent by users on Facebook, the number of friends an individual had, and attitude toward the application. Shy indi-viduals have fewer friends than more gregarious individuals; Further, shy users spend more time on their Facebook accounts relative to non-shy individuals. While it may be inaccurate to conclude that shy people are more likely to use Facebook based on this study; what is important to note is that social media tools like Facebook can encourage even shy individu-als to interact. Such are the capabilities of social media tools. In a similar vein, Madell and Muncer (2006) studied usage patterns of e-mail, chat rooms, and instant messaging (IM) by shy individuals. The authors reported that shy individuals, in comparison to nonshy individuals, were less frequent users of e-mail primarily because these shy users did not have many contacts with whom to exchange messages. However, Sheeks and Birchmeier (2007) assert that a direct relation between shyness and online communication should exist because shy individuals were found more likely to report satisfying online relationships.

Learner-Rest of the World

Unlike small group formation in the traditional learning model, this dimension of relationship is developed organically (Kozinets, Valck, Wojnicki, & Wilner, 2010). Relationships are formed without direct inter-vention or incentive from the instructor; the formation of this relation-ship is rather driven by the enthusiasm of the individuals in the subject matter and the overall goals of the community.

In what emerges as an outcome of the Learner-Learner, Learner-Instructor, and Learner-Rest-of-the-world relationships is a unique definition of the user within the social media domain. Each user or learner has the opportunity to craft for himself or herself a space in the environment which is a form of self-representation. Thus, the learning relationship is now no longer linear. Since a single individual cannot experience and acquire all the knowledge that may be related to a concept, forming connections with others augments the multidimensional learning experience. For example, the Web 2.0 tool, Facebook and Myspace.com, all allow users to create, develop, manage, and maintain their identities by posting user profiles. Other forms of self-expression in the Facebook domain include individuals' selection of friends, posting a status, and commenting on status of friends or crafting one's own status.

The S-S dimension in learning can be said to exist in the traditional learning model; however, it has been radically transformed by the social media arena. At the solitary end of the traditional learning model the learner may choose to work independently, or at the other social end of the spectrum one may choose to embark on learning the material in a study group. Social media software alters the solitary dimension so that the learner can now work independently being fully aware of the social interactions that exist at the social end of this dimension. At the social end of the spectrum, social media allow for greater interaction among users in the learning environment, and provide a means for collaborating with anyone across the globe who might be interested in the content being explored.

Critics of social media tools express concern about trust and confidentiality. Trustworthiness is an important element in online transactions. In the context of the educational transaction, trust is crucial to inspiring people to share information and ideas (Mason & Rennie, 2008). The S-S dimension also works to define the social identity of an individual. Humans are a complex mix of their personal and public selves. In the presence of social media, individuals can choose to represent and express multiple aspects of their personalities. For example, the social networking sites Facebook and Myspace.com are platforms where an individual chooses to interact with people, share pictures and post comments. The e-portfolio, an electronic document, makes a statement about the achievements of an individual and is a form of representing one's professional self via social media tools. E-portfolios can be used as a tool for preparing for job interviews and as a means of maintaining lifelong record of achievements. The content of the e-portfolio is typically linked to the professional goals of an individual. People might also represent their professional identity by setting up a LinkedIn account which is qualitatively substantially different from their personal self representation using a Facebook account.

Interestingly, Ling (2007) points out that social talk that occurs on social networking sites might be effective for discussions and pedagogical development, even though they are not necessarily directly related to traditional learning activities. This is because social dynamics are crucial for effective group action (Hobaugh, 1997). The first step toward collaborative learning is forming a sense of community among members without, which anxiety or a lack of willingness to take risks associated with learning may exist. Thus the S-S dimension has important implications for individuals' location on the collaborator-observer dimension, to be discussed in the next section.

Social networking enables building, strengthening, and maintaining relationships. Interaction between two or more users can take place in the form of online, real-time IM interaction where users send videos, images, audio files and other attachments. Vratulis and Dobson (2008) reported that learners develop social relationships through the identities they represent in a wiki environment. The exchanging and sharing of information on the wiki website results in people creating their own identity, which they subsequently use to confirm mental models exchanged among other people. Similar to wiki technology, a blogosphere also encourages formation of user identity based on the views one shares with other individuals.

Collaborator-Observer

This collaborator-observer dimension focuses on the nature of social interaction among learners. The relationships are defined by the type and the level of interaction constituting the social relationships that the individual has forged for him- or herself. At one end of the bipolar dimension lies collaboration in which the learner actively engages in coconstructing material with other users of the new media; on other end lies a learner who chooses not to engage in the process of contributing and formulating mental models of the material. As in the previous two dimensions discussed, visual-verbal and solitary-social, each learner chooses a specific level of instructiveness based on his or her preferred vehicle of social interaction.

This spectrum defines the interaction in terms of higher levels of involvement with others to meet a particular goal (Figure 2.3): Collaborative learning at one end of the spectrum is defined as a mutual engagement of individuals who exert a coordinated effort to solve a problem together by networking. Collaboration might take place in the form of editing, creating, reconstructing and maintaining knowledge structures. For example, collaborative editing tools such as Google docs and Zoho allow people to share documents and edit them either one at a time or simultaneously. Somewhere in the middle of the spectrum lies coopera-tive learning where there is a division of labor such that each individual is responsible for a part of the problem within the group (Roschelle & Teas-ley, 1995). Social networking might also promote individual learning, engaging the individual in the learning process alone even though social media encourages collective contribution over individual ownership (Mason & Rennie, 2008).

The nature of the interaction among the learners in a particular envi-ronment might follow definitive stages that reflect how an individual gradually incorporates herself into the interactive learning process through careful interactions. Salmon (2003) describes five stages before which a student becomes an effective participant in an online social set-ting such as a group discussion. Stage 1 is merely represented by the stu-dent/ learner joining the discussion group. In Stage 2, he acknowledges his motivation in doing so. After the student begins to share knowledge in Stage 3, he moves to Stage 4 where he participates in the mutual con-struction of knowledge. Within this stage, the learner "explores the issue, takes positions, discusses others positions in an argumentative format, reflects on and re-evaluates their positions" (Salmon, 2003, p. 33). There-fore the student, in Stage 5, becomes an active coproducer of content and meaning.

This collaborative process of active learning engaging the student as coproducer creates and develops a "collective intelligence" which in turn promotes a sense of community and empowerment. Collective intelli-gence is defined as groups of individuals who can occasionally and under certain circumstances meld their thinking into a coherent whole. The movement from a traditional means of learning in which the instructor "gives" and the student "takes" is dramatically altered to become a real-time engineered interaction wherein the responsibility for learning is now shared if not transferred to the learner.

A central tenet in the success of cooperative learning is transparency among students. Transparency is defined as the ability of all collaborating members to be aware of and have access to one another's thoughts, inter-ests, ideas, writings, references and assignments (Dalsgaard & Paulsen,

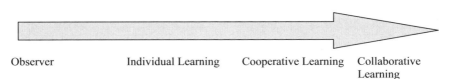

Observer   Individual Learning   Cooperative Learning   Collaborative
                                                                       Learning

Figure 2.3.   The collaborator-observer dimension.

2009). Several researchers have discussed the potential of different forms of interaction ranging from groups, communities, collectives, connections, and network. A comprehensive review of these forms of interaction is outside the scope of this chapter but brief summary of some of the selected forms is presented below:

- *Groups.*   Dron and Anderson (2007) define a group as a collection of individuals who are engaged in a collaborative work. A network is a loosely organized structure that does not involve direct communication or collaboration.

- *Communities.*   Wenger, McDermott, and Snyder (2002) defined communities of practice (CoP) as groups of people sharing a concern or deep interest in a topic and interacting with one another to deepen their knowledge and experience of the content matter. These individuals have a common goal, and the contribution of each member is valued. Gunawardena et al. (2009) defined the three components of a CoP as domain, community and practice that work together to form a social knowledge structure with an objective of developing and sharing knowledge. Domain refers to the specific topic of interest to the community, where community is defined as individuals convening through dialogue and conversation and making sense of a body of knowledge. Practice refers to the specific knowledge created, maintained and shared by the members of the community. CoP rests on the principles of socioconstructivist theory, which asserts that knowledge structures are not owned by individual minds but are distributed across individuals and environments. Knowledge structures created in this manner are generated by reflecting on the other group members' ideas organizing resources, formulating one's own ideas and providing evaluative feedback to other members.

It must be acknowledged that any given social media tool is flexible enough to serve at each end of the spectrum. For example, a blog on its own supports an individual's work, yet, increased interactivity in the form of commentary/ response, and the addition of suggested hyperlinks can make the same blog an increasingly interactive tool. Furthermore, RSS feeds can be used in consonance with blogs to promote reflective thinking, writing and student dialogue (Dalsgaard, 2006). In addition, wiki, a simple website that allows for editing by different users can be left untouched by anyone other than the author, when there is no collaboration; however, when learners employ team-building skills and contribute to the material on the wiki, its content can reflect the collaboration of several others. Mason and Rennie (2008) note that a wiki can be used for group project work. Each member of the group can contribute at his convenience to collate, review, and produce refined iterations of their group work. Information is fluid, flexible, and communally constructed and owned.

Really Simple Syndication (or RSS), defined as a "poor cousin" of the Web 2.0 technologies, promotes rich, active social learning experiences that emphasize personalization and autonomy among users. An RSS-enabled website generates data which summarizes the content of any selected website and delivers updates directly to the user's desktop via web-based aggregators such as GoogleReader. RSS underscores transfer pedagogy: It acts as a source for a student-centered approach to learning in which the student gathers information disseminated by the instructor and beyond, with the objective of either deeply understanding the materials and to pursue future research in the identified area, than to merely receive course announcements (Lee et al., 2008). Students can quickly skim new content on websites of interest and later choose to read in detail material they consider important. In fact, the collaborative capabilities of RSS extend to the learner-teacher interactions described by Laurillard. On the other hand, users can choose limited "interference" from RSS by opting to only receive course announcements.

Students and educators can further combine shared information and feeds across various sources. Thus RSS serves as a collaborative tool that permits and facilitates relationships among and between students, educators and the community. Integrated with other social media tools, RSS, when combined with wiki or blogs, can aid in tracking discussions or updates on other websites maintained by individuals or groups of individuals, and facilitate and strengthen connections among people (see Figure 2.4).

Soon to supplant the static Internet, Wiki are collaborative tools that enable students to become active learners rather than passive receivers of knowledge. Students can edit a wiki and/or add hyperlinks to other pages. The final "quality output" of the wiki is the result of collaboration of students who monitor and review the wiki content as deemed necessary. Collaborative editing, therefore, is the defining feature of a wiki. Much work needs to be done in understanding foolproof methods of wiki assessment (Cronin, 2009).

Blogs can also be used as a community building tool. Individuals can share views, make comments, post messages, add pictures and audio files, or discuss a topic of mutual interest. Blogs encourage student-centered learning where beginners are not scaffolded to higher levels of learning, and are allowed to learn at their own pace. Moreover, blogs introduce members to different perspectives on the topic of interest (Yang, 2009).

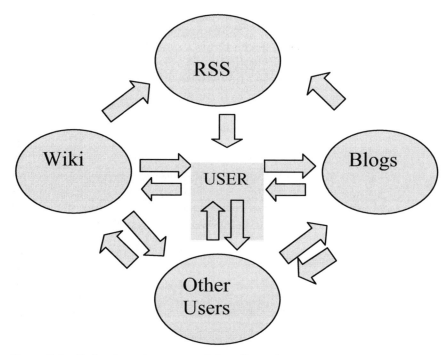

Figure 2.4.   Relatedness between social media tools.

Participatory Web tools can transform the way in which we engage in scholarship. Social bookmarking sites such as Delicious provide a central networked location where an individual's bookmarks and tags (or keywords) are assembled chronologically, annotated, shared or recommended to either the user or a collection of users that the user chooses to reciprocate with. For example, the sharing of bookmarks can be very helpful. Students can build on bookmarks made available to them by a researcher of their interest. Social bookmarking sites have the potential to transform traditional scholarship practice in which an individual writes a research piece in isolation; networks such as Delicious, CiteULike, and Diigo, allows writers to post an unfinished work in a collaborative space. Tagging or labeling content enables users to generate unique identification tabs to provide easy and quick access to the labeled resource. Tags might be depicted in a visual format known as a "tag cloud" for ease of visibility to the participants. Participatory web tools lead to the development of what is called social scholarship, which operates on the principles of "openness, conversation, collaboration, access, sharing and transparent revision" (Cohen, 2007).

Mash-ups are a social networking tool which present content from various sites such that one is able to combine and contrast the information from the different resources.

Instructor Dimensions

In a formal educational context instructors have the ability to heavily influence learner-media interactions through a variety of strategies and tactics. There are at least three specific dimensions that shape the nature and scope of instructor control. The first dimension is the extent to which an instructor filters, moderates, or otherwise manipulates the information transmitted to learners within a given medium. For example, interactions might be heavily moderated, modestly moderated or not moderated at all. Similarly, access to some information or some types of interaction may require the instructor's permission or presence. A second dimension that is related to the first is the degree to which a given medium is controlled by the instructor or the learners. For example, the instructor might provide specific protocols or scripts that learners, teaching assistants or others must follow. On the other hand, a collaborative tool used by a group to complete an assignment might be completely under the control of the group. A third dimension is the breadth and variety of content available within a specific media. A specific medium might be narrowly focused on a particular assignment or activity, such as, a negotiation exercise, or provide a broad array of content, such as a learning portal.

Collectively, these media, learner, and instructor characteristics offer a broad-based set of variables for characterizing interactive social media within an educational content. These variables are intended to be illustrative rather than exhaustive but they can serve to organize and direct educational researchers in generating theoretically interesting and practically useful research questions.

INTERRELATEDNESS AMONG THE DIMENSIONS

Social media software tools offer a tremendous opportunity to identify, design, and locate the ideal array of verbal and visual content best suited to a specific learner. While the task of identifying and matching user-specific characteristics to an application is commonly used in commercial applications, the development of social software for the use of education is imminent. For example, at Amazon, choices and preferences of individuals are recorded and matched with the choices of similar users. This matched information is then used to predict potential choices for a user in the future. In educational terms, the complex profile information of an individual is drawn upon to gather sufficient data in order to compile the participatory Web tools that could be most suitable for the learner (based on his or her profile).

Web 2.0 allows for the interactive use of a variety of web participatory tools. The convergence of these tools in the domain of pedagogy can create new synergistic possibilities to better assist students. Jonassen, Peck, and Wilson (1999) define these tools as 'mind tools' to promote interaction, cognitive reflection, construction of meaning, and deep engagement with learning materials. Wikis and blogs aid in actively creating knowledge structures; Podcasts provide a constant stream of knowledge and information. Any information updated on wikis and blogs can be obtained with little effort via RSS feeds. At the same time, learners interact with one another to create a dynamic learning ecosystem.

Some Web participatory tools utilize the dimensions defined above to a different extent. For example, Second Life (SL) is a 3-D Multi-User Virtual Environment (MUVE) in which users interact simultaneously with one another through avatars, user-designed representations of the self. Users create their own context for interaction which is an integral force in the use of SL in higher education. Individual members can create objects complete with audio, video, and text and proceed to interact spontaneously with these objects in the 3D environment. In the higher education arena, SL can be used to simulate real life conditions such as debates, discussions, conversations and presentations. In fact, some authors reported a strong correlation of virtual world avatars to mutual gaze. While SL provides the opportunity to closely represent the real life scenario, it is not equipped to provide information such as emotional response, facial expression and body language, which are important sources of information in real life. In this regard, Sullivan, Deutschmann, and Steinvall (2009) suggest that linguistic cues take on the role of providing visual communicative cues and signals. SL provides a low anxiety immersive arena where individuals convene and practice new skills such as language acquisition. Kay and Fitzgerald (2009) identified a set of categories that SL can be used for educational activities which include self-paced tutorials, display and exhibits, immersive exhibits, role plays and simulations, data simulations, treasure hunts and quests, language and cultural immersion, and creative writing.

ISSUES FOR RESEARCH AND APPLICATION

While social interaction has a long history within an educational context the development and use of computer mediated interactive social media is of very recent origin. Technologies and tools continue to evolve, and new tools and media often give rise to yet additional tools and media. For example, Facebook, was launched in early 2004 and has subsequently given rise to a host of interactive games, applications, and add-on tools that further expand opportunities for interaction, sharing of information, and expansion of social networks; it has also migrated to mobile media. Various efforts to use interactive social media in the service of education have been documented (Reuben, 2008). However, much of the current literature is largely descriptive, offering discussions of demonstrations projects, efforts by individual faculty members, and examples of use. While such catalogs are useful there is clearly a need for a more theoretically grounded examination of these media as tools for the service of education. A starting point for such an examination is the development and testing of the types of taxonomies that have been offered in this chapter. Such taxonomies need to go beyond simple listings of alternative social media to identification of underlying dimensions of media, actors and interactions. This establishes similarities and differences that can be linked to the learning processes and learning outcomes.

There is little doubt that interactive social media have already become a significant part of the media landscape. They already play a significant role in the delivery of educational content in both formal and informal contexts. However, their advent has also raised a host of issues. The enormous access and ready availability of these media create a need for verification of content. Merely because information is shared, even if shared on a wide scale, it is not necessarily accurate or correct. Thus there is a need for certifying the authenticity and credibility of information. At the same time there is need to authenticate original work by individuals both to protect intellectual property and to reduce the potential for plagiarism.

Computer mediated social media also raise new issues with respect to privacy and the confidentiality of personal information. Linking one social medium tool to another may require the user to submit user details and other user-related information. Thus, the dimensions of control and access are especially important when considering the use of these tools. Virtual learning environments also have the potential to introduce individuals into the learning process who are not part of the formal institution or learning process.

The success of social media in the field of education also depends on its adoption by both instructors and learners. There are potential barriers to such adoption. Such media tend to blur the relationship of private and public life, of work, study and leisure, and meaning of "relationship." By their very nature social media create collaborative environments that are highly context dependent. This makes assessment of the independent performance of a learner difficult to evaluate. Thus final evaluations may be tedious and create a barrier to adoption of the media.

Finally, there are important questions about which types of media to use in the service of specific learning objectives. The answers to these questions depend on which media are most effective for delivering specific types of content for particular types of learners. These questions include not only the selection of specific social media but also what might better be delivered in the more traditional interactive social medium of the classroom and what might be the optimal mix of traditional versus social media for specific learning outcomes.

REFERENCES

Anon. (n.d.). *About podagogy.com.* Retrieved from http://www.podagogy.com

Arabaugh, J. B. (2005). Is there an optimal design for on-line MBA courses. *Academy of Management Learning and Education, 4*(2), 125-149.

Balasubramanian, S., Raghunathan, R., & Mahajan, V. (2005). Consumers in a multichannel environment: Product utility, process utility, and channel Choice. *Journal of Interactive Marketing, 19*(2), 12-30.

Beldarrain, Y. (2006). Distance education trends: Integrating new technologies to foster student interaction and collaboration. *Distance Education, 21*(2), 139-153.

Bober, M. J., & Dennen, V. P. (2001). Intersubjectivity: Facilitating knowledge construction in online environments. *Education Media International, 38*(4), 241-250.

Boles, W. W., Pillay, H., & Raj, L. (1999, December). Matching cognitive styles to computer-based instruction: An approach for enhanced learning in electrical engineering. *European Journal of Engineering Education, 24,* 371-383.

Boulos, M., Maramba, I., & Wheeler, S. (2006). Wikis, blogs and podcasts: A new generation of web-based tools for virtual collaborative clinical practice and education. *BMC Medical Education, 6*(41). Retrieved from http://www.biomedcentral.com/1472-6920/6/41

Cambiano, R. L., De Vore, J. B., & Harvey, R. (2001). Leaning style preferences of the cohorts: Generation X, baby boomers, and the silent generation. *PAACE Journal of Lifelong Learning, 10,* 31-39.

Carver, C. A., Howard, A. R., & Lane, W. D. (1999). Enhnacing student learning through hypermedia courseware and incorporation of student learning style. *IEEE Transactions on Education, 42*(1), 33-38.

Cavazza, F. (2008). *Social media landscape.* Retrieved from http://www.fredcavazza.net/2008/06/09/social-media-landscape/

Chan, A., & Lee, M. J. W. (2005). An MP3 a day keeps the worries away: Exploring the use of podcasting to address preconceptions and alleviate pre-class anxiety amongst undergraduate information technology students. In D. H. R. Spennemann & L. Burr (Eds.), *Good practice in practice: Proceedings of the Student Experience Conference* (pp. 58-70). Wagga Wagga, New South Wales, Australia: Charles Sturt University.

Cronin, J. J. (2009). Upgrading to web 2.0: An experiential project to build a marketing wiki. *Journal of Marketing Education, 31*(1), 66-75.

Cohen, L. (2007, May 1). Social scholarship on the rise [Web log message]. *Library 2.0: An academic's perspective* Retrieved from http://liblogs.albany.edu/library20/2007/04/social_scholarship_on_the_rise.html

Dale, C., & Pymm, J. M. (2009). Podagogy: The i-Pod as a learning technology. *Active Learning in Higher Education, 10*(1), 84-96.

Dalsgaard, C. (2006). Social software: E-learning beyond learning management systems. *European Journal of Open, Distance and E-Learning, 2006/II*. Retrieved from http://www.eurodl.org/materials/contrib/2006/Christian_Dalsgaard.htm

Dalsgaard, C., & Paulsen, M. F. (2009). Transparency in cooperatibe online education. *International Review of Research in Open and Distance Learning, 10*(3), 1-22.

Dewey, J. (1938). *Experience and education*. New York, NY: Macmillan.

Dholakia, U., Kahn, B. E., Reeves, R., Rindfleisch, A., Stewart, D. W., & Taylor, E. (in press). Consumer behavior in a multichannel, multimedia retailing environment. *Journal of Interactive Marketing*.

Dron, J., & Anderson, T. (2007, October). *Collectives, networks and groups in social software for e-learning*. Paper presented at the Proceedings of World Conference on E-Learning in Corporate, Government, Healthcare, and Higher Education Quebec.

Duff, A. (2000). Learning styles measurement: the revised approaches to studying inventory (RASI). *Bristol Business School Teaching and Research Review, 3*(Summer). Retrieved from http://www.uwe.ac.uk/bbs/trr/Issue3/Is3-1_5.htm

Duffy, T. M., & Cunningham, D. J. (1996) Constructivism: Implications for the design and delivery of instruction. In D. H. Jonassen (Ed.), *Handbook of research for educational communications and technology* (pp. 170-198). New York, NY: Simon & Shuster Macmillan.

Dunn, R., Bruno, J., Sklar, R. I., Zenhausern, R., & Beaudry, J. (1990) Effects of matching and mismatching minority developmental college students' hemispheric preferences on mathematics scores. *Journal of Educational Research, 83*(5), 283-288.

Dunn, R., & Dunn, K. (1978). Teaching students through their individual learning styles. Reston, VA: Reston.

Engstrom, Y. (1987). *Learning by expanding: An activity-theoretical approach to developmental research*. Helsinki, Finland: Orienta-Konsultit.

Farnsworth, J., & Austin, T. (2005). Mobile social networks assembling portable talk and mobile worlds: Sound technologies and mobile social networks. *Convergence, 11*(2), 14-22.

Felder, R. M., & Brent, R. (2005). Understanding student differences. *Journal of Engineering Education, 94*(1), 57-72.

Felder, R. M., & Silverman, L. K. (1988). Learning and teaching styles in engineering education. *Engineering Education, 78*(7), 674-681.

Garrison, D. R. (1990). An analysis and evaluation of audioteleconferencing to facilitate education at a distance. *The American Journal of Distance Education, 4*(3), 13-24.

Garrison, D. R., & Anderson, T. (2003). *E-learning in the 21st century: A framework for research and practice*. London, England: RoutledgeFalmer.

Garrison, D. R., Anderson, T., & Archer, W. (1999). Critical inquiry in a text-based environment: Computer conferencing in higher education. *Internet and Higher Education*, *2*(2-3), 87-105.

Gee, J. P. (2004). *Situated language and learning: a critique of traditional schooling.* New York, NY: Routledge.

Gunawardena, C. N., Hermans, M. B., Sanchez, D., Richmond, C., Bohley, M., & Tuttle, R. (2009). A theoretical framework for building online communities of practice with social networking tools. *Education Media International*, *46*(1), 3-16.

Hobaugh, C. F. (1997). Interactive strategies for collaborative learning. In *Competition, Connection, Collaboration: 13th annual conference on distance teaching & learning: August 6-8, 1997, Holiday Inn Madison West, Madison, Wisconsin, proceedings* (pp. 121-125). Madison, WI: University of Wisconsin-Madison.

Hutchinson, J. W., & Eisenstein, E. M. (2008). Consumer learning and expertise. In C. P. Haugtvedt, P. M. Herr, & F. R. Kardes (Eds.), *Handbook of consumer psychology* (pp. 103-132.) New York, NY: Psychology Press.

Jonassen, D. H., Peck, K. L., & Wilson, B. G. (1999). *Learning with technology: A constructivist perspective.* Upper Saddle River, NJ: Merrill.

Kaplan, A. M., & Haenlein, M. (2010). Users of the world, unite! The challenges and opportunities of social media. *Business Horizons*, *53*(1), 59-68.

Kay, J., & Fitzgerald, S. (2009). *Second Life in education.* Retrieved from SLEDUCATION: http://sleducation.wikispaces.com/educationaluses

Keefe, J. W. (1979). *Student learning styles: diagnosing and prescribing programs.* Reston, VA: National Association of Secondary School Principals.

Kolb, D. A. (1971). *Organizational psychology.* Englewood Cliffs, NJ: Prentice-Hall.

Kozinets, R. V., Valck, K. D., Wojnicki, A. C., & Wilner, S. J. (2010). Networked narratives: Understanding word-of-mouth marketing in online communitied. *Journal of Marketing*, *73*(March), 71-89.

Laurillard, D. (1995). *Rethinking university teaching a framework for the effective use of educational technology.* London, England: Routledge.

Lee, M. J., Miller, C., & Newnham, L. (2008). RSS and content syndication in higher education: Subscribing to a new model of teaching and learning. *Educational Media International*, *45*(4), 311-322.

Ling, L. H. (2007). Community of inquiry in an online undergraduate information technology course. *Journal of Information Technology Education*, *6*, 153-168.

Madell, D., & Muncer, S. (2006). Internet communication: An activity that appeals to shy and socially phobic people? *CyberPsyhcology & Behavior*, *9*, 618-622.

Mandel, N., & Johnson, E. (2002). When Web pages influence choice: Effects of visual primes on experts and novices. *Journal of Consumer Research*, *29*(2), 235-245.

Mason, R., & Rennie, F. (2008). *E-learning and social networking handbook: Resources for higher education.* New York, NY: Routledge.

Mayer, R. E. (2001). *Multimedia learning.* Cambridge, England: Cambridge University Press.

Norman, D. A. (1999). Affordances, conventions and design. *Interactions*, *6*(3), 38-43.

O'Reilly, T. (2005). *What is web 2.0: Design patterns and business models for the next generation of software.* Retrieved from http://www.oreillynet.com

O'Reilly, T., & Battelle, J. (2004, October). *Opening welcome: State of the Internet industry.* Presented at Web 2.0 conference, San Francisco, CA.

Orr, E. S., Sisic, M., Ross, C., Simmering, M. G., Arseneault, J. M., & Orr, R. R. (2009). The influence of shyness on the use of Facebook in an undergraduate sample. *CyberPsychology & Behavior, 12*(3), 337-340.

Riva, G. (2007). Virtual reality and Telepresence. *Science, 318,* 1241-1242.

Reuben, R. (2008). *The use of social media in higher education for marketing and communications: A guide for professionals in higher education.* Retrieved from http://doteduguru.com/wp-content/uploads/2008/08/social-media-in-higher-education.pdf

Roschelle, J., & Teasley, S. (1995). The construction of shared knowledge in collaborative problem solving. (1995). In J. Roschelle & S. D. Teasley (Authors), *Computer supported collaborative learning* (pp. 69-97). Berlin, Germany: Springer-Verlag.

Safko, L., & Brake, D. K. (2009). *The social media bible: tactics, tools, and strategies for business success.* Hoboken, NJ: John Wiley & Sons.

Salmon, G. (2003). *E-moderating: The key to teaching and learning online.* London, England: RoutledgeFalmer.

Sheeks, M. S., & Birchmeier, Z. P. (2007). Shyness, sociability, and the use of computer-mediated communication in relation development. *CyberPsychology & Behavior, 10,* 64-70.

Solis, B. (2008a). *Introducing the conversation prism.* Retrieved from http://www.briansolis.com/2008/08/introducing-conversationprism.html

Solis, B. (2008b). *The essential guide to social media.* Retrieved from http://www.briansolis.com/2008/06/essential-guide-to-social-media-free/

Stewart, D. W., & Pavlou, P. (2002). From consumer response to active consumer: Measuring the effectiveness of interactive media. *Journal of the Academy of Marketing Science, 30*(4), 376-396.

Stewart D. W., & Pavlou, P. (2007). Measuring the effects of interactive media. In D. Schumann & E. Thorsen (Eds.), *Internet advertising, theory and research* (pp. 225-257). Mahwah, NJ: Erlbaum.

Stewart, D. W., & Pavlou, P. (2008). The effects of media on marketing communications. In J. Bryant & M. B. Oliver (Eds.), *Media effects: Advances in theory and research* (3rd ed., pp. 363-402). New York, NY: Taylor and Francis Group.

Suler, J. (2008). Image, word, action: Interpersonal dynamics in a photo-sharing community. *CyberPsychology and Behavior, 11*(5), 555-560.

Sullivan, E., Deutschmann, K., & Steinvall, A. (2009). Supporting learning reflection in the language translation class. *International Journal of Information Communication Technologies and Human Development, 2*(3), 26-48.

Vermaas, K., & Van de Wijngaert, L. (2004, May). *Internet and the uses of uses and gratitifaction.* Paper presented to the 2004 annual meeting of the International Communication Association, New Orleans, LA.

Vratulis, V., & Dobson, T. M. (2008). Social negotiations in a wiki environment. *Educational Media International, 45*(4), 285-294.

Vygotsky, L. S. (1962). *Thought and language.* Cambridge, MA: The MIT Press

Wenger, E., McDermott, R., & Snyder, W. (2002). *Cultivating communities of practice: A guide to managing knowledge.* Boston, MA: Harvard Business School Press.

Yang, S. H. (2009). Using blogs to enhance critical reflection and community of practice. *Educational Technology & Society, 12*(2), 11-21.

CHAPTER 3

TEACHING AND LEARNING WITH SKYPE

Alanah Mitchell, Charlie Chen, and B. Dawn Medlin

Electronic learning, or e-learning, is becoming an increasingly common way to educate and train individuals. However, along with the benefits of e-learning there are some challenges. This chapter presents a process which uses Skype and VoIP (voice over Internet protocol) technology as an e-learning system. As such, this chapter discusses the background of e-learning systems. We then present a collaboration process for teaching and learning with Skype and discuss the application of the process in relation to intercultural communication. As education and organizations become more global, the ability to work with diverse cultures is increasingly important. To address this challenge, this chapter presents the application and use of Skype to teach and learn intercultural communication between U.S. and Taiwanese students. The chapter describes the process in detail and highlights research results from this experience which suggest that VoIP technology provides a good fit for one-on-one e-learning in addressing an intercultural communication task.

Cutting-Edge Social Media Approaches to Business Education:
Teaching With LinkedIn, Facebook, Twitter, Second Life, and Blogs, pp. 39–56
Copyright © 2010 by Information Age Publishing
All rights of reproduction in any form reserved.

INTRODUCTION

Electronic learning, or e-learning, systems allow for education and training to be delivered electronically, through the use of information and communication technologies (Chen, Wu, & Yang, 2006). E-learning is becoming increasingly popular for academic institutions as well as other organizations because the process provides consistent education and reduces time, information overload, and expenses, as well as increases learner convenience and improves tracking (Welsh, Wanberg, Brown, & Simmering, 2003). The use of electronic learning systems not only allows for the education and training of students, but the process of learning through an e-learning system also provides students with the skills necessary to work in a virtual environment. Increasingly, practitioners are experiencing what it means to work within a virtual team and e-learning systems are an option for preparing practitioners for this experience (Davis & Zigurs, 2008; Robey, Khoo, & Powers, 2000).

Despite the benefits of e-learning systems, there are some drawbacks in relation to upfront system costs and the lack of learner interaction (Welsh, et al., 2003). Due to its accessibility and interaction capabilities, an e-learning system which relies strictly on voice over Internet protocol (VoIP) technology offers a way to address these two drawbacks. Based on this idea, our research has resulted in the design and field test of a collaborative process for teaching and learning over Skype.[1] As education and organizations become more global the ability to work with diverse cultures is increasingly important. Therefore, we tested our process in relation to an intercultural communication task. This chapter presents the application of using Skype to teach and learn intercultural communication between U.S. and Taiwanese students.

The chapter begins with a background of e-learning. Next, the chapter describes the collaborative process for teaching and learning with Skype as well as the research results obtained during the application of the process in relation to intercultural communication. The chapter then presents a discussion of future trends and research issues as well as our conclusions.

BACKGROUND ON E-LEARNING

An extensive body of research exists in the area of teaching in online environments (e.g., Alavi, 1994; Hiltz, 1997; Leidner & Jarvenpaa, 1995; Shen, Hiltz, & Bieber, 2006; Sloffer, Dueber, & Duffy, 1999). E-learning is one example of this form of teaching. By definition, e-learning is the use of information and communication technologies over the Internet to deliver information and instruction to individuals (Welsh et al., 2003). E-learning systems increase the ability to collaborate asynchronously or synchronously by relying on technology features that allow for video conferencing and collaboratively accessing web applications and information repositories (Chen et al., 2006; Welsh et al., 2003).

E-learning systems allow for collaborative learning which has been defined as "a learning process that emphasizes group or cooperative efforts among faculty and students" (Hiltz, 1997). This type of approach centers on learning and implies that different people with different backgrounds can work together to address challenges and solve problems (Kirschner & Van Bruggen, 2004; Shen et al., 2006). Learning emerges through the interaction that collaboration learning requires (Kirschner & Van Bruggen, 2004; Shen et al., 2006). The diverse backgrounds of collaborative learners allows for rich problem analysis and rich solutions (Kirschner & Van Bruggen, 2004). However, collaborative learner diversity can lead to challenges such as conflicting perspectives (Kirschner & Van Bruggen, 2004). Despite challenges collaborative learning results in more student involvement and more learning engagement, problem solving, and critical thinking (Alavi, 1994; Leidner & Fuller, 1997; Shen et al., 2006; Sloffer et al., 1999).

Common, asynchronous e-learning environments include Blackboard[2] (e.g., O'Dwyer, Carey, & Kleiman, 2007), WebCT[3] (e.g. Shen et al., 2006), and Moodle.[4] However, a simple asynchronous e-learning example might only include PowerPoint slides posted to a website (Welsh et al., 2003).

As an alternative to an asynchronous learning environment, synchronous e-learning environments might involve the use of WebEx,[5] GoToMeeting,[6] or another electronic meeting system. With this type of set-up, learners from different locations log in, as an instructor facilitates a discussion with the use of slides and/or a whiteboard (Welsh et al., 2003). There have been numerous studies on the use of electronic meeting systems and groupware to support group processes and enhance learning (Fjermestad & Hiltz, 2000/2001); therefore with this chapter we are focusing on the most basic type of synchronous e-learning: VoIP. VoIP technology, specifically an online synchronous audio and video system, provides the most basic type of real time audio or video conferencing necessary for e-learning. VoIP technology enables one-to-one, one-to-many, or many-to-many interactions between people who are geographically dispersed. Previous research of electronic group work has found that the use of Skype, or any other VoIP technology, is a useful way to establish learning (Davis, Germonprez, Petter, Drum, & Kolstad, 2009).

As suggested above, e-learning is becoming increasingly popular for academic institutions as well as organizations due to the educational consistency, learner convenience and tracking, and the reduction of information overload and expense (Welsh et al., 2003). Furthermore, the use of electronic learning systems not only allows for the education and training of students, but it also prepares practitioners to work in a virtual team, a skill that is growing in necessity (Davis & Zigurs, 2008; Robey et al., 2000). With this chapter, we also explore this factor.

A COLLABORATIVE PROCESS FOR TEACHING AND LEARNING WITH SKYPE

We developed a collaborative process for teaching and learning with Skype. Our process, shown in Figure 3.1, consists of four steps: identifying, brainstorming, connecting, and concluding. The following subsections discuss each step in detail.

Step 1: Identify the Participants and the Task

The teaching and learning process using Skype begins with the identification of the participants and the task. In relation to task, the theory of task-technology fit (TTF) suggests that technology is more likely to have a positive impact on performance and is more likely to be used if the technology capabilities match the user's task (Goodhue & Thompson, 1995; Zigurs & Buckland, 1998). The basic premise of task-technology fit suggests that user perceptions of task-technology fit are impacted by the task and the technology characteristics (Goodhue & Thompson, 1995). Additionally, the theory suggests that task-technology fit impacts performance and is mediated by utilization.

A group level analysis of task-technology fit suggests that group performance is impacted by the fit profile between the task and a group technology (Zigurs & Buckland, 1998). In this theory of task-technology fit, tasks are characterized as simple, problem, decision, judgment, or fuzzy, while technologies are characterized according to the degree of support for communication, process structuring, and information processing (Zigurs

Figure 3.1.   Collaborative process for teaching and learning with Skype.

& Buckland, 1998; Zigurs, Buckland, Connolly, & Wilson, 1999). Each task type is then associated with a technology which best fits the task. For example, simple tasks are associated with a single outcome and are best fit with a technology that offers high communication support, low process structuring, and low information processing so that team members can easily communicate their ideas. Problem and decision tasks technology should allow for low communication support, low process structuring, and high information processing. Finally, for fuzzy tasks, high communication support, medium process structuring, and high information processing is necessary from the team technology.

With our process, we are using Skype, a VoIP system, which offers high communication support, low process structuring, and low information processing. According to task-technology fit, this means the technology is best suited for a simple task. Therefore, with this process, it is critical that a simple task is chosen.

We identified approximately 60 students from Taiwan who were interested in learning English (the learners), a task that can be classified as a simple task. We then identified approximately 100 students from the United States who could also participate in this process (as the teachers). These students were brought together to work one-on-one in order to increase their intercultural communication competency. The students from Taiwan were volunteers interested in learning English, while the students from the United States were undergraduates taking an introductory MIS course.

As mentioned above, the use of electronic learning systems not only allows for the education and training of students, but it also prepares practitioners to work in a virtual team, a skill that is growing in necessity (Davis & Zigurs, 2008; Robey et al., 2000). Virtual teams are comprised of individuals who work in different geographic locations, time zones, organizations, and/or cultures (Dubé & Paré, 2004; Lipnack & Stamps, 1997). As a part of this collaboration, team members are often faced with intercultural communication challenges (Avison & Banks, 2008; Cramton, 2002). Therefore, a simple task which addresses improving students' intercultural communication competency fits with our VoIP technology selection. In fact, VoIP has become the choice technology for people who are interested in improving their intercultural communication competence (Scott, 2008). VoIP technology adds realism and life to intercultural interactions without geographical limitations. This excites and motivates students during the learning process (Scott, 2008). With VoIP, real-time conversation exchange can directly and indirectly develop second-language speaking abilities by allowing native speakers to provide immediate phonetic feedback and authentic interactions to the learners (Payne & Whitney, 2002). Depending on the participants and their goals, other simple tasks can be chosen for the process of teaching and learning in Skype.

Step 2: Brainstorm Topics for Conversation

The second step in the process focuses on what will be achieved while working in Skype. To this end, the brainstorming needs to take place. Prior to the Skype sessions, lists of cultural topics were created for all of the students. The goal of this list was to give the students something to think about discussing. The U.S. students collaborated using GoogleDocuments[7] (an online collaborative document tool) in order to brainstorm and come up with content and questions for discussion. Overall, 41 topics were identified in the areas of personal experience (e.g., places, people, culture, food, and hobbies), personal preference (e.g., cars, vacations, cash or gift, and indoors or outdoors), personal opinions (e.g., chores, beauty, decisions, and zoos), and personal comparisons (e.g., summer jobs, travel, language, news, and food). The final list was posted online for all of the students (in the United States and Taiwan) to review prior to the sessions.

Step 3: Provide Instruction and Connect Participants

Once all the preparation has been completed, the next step is to connect the participants in Skype. To initiate this connection, we provided our students with computers that had Skype installed, headphones, and webcams (see Figure 3.2). Additionally, instructions should be provided. In our case, we used the following five step instructions for our U.S. students:

1. Log into Skype with your assigned username and password;
2. Add the corresponding Taiwanese student's Skype username as a new contact;
3. Wait for the Taiwanese student to accept your invitation;
4. Start discussing with each other according to the handout/website; and
5. Wrap up your discussion.

Sessions were held following these instructions, with each session lasting around 50 minutes. There were many sessions held, with approximately 30 students from the United States and 30 from Taiwan in each

Figure 3.2.   Picture of U.S. student working with student from Taiwan.

session. This means that even though there were fewer students from Taiwan overall, the pairings were equal for the sessions and some Taiwanese students participated more than once. The sessions included simple conversations which allowed the Taiwanese students the opportunity to practice speaking in English as well as discussions beyond this interaction where U.S. students corrected pronunciation and did more teaching. Table 3.1 shows a couple of sample questions and answers that took place during the sessions.

Step 4: Wrap-up and Discussion

Once the exercise has taken place, the final step is to close with a wrap-up and discussion. Following our sessions and Skype conversations, a post-survey was given to the students using SurveyMonkey[8] (see Table 3.2). Students completed the survey after their first session only. Our primary purpose of this survey was to gain an understanding of the e-learning process and whether Skype and VoIP technology can be useful for this type of teaching and learning.

Table 3.1. Sample Questions and Answers
From the One-on-One Sessions

- **Question**: Who is the person who has influenced your life the most?
- **Answer**: The person who has most influenced my life is my mother. She raised two girls on her own for 15 years and also battled cancer for 3 of those 15 years. She is a very strong and admirable woman who keeps a positive outlook on life. I can only hope to one day possess the courage and grace which she displays on a daily basis.
- **Question**: Who is the biggest role model in your life? Explain how he/she has helped you to become the person you are today. Is this person related to you? Do you have a role-model that is famous? How did they become your role model? How long have you known this person?
- **Answer**: In my family, my mother has influenced me greatly because she has so many good qualities. She is very well educated and keeps an open mind. Her thinking is very modern. She is able to understand people from different generations. In addition, she is a good listener. This makes her tolerant of other people's opinions. Her personal values set a good example for me to follow in my own life. The way she treats people and thinks makes me want to become the best person I can be. This is why I think my mother has influenced me the most in my life.

Table 3.2. Postsurvey Questions

1. Do you think that Skype is a useful way to teach another language (in this case English)? Why or why not?

2. Do you think that you were able to successfully teach another language to the person you worked with today? Why or why not?

3. How many more sessions would you need till the person you worked with was able to easily hold a conversation in English?

    a. None, They Can Hold A Conversation Now/Less Than 5/5-10/10-20/20+

4. Do you think that Skype is a useful way to get to know individuals? Why or why not?

5. What are some of the things that you learned about the individuals you talked with on Skype?

6. What technology capabilities did you use to teach these individuals?

    a. Text Chat/Video Chat/Other (Specify)

7. What technology capabilities did you not use that you think would have been helpful to have access to?

    a. Text Chat/Video Chat/Other (Specify)

8. Describe the experience that you just had. What did you talk about, what was your method or process for teaching another language, etc? Be detailed.

9. Describe the most positive aspects of the experience you just had?

10. Describe the most negative aspects of the experience you just had?

11. Is this your first time using Skype? If not, how long have you been experienced with Skype?

    a. 0-6 Months/6 Months-1 Year/1-2 Years/2+ Years

The following section presents many viewpoints submitted by the students who were surveyed.

APPLICATION EXPERIENCE: INTERCULTURAL COMMUNICATION

In the process presented above, we included the details of an actual application of our process focused on the task of intercultural communication. The following subsections describe the analysis and results of the data that were collected using the approach explained in the previous section. We begin by presenting the findings from the questionnaire in relation to demographics.

As Table 3.3 shows, the subjects in this study were student age and only half of them had used Skype prior to this experience. Of those that had used Skype they either had very little experience (i.e., less than 6 months) or significant experience (i.e., 1 to 2 years).

The remainder of this section focuses on the students' perceptions of Skype as an e-learning tool for teaching and learning intercultural communication, their relationship development, the role of the technology in this learning process, and the overall experience findings.

Teaching and Learning

Our primary goal was to investigate whether Skype could be a useful e-learning system to foster an innovative learning environment for the teaching and learning of a language (i.e., English) in order to improve

Table 3.3.   Profile of Study Participants

Demographic Variable	N	Frequency: U.S.	N	Frequency: Taiwan
Age	84	18-20 (14.3%) 20-22 (71.4%) 22-25 (10.7%) 25-30 (2.4%) 30-40 (1.2%)	25	18-20 (92.0%) 20-22 (8.0%)
First time using Skype	84	Yes (53.5%) No (46.4%)	25	Yes (52.0%) No (48.0%)
Of those experienced, length of experience	39	0-6 months (33.3%) 6 months (15.4%) 1-2 years (35.9%) 2+ years (15.4%)	12	0-6 months (33.3%) 6 months (25.0%) 1-2 years (33.3%) 2+ years (8.3%)

**Table 3.4.   Usefulness and Success of Sessions
With Regard to Teaching and Learning**

Variable	N	Frequency: U.S.	N	Frequency: Taiwan
Usefulness	84	• Yes (78.6%) • No (21.4%)	25	• Yes (88.0%) • No (12.0%)
Successful	84	• Yes (42.9%) • No (57.1%)	25	• Yes (84.0%) • No (16.0%)
More sessions required to be successful	84	• None, they can hold a conversation now (50.0%) • Less than 5 (20.2%) • 5-10 (16.7%) • 10-20 (7.1%) • 20+ (6.0%)	25	• None, I can hold a conversation now (12.0%) • Less than 5 (36.0%) • 5-10 (44.0%) • 10-20 (8.0%) • 20+ (0.0%)

intercultural communications. At the end of the sessions, 78.6% of the U.S. students and 88.0% of the Taiwanese students found that Skype was indeed a useful way to teach (from the U.S. perspective) and learn (from the Taiwanese perspective) another language (see Table 3.4).

The positive comments from the students suggested that the ability to practice another language was the greatest benefit of using Skype. For example, one U.S. student made the following comment: "*It helps non-English students hear how the language is spoken and words that are typically used. Sometimes when learning a different language it's hard to know which words to use in certain situations and hearing a native person speak is very helpful. Gives practice that is also fun.*" Another student commented, that Skype was an excellent tool because of the accessibility: "*It is cheap and allows communication across great distances.*" Despite the positive comments 8.2% of the students that commented were concerned with the technology and potential issues that might occur: "*I think it could be a very good way to teach a language. However, if someone were to have a problem with their microphone then it could be a small problem but other than that I think that this could be a good way. That is because you can interact and learn from someone online and you do not actually have to be near that person.*"

When asked if they were successful in teaching and learning, only 42.9% of the U.S. students thought that they did a good job teaching the person that they worked with. This is an interesting point, considering that 84.0% of the Taiwanese students felt that they were successful in learning during the session. In fact, 50.0% of the U.S. students felt like they did not need to hold any more sessions to teach their partners because they felt that the Taiwanese students were able to easily hold a conversation in English. One student commented: "*The students I talked to were pretty fluent in English, but both seemed to doubt themselves when it came to speaking English. I think more interaction would boost their confidence and give them good experience. Learning a language from a book is very different than talking to someone with a genuine accent or dialect.*"

Despite the U.S. students' confidence in the Taiwanese students, only 12.0% of the Taiwanese students felt that they were able to hold a conversation. Many of them made comments like: "*My English is so poor.*" Along with the English teaching and learning, there was also teaching about different slang terms. One U.S. student commented: "*I said a few words that he was not sure what they mean so I had to explain to him what they were. Such as the NFL, he knew about American Football but he really did not know what the NFL was or what it stood for.*" Additionally, 3.6% of the U.S. students commented that they learned something themselves. For example: "*I learned how to say Hi and how are you in Taiwanese (Niho and niho ma).*" Overall, the students attributed the usefulness and success of teaching and learning in Skype to (1) the ability to practice another language, (2) the ability to see the person you are talking to, and (3) the accessibility of the technology. Any concerns of the process were related to (1) technical concerns or (2) communication challenges and misunderstandings.

Relationship Development

As we mentioned in the previous section, the students learned more than just English. When asked whether they found the use of Skype to be a good way to get to know individuals, the result was almost unanimous among both groups of students (see Table 3.5).

Interestingly, 13.8% of the students commented on how easy the process was and how easy it was to talk to people from a different culture through Skype: "*I think it is an easy way to be able to interact with people that are thousands of miles away. You can talk to just about anyone, anywhere. Even if the language barrier is there to an extent you can still learn a lot of information about that person.*"

Many of the topics discussed were related to hobbies, travel, food, family, and school or job related factors. This makes sense considering the pretask list of topics that each student had to review. Pop culture topics

Table 3.5.   Usefulness of Sessions in Terms of Relationships

Variable	N	Frequency: U.S.	N	Frequency: Taiwan
Usefulness	84	Yes (100.0%) No (0.0%)	25	Yes (96.0%) No (4.0%)

were discussed which showed some of the students that their cultures are not that much different. For example, one U.S. girl mentioned that the girl she talked to was much like her: "*She likes the movie Twilight and thinks the actor Robert Pattinson is hot. She enjoys swimming for fun. She drives a motorcycle 100cc for transportation. She also likes American food, mostly fast food.*" In fact, many of the students found that they were very similar: "*They are more similar to me than I thought. They do the same things I do and like the same things.*"

There were also comments from students who discussed aspects that differ between the cultures. For example, one U.S. student commented: "*In this study you are kind of forced to discuss issues, though I was nervous at the beginning it was very interesting to learn about a different culture.*" Whether they found similarities or differences it is interesting to note that such a high percentage of the students were able to foster an innovative learning environment for not only the teaching and learning of a language, but relationship development as well.

Role of Information Technology

During the sessions, students were allowed to use the text, audio, and video features offered in Skype. As Table 3.6 shows, the students relied more on the video feature of Skype than the texting feature. After the session, a few students mentioned that they were unaware that texting was an option: "*I didn't know that we had the ability to use text chat, I think that would have helped immensely.*" Those who did not use texting though that it would have been helpful to do so: "*Sometimes it was hard to understand what he was saying so it would have been easier if he were to just type those words.*"

Other students commented that they used every feature they could, and would have preferred more features outside of Skype. For example: "*Being able to quickly reference internet and pull up pictures, maps and other useful things to make the conversation more productive. Easier to show examples than to just talk about things.*" Due to the fact that all of the communication took place through the use of technology, IT did play a critical role in both the teaching and learning and the relationship development among the students.

Table 3.6. Technology Capabilities Used

Variable	N	Frequency: U.S.	N	Frequency: Taiwan
Used	84	Text (26.2%) Video (96.4%)	25	Text (32.0%) Video (72.0%)

Overall Experience Findings

For the most part the students were very happy with the experience. In fact, all of the students were able to identify a positive aspect of the experience, whether it was related to the use of Skype, the chance to meet and talk with someone from so far away who has a different culture, or the chance to make a new friend. One student commented: "*The most positive aspect of the experience was just knowing that I was talking to someone thousands of miles away in a completely different time zone and I was able to understand him and see him as if he were just a few feet away.*" A couple of students also commented on the learning/teaching aspect of the experience and how they were most excited to have helped someone out. For example, one student mentioned that they were most happy about: "*Encouraging the person to be confident about learning English.*"

When asked what the negative aspects of the experience were, 23.8% of students commented on the language barrier or accent issues causing communication challenges, 19.2% of students commented that they had trouble hearing due to the background noise (with everyone talking in the computer lab at the same time), 18.3% of students said there was nothing negative about the experience as it was mostly positive, and six students commented on technical challenges that occurred such as microphones or webcams not working correctly. Despite these negative comments, the overwhelming feeling regarding the experience was a positive one.

FUTURE TRENDS AND RESEARCH ISSUES

In terms of future trends and research issues, the application experience of this process opens various avenues for future research. For example, there are many opportunities to expand and refine this work. In fact, recent research recommends using both asynchronous and synchronous e-learning systems for teaching and learning (Ferratt & Hall, 2009). Therefore, future research should consider exploring this possibility with a different technology. The collaborative process used in this study may be generalizable to other social media technologies such as blogs, wikis, or discussion boards. Skype could also be combined with an asynchronous e-learning system to address teaching and learning to improve intercultural communication.

Further studies of teaching and learning could also be completed. For example, in regards to teaching, future research might explore how professors or instructors are using Skype (e.g., lectures, office hours, review sessions, etc.). Student perspectives on this use could then be assessed. Additional studies of how the technology is related to learning styles would also be valuable. A future study could begin by having respondents complete a learning styles inventory to identify the way in which they learn. The different learning styles might have an impact the success of this technology.

Additional comparison of the technology capabilities might result in additional interesting findings. For example, to further explore the technology capabilities, an experiment could be set up where half of the students are allowed to use voice and half are allowed to use voice and video. Analysis could then determine the benefits of one approach over the other. Addressing the technology concerns that we uncovered in this study would be another future research consideration. Like the social networking site, Facebook,[9] some universities are limiting or discouraging Skype use due to Skype's built-in feature that can turn a user's computer into a relay station for other users consuming bandwidth. However, as a result of this study it is clear that there are educational benefits from the technology and future studies could address making this option available at all universities.

Ultimately, we hope that the process design presented in this chapter ignites a stream of research that focuses on the use of Skype for teaching and learning. We expect that there are many simple tasks, beyond language, that can be addressed through the use of Skype. In fact, Skype has been used to talk to CEOS, scientific experts, officials, and political leaders in the classroom. Studies of culture in different countries and the comparison of education or holiday celebrations could also be undertaken to address cultural difference. Additionally, students could give presentations beyond their own classroom or collaborate on a project using Skype (Davis et al., 2009). Our process can be used to address these different task types.

CONCLUSIONS

Ultimately, we wanted to investigate whether or not Skype could be a useful e-learning system to foster an innovative learning environment for the teaching and learning of a language in order to improve intercultural communications. The findings from our process application show that students are able to use Skype and its capabilities to achieve the learning goals. Overall, the students attributed the usefulness and success of teaching and learning in Skype to the ability to practice another language, the ability to see the person you are talking to, and the accessibility of the technology. Any concerns of the process were related to technical concerns or communication challenges and misunderstandings. Whether the students found cultural similarities or differences they overwhelming were able to foster an innovative learning environment for not only the teaching and learning of a language, but relationship development as well. Overall, teaching and learning with Skype worked and students who participated in the experience acquired: (1) problem-solving skills, (2) a passion and appreciation for diversity, (3) self-assurance, (4) an understanding of a global economy, (5) global business terminology and savvy, (6) intercultural empathy and diplomacy, and (7) communication skills and possibly foreign language skills.

In term of contributions, our findings suggest that VoIP technology provides a good fit for one-on-one e-learning in addressing an intercultural communication task. Educators can use this technology to provide students with a similar experience to prepare them for their likely future work as a virtual team member (Davis & Zigurs, 2008; Robey et al., 2000). From the instructor perspective Skype was not time-consuming to download and it was not difficult to use in the classroom. To use Skype in the classroom a few simple steps need to be followed: (1) download Skype on the lab computers remembering to consider privacy settings, (2) test the connection beforehand to ensure everything is working, (3) prepare the lecture regarding the task, (4) prepare the participants, task, topics, and instructions for the Skype exercise according to the process presented in this chapter, and (5) prepare discussion questions for the exercise conclusion and wrap-up. Outside of the educational environment, organizations can also use this process to prepare their employees to face intercultural communication competency challenges when working in virtual teams or managing offshore projects (Avison & Banks, 2008).

TERMS AND DEFINITIONS

- e-learning: the use of information and communication technologies over the Internet to deliver information and instruction to individuals (Welsh, et al., 2003).
- Information and communication technologies: an integrated set of tools that supports team communication, process, and information sharing.
- Task-technology fit: the extent that the functionality of a technology matches task requirements (Goodhue & Thompson, 1995; Zigurs & Buckland, 1998).
- Virtual team: a group of individuals who work together from different geographic locations, time zones, organizations, and/or cultures (Dubé & Paré, 2004; Lipnack & Stamps, 1997).

- Voice over Internet protocol (VoIP) technology: an online synchronous audio and/or video system which provides the most basic type of real time audio and/or video conferencing necessary for e-learning. This type of technology enables one-to-one, one-to-many, or many-to-many interactions between people who are geographically dispersed.

ACKNOWLEDGMENT

Some of the ideas in this chapter will be presented at the 16th Americas Conference on Information Systems, Lima, Peru.

NOTES

1. http://www.skype.com/
2. http://blackboard.com/
3. Now owned by Blackboard.
4. http://moodle.org/
5. http://webex.com/
6. http://www.gotomeeting.com/
7. http://docs.google.com/
8. http://www.surveymonkey.com/
9. http://www.facebook.com/

REFERENCES

Alavi, M. (1994). Computer-mediated collaborative learning: An empirical evaluation. *MIS Quarterly, 18*(2), 159-165.

Avison, D., & Banks, P. (2008). Cross-cultural (mis)communication in IS offshoring: understanding through conversation analysis. *Journal of Information Technology, 23*(4), 249-268.

Chen, C. C., Wu, J., & Yang, S. (2006). The efficacy of online cooperative learning systems: The perspective of task-technology fit. *Campus-Wide Information Systems, 23*(3), 112-127.

Cramton, C. D. (2002). Finding common ground in dispersed collaboration. *Organizational Dynamics, 30*(4), 356.

Davis, A., Germonprez, M., Petter, S., Drum, D., & Kolstad, J. (2009). A case study of offshore development across IS courses: Lessons learned from a global student project. *Communications of the Association for Information Systems, 24*(21), 351-372.

Davis, A., & Zigurs, I. (2008, August). *Teaching and learning about virtual collaboration: What we know and need to know.* Paper presented at the 14th Americas Conference on Information Systems, Toronto, Ontario.

Dubé, L., & Paré, G. (2004). The multi-faceted nature of virtual teams. In D. J. Pauleen (Ed.), *Virtual teams: Projects, protocols, and processes* (pp. 1-39). Hershey, PA: Idea Group.

Ferratt, T. W., & Hall, S. R. (2009). Extending the vision of distance education to learning via virtually being there and beyond. *Communications of the Association for Information Systems, 25*(35), 425-436.

Fjermestad, J., & Hiltz, S. R. (2000/2001). Group support systems: A descriptive evaluation of case and field studies. *Journal of Management Information Systems, 17*(3), 115-159.

Goodhue, D. L., & Thompson, R. L. (1995). Task-technology fit and individual performance. *MIS Quarterly, 19*(2), 213-236.

Hiltz, S. R. (1997). Impacts of college-level courses via asynchronous learning networks: Some preliminary results. *Journal of Asynchronous Learning Networks, 1*(2), 1-19.

Kirschner, P. A., & Van Bruggen, J. (2004). Learning and understanding in virtual teams. *CyberPsychology & Behavior, 7*(2), 135-139.

Leidner, D., & Fuller, M. (1997). Improving student learning of conceptual information: GSS supported collaborative learning vs. individual constructive learning. *Decision Support Systems, 20*(2), 149-163.

Leidner, D. E., & Jarvenpaa, S. L. (1995). The use of information technology to enhance management school education: A theoretical view. *MIS Quarterly, 19*(3), 265-292.

Lipnack, J., & Stamps, J. (1997). *Virtual teams: Reaching across space, time, and organizations with technology.* New York, NY: John Wiley and Sons.

O'Dwyer, L. M., Carey, R., & Kleiman, G. (2007). A study of the effectiveness of the Louisiana algebra I online course. *Journal of Research on Technology in Education, 39*(3), 289-306.

Payne, J., & Whitney, J. (2002). Developing L2 oral proficiency through synchronous CMC: Output, working memory, and interlanguage development *CALICO Journal, 20*(1), 7-32.

Robey, D., Khoo, H. M., & Powers, C. (2000). Situated learning in cross-functional virtual teams. *IEEE Transactions on Professional Communication, 43*(1), 51-66.

Scott, D. (2008). Effective VoIP learning experiences: The relationship between adult Learners' motivation, multiple intelligences, and learning styles. *International Journal of Learning, 15*(3), 63-78.

Shen, J., Hiltz, S. R., & Bieber, M. (2006). Collaborative online examinations: Impacts on interaction, learning, and student satisfaction. *IEEE Transactions on Systems, Man and Cybernetics, 36*(6), 1045-1053.

Sloffer, S. J., Dueber, B., & Duffy, T. M. (1999, January). *Using asynchronous conferencing to promote critical thinking: Two implementations in higher education.* Paper presented at the 32nd Annual Hawaii International Conference on System Science.

Welsh, E., Wanberg, C. R., Brown, K. G., & Simmering, M. J. (2003). E-learning: emerging uses, empirical results and future directions. *International Journal of Training and Development, 7*(4), 245-258.

Zigurs, I., & Buckland, B. K. (1998). A theory of task/technology fit and group support systems effectiveness. *MIS Quarterly, 22*(3), 313-334.

Zigurs, I., Buckland, B. K., Connolly, J. R., & Wilson, E. V. (1999). A test of task-technology fit theory for group support systems. *The Data Base for Advances in Information Systems, 30*(3/4), 34-50.

CHAPTER 4

SOCIAL MEDIA
FOR THE MBA PROFESSOR

A Strategy for Increasing
Teacher-Student Communication
and the Tactics for Implementation

Allen H. Kupetz

Anything that gets invented after you're 30 is against the natural order of things and the beginning of the end of civilization as we know it until it's been around for about 10 years when it gradually turns out to be alright really.

—Douglas Adams (1999)

Teaching students in an MBA program is different to teaching undergraduates because there is such a wide age range. Students in their early 20s have a lifetime of experience with social media and can't imagine any aspect of their life without it. MBA students older than 40 might be more reluctant to embrace social media, as Adams suggests. As such, incorporating the suite of social technologies into MBA curriculum brings unique

Cutting-Edge Social Media Approaches to Business Education:
Teaching With LinkedIn, Facebook, Twitter, Second Life, and Blogs, pp. 57–71
Copyright © 2010 by Information Age Publishing
57

challenges when compared with undergraduate and nonprofessional graduate programs.

Certainly age is not the only difference between MBA students and undergraduates. Many MBA students have worked all day before they arrive in class. A bad day at the office may distract totally from that evening's class. And many MBA students have spouses, children, and/or aging parents that compete for their time, attention, and focus. Former Apple and Microsoft executive Linda Stone coined the phrase "continuous partial attention,"[1] which to me describes a particular challenge that MBA professors have: MBA students are subject to all the distractions that all students face, plus the time constraints placed on them due to family and career obligations.

How then to deal with *continuous partial attention*, which, by the way, social media often contributes to as students update their Facebook status and instant message each other in class. Ironically, social media is a good solution to this challenge. Instead of trying to get students to pay attention more closely in class—or to pay attention at all for a longer period of time—use social media to extend the class beyond the scheduled time. If your course is 3-hours long and students are focused a third of the time, they will get 1 hour of content. Rather than fighting this, use social media to allow students to learn and participate after they leave the classroom. If students are awake 16 hours a day and you have their continuous partial attention just 20% of the time, you can deliver the 3 hours of class content you wanted to.

> It's (social media is) really forcing university professors to think about their teaching style and the pedagogical techniques that they use in the classroom. In other words, I've become increasingly dissatisfied with simply delivering a traditional lecture in the classroom. I'm beginning to debate whether or not it's effective, whether or not it works, whether or not it's a useful tool or a useful way to engage and create a kind of learning space or a learning environment. They're active learners, as opposed to passive learners. That one-way flow of content—I don't know how effective that is anymore. (S. Craig Watkins, associate professor of radio, TV, and film at the University of Texas [Beja, 2009])

This is not a theory. It has been my experience that using the tools and tactics described below, I am engaged with some students nearly around the clock. And, thankfully, even when I'm sleeping, they are still engaged with each other on topics relevant to what I'm trying to teach.

This chapter will be solely focused on the use of social media for MBA professors, but certainly many of these ideas may be applicable to other programs. These are techniques I've used with my own MBA students. What these ideas won't do—because social media can't—is make a bad teacher better. But social media does offer good teachers ways to make their classes better, to increase both the quantity and quality of student participation, and to get students focused on key course objectives even when they are not in class.

TOOLS FOR TEACHING AFTER CLASS

We invariably overestimate the short-term impact of new technologies, while underestimating their long-term effects.

—Amara's Law (Roy Amara)

There are thousands of social media applications and listing them all would be pointless, as there would be hundreds more created before one could finish the list. Below are five types of activities an MBA professor can use to extend the amount of time you are trying to engage students.

Blogging

The word blog is irrelevant, what's important is that it is now common, and will soon be expected, that every intelligent person (and quite a few unintelligent ones) will have a media platform where they share what they care about with the world. (Seth Godin)[2]

Of the thousands of applications, my experience has shown that blogging is the best social media tool that MBA professors can integrate into their courses. A blog gives the MBA professor an opportunity to post his/her own thoughts, or an article from someone else, and allow students to read it and comment on it outside of class. While some of this functionality exists in many course management tools like Blackboard, a blog hosted externally from the school generally has better tools to integrate text, pictures, and video into a single message. Students can read the content outside of class, comment on it, and comment on the comments of other students.

You can easily create and manage a blog with two of the most popular sites, Blogger (www.blogger.com) or WordPress (www.wordpress.com). Both are free and relatively easy to use, but WordPress offers a broader suite of applications.

Something else that may motivate MBA professors to start a blog is to enhance their personal brand. As Godin pointed out, intelligent people are all but expected to have a blog. When someone searches for you online, often your blog will be near the top of the results after your college's website. You can share your ideas with a far broader audience than just those in your class. You can promote your school by showing prospective students what kind of teaching talent is resident there. You can promote a new book or article. You can write about things that are outside your teaching discipline—extending your current brand to a whole new set of people who want to learn.

In August 2008, a book I wrote, *The Future of Less*, was published. It is about the wireless, paperless, and cashless revolutions underway globally and was used in a class I taught on managing technology. I created a website to promote the book, www.futureofless.com, with a link to my blog on these topics, www.futureofless.blogspot.com. I put over 160 articles on that blog for my students and other readers to comment on. In addition to adding current content to my course, the blog also helped me sell over 4,000 copies of the book through a direct channel, promote my public speaking engagements, and brand myself as "a recognized thought leader on the impact of technology on individuals, organizations, and corporations."[3]

In another example, my school is developing a new MBA program targeted at students outside our core geographic vicinity. In a first for us, the 36 face-to-face hours all our courses are will be changed to 16 face-to-face hours with the balance being distance learning with an online component. As such, the faculty has had to rethink everything from team projects to physical versus digital textbooks. We created a blog so that faculty could share their ideas with each other.

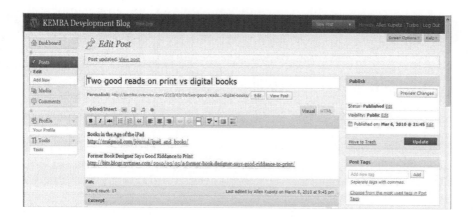

Figure 4.1.   KEMBA blog example.

Twitter

The qualities that make Twitter seem inane and half-baked are what makes it so powerful.

—Jonathan Zittrain, law professor at Harvard (Cohen, 2009)

Twitter (www.twitter.com) is a form of blogging (sometimes called *micro-blogging*) where entries are limited to 140 characters. Companies that use Twitter well get followers to engage with their brands in manner that is much more dynamic than their website content. Twitter accounts from other than product or service-based entities produce a constant volume of information on current topics. Students can follow traditional print and media sources, but also more scholarly posts like the McKinsey Quarterly (twitter.com/MckQuarterly) and the excellent Knowledge@Wharton (twitter.com/knowledgwharton).

> The first thing I noticed when the class started using Twitter was how conversations continued inside and outside of class. Once students started Twittering I think they developed a sense of each other as people beyond the classroom space, rather than just students they saw twice a week for an hour and a half. As a result, classroom conversation became more productive as people were more willing to talk, and [be] more respectful of others. (David Parry, professor of emerging media at the University of Texas [Ferenstein, 2010])

Different social media sites have different cultures, much like different countries do. I recommend creating an account and following a few other people on Twitter in areas that interest you, are relevant to your academic specialty, or might benefit your students. After you are more familiar with the unwritten protocols, then start Tweeting yourself.

How do you find such people to follow? Many people on Twitter make use of the # key, called *hash tagging* in the Twitter community. Let's say a Tweet discusses something about 10-year treasuries without specially mentioning *bonds*, the author might put a #bond at the end of the Tweet to make it easier to find all the Tweets that posted on that topic. For example:

> US Treasury 10-Year Yield Rises Most in 2010 after Note Auctions (Bloomberg) http://bit.ly/b02lA1 #bonds #futures

If you want to make sure you see all the Tweets from your students, ask them to use the @ sign in front of your Twitter name somewhere in their Tweet. For example:

@FinProf US Treasury 10-Year Yield Rises after Note Auctions http://bit.ly/
b02lA1 – I wonder why, given no change in Fed policy or rates #bonds

There are ways you can reply (i.e., direct messaging) so that only that student sees the answers or such that anyone following you can see your reply. And if you have several different Twitter accounts for different courses, you can download a tool like TweetDeck (www.tweetdeck.com) so you are alerted anytime anyone sends you a personal message.

Wikis

Wikipedia is the best thing ever. Anyone in the world can write anything they want about any subject so you know you are getting the best possible information.

—Michael Scott in *The Office*

Wikis, of which Wikipedia is just the most famous example, are a way to develop a classwide collaborative project. Unlike blogs where the original content is unchanged and people can comment on it, wikis have a single document on that topic that changes as people edit it. Based on the premise of the wisdom of crowds, if enough of your students edit this document, the final product will be much better than its first version. The software to create and manage a wiki is available at no charge from multiple sources. Search for "free wiki software" to find the best tool for your course or contact your IT director.

Ning

Users create knowledge, but only if we let them.

—John Thackara

You may be familiar with social networking sites like Facebook (www.facebook.com) and the more professionally oriented LinkedIn (www.linkedin.com). Students are likely posting things on Facebook that they would not want their professors to see, but this kind of tool can be used to create a sense of community in the course that furthers discussion and collaboration. You can create your own social networking site for a particular course using Ning (www.ning.com). You send invitations to your students to join and can close the posting to only those in the course. This allows students to post items of interest to the course that wouldn't be interesting to their broader network of Facebook friends and keeps the professor from having to wade through the pool of less-focused ideas that students post to Facebook. On the downside, Ning recently announced it would start charging for its service. It is likely a similar free service will sprout up. As an alternative, private group pages in Facebook can be created as a social networking learning platform.

Hotseat

In the theatre, the actor is given immediate feedback.

—Charles Keating

For the most adventurous MBA professors, or at least those teaching large classes, Purdue University invented Hotseat to "enable collaborative microdiscussion in and out of the classroom."[4] The application allows students to comment on the class and then enables other participants—including professors, students, and teaching assistants—to view those messages. Students either use their Twitter, Facebook, or MySpace accounts to post the messages or log in to the Hotseat website to send text messages. The application resides on the web so there is no software for professors or students to install (McCrea, 2009).

I haven't used Hotseat, but see some value. Teaching a quantitative course like finance or accounting and want to know if the students are with you before you move on? Students may be reluctant to raise their hands and be the minority who want to see it one more time. But if you could poll the room in real time and students could reply without the other students knowing who they were, you might get a more accurate status report. And since most MBA quantitative courses are taught with laptops open, Hotseat would seem to offer minimal disruption.

There is benefit for qualitative courses too. Similar to the way a blog allows for nonnative speakers to contribute to a discussion nonverbally, the developers of Hotseat promote it by noting that it "allows students to discuss controversial topics without the fear of embarrassment that comes from standing up and speaking in front of a class of 100-plus students" (McCrea, 2009)

THE *ME* IN SOCIAL MEDIA

Social media is like teen sex. Everyone wants to do it. Nobody knows how. When it's finally done there is surprise it's not better.

—Avinash Kaushik[5]

In March 2009, Kaushik tweeted that he overheard this observation. He shared it using 136 of the 140 characters and spaces allowed by Twitter in any single tweet (i.e., message or post).

Most MBA professors are likely as far removed from Twitter as they are from teen sex. But Twitter—and other social media including blogs, social networking, and picture and video sharing sites—are integral parts of most of young students' lives and can easily be incorporated into your existing pedagogy and syllabi.

According to *Groundswell*, a must read for MBA faculty and students interested in social media, social media is, "A social trend in which people use technologies to get the things they need from each other, rather than from traditional institutions like corporations" (Li & Bernoff, 2008, p. 9). This is a useful definition because "traditional institutions" might include colleges and universities. It can feel threatening that students are now learning—or, at least, seeking answers—from each other rather than solely from you. In fact, this is hugely advantageous if integrated into the strategic plan you have for where you want your course to go.

Kelly LeBlanc, the founder of Aleuromedia, presented in 2009 on things that surprised her most about social media in education:

- Faculty engaging in social media platforms without a defined social media policy or plan;
- Faculty without their demonstrated thought leadership available or accessible online; and
- Faculty unaware of how social media has evolved and the resulting changes in communication.

Does your institution—or even your department—have a well-defined social media policy? Can the absence of one be considered a green light to use the whole suite of social media tools?

Why isn't more of your content and more of ideas easily accessible online—not just for the benefit of your students, but also to support your school's recruiting efforts. There is also the issue of your school and your personal brand.

STRATEGY AND TACTICS FOR THE MBA PROFESSOR

Strategy without tactics is the slowest route to victory. Tactics without strategy is the noise before defeat.

—Sun Tzu

The authors of *Groundswell* advise that companies should first makes sure they understand what their customers (People) are ready for, define their Objectives, create a Strategy, and only then choose a Technology— what they call the POST process (LeBlanc, 2009). So too with social media in the classroom: choose the particular technology last after you have decided what you want to accomplish.

I think you'll agree that social media is hardly a panacea for students' continuous partial attention. But the fact that you are reading this chapter is probably an indication that you know that the current generations of MBA students cannot be taught exactly the same way you have been teaching.

> "Unlike those of us a shade older, this new generation didn't have to relearn anything to live lives of digital immersion. They learned in digital the first time around," declare John Palfrey and Urs Gasser of the Berkman Centre at Harvard Law School in their 2008 book, *Born Digital*, one of many recent tomes about digital natives. The authors argue that young people like to use new, digital ways to express themselves: shooting a YouTube video where their parents would have written an essay, for instance. ("The Net," 2010)

And you see this in the work of MBA students. Their ability to mash up words, images, and video into a PowerPoint presentation on a case study would shame any professor still using bullet points and Microsoft Clipart. Just as effortlessly, MBA students mash up with in-class time with a combination of listening to the professor and instant messaging, watch streaming sporting events, and doing work for other classes.

I've decided not to try to fight their need (and ability) to multitask in class. Instead, I try to use social media when they are not in class to extend the time I'm engaged with them. The goal is to have their partial attention throughout the whole day instead of having their undivided attention for 3 hours.

Following are several broad categories of objectives and some ways to use social media to achieve them.

Discussion

A conversation is a dialog, not a monolog.

—Truman Copote

Most syllabi have a participation component as part of the final grade. Many students—particularly those whose native language is not being used in class or whose culture discourages engaging with professors—are reluctant to raise their hands. A blog is one way to increase their level of participation because students can collect and process their thoughts before sharing them (something many native-speaking MBA students might also benefit from).

Course Example

You have a textbook and cases in your syllabus, but try posting a current article from the business press and having your students comment on it and the other students' comments. The students can also post links to other related articles that may have a different perspective. Blogs are a useful way to promote discussion and keep the subject matter fresh. E-mailing students the article doesn't allow for an interactive response. And photocopying the article and handing it out in class doesn't increase the participation. Creating a blog takes less than 5 minutes and posting an article to it takes less than that.

I take students abroad to meet with senior executives as part of my school's mission to prepare students for the global world through experiential learning. In preparation for a trip to Singapore, for example, I created a blog called Singaporeality ("Singapore" plus "reality") at Blogger.com, www.singaporeality.blogspot.com. I posted over 50 articles in 12 months, but only occasionally more than one per week. The student response was very positive, both in terms of the quantity and quality of their comments. Students also sent me content to post and for others students to respond to—everything from deep discussions on whether immigrants were still benefiting Singaporean society to a heads up that the World Cuisine Show would occurring while we were there.

Figure 4.2.   Singaporeality blog.

Some items are simply too thin for a blog spot, so I also created a Twitter account with the same name, www.twitter.com/singaporeality. Twitter is not as useful as a blog in promoting discussion, but it is a great way to share quick tidbits with students rather than sending email.

Collaboration

The value of a network increases in proportion to the square of the number of nodes on the network.

—Metcalfe's Law (Robert Metcalfe)

Often qualitative business courses like organizational behavior, marketing, and international business have teams of students that research topics and present their findings to the rest of the class.

Course Example

An entrepreneurship class is preparing a business plan for a local business. Teams of students have been assigned the lead on particular elements, but everyone must work together on the final document. Instead of sending various drafts around and having students edit a version that is already outdated, a wiki will keep a single, current version for all the students to edit. The professor can observe the process by getting automatic updates when changes are made and seeing which students are making the substantive edits.

Research

The dynamic of an intellectual ecosystem, where students dive deep into class readings and argue contentious issues outside of class, is difficult to create if discussion ends when class is over. Fortunately, Twitter has no time limit.

—Greg Ferenstein (2010)

Google has seemingly replaced other traditional student research tools and the quantity of information available is impressive, even if the quality is occasionally suspect. Search was one of most disruptive technologies in the Internet Age, but may now be burdened by its own success—there may be too much information to sift through. Twitter can be used as a complement to traditional online research when a student needs to measure an issue that is particularly dynamic. Twitter is not terribly useful in finding the current exchange rate of the Singapore dollar versus the U.S. dollar, but it can offer real-time information on the reaction to revaluations, unexpected interest rate changes, et cetera.

Course Example

You can go to Twitter and without even creating an account can type a search term and see what others are posting on that topic. Taking a class to Buenos Aires and want to expose your students to a very wide range of information? Have them type in *Argentina* and find a useful tweet or link and post it to the blog you created for the course.

Community

> *It is the function of creative man to perceive and to connect the seemingly unconnected.*
>
> —William Plomer

An MBA class can become a small community that exists long after the course is over. And social media is better at fostering this community since, for example, Blackboard is neither archival nor available after a course has ended or a student has graduated.

Course Example

Not sure what social media tools your students will best respond to? Use Ning as a single site to try blogging, Twitter-like messaging, and tra- ditional social networking tools. Post content using all of these compo- nents and then decide what seems to get students involved in the discussion. And, unlike Blackboard, this Ning community can exist long after graduation and allow former students to engage you and their fellow alumni in some real-world issues they are facing and are in need of help to solve. This may have the added benefit of helping alumni stay engaged —a resource that can then be tapped by your development office.

THE *YOU* IN SOCIAL MEDIA: MISTAKES TO AVOID

> *Experience is the name every one gives to their mistakes.*
>
> —Oscar Wilde

By now, I hope you have decided there is a place for one or more social media tools in your courses because you believe they will enhance the learning process. You could continue to use the same syllabus you used 5 years ago, but you're not. That's good for you, and it's good for your students. In fact, I'm convinced that students now expect professors to use technologies that go beyond PowerPoint and Blackboard. And they likely will appreciate the fact that you are looking for new ways to reach them in and out of the classroom.

As powerful as many social media tools can be, however, they also present some pitfalls. But by keeping the following suggestions in mind, you'll keep the technology under control and your students on task.

Focus on your strategy, not the technology. Like blackboards and textbooks, social media applications are aids to the learning process. Use them to enhance the course, not just to say you use them. For instance, outside of class, use social media to increase the level of discussion and collaboration on new or tangential topics. This will help you free up in-class time for more central topics.

Don't drive the bus—take a seat in back with your students. Don't create a blog post and then just sit back and wait; continue to be a part of the conversation. Respond to students' comments. Ask "Have you considered this idea?" or "How does your comment relate to this link?" Encourage responses to your response to their responses – and so on. Social media is about having a conversation, even if you are the professor.

On the first day of class, I share with students this quote by Marshall McLuhan: "I don't necessarily agree with everything I say." I tell them that I will try to provoke them. I want them to be comfortable posting their opinions, especially when more objective information might not be available.

Participate, but don't officiate. Social media tends to lower inhibitions —students will write things about others that they would never say face-to-face, even when each post is attributed to its writer. Why the most egregious violations of civil discourse are less likely from MBA students, you should still set guidelines for what is appropriate and what isn't. Make it clear that students should challenge ideas, not attack other students' motives or intelligence. Writing "a better choice might have been" is, well, a better choice than "only an idiot would have reached that conclusion."

Also remind them of the level of discourse expected. Using a Twitter feed to post what they had for lunch does not move the discussion forward, unless the comment is meant to highlight a facet of customer service, marketing, or pricing strategy.

On the other hand, you also should avoid being too restrictive. Most blog sites allow you to approve comments before they are posted to the broader audience, but I recommend against that. You risk giving students the impression that they can post ideas only if you approve of them. Or worse, that all the ideas posted are in fact things you do agree with. Let them post whatever they want. If a comment is completely out of bounds or overly confrontational, you can easily delete it. Otherwise, let students respond to offending comments.

CONCLUSION

Innumerable confusions and a feeling of despair invariably emerge in periods of great technological and cultural transition.

—Marshall McLuhan

At the 1939 World's Fair in New York City, then-mayor Fiorello LaGuardia encountered a new technology called television. He reportedly commented that he doubted Americans would find the time to sit in front of such a box in their living rooms.

It would be just as easy to dismiss social media as a fad that will diminish or disappear in the years ahead. But I think its rapid adoption is a clear signal that the digital generation of students would be unable to imagine life without a Facebook page. Like television, social media promises to have staying power if only because this generation of students—these multitasking students—would be lost without it. I realize, however, that my view is almost certain still a minority one for professors my age.

Writing in the *British Journal of Education Technology* in 2008, a group of academics led by Sue Bennett of the University of Wollongong set out to debunk the whole idea of digital natives, arguing that there may be "as much variation within the digital native generation as between the generations." They caution that the idea of a new generation that learns in a different way might actually be counterproductive in education, because such sweeping generalizations "fail to recognize cognitive differences in young people of different ages, and variation within age groups." The young do not really have different kinds of brains that require new approaches to school and work, in short. ("The Net," 2010, p. 10)

I disagree. I teach over 100 under-24 year old MBA students every year and they are different compared to older students and from students their age a generation ago. I contend that we must use social media to extend the time we're engaged with them, even when they're not in class. I want to have their partial attention throughout the whole day since it is all but impossible to have their undivided attention for even a few hours.

If your goal is to help prepare students for business in the real world, then you must acknowledge that businesses are using social media in all kinds of ways. I know my students see the value in using social media as a complement to other course materials. Better yet, these tools are not time-consuming. Most weeks, I spend less than two additional hours posting articles to social media sites for my courses. I am reading those articles anyway, and the time I spend to cut and paste them into a blog is small. Reading student comments might add another hour per week.

Finally, MBA students are different from undergraduates and even other graduate students in many ways. Certainly they differ from undergraduates in that they are working or know that they will need to find jobs when they do graduate. Not only do they want to be engaged in and out of the classroom, they want exposure to tools that they will use to engage the customers, colleagues, and shareholders. And they differ from other graduate students in that their degree is less vocational than a lawyer or a doctor. MBA graduates know they will need to hunt to survive. Social media skills give them another arrow in the quiver and the access to learn from other MBA graduates about the hunt. Give MBA students what they want and need to be successful and you'll have done your job.

NOTES

1. Retrieved from http://www.lindastone.net/
2. Retrieved from http://www.slideshare.net/arlton/social-media-brownbag-presentation
3. Retrieved from http://www.futureofless.com/files/speaker.pdf
4. Retrieved from http://www.itap.purdue.edu/tlt/hotseat/
5. Retrieved rom http://twitter.com/avinashkaushik/status/1270289378

REFERENCES

Adams, Doug. (1999). *How to stop worrying and learn to love the Internet.* Retrieved from http://www.douglasadams.com/dna/19990901-00-a.html

Beja, M. (2009). *How students, professors, and colleges are, and should be, using social media.* Retrieved from http://chronicle.com/blogPost/How-Students-Professors-and/7787/

Cohen, N. (2009). *Twitter on the barricades: Six lessons learned.* Retrieved from http://www.nytimes.com/2009/06/21/weekinreview/21cohenweb.html

Ferenstein, G. (2010). *How Twitter in the classroom is boosting student engagement.* Retrieved from http://mashable.com/2010/03/01/twitter-classroom/

LeBlanc, K. -S. (2009). *Social media in education.* Retrieved from http://www.slideshare.net/KSLeBlanc/teaching-the-teachers-about-social-media

Li, C., & Bernoff, J. (2008). *Groundswell.* Boston, MA: Harvard Business Press.

McCrea, B. (2009). Purdue U brings social networking to the classroom. *Campus Technology.* Retrieved from http://campustechnology.com/articles/2009/11/18/purdue-u-brings-social-networking-to-the-classroom.aspx?sc_lang=en

The net generation, unplugged. (2010, March 6). *The Economist,* p. 10.

CHAPTER 5

APPLICATIONS OF SOCIAL NETWORKING IN STUDENTS' LIFE CYCLE

Vladlena Benson, Fragkiskos Filippaios, and Stephanie Morgan

Over the past few years online social networks have become one of the most popular Internet applications. Naturally, social media is attracting a significant attention from researchers probing its applicability in Higher Education. Although results of studies exploring pedagogical use of social networks prevail, currently there is a lack of literature addressing the issues of graduates using social networking connections to build their social capital and enhance their employability prospects. Moreover, social media has the potential of providing an easy-to use platform to connect students throughout their entire life cycle—from aspiration rising, enrollment, learning and teaching leading on to employment, alumni communication and life-long learning. This chapter summarizes the results of a quantitative study of 272 business students from the United Kingdom and 4 international universities in Europe. This research is a part of a wider study into the use of social networks by students. Results of the data analysis reveal significant differences in how students perceive the benefits of social media. Use of online social networking for career management is virtually unknown to undergraduate U.K. students, while postgraduate students and international graduates reveal a higher level of exploitation of social capital

Cutting-Edge Social Media Approaches to Business Education:
Teaching With LinkedIn, Facebook, Twitter, Second Life, and Blogs, pp. 73–93
Copyright © 2010 by Information Age Publishing
73

through social media. The chapter attempts to provide a framework for applications of social media in student's life cycle. It provokes a discussion into issues of career development in connection with the notion of the digital footprint which online users leave as a result of social networking activity. Future research directions are discussed.

INTRODUCTION

Online social networking services (SNS) offer a straightforward way to connect people and support information sharing and communication. University students are often ahead of the rest in the adoption of new technologies, and according to (Quan-Haase, 2007) their communication networks tend to be dense and multilayered. Extant literature abounds with evidence of business opportunities (e.g., Aldrich & Kim, 2007) and educational use (e.g., Mastrodicasa, 2008)) of social networks. However, very little research attention has been paid toward a systematic adoption of SNS throughout the complete student life cycle geared towards achieving higher employability and improved career progression. Defined in its broadest sense, the student life cycle means from the first point of contact with potential students to graduation and lifelong learning and career management for graduates (Kingston University, 2007). The first point of contact can precede the application process considerably and comprise of awareness and aspiration rising stage. Moving on to the application and recruitment and preentry support, the student life cycle process then transits to induction, on-course support, learning, teaching and assessment. Final stages of the life cycle involve career management and lifelong learning. Popularity of social networks among students, especially Facebook, has been unprecedented. Social nature of SNS maps face-to-face social behavior into online environments incredibly well. Recent literature draws attention to the potential of online networking services while studying at the university (e.g., Ellison, Steinfield, & Lampe, 2007). However, little research attention has been drawn to the significance of social networks in the student life cycle in its entirety. This is especially important as the stages of employability management and life-long learning take a centre stage in managing student expectations and influencing their decision of taking up places at which university. As shown in Figure 5.1, stages involved in the student life cycle begin with aspiration rising and conclude with employability and life-long learning opportunities, reaching beyond the time of class attendance.

This chapter constructs a framework of social networking use and benefits offered by their application at each stage of the student life cycle as well as discusses issues often overlooked in newer applications of technol-

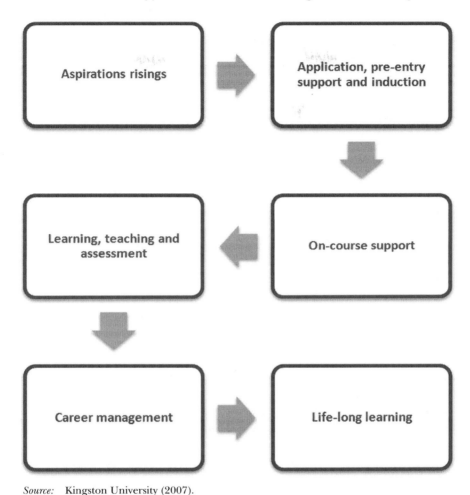

Source: Kingston University (2007).

Figure 5.1.   Student life cycle.

ogy and their impact on users. The chapter draws from the results of a wider study into the use of social networks in higher education (HE) which employed qualitative methods (focus groups) and a quantitative instrument, a survey of over 270 respondents. The survey was designed from the focus group findings to assess a wide range of aspects related to the use of online social networks, including the reasons why students joined and used particular SNS (indicating awareness of social capital use) and the number of networks and amount of time spent taking part in SNS, to assess the digital footprint.

The chapter is organized as follows. After definition of the student life cycle, we apply theories of social capital to develop a model for examining the impact of social media on various stages of the student life cycle, focusing on knowledge sharing and career progression. We introduce the concept of online social media in HE settings and discuss the key issues for understanding motivations for use of these networks among students. Empirical evidence is then examined in relation to students in business studies and their perceptions about the use of social networking. Finally we discuss how our empirical findings contribute to theory development and improve our understanding of how online social technologies can support and enhance individuals through the student life cycle and beyond.

LITERATURE REVIEW

Social Capital and Knowledge Sharing

The notion of social capital has received considerable attention from researchers in a variety of fields and has been broadly defined as "resources embedded in a social structure that are accessed and/or mobilized in purposive action" (Lin, 2001, p. 29). Scholars have used the term habitually and frequently in contradictory ways (Leana & Van Buren, 1999). Some literature (e.g., Useem & Karabel, 1986) suggests that social capital is an individual attribute which offers advantages to a person in a group because of his or her status, reputation, et cetera. Others (e.g., Putnam, 1993) described social capital as a common attribute of communities and societies (Coleman, 1990), while networking researchers, such as (Burt, 1997) suggest that forming various types of social network present benefits to individuals. The main differences between social and other forms of capital lie in that it is "an asset which inheres in social relationships and networks" (Leana & Van Buren, 1999, p. 538). Stone, Gray, & Hughes (2003) emphasizes that the nature of individual social capital is largely influenced by different patterns of their network characteristics. Connections in these networks can be categorized into bonding ties encompassing family, friendship and neighborhood relationships; civic linkages and other more distant ties are termed as bridging, since these often provide contact with people different from one's self and with varied opportunities; and institutional connections are linking ties. It is widely accepted that social capital can be divided into three types—bonding, bridging, and linking (Narayan, 1999; Woolcock, 2000). While bonding social capital manifests itself in dense or closed networks, it helps people "get by" in life on a daily basis. Bridging social capital makes accessible the resources and opportunities which exist in one network to a member of another. This type of social capital is particularly useful in helping people to "get ahead." Linking social capital entails social relationships with those in authority or positions of power and is useful for gaining resources. Knowledge as an asset embedded in the fabric of relationships between individuals in a social network is a valuable resource. Extant research (e.g., Wasko & Faraj, 2005) continually draws attention to opportunities of knowledge sharing through online social networks, enabling individuals to exchange advice and ideas with others based on common interests. Online networking makes it possible to share information with large numbers of users quickly and on a global scale. In the business world, people contribute to their knowledge as they perceive that it enhances their professional reputation, when they have experience and stature to do so. Can social networks have a similar impact on knowledge contribution and sharing among students? Will this help graduates be better prepared for their future employment? Brown and Duguid (2001) argue that when individuals have a common interest or are engaged in a similar practice, knowledge readily flows across that practice, enabling individuals to create social networks to support knowledge exchange. According to (Powell, Koput, & Smtih-Doer, 1996) knowledge exchange networks often emerge in fields where the pace of technological change requires access to knowledge outside of any one network. With the proliferation of information and communication technology (ICT) in HE and recognition of continuous improvement of ICT skills as core learner competencies, the pace of technology emphasizes the importance of knowledge sharing during the student life cycle. Furthermore, the international mix of the student population can benefit from knowledge sharing across borders, as reiterated in Constant, Sproull, and Kiesler (1996), online networks have been found to support knowledge flows between geographically dispersed users. Brown and Duguid (2001) suggest thinking about knowledge and learning as an outcome of actual engagement in practice, and online social networks have the capability to be the ideal enabler of the knowledge flow.

Social Capital and Career Progression

Considerable evidence has been collected by organizational researchers that demonstrates social capital is one of the determinants of career success (e.g., Dreher & Ash, 1990). The roles of bridging and bonding capital, including informal interpersonal behaviors (Judge & Bretz, 1994) have been explored far less. Popular advice for career success emphasizes the importance of networking for the achievement of career goals (Bolles, 1992). Studies among managers (Luthans, Hodgetts, & Rosenkrantz, 1988) found that networking and communication activities are major determinants of their success. Social capital theory and career success have been linked by Seibert, Kraimer, and Liden (2001) who integrated three competing theories of social capital, namely weak tie theory (Granovetter, 1973), structural hole theory (Burt, 1992) and social resource theory (Lin, 1999). Relationships between individuals in a network help formalize social networking analysis. The weak tie theory considers the strengths of ties or links between individuals and proves that weak ties are indispensable to individuals' opportunities, for instance in the process of finding a job. In particular (Granovetter, 1973) showed that ties between members of a given network can be intense such as those between co-workers, advisors and friends. Knowledge and information shared between the members of a network with strong ties already exists internally or is assimilated and shared quickly. On the other hand, infrequent and emotionally uninvolved relationships between an individual and another in an internally strongly interconnected network are expected to be weak. These weak ties frequently bridge interconnected networks thereby serving as sources of unique information and resources to others. Granovetter (1973) argues that weak ties were more useful than strong ties as a source of information about job openings helping individuals with connections to external networks to gain access to better job opportunities. Another view, the structural hole theory, focuses on the impact of network connections of individuals or the opposite of them (structural holes) and their influence on formation of social network has been shaped by Burt (1992, 1997). A structural hole exists where two individuals are not connected to each other. Structural holes theory argues that it is beneficial for an individual to be connected to others who are themselves unconnected within the network. According to Burt (1992, 1997) social networks rich in structural holes provide an individual with better access to information, bargaining power and therefore lead to exercising greater control over resources and opening career opportunities throughout the social system. Although contested by the weak ties theory the structural hole argument is that "social capital is created by a network in which people can broker connections between otherwise disconnected segments" (Burt, 2001, p. 1) The third key theory of social capital concentrates on the nature of the resources embedded inside the social network (Lin, Ensel, & Voughn, 1981). Social capital is considered to be vital in giving access to knowledge, resources and referrals. These resources are viewed as finite, and therefore people must compete for them.

So there is a point of general agreement between researchers (e.g., Burt, 2001; Coleman, 1990; Putnam, 1993) in the discussion of social capital. Diversely expressed but converging perspectives cited above agree that social capital is a metaphor in which social network is a type of asset which can create certain competitive advantage to some individuals or groups in pursuing their goals. Pfeil, Arjan, and Zaphiris (2009) highlight that younger people tend to have more contacts, but mainly in the same age group. This may reduce the usefulness of their network in terms of social capital. However, for our discussion, with the general agreement that "better connected people enjoy higher returns" (Burt, 2000, p. 3) we proceed to the consideration the notion of the digital footprint generated as a result of networking on social media and its impact on career management.

Aftermath of Online Social Networking

Traditional social networks could be viewed as footprints in the sand that can be washed away by the tide, whereas a digital footprint stays behind longer and is far more difficult to wash away than to create. A growing number of publications (e.g., Barnes & Barnes, 2009; Lange, 2007, Lewis & West, 2009; Livingstone, 2008) continuously draw attention to issues of privacy of individual information that becomes available as a result of social networking use. Informally chatting with friends or sharing personal multimedia on Facebook has become a part of a daily routine for many users. However, the prospect of personal content becoming available to the outsiders of an informal social circle is more than probable. Research indicates that many people view any online contact as a "friend" and indeed there is some competition around having a large number of these. Studies have also shown that people have a limited understanding of privacy issues and tend not to use their privacy settings as well as they should (see Debatin, Lovejoy, Horn, & Hughes, 2009). They are also far more likely to assume that the risk is to other people, not themselves, known as "the perceptual hypothesis" (Brosius & Engel, 1996). Many users maintain separation of their private informal profile and a public business profile (Lyne, 2009), using an informal SNS, such as Facebook, for the former and a business-centred one, such as LinkedIn, for the latter. Lange (2007) provides a useful lens on the technological impact on what is considered private versus public information and shared content. According to Lange, context determines whether certain content shared through SNS is viewed as private or public. For example, photos or videos taken at home are private when contrasted with media related to a town or a neighborhood. At the same time, public and private content may exist within the same piece of media in a broader context. Gal (2002) argues that "public" and "private" are relative terms and shift according to individual perspectives. Recent studies (e.g., Madden, Fox, Smith & Vittak, 2007) has shown a growing concern among Internet users about the control over the public and private information available whether through third parties or self-generated. Increasingly, search engines are used to discover contacts, personal information and for background checks on individuals. Internet identity, the information available online connected to an individual's name, has been reportedly used by employers for background checks on current or perspective employees (Dutta & Fraser, 2009), coworkers, friends (Madden et al., 2007) and even as evidence of expert's proficiency by cross-examining attorneys in the court of law. Social networking users produce an estimated 10 billion pieces of content (Peluchette & Karl, 2010), including messaging, emails, multimedia, per week. Hough (2009) highlights that people generally neglect to assess the impact of technology on information disclosure. It is perhaps time to raise awareness and caution among students over how digital footprints remaining on social media can affect current and future employment prospects. Furthermore, there is still little understanding of how students perceive social networking in terms of knowledge sharing or career progression, across the students' life cycle.

METHOD

As a part of a wider study of online social networking in HE, a two phase approach to data collection was adopted, with two focus groups informing the development of a survey. The sample for the focus group was drawn ad hoc from the student population at a post-92 university in the United Kingdom. Stage one of the study included two focus groups for undergraduate and postgraduate students conducted with four participants each. Undergraduate students participants were drawn from the second year courses, while postgraduate participants studied on the MBA programme. Each focus group discussion was structured around nine open ended questions and lasted for approximately an hour. The discussions were digitally recorded and transcribed. The focus group transcripts were processed and categories were derived to form the themes for the survey questions. Focus group transcripts were initially analyzed using open coding to divide the data into concepts. Students at both undergraduate and postgraduate levels indicated that they would like to use social networking before joining a university to make contact with other students, find out who is joining from their area/country, and also to gain a feeling of belonging before they attend. Postgraduates were particularly keen to find out more about their courses and lecturers, and also were more likely to discuss gaining access to alumni and potential job opportunities from networking. All students indicated that they would be interested in using online social networks to find out more about their modules and course content during their studies, and would be keen to read more about staff activities. There seemed little resistance to the idea of mixing social and learning activities, although some did indicate that they would like to keep some aspects of their social life private. Postgraduate students were more positive about keeping in touch with other students and trying to make business contacts after they had graduated. A wide range of issues were raised, including overuse of social networking and pressure to use from friends. These elements were included in the survey but will not be the focus of this chapter.

The analysis of the focus group transcripts provided the starting point for developing a range of questions covering various aspects and concerns of social networking use. In the second stage of data collection a draft survey was piloted on twenty individual students at the research site. Based on the feedback from the pilot the questionnaire was amended and formatted into its final version. The questionnaire in paper format was distributed to a random sample of undergraduate and postgraduate students including United Kingdom and European universities. The sample was drawn entirely from students studying on business courses. The total number of respondents comprised of 272 individuals. The demographic data collected included information on age, nationality, number of years of work experience, first language, year and type of degree. Further questions covered a range of expectations and motivation for persistent use of various networks. The questions worded ("Why did you join this social network" with answer options including "Find a job," "Make business contacts" as well as "To find contacts at the university" and "To be generally sociable," etc.) were provided for each network type. A Likert scale was used (1 = *strongly agree* to 5 = *strongly disagree*).The average age of our sample is 25 years while the postgraduate students have an average of 29 years and the undergraduates 22 years. The proportion of males and females in our sample is 50.5% and 49.5% respectively. The full time students represent the 55% of our sample while the part time students are 45%. The average work experience for the total of our sample is almost 5 years but there is a substantial difference between the undergraduate students with an average of less than 3 years and the postgraduate students with almost 7.5 years. The English speaking participants are dominating our sample representing the 43% of the total number of participants. We also have 47 different nationalities participating in our sample with the British being the dominant one representing 38% of our sample. They are followed by Cypriots at 8%, Russians and Indians at 6%, and Chinese at 4%.

FINDINGS

The survey results were wide ranging, therefore first we focus on the potential life cycle implications. Students were quite positive about enjoying access to a wide range of university services online, starting from finding out about the university through to helping each other share information and then keeping in touch later, supporting the idea of utilizing the full life cycle. As a first step we wanted to associate the use of each of the four key SNS, that is, Facebook, Bebo, Myspace, and LinkedIn with the degree status of the students to identify differences between undergraduate and postgraduate students. The first three networks are primarily associated with social aspects of SNS use while the fourth one (LinkedIn) with a more business oriented and professional use. To do so a one-way ANOVA estimation was used. Results presented in Tables 5.1 to 5.4 show that there is a clear difference in the participation of all SNS between undergraduate and postgraduate students. This difference though is even stronger when it comes to the two extremes as we call them, that is, Facebook and LinkedIn.

As a second step of our analysis we would like to explore differences in the use of SNS between the two sets of students. Although in some cases some students provided evidence for the use of up to four different SNS, in this chapter we will only report their responses regarding the use of their primary and secondary network. The vast majority of students report Facebook as their primary network.

Table 5.1.   Comparison Between Undergraduate and Postgraduate Participation (Facebook)

Type	Mean	SD	Freq.		
Undergraduate	.765	.425	132		
Postgraduate	.585	.495	99		
Total	.688	.464	231		

Source	SS	df	MS	F	Prob > F
Between groups	1.818	1	1.818	8.72	0.0035
Within groups	47.739	229	0.208		
Total	49.558	230	0.215		

**Table 5.2.   Comparison Between Undergraduate
and Postgraduate Participation (Bebo)**

Type	Mean	SD	Freq.		
Undergraduate	0.060	0.239	132		
Postgraduate	0.010	0.100	99		
Total	0.038	0.193	231		

Source	SS	df	MS	F	Prob > F
Between groups	0.144	1	0.144	3.89	0.0499
Within groups	8.505	229	0.037		
Total	8.649	230	0.037		

**Table 5.3.   Comparison Between Undergraduate
and Postgraduate Participation (MySpace)**

Type	Mean	SD	Freq.		
Undergraduate	0.151	0.359	132		
Postgraduate	0.050	0.220	99		
Total	0.108	0.311	231		

Source	SS	df	MS	F	Prob > F
Between groups	0.577	1	0.577	6.09	0.0144
Within groups	21.717	229	0.094		
Total	22.294	230	0.096		

**Table 5.4.   Comparison Between Undergraduate
and Postgraduate participation (LinkedIn)**

Type	Mean	SD	Freq.		
Undergraduate	0.030	0.172	132		
Postgraduate	0.171	0.379	99		
Total	0.090	0.288	231		

Source	SS	df	MS	F	Prob > F
Between groups	1.131	1	1.131	14.43	0.0002
Within groups	17.959	229	0.078		
Total	19.090	230	0.083		

Table 5.5 presents tabulation between undergraduates, postgraduates and their primary network. The total number of students is lower that the total sample as the rest of the students reported other SNS. The chi-square statistic shows a clear association between the status and the use of a specific network.

Table 5.6 presents the results for the secondary SNS. Again the Chi-square statistic shows an association between the degree type and the participation to a specific SNS. It is worth highlighting that when one compares Tables 5.5 and 5.6 an interesting pattern emerges. None of the undergraduate students reported LinkedIn as their primary SNS, while a large number of postgraduate students use Facebook.

Our last step in the empirical investigation is to clarify the motivations for the use of the primary and secondary networks and examine whether any patterns emerge around their use from undergraduate or postgraduate students. Students were asked to provide their key motivations around the use and participation in SNS. Table 5.7 presents a summary of ANOVA analysis between the two groups, their responses and the different motivations for both primary and secondary networks. Students as

**Table 5.5.   Tabulation of SNS Participation
and Degree Level (Primary Network)**

	Undergraduate	Postgraduate	Total
Facebook	87	57	144
MySpace	2	0	2
LinkedIn	0	6	6
Total	89	63	152
Chi-square = 10.098***			

**Table 5.6.   Tabulation of SNS Participation
and Degree Level (Secondary Network)**

	Undergraduate	Postgraduate	Total
Facebook	2	6	8
Bebo	7	1	8
MySpace	14	5	19
LinkedIn	3	12	15
Total	26	24	50
Chi-square = 16.10***			

**Table 5.7.   Key Differences in Motivations Between
Undergraduate and Postgraduate Students
for Primary and Secondary Networks**

Primary Network

Motivations	Undergraduate	Postgraduate	ANOVA F-stat	Prob>F
To be generally sociable	2.30	2.42	0.45	0.50
Peer pressure (old friends)	3.29	2.78	5.84	0.02
Peer pressure (new friends)	3.43	3.06	3.31	0.07
Find a job	4.07	4.14	0.13	0.72
Find Business	4.14	4.10	0.04	0.85
Curiosity	2.74	2.81	0.11	0.75
Keeping in touch with new friends	1.93	1.97	0.05	0.82
Making contact with people from university	2.56	2.52	0.03	0.86
Making new friends	3.12	3.28	0.68	0.41

Secondary Network

Motivations	Undergraduate	Postgraduate	ANOVA F-stat	Prob>F
To be generally sociable	2.60	3.00	1.66	0.20
Peer pressure (old friends)	2.81	2.81	0.00	0.98
Peer pressure (new friends)	3.41	3.29	0.11	0.74
Find a job	4.27	3.56	4.54	0.04
Find business	4.32	3.81	2.53	0.12
Curiosity	2.97	2.61	1.62	0.21
Keeping in touch with new friends	2.70	3.03	0.48	0.49
Making contact with people from university	3.60	3.05	2.69	0.11
Making new friends	3.47	3.29	0.34	0.56

mentioned before used a Likert scale (1-5) with lower values representing higher motivations.

An interesting pattern emerges from Table 5.7 (highlighted elements). While when it comes to the use of primary network (with Facebook being the dominant SNS), the difference can be summarized in peer pressure either by new or old friends. In both cases, postgraduates feel higher pressure from new or old friends to join a SNS. Results differ in the use of the secondary network (where LinkedIn has a substantial share). Three key factors differentiate the undergraduate from the postgraduate students with the latter group indicating a much higher motivation for finding a job, finding business general but also making contact with people from the University either fellow students or even members of staff.

Limitations

The study aimed to obtain a sample as close to representative of undergraduate and postgraduate students. The research has been conducted using a sample drawn from several research sites and demographically diverse. However, it is conceivable that a different choice of participating universities could have a different set of results. As stated earlier in the chapter the study is mainly exploratory and attempts to provide a practical lens on the potential of social networking in educational settings. It opens a useful discussion and suggests some directions for future research.

SOCIAL MEDIA AND ITS PRACTICAL APPLICATIONS IN STUDENTS' LIFE CYCLE

Recent trends in SNS saw a distinctive shift toward specialization of online social networks into formal, or business related, and informal, pure social, types. Possibly the most popular online SNS, Facebook, is generally regarded as a means for informal communications between people. On the other hand, LinkedIn has been specifically designated for finding and maintaining business connections. This type of social networks is much more aimed at developing business links, finding employment and consultancy opportunities. Regardless of network specialization one distinctive advantage offered by social networking services is their user-friendliness and wide acceptance. As seen from the survey results students ate comfortable users of social technologies. The potential of a structured application of social networking services by universities is yet to be realized. Table 5.8 provides the lens on the applications of social networking services and their benefits at each stage in the student life cycle as detailed in subsequent sections.

Awareness and Aspiration Rising

Increasingly individuals turn to the Internet in search of information about courses offered by universities. The aim of the initial stage in the students life cycle is to generate interest and engage potential entrants from a range of sectors from schools to workplace. Social networking services strategically aligned with the Internet presence of a higher education institution can deliver such engagement. Moreover, the enhanced capabilities of digital marketing can help universities target specific groups of users and make recruitment process more efficient leading to the next stage in the student life cycle—application and preentry.

Application, Preentry, and Induction

The focus group analysis highlighted that students would like to make more use of social networking at the early stages of the student life cycle. Their preference is to communicate with current students as well as those joining at the same time, this supports the findings of (Pfeil et al., 2009) in that young people tend to reach out to people of their own age. However it does suggest that higher education institutions could use social networking in the first stage of the life cycle to maintain student interest and initiate early feelings of belonging. Connecting students and university by means of social networking services may lead to improving advice and guidance services as well as facilitate implementation of an information and communication plan of universities with their future students.

On-Course Support

Network structure of student community may be effectively supported through social media. Such processes as helping students to fully engage with their courses and the broader learning community can be facilitated through a social network. University services connecting with students offer only one side of the benefits. Knowledge sharing between peers may enhance student engagement and promote formation of interest groups and on-course communication. This may be delivered not only by the formal, university lead, networking but also informal peer-driven communication.

Learning, Teaching, and Assessment

This stage of the student life cycle has attracted possibly the most research attention so far. To ensure that students have the best possible learning experience universities attempt to go beyond traditional virtual learning environment for on course communication, and teaching tools.

Increasingly, social networking platforms open opportunities for third party application development. In higher education settings learning and teaching tools are enhanced by social interactions among students and with their instructors offer tremendous capabilities. These broadening opportunities are based upon knowledge sharing. However, one of the barriers to a successful integration of social networking in teaching is achievement of student engagement in the more formal communication process. Some participants of the focus groups indicated that they perceive study-related communication as formal and may resent sharing their informal space while on course.

Career Management and Employability

As reported in (Dutta & Fraser, 2009) Facebook has recently seen an increase in the registrations of people in their mid careers. It has been suggested that with the downturn in the global economy, people turn to Facebook in search of business contacts and safer employment prospects. According to (Zhiwen & van der Heijden, 2008) employability enhancement and career management among a diverse range of core university processes can be facilitated through application of social networks. Our findings suggest that undergraduate students in particular are less likely to be members of business-focused networks such as LinkedIn, but that postgraduate students are keen to exploit entrepreneurial and business opportunities through resources embedded in social networks.

Both the focus groups and the survey results also indicate that students would like to use social networks to make contact with alumni who may help them find jobs, but were a little uncertain as to how best to achieve this.

Life-Long Learning

Results of the study suggest that students are eager to maintain contacts with fellow students after leaving university walls. This again supports the view that the entire life cycle must be considered when developing online student support systems.

Finally, our study also suggests that particularly undergraduate students are rather naïve about the use of social networks, supporting recent research findings emphasizing that networking users are unaware of privacy issues and risk (Debatin et al., 2009). Universities should consider educating students in both the risks and the advantages, particularly of social capital development, of online social networking.

Table 5.8. Potential Applications of Social Media in Student's Life Cycle

Life Cycle Stages	Objectives	Social Networking Enablement	Key Implications
Aspirations risings	• Ensure that potential entrants into HE whether currently at school, in HE, in the community or in the workplace are engaged with by the university to raise their awareness of undergraduate, post-graduate and CPD opportunities.	• Delivering interventions in all sectors including: school, college, HE, community, workplace; • Digital marketing, engagement of potential entrants by means of online social communication	• Maintaining social networking presence of the office university sites
Application, preentry support and induction	• Prove increased opportunities for students from more diverse backgrounds to enter university	• Improving advice and guidance service; • Implementing an information and communication plan	• Monitoring the Internet identity of HE institution • Digital marketing through targeted social networks
On-course support	• Support students in fully engaging with their courses and the broader learning community	• Common interest groups; • Knowledge dissemination through social media	• Support through formal and informal social networks
Learning, teaching and assessment	• Ensure that students have the best possible learning experience	• Integration of social media into learning and teaching strategies	• Difficulties in student engagement
Career management	• Continually improve the employability of students; • Equip students with employability skills; • Support their transition into the workplace or further study	• Alumni network management; • Social capital building and exploitation	• Awareness of the effects of digital footprint and Internet identity and their implication upon career progression
Life-long learning	• Continually improve and develop personal and professional skills, engage with communities of best practice; development of career management skills	• Communities of best practice; • Knowledge contribution and idea sharing; • Engagement with younger generations; • Broadening business opportunities within social media	• Knowledge and idea contribution; building and exploitation of cooperative knowledge online.

CONCLUSION

Although diversely defined (Coleman, 1990; Putnam, 1993), social capital is a metaphor about advantage (Burt, 2001). The model offered here is a limited step in linking of social capital theory and social media applications in higher educational settings. Graduates who are coming into business for the first time are almost expected to be comfortable with interactions using social networks. This brings new challenges to graduates in the way they use social networks and how they enhance their career development and relationships with employers. This study reports the findings of a survey of 272 United Kingdom and international business school students on career development and entrepreneurship as a part of a wider study of online social networking use. This research bridges the gap in literature by evaluating the use of social networks among students, focusing on their reasons to join, expectations from, and actual use of social networking for career development in a higher education settings. Treating social media use only in learning and teaching, for instance, ignores the importance of social capital in the rest of the phases in the student life cycle. What is the relationship between the on course support and social capital formation, or between attaining higher employability and integrating networking skills into HE curriculum? Should digital footprint awareness be developed as a theme in ICT education? What is the development of students' networks over time which maximizes the use of bridging social capital and help them "go ahead" in their careers and lifelong learning?

As such questions are resolved, others will arise. The digital divide, mobility and engagement are just a few of the variables which would be of particular importance in the development of micro-macro linkage between student life cycle and networking analysis for career success. The conclusions of the study help better understand motivations and barriers to an effective application of social networks in business. Our contribution here is mainly exploratory, its primary purpose being to generate interest in the proposed e-social capital theory and research.

REFERENCES

Aldrich, H., & Kim, P. (2007). Small worlds, infinite possibilities? How social networks affect entrepreneurial team formation and search. *Strategic Entrepreneurship Journal, 1,* 147-165.

Barnes, N. D., & Barnes, F. R. (2009). Equipping your organization for the social networking game. *Information Management, 43*(6), 28-33.

Bolles, R. N. (1992). *What color is your parachute?* Berkeley, CA: Ten Speed Press.

Brosius, H. B., & Engel, D. (1996). The causes of third-person effects: Unrealistic optimism, impersonal impact, or generalized negative attitudes towards media influence? *International Journal of Public Opinion Research, 8*(2), 142-162.

Brown, J. S., & Duguid, P. (2001). Knowledge and organization: A social-practice perspective. *Organization Science, 12*(2), 198-213.

Burt, R. (1992). *Structural holes: The social structure of competition.* Cambridge, MA: Harvard University Press.

Burt, R. (1997). The contingent value of social capital. *Administrative Science Quarterly, 42*, 339-365.

Burt, R. (2001). The social capital of structural holes. In M. Guillen, R. Collins, P. England, & M. Meyer (Eds.), *New directions in economic sociology.* New York, NY: Russell Sage Foundation.

Coleman, J. (1990). *Foundations of social theory.* Cambridge, MA: Harvard University Press.

Constant, D., Sproull, L., & Kiesler, S. (1996). The kindness of strangers: The usefulness of electronic weak ties for technical advice. *Organization Science, 7*(2), 119-135.

Debatin, B., Lovejoy, J. P., Horn, A. K., & Hughes, B. N. (2009). Facebook and online privacy: Attitudes, behaviors, and unintended consequences. *Journal of Computer-Mediated Communication, 15*, 83-108.

Dreher, G. F., & Ash, R. A. (1990). A comparative study of mentoring among men and women in managerial, professional, and technical positions. *Journal of Applied Psychology, 75*, 539-546.

Dutta, S., & Fraser, M. (2009). When job seekers invade Facebook. *The McKinsey Quarterly, 3*, 16-17.

Ellison, N. B., Steinfield, C., & Lampe, C. (2007). The benefits of Facebook "friends": Social capital and college students' use of online social network sites. *Journal of Computer-Mediated Communication, 12*(4), 1143-1168.

Gal, S. (2002). A semiotics of the public/private distinction. *Journal of Feminist Cultural Studies, 13*(1), 77-95.

Granovetter, M. (1973) The strength of weak ties. *American Journal of Sociology, 6*, 1360-1380.

Hough, M. G. (2009). Keeping it to ourselves: Technology, privacy and the loss of reserve. *Technology in Society, 31*, 406-413.

Judge, T. A., & Bretz, R. D. (1994). Political influence behavior and career success. *Journal of Management, 20*, 43-65.

Kingston University. (2007). *Quality enhancement startegy.* London, England: Kingston Academic Development Centre.

Leana, C. R., & van Buren, H. (1999). Organizational social capital and employment practices. *The Academy of Management Review, 24*(3), 538-555.

Lange, P. G. (2007). Publicly private and privately public: Social networking on YouTube. *Journal of Computer-Mediated Communication, 13*(1). Retrieved from http://jcmc.indiana.edu/vol13/issue1/lange.html

Lewis, J., & West, A. (2009). 'Friending': London-based undergraduates' experience of Facebook. *New Media Society, 11*(7), 1209-1229.

Lin, N. (2001). *Social capital: A theory of social structure and action.* New York, NY: Cambridge University Press.

Lin, N., Ensel, W., & Vaughn, J. (1981). Social resources and StrenTies: Structural factors in occupational status attainment. *American Sociological Review, 46*(4), 393-405.

Livingstone, S. (2008). Taking risky opportunities in youthful content creation: Teenagers' use of social networking sites for intimacy, privacy and self-expression. *New Media Society, 10,* 393-411.

Luthans, F., Hodgetts, R. M., & Rosenkrantz, S. A. (1988). *Real managers.* Cambridge, MA: Ballinger.

Lyne, N. (2009, November). Ten tips to raise your business visibility through social networks. *Financial Executive, 25*(9), 17.

Madden, M., Fox, S., Smith, A., & Vittak, J. (2007). *Digital footprints: Online Identity management and search in the age of transparency.* Washington, DC: Pew Research Center Publications.

Mastrodicasa, J. (2008). Technology use in campus crisis. *New Directions for Student Services, Winter*(124), 37-53.

Narayan, D. (1999). *Bonds and bridges: Social capital and poverty.* Washington, DC: World Bank.

Peluchette, J., & Karl, K. (2010). Examining students' intended image on Facebook: "What were they thinking?!" *Journal of Education for Business, 85*(1), 30-37.

Pfeil, U., Arjan, R., & Zaphiris, P. (2009). Age differences in online social networking—A study of user profiles and the social capital divide among teenagers and older users in MySpace. *Computers in Human Behavior, 25,* 643-654.

Powell, W. W., Koput, K., & Smtih-Doer, L. (1996). Interorganizational collaboration and the locus of innovation: Networks of learning in biotechnology. *Administrative Science Quarterly, 41,* 116-145.

Putnam, R. (1993). The prosperous community: Social capital and public life. The *American Prospect, 13,* 35-42.

Quan-Haase, A. (2007). University students' local and distant social ties: Using and integrating modes of communication on campus. *Information, Communication & Society, 10*(5), 671-693.

Seibert, S., Kraimer, M., & Liden, R. (2001). A social capital theory of career success. *Academy of Management Journal, 44*(2), 219-237.

Stone, W., Gray, M., & Hughes, J. (2003). Social capital at work. How family, friends and civic ties relate to labour market outcomes. Melbourne, Australia: Australian Institute of Family Studies. Retrieved from http://www.aifs.gov.au/institute/pubs/respaper/RP31.pdf

Useem, M., & Karabel, J. (1986). Pathways to top corporate management. *American Sociological Review, 51,* 184-200.

Wasko, M., & Faraj, S. (2005). Why should I share: Examining social capital and knowledge contribution in electronic networks of practice. *MIS Quarterly, Vol. 29,* 35-57.

Woolcock, M. (2000). Social capital and its meanings. *Canberra Bulletin of Public Administration, Vol. 98,* 17-19.

Zhiwen, G., & van der Heijden, B. (2008) Employability enhancement of business graduates in China: Reacting upon challenges of globalization and labour market demands. *Education and Training, 50*(4), 289-304.

CHAPTER 6

USER-GENERATED CONTENT IN BUSINESS EDUCATION

Domen Bajde

By significantly reducing the limitations of traditional media, social media offer new possibilities for individuals and groups to actively participate in mediated communication by creating and sharing user-generated content (UGC). Business education is faced with the challenging task of educating students about the ways of the "new" participatory consumer, while at the same time being blessed with the opportunities offered by the blossoming UGC culture and technologies. We aim to provide support on both fronts by: (1) defining and categorizing UGC, (2) sketching out its vital role in social media, and (3) addressing the implications and challenges it holds for business education.

Social media remove many traditional obstacles to public expression, supplementing the traditional one-to-many mass media with decentralized many-to-many media. The multiplication of media is owed both to new professional media entrants and to a process Shirky (2008) calls "mass amateurization," the shift in cultural production from editorially filtered professional production (i.e., quality is guaranteed through the choice of professional "gatekeepers") to the amateur production operating by the "publish first-filter later" principle. This new modus operandi relies upon

Cutting-Edge Social Media Approaches to Business Education:
Teaching With LinkedIn, Facebook, Twitter, Second Life, and Blogs, pp. 95–115
Copyright © 2010 by Information Age Publishing
All rights of reproduction in any form reserved.

the consumers' ability and willingness to not only create and publish, but also to actively share and filter content (rate, tag, comment, recommend, flame, etc.). In other words, consumption of information becomes inseparable from production and the remarkable increase in the ability to share content, to communicate and cooperate transforms the passive consumer audience into today's producer-consumers (Kozinets, Hemetsberger, & Schau, 2008). In this sense the world in which some produce and many consume media is gradually being transformed into one where "many" have a more active stake in the production of cultural products (Jenkins, 2006a, 2006b).

These profound shifts have also been observed in nonacademic circles. In 2006 The Times Person of the Year award went to the "new" participatory consumers (i.e., "You") who were honored for "seizing the reins of the global media, for founding and framing the new digital democracy, for working for nothing and beating the pros at their own game" (Grossman, 2007). Following suit, Advertising Age named "The consumer" as the ad agency of the year, arguing that in 2006 "consumer-generated commercial content ... would easily trump any single agency's offering" (Creamer 2007). These prominent recognitions of the rising consumer participation were preceded by earlier expositions such as Garfield's (2005) "Listenomics" manifesto, wherein the author heralds "the emerging open-source world of communications" driven by "a crowd of what you used to call your 'audience.' "[1] Despite Garfield's doomsday rhetoric, it is not very likely that the emergent (social) media will utterly replace traditional media or that consumers will take over the realm of cultural production altogether, but rather reaffirms the dramatic increase in consumers' communicative opportunities and the need for more energetic cooperation between companies and consumers (McCracken, 2009).

The need for such cooperation is addressed by Jenkins (2006a) who introduces the notion of "participatory culture," a culture characterized by its low barriers to expression and civic engagement and by its supportiveness for creating and sharing of content (Jenkins, 2006b). This culture stimulates consumers to constantly learn how to use internet communication technology (ICT) to bring the flow of content more under their control, thus necessitating companies to more actively engage with the newly-formed participatory consumer communities (Jenkins, 2006a). Such engagement proves to be a haunting task due to the decreased level of corporate control over "participatory" communication and the highly divergent and unpredictable nature of these new participatory audiences.

According to Jenkins (2006b) participatory culture comes in at least four forms: affiliations (participation centered on socializing and community membership), expressions (participation in the form of novel creative works), collaborative problem solving (participation in teams and groups) and circulations (continuous flow of participation). All of these forms are directly or indirectly associated with the user generated-content created by consumers outside their professional routines.[2] UGC represents the most evocative form of consumer participation in digital environments, social media in particular. As a result, business education is faced with the challenging task of educating students about the ways of the "new" participatory consumer and UGC culture, while at the same time being blessed with the opportunities offered by the blossoming participatory culture and UGC technologies. We aim to provide support on both fronts by: (1) defining and categorizing UGC, (2) sketching out the vital role of UGC in social media and (3) addressing the implications and challenges it holds for business education.

DEFINING AND CATEGORIZING UGC

The term user-generated content has been used in various contexts, designating different aspects of user activity to different authors. In its broadest usage UGC can be taken to envelop all the information and content extracted by internet service providers from their users. The term can be applied both to content in its narrow sense (e.g., texts, videos, pictures) or, more broadly, also to the more structural contributions of users (e.g., hyperlinking, tagging, rating, mapping). As used here, UGC encompasses various forms of creative products (be it in written, visual, video or audio mode) that have been created and shared by consumers themselves. More precisely, we follow Vickery and Wunsch-Vincent (2007), who in their OECD report define UGC (or in their terminology user-created content) as *content made publicly available over the Internet, which reflects a certain amount of creative effort and is created outside of professional routines and practices*.

UGC takes many diverse shapes and forms and flows across various platforms. It can perhaps most readily be classified based on its dominant mode of presentation. Predominately *textual content* is typically, but not exclusively, found on blogs, prose or poetry sites, citizen journalism sites and in the educational contexts. *Audio content* represents the dominant mode of expression in user-generated podcasts and social media contexts devoted to music. *Image-dominant* UGC (e.g., user video and photo collections, photo blogs, video blogs) can be found on photo and video sharing platforms. As evidenced by this short and simplified overview, the modes of expression used in UGC are inextricably tied to the nature of the respective UGC hosting platform. Accordingly, UGC could also be classified based on the platforms hosting it (e.g., blogs, wikis, virtual worlds, social networks, video/photo sharing platforms).

Another way of categorizing UGC content involves the consideration of the motives that underpin its creation. UGC can perform a number of pragmatic functions relevant to its authors and the respective user community. While a considerable proportion of user created content seeks to entertain, it can also serve as a problem-solving tool, an educational device, or as a gift or tribute to other users, professional content creators, organizations and their brands. UGC can be employed to entice others to particular actions (e.g., collective problem solving, user resistance, social gathering). It can also voice artistic expressions, serve as a transient social lubricant (e.g., greeting, sharing personal news and opinions), et cetera.

We must note that user *motivations* for creating are multifaceted and often intertwined inasmuch as particular creators will likely be driven by divergent mixtures of the proposed motives. Although the respective "mixtures" of user motivation will likely differ across individual creators as well as across specific situations, several general observations can be offered. Consumers have been found to primarily create content in order to lessen their insecurities about themselves and to be recognized by peers who share similar beliefs and values (Daugherty, Eastin, & Bright, 2008). Along these lines, Vickery and Wunsch-Vincent (2007) list connecting with peers and achieving a certain level of fame, notoriety, or prestige, and the intrinsic desire to express oneself as the chief motivating factors in UGC creation. These general descriptions of user motives share an apparent emphasis on the social nature of UGC.

UGC AND SOCIAL MEDIA

Whereas the notion of UGC has been associated with the Internet at least since the early 1990s (Sawyer, 2010), the sociocultural and economic role of UGC increased dramatically with the rise of Web 2.0 and the advent of social media. According to O'Reilly (2005), the "architecture of [user] participation" represents one of the vital pillars of Web 2.0. Social media heavily rely on the participation of large-scale communities of consumers who invest effort into navigating and filtering the Web and creating content for other users to enjoy (Jenkins, 2006b). Evidently, social media like YouTube, Flickr or Facebook are inconceivable in absence of user videos, photos, texts, and other forms of UGC.

Social media platforms are well-suited to the creation and exchange of content (Kaplan & Haenlein, 2010). UGC is inherently social inasmuch as it is created to be published and shared across the (often broad) social networks (Vickery and Wunsch-Vincent, 2007). Be it in its more egoistic or altruistic form, the notion of sharing remains vital to the UGC culture.[3] As soon as UGC starts to partake in commodity exchange (as opposed to voluntary sharing), it becomes harder to conceive it as being created and distributed outside of professional routines. The social element found in sharing resources, clearly represents one of the pillars of the UGC culture. It is precisely the voluntary sharing of digital resources (UGC included) that social media facilitate so effectively.

There are good reasons for calling social media social. As pointed out by Garfield (2005), the users of social media are "still an audience, but they aren't necessarily listening to you [the company]. They're listening to each other." Although the "talking and listening" referred to by Garfield does not necessarily involve UGC,[4] social media do heavily rely on the more deliberate and laboriously creative contributions made by their users. For example, platforms like Wikipedia or YouTube invite users to voluntarily create, publish and share content. One could argue that the success of social media largely depends on their ability to effectively facilitate the flow of UGC.

A further consideration of the role of social (media) in UGC flows involves the collective intelligence aspect of UGC creation. The creativity pertaining to UGC is often collective in the sense of being triggered by social interactions and collaborative practices (Kozinets et al., 2008). Social media provide the vital social hotbed for UGC creation by helping users locate similar others and receive the support (e.g., mentoring, reflection) crucial to successful content creation (Jenkins, 2006b). In addition, social media also help facilitate user coordination (Shirky, 2008), localized user cooperation (i.e., creating in groups) and make possible the collective filtering, essential in 'taming' the seemingly endless mass of UGC.

Kozinets et al. (2008) divide creative online communities across two dimensions of collective user creativity: the concentration and orientation of creation. Social media can thus facilitate highly concentrated UGC creation, where a very small group of individuals creates the majority of the content, or more dispersed creation where a larger number of users engage in creation. Next, social media can encourage creation driven by a specific goal, or contributions of more unstructured nature. Figure 6.1 presents the four resulting types of UGC communities by applying Kozinets et al.'s (2008) typology of online creative communities to the context of UGC.

Having devoted considerable attention to questions of what, where, why and how UGC "happens," it is now time to discuss the relevance of this phenomenon to business education. There are several reasons for seriously considering the UGC culture from a business. First, there is the sheer extent of the UGC phenomenon. According to eMarketer (2008) 82,5 million U.S. consumers (42,8% of U.S. Internet users) have created UGC in 2008, while 116 million (60%) have consumed it. Although the

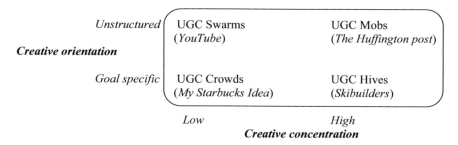

Source: Adapted from Kozinets et al. (2008).

Figure 6.1.   Types of UGC communities based on creative orientation and concentration.

more recent statistics indicate a significant drop in teen user engagement in blogging, teens' participation in other forms of UGC creation as well as overall adult participation remain stable or are still on the rise (Lenhart, Purcell, Smith, & Zickuhr, 2010). What is more, at least among teens, UGC-related activities have become mainstream as the previously found variations in user participation across gender, race, ethnicity or socioeconomic status disappeared by 2010. In the more specific areas of news consumption and health care, recent studies show that more than a third of U.S. Internet users (i.e., 37%) have actively contributed to the creation of news, commentary or distribution of news via social media sites (Purcell, Lee, Mitchell, Rosenstiel, & Olmstead, 2010), and that user participation is on the rise in areas such as healthcare, where patients increasingly create UGC to share their opinions and experiences (Fox, 2009).

Second, Vickery and Wunsch-Vincent's (2007) review of the economic impacts, confirms that UGC exerts a significant impact on a number of industries. More specifically, the emergent participatory culture and the rising production of UGC have been heralded as "a significant disruptive force for how content is created, consumed and for the industries traditionally supplying content" (Vickery & Wunsch-Vincent, 2007, p. 5). In his recent book, *The Chaos Scenario*, Garfield (2009, p. 430) presents UGC as an important contributor to the overall "disintegration of the critical audience mass" required for corporate content producers and mass media to operate profitably. The growing mass of free (or close to free) UGC is suggested to have subverted the "economics of scarcity," upon which the traditional business models for content creation and distribution, advertising and mass marketing are largely founded. Conversely, the abundant[5] and diverse UGC is well-suited to the progressively fragmented audiences, composed of consumers who are less willing and less compelled to pay for content (in money or in their attention to advertising).

On the other hand, it is shortsighted to cast UGC as the annihilator of the content industry, traditional media and mass advertising. For one, a significant proportion of UGC is derivative in nature, and users often remix and build upon commercial content during the process of (re)creation. At least indirectly the burgeoning creation of UGC increases the need for commercial content. Next, UGC platforms largely rely on advertising revenues, which are difficult to generate in the milieu of unpredictable and potentially offensive UGC. Advertisers generally prefer the more conventional and corporate-friendly commercial content, which has increasingly led UGC platforms such as YouTube not only to partner with commercial content creators (e.g., recording labels) and traditional media (e.g., TV networks), but also to "commoditize" their relationship with the more popular user creators (Wasko & Erickson, 2009). When users get enlisted as quasi-commercial partners, they receive financial incentives to conform to YouTube's content guidelines, consequently making it easier for YouTube to monetize their content through advertising. These developments indicate that UGC is more likely to increase the reformation of the media and content industries, than it is to destroy or replace them.

Third, although the earnings generated by the UGC platforms fall far short from the revenues generated by the traditional media and content industries, UGC-related earnings are far from negligible. UGC platforms rely on various monetization models including: the user donations model, the charging for services model (per item or subscription payments), the merchandise sale model and the advertising-based model (Vickery & Wunsch-Vincent, 2007). Platforms often combine these models in their uphill quest to monetize their user-base. The photo-sharing platform Flickr, for instance, combines the advertising-based model with subscription charges to user who elect to upgrade their account to receive a premium service (i.e., unlimited storage, upload, bandwidth, permanent archiving and an ad-free service). Advertising remains the dominant revenue stream for UGC sites. In one of the few available reports on UGC-related revenue, eMarketer (2007) estimates the 2007 UGC advertising revenue in the United States at $1.042 million, predicting that it will quadruple by 2011.

Although the rising ranks of user creators and consumers of UGC increase the potential for revenue, they often increase costs at an even higher rate. UGC platforms like YouTube are burdened by tremendous band-width costs, which often exceed the incoming advertising revenue. As a result, despite its incredible popularity, YouTube has not yet managed to generate the profitability that would justify the hefty price paid for it by Google. This (among other things) leads Garfield (2009) to describe it as "the world's most successful failure." In light of such high investments and expectations, it is not hard to conceive the mounting pressure on UGC platforms to more aggressively monetize their user-base. These pressures are all the more problematic, because these platforms operate in two-sided markets, having to satisfy their user and advertiser customers, whose interests are a times directly opposed.[6]

Fourth, there are significant economic impacts of UGC on companies that might have no direct interest in creating or selling content as such. The more immediate positive impacts in terms of growth, market entry of new firms and employment are currently with ICT goods and service providers such as search engines, portals, and aggregators monetizing on the increasing needs to search, aggregate and distribute UGC content (Vickery & Wunsch-Vincent, 2007). Novel opportunities, spawned by the UGC trend, await consumer electronics and ICT hardware producers and software producers offering product that facilitate the creation and sharing of content.

Fifth, in addition to the discussed economic impacts, the rising UGC phenomenon also exerts profound sociocultural impacts, which significantly affect the way companies conduct their business. The recent changes in the way users produce, distribute, share, and (re)use content has led to profound shifts in the relationship between companies and consumers. As suggested earlier, the increase in opportunities for consumer to create and share content have led to increased user empowerment and participation. As a result, the past conceptions of consumers as passive destroyers of goods need to be revised to make way for today's producer-consumers. With the advent of social media and UGC technologies consumers can more effectively interact with intimate and distant others and take unprecedented charge of their media experiences (Daugherty, 2008). The rise in user participation and the increasing consumer reliance on UGC, shift the balance of power between the company and the consumer in the favor of the latter as UGC begins to play more and more prominent role in consumer communication, media consumption and ultimately purchase decision making (Kucuka & Krishnamurthy, 2007). These changes call for revisions in marketing and communicating with consumers, novel approaches to consumer research and offer new opportunities to leverage the UGC culture as an innovation-driving force.

Learning About the UGC Culture
(the Marketing Perspective)

A detailed review of the extensive literature focusing on the impacts of the recent developments in ICT and social media which would extend far beyond the scope of this treatise. Instead, we start with some basic observations. There is considerable consensus among marketing academics and practitioners that the opportunities for consumers to acquire and share information have increased dramatically (Kucuka & Krishnamurthy, 2007; Urban, 2005). The increased communication between consumers coupled with the improved consumer control in consuming media and information reduces the effectiveness of traditional push and pull marketing tools, encouraging marketers to rely more on nurturing a mutual dialogue with customers as opposed to "speaking at customers" (Urban, 2005). Such "dialogue" strategies are largely dependent on transparency and trust (openly and honestly sharing information) as well as a genuine societal orientation (striving to benefit customers, communities and the society).

With the rising role of consumer-to-consumer interaction in purchase decision making, marketers are encouraged to rethink the role of so called word of mouth (WOM), in particular in its digital forms (at times dubbed "word of mouse"). UGC represents one of the most evocative forms of today's WOM (Hutton, 2009). Universal McCann's (2008) report on the new consumer influence landscape, marked by the advent of social media, describes an emergent breed of "super influencers." The report shows that the "democratization of influence" (i.e., a shift from top-down, mainstream media-driven influence to the web-enabled peer to peer influence) spawns a group of super-influencers, who are (not surprisingly) dominated by the ranks of users, who create and share content online (in particular video UGC and blogs). Similar conclusions are drawn in a recent Forrester report (Ray, 2010) which finds that a segment of mass influencers, representing 16% of the U.S. population, is responsible for 80% of the influence impressions and posts about products and services in social media. Within this influential segment of consumers, the report highlights the segment of "Mass mavens who create and share content about products and services in other social channels such as YouTube, blogs, forums, or ratings and review sites." Mass mavens represent only 13.4% of U.S. online users, but create roughly 80% of all influential online posts related to product and services (Ray, 2010).

As a result, it is essential for companies to engage with the social media users, in particular the influential UGC creators. These users do not only represent a cost effective and trust-inspiring channel to get the company's "message" across, they also represent the ranks of potential innovators. The rise of UGC culture has led many companies to more energetically invite consumers to partake in the creation of marketing communication as well as in the process of product development (von Hippel, 2005). In their review of breakthrough advertising campaigns conducted in 2008, Bernardin et al. (2008) find that these campaigns often relied on active consumer participation and UGC. Prominent examples of user participation in creating advertising content include UGC-based contest such as Frito Lay's "Crash the Super Bowl," Converse's conversegallery.com or Mastercard's "Write a Priceless Ad Contest." A more recent example of "crowd sourcing"[7] can be found in Ford's efforts to promote Fiesta. McCracken (2010) describes it as three-step process which involves: engaging culturally creative consumers to create content, encouraging them to distribute this content across their social networks, and crafting this in a way that turns the established digital currency into value for the brand.

However, harnessing the UGC culture is difficult. Slapdash attempts often prove ineffective, or worse, counterproductive. For example, Chevrolet's infamous Tahoe campaign backfired as users invited to promote the Tahoe SUV, opted to create anti-SUV content instead. Hutton (2010) cautions marketers to avoid the pitfall of inviting consumers to create content centered to narrowly around the products; instead companies should strive to "rouse consumers" genuine curiosity and invite an authentic response that isn't transparently self-serving to the needs of the brand' (Hutton, 2010).

Similar conclusions also apply to company efforts to involve consumers in the product development process. While, consumers definitely do posses a unique vantage point when it comes to their product experiences and while it would be unwise to dismiss the creative potential of individual consumers and online communities, consumers will seriously engage in product development only when their existent involvement in the product or brand is high and the required investment is perceived as meaningful and worthwhile to them, not to the company alone. Successful examples of harnessing the UGC culture for product development purposes include consumer idea generating campaigns such as Dell's Idea Storm or Starbuck's My Starbucks Idea, or examples of more sophisticated consumer-sourcing such as Lego's Mindstorm program. As explained by Garfield (2010) in a radio interview, Lego:

> went out to this fan base, which they located on chat rooms and Web sites around the world, and they invited them to come to Billund at their own expense and to participate in the redesign of the Mindstorm's line of products ... and the next thing you know, people were flying to Denmark, and they spent, I don't know what it was, I think six weeks there, again at their own expense, went in every day, got into the inner sanctum at LEGO, where no civilians hitherto had ever ventured and redesigned this line and then worked on it for another 14 months when they got home at their computers. And when the new line was launched after about two years, it was almost entirely the work of these volunteers who were nothing more than LEGO fans. And not only did they redesign the brand, they were 100 percent of the marketing force because using those very chat rooms and Web sites.

In order to tap the creative and communicative potential of consumers, companies need to obtain a thorough understanding of the participatory communities. For this to happen, consumer research theory and need to actively engage with the UGC culture and its diverse manifestations. The need to explore user engagement in user-generated content has been stressed by various authors (Blythe & Cairns, 2009; Garfield, 2005; Muniz & Schau, 2006; Pace 2008). When properly studied UGC allows the researchers an invaluable view into the frustrations and joys of consumers (i.e., what matters to consumers, and the problems they might have)—the naturally occurring responses of consumers to products and companies. For example, Muniz and Schau (2006) explicitly stress the importance of surveying UGC communities to better understand how users engage with brands and marketing. Their study shows how consumers sometimes use social media and UGC in an attempt to control 'the destiny' of a beloved brand and how UGC can reveal the complex relations that bind the users together as well as connecting them with the brand and the respective company.

Despite the relatively early stage of this research stream's development, a multitude of methodological tools have already been used or suggested by consume researchers. UGC and the social contexts surrounding it, have been studied by way of content analysis (Blythe & Cairns, 2009), net-nographic research (Muniz & Schau, 2006), narrative analysis (Pace, 2008), lexical semantics (Aggarwal, Vaidyanathan, & Venkatesh, 2009) and multimodal discourse analysis (Bajde & Culiberg, 2010). Similarly the marketing research industry has been very active in devising tools that measure and mine UGC content. However, while proprietary research has been relatively proficient in measuring UGC's reach and quantifying the spread and consumption of UGC, in-depth research in the UGC context remains scarce and the methodological approaches are still in their infancy.

Learning From/With UGC Culture (the Educational Perspective)

In addition to its relevance in the context of marketing communication, product development and consumer research, the UGC culture also carries broader implications for management education. Foremost, incorporating UGC into educational practices contributes toward creating a more "constructivist learning environment," wherein students not only engage in more active learning, but also actively contribute toward the learning of others (vom Brocke et al. 2010, p. 150). Auvinen (2008) calls this aspect of learning "peer production of learning." My contention is not that students can/should replace professors, but rather that students and other nonacademic stakeholders can produce content that: (1) supports peer-to-peer learning, (2) enriches the communication occurring in the process of learning and (3) creates new connections between various "content" produced by educators.

Similar to other forms of social media-inspired learning, incorporating UGC into higher education challenges the traditional borders between author and "reader," teacher and student (Auvinen, 2008). The UGC culture supports a hierarchy-averse creative ethos, distinguished by its emphasis on sharing and play. The social and playful nature of UGC possesses the ability to free the creation process from the "burdens" of formalized reward and punishment systems and enrich it with the momentum of social engagement. Put differently, the UGC culture encourages creative experimentation and intensifies engagement through sharing (i.e., creating for others and with others).

Unfortunately, it is all but impossible to find comprehensive empirical data on the actual extent of UGC's integration in higher education. Rather than measuring the extent of this elusive phenomenon, the pertinent literature offers various case studies. For instance, vom Brocke et al. (2010) report of bringing together students groups from Germany and New Zealand by forming a UGC community devoted to exploring themes such as "globalization and localization." Media reports touching upon instances of local traditions from both countries were used as a stimulant for students' creation of UGC debating various perspectives on the topic. For instance, a discussion of tattoo consumption practices in New Zealand and Germany greatly enhanced the students' understanding of divergent cultural meanings assigned to tattoos in both cultures, the impact of global fashion trends on local traditions, and significantly improved the student's German/English language skills through the process of creating for and communicating with native German/English speakers. Parallel qualitative studies report on the educational use of student-generated web-blogs and wikis (Hemmi, Bayne, & Land, 2009), podcasts, UGC on social networking sites (Minocha, 2009) and UGC in virtual worlds (Antonacci & Modaress, 2008). Among the more prominent examples of integrating the UGC culture into higher education one also needs to mention Michael Wesch's inspiring work with UGC (in particular with respect to the YouTube platform), eloquently outlined on his Kansas University Digital Ethnography blog (http://mediatedcultures.net). Wesch equips and stimulates students to study digital UGC environments as well as initiates various UGC-driven student projects. For example, the recent 'Students helping students' project lead the students toward creating short video vignettes devoted to past "K-State Proud" scholarship winners. According to Wesch, the project not only promoted a socially beneficial cause, but more importantly gave "students some experience in online organizing and planning, handling a camera ..., allowing them to bond with each other through a fun experience" (Wesch, 2010).

The playful creative engagement and communal sharing associated with the UGC culture help its proponents to acquire a number of skills invaluable to modern-day managers. We have devoted considerable attention to demonstrate the vital economic and socio-cultural role of UGC in today's environment, thus indicating the need for business educators to pay notice to the rising UGC culture. More specifically, we have sketched out some specific implications this culture holds for marketing, product development and consumer research. In the paragraphs that follow, we focus on how educators can help students better develop a set of skills by integrating the UGC culture into business education. These skills largely intersect with the notion of new media literacy, skills "that enable participation in the new communities emerging within a networked society... exploit new simulation tools, information appliances, and social networks ... exchange information between diverse communities and ... move easily across different media platforms and social networks" (Jenkins, 2006b, p. 55). In their report on the challenges facing educators in the twenty-first century education Jenkins (2006b) lists eleven the socio-cultural skills and competencies that are emerging in the new participatory media landscape. Several of these skills are highly relevant to the UGC context and will be discussed in more detail. We present three clusters of such skills that could be described as the three interconnected pillars of the UGC culture: its playful creativity, its promiscuous foraging and remixing of content, and its networked sociality.

The UGC culture is inherently tied to the *notion of play* and the capacity to experiment with one's surroundings as a form of fun but also a form of problem solving. Because the creation and sharing of UGC takes place outside of the formal/professional routines, the stakes of failing are lowered and learning through trial and error is encouraged. Educators would do well not to reduce the UGC culture to "fleeting fun," but also recognize it as a potentially powerful form of learning. The playfully subversive nature of UGC can be channeled towards constructive criticism and creativity instead of being avoided or muffled due to its seditious disrespect to formal authority and conventions. The playful learning potential of UGC can readily be destroyed by over-formalizing UGC-inspired teaching. For instance, students can learn much about wikis through carefully structured and formalized assignments to post entries or engage in discussions on pre-chosen sites. But such activities are unlikely to retain the playful essence of the UGC culture and encourage the students to engage in free experimentation. Less structured, "bonus" assignments, inviting students to experiment with media platforms within loosely defined research questions (e.g., How does particular UGC content reach popularity on this site?) can be more effective in this regard.

The UGC culture encourages *creative reappropriation* of exiting creative products. The escalating abundance of content, the growing access to a multitude of content archives, as well as the increased ease of archiving, editing, sampling and remixing content, encourage users to engage in various forms of content reappropriation, ranging from activist satire to homemade parodies and tribute works. Closely associated with reappropriation are also skills of "transmedia navigation," or the abilities to follow and actively contribute to the flow of content and information across multiple modalities both in the sense of multiple media outlets and in the sense of multiple representation modes. Accordingly, students should be encouraged to actively forage the emergent UGC platforms for valuable resources, to reappropriate and build upon those resources and to ultimately take advantage of these same platforms to disseminate their ideas and encourage others to engage with their work. Reappropriation also raises a number of ethical and legal concerns (e.g., author's moral and legal rights to control the distribution and use of his creations), which will be discussed in the last section of this chapter.

The third *assortment of social skills* related to UGC endeavors entails the closely aligned abilities to pool knowledge and interact with others in the process of learning (i.e., collective intelligence) and the abilities to partake in diverse communities in order to search for, synthesize, and disseminate content and information (i.e., networking). Such transcommunal engagement demands that the creator/communicators are able to take in and respect a multitude of (often conflicting) perspectives and norms (Jenkins, 2006b). A genuine appreciation of the practices and norms associated with cooperation and sharing, in particular, are essential to effectively partaking in UGC communities. Although UGC-related cooperation and sharing generally proceed in conditions of ad-hocratic organization and, to use Turner and Rojek's terminology (2001), "thin" social relations, the often loose and transient social ordering of UGC communities should not be confused with the absence of sociality. Individuals and groups who are unable to recognize the social aspect of UGC are unlikely to be successful at creating and disseminating content that will be meaningful to and appreciated by others. Along these lines, students can be encouraged to partake in relevant UGC communities, systematically reflecting on the social arrangements, discourses, practices and norms prevalent in the community. The problems communities face in engaging with established businesses and the respective platform owners can provide useful entries into the study of UGC culture and its relevance to business.[8] UGC communities can also help the students to more readily cooperate with distant others on projects, adding expertise and cultural depth to their work.

THE CHALLENGES OF UGC-INSPIRED EDUCATION

We round up our discussion of UGC's role in business education by reviewing some of the pertinent challenges faced by educators. The core challenge awaiting educators who wish to "incorporate" the UCG culture in their interaction with students pertains to achieving a balance between an overly romanticized understanding of the UGC culture and the drive to excessively normalize it to the existent teaching/management norms and practices. In this final section we provide some preliminary observations on achieving this problematic balance, and discuss several remaining challenges in "going UGC" in business education.

Without engaging in lengthy and knotty negotiation of the critical and the celebratory perspectives on the contemporary web-culture and its impacts on society, let us make some basic observations. To a significant degree, the UGC culture rests on ideologies of democratization, empowerment and community. UGC platforms have undoubtedly provided users with unprecedented opportunities to pool knowledge, to cooperate in their creative efforts and "broadcast" themselves and their content. Yet, these platforms are neither spaces of unrestricted freedom nor utopian communities of equals unscathed by political or commercial interests. It is paramount for educators and students to recognize how UGC platforms empower users by giving them voice and opportunities to connect with other users, but to also how UGC platforms and communities are inevitably enmeshed in commercial and political interests of the pertinent stakeholders (e.g., platform owners, users, advertisers, political elite). Even within the user communities, users are far from equal or all-powerful. As is the case in all social groupings, hierarchies, power disparity and restrictive conventions are prone to emerge.

Second, the fact that students are likely to be more "native" to the UGC world than educators tends to dissuade educators from engaging with this culture. Jenkins (2006b) provides three important reasons for refraining from such reasoning. The students' active participation in the UGC culture does not necessarily lead to active reflection on their UGC experiences. Education is necessary to put UGC into perspective by discussing its economic and sociocultural significance and helping students to articulate what they learn and experience from their participation in UGC communities. Education in this area is also necessary to tackle the likely inequalities in students' mastery of UGC technologies and opportunities for participation in UGC communities. Last, education can help establish and ingrain the ethical norms needed to cope with the complex and varied UGC environments.

Third, the presented arguments should not lead educators to excessively 'normalize' the UGC ethos. The UGC culture represents an appealing alternative learning culture precisely because it differs from the more formal learning cultures instilled by the established educational systems. It is worthwhile to recognize the essential role that communal reinforcement and playful engagement with popular culture play in UGC creativity. Assignments structured in the traditional manner, where students are rewarded exclusively by professors and the students' primary concern is not to "fail," where popular culture and the "trivia of the day" are frowned-upon, are likely to stifle the UGC culture's ability to inspire and engage.

Fourth, as of yet, notions such as UGC, let alone the hazy concept of UGC culture, are difficult to pin down. Due to the diverse understandings of these terms, the available data describing these phenomena needs to be approached with heightened awareness. There is much need for additional academic research in this area which could help us tackle these topics more systematically while at the same time keep us abreast with the fast-paced developments in this area. In particular, the intersection of the commercial and noncommercial aspects of the UGC culture need to be given additional thought. While, the existent debates have largely been dominated by the noncommercial ideologies of democratization and community, it is clear that UGC predominately takes place on commercial platforms and the user's propensity to create and consume UGC are increasingly subjected to attempts of monetization. Business researchers can provide important contributions to a more comprehensive understanding of this emerging 'social hybrid economy' (Wasko & Ericson, 2009).

Fifth, the UGC culture also raises manifold ethical and legal issues. UGC platforms enable novel forms of expression and sharing which can lead to various ethical predicaments. While many ethically questionable practices are effectively addressed by the UGC platform's managers and the user communities, others demand broader, more coordinated efforts. Specifically, we would like to point to several pertinent consumer rights issues and the problematic of copyright in UGC contexts. Many authors have recently tackled the problems of consumer rights in relation to privacy protection and commercial abuse of consumer data (see Langenderfer & Miyazaki, 2009). Unfortunately, consumer rights violations also occur in contexts of intentional user participation (e.g., creating and sharing UGC). Although in comparison to traditional media, UGC platforms considerably increase consumer freedom to create, publish and share content, these freedoms are neither absolute, nor are they safe from various attempts to exploit or abuse them (Miller, 2009).

According to Poster (2006), copyright represents one of the central tools used by the web platforms and their corporate stakeholders to rein in the "empowered" consumer in. TACD's (2008) Charter for Consumer Rights in the Digital World emphasizes the tendencies of copyright holders and service providers to restrict users' freedom of access, use and content transformation beyond the limits of reasonable protection of copyright.

On the other hand, copyright law imposes legal restrictions on copying, distribution and/or sale of copyrighted content in order to protect the rights of the copyright holder (Yar, 2005). Users have been known to violate these rights by massively uploading copyrighted materials and UGC platforms are often faced with the taunting task of balancing the intellectual property owners' interests with the users' whishes for unrestricted access to existent content (i.e., to consume and transform it). This task is all the more difficult due to various territorial differences in copyright law and the relatively loosely defined exceptions/limitations to copyright that often apply to UGC contexts (e.g., the US doctrine of 'Fair use').[9] Here again much additional effort is needed to provide users and educators with guidelines regarding lawful uses of existent content. Among the invaluable resources that do exist already we would point out European Commission's eYouGuide (2010) and American University Center for Social Media's a Code of best practices in Fair Use for Online Video (CSM, 2008).

In retrospect, despite the manifold challenges and obstacles awaiting educators who wish to engage with the rising UGC culture, our treatise aimed to demonstrate that the opportunities offered by the diverse UGC platforms, the thriving UGC communities and the inspiring UGC ethos warrant the business educators' attention. We strived to provide encouragement and support for addressing the role of UGC in today's cultural and economic setting. Some preliminary reflections of the more specific impacts of the "UGC turn" in the area of marketing and consumer research were also presented to encourage parallel contemplation in other areas of management studies. In the concluding part we extrapolate three sets of skills pertinent to the UGC culture and invaluable to modern-day managers. It is our hope that these humble initial steps will lead towards heightened awareness, new ideas for teaching and learning as well as stimulate the much needed additional research in this area.

NOTES

1. In his later work, Garfield (2009) refers to Listenomics as "the art and science of cultivating relationships in a connected, increasingly open-source

environment." The notion of open-source is used very broadly, defining it as "any creative work that is not treated as proprietary by its originators" (Garfield, 2005).

2. While UGC could in Jenkins' terminology be categorized as "expressions" or creative works, it is also a vitally associated with affiliation, collaboration and circulation inasmuch as the processes of creating and sharing UGC are inherently social (affiliation), often involve collaborative efforts and often take the form of recurring flows (e.g., blogs, vlogs).

3. The term "UGC culture" is used to designate the dimensions of "participatory culture" (Jenkins, 2006b) pertaining to the creation and sharing of UGC.

4. Much of the users communication in social media takes the form of short, fragmented articulations that are not accessible to a broader audience, and thus do not qualify as UGC in the sense used here (i.e., published content reflecting a certain amount of creative effort). What is more, user "participation" can also occur in absence of consumer intention and at times also in absence of consumer awareness. For instance, this is often the case with automated systems for tracking and aggregating user behavior on social media platforms.

5. The digital age has been suggested to usher in the "economy of abundance" as cultural resources are so easily copied, remixed, and disseminated (Hemmungs Wirtén, 2008).

6. For instance, UGC platforms seek to connect the users' interests (i.e., free access to content consumption and sharing) with the advertisers' readiness to subsidy them, which is often based on the desire to command user attention and behavior (Farchy, 2009).

7. Crowd-sourcing is a popular term describing the companies' efforts to 'tap the latent talent of the crowd' by encouraging online communities to contribute UGC to help the company is some way or another (Howe, 2006).

8. For a fairly recent example of a clash between a UGC community and the existent content industry see Sandoval (2009). A more graphic representation of the events can be found on http://tinyurl.com/yd8tnv7

9. See Postigo (2008) for additional information on the subject of copyright and fair use in the context of UGC as well as for further illustrations of these issues in the context of video-sharing platforms such as YouTube.

REFERENCES

Aggarwal, P., Vaidyanathan, R., & Venkatesh, A. (2009). Using lexical semantic analysis to derive online brand positions: An application to retail marketing research. *Journal of Retailing, 85*(2), 145-158.

Antonacci, D. M., & Modaress, N. (2008). Envisioning the educational possibilities of user-created virtual worlds. *AACE Journal, 16*(2), 115-126.

Auvinen, A. M. (2008). *Setting the scene—Introduction to quality in peer production of eLearning.* Retrieved from http://www.eric.ed.gov/ERICDocs/data/ericdocs2sql/content_storage_01/0000019b/80/43/77/df.pdf

Bajde, D., & Culiberg, B. (2010). *Exploring user-generated content: A multimodal analysis of consumer responses to advertising.* Unpublished.

Bernardin, T., Kemp-Robinson, P., Stewart, D.W., Cheng, Y., Wan, H., Rossiter, J. R., et al. (2008). Envisioning the future of advertising creativity research. *Journal of Advertising, 37*(4), 131-149.

Blythe, M., & Cairns, P. (2009). Critical methods and user generated content: The iPhone on YouTube. In *Proceedings of the 27th international conference on human factors in computing systems* (pp. 1467-1476). Boston, MA: ACM.

Creamer, M. (2007, January 8). Ad age agency of the year: The consumer. *Advertising Age.* Retrieved from http://www.drewsmarketingminute.com/files/adagestory.pdf

CSM. (2008). *Code of best practices in fair use for online video.* Retrieved from http://www.centerforsocialmedia.org/files/pdf/online_best_practices_in_fair_use.pdf

Daugherty, T., Eastin, M. S., & Bright, L. (2008). Exploring consumer motivations for creating user-generated content. *Journal of Interactive Advertising, 8*(2). Retrieved from http://www.jiad.org/article101

eYouGuide. (2010). Retrieved from http://ec.europa.eu/information_society/eyouguide/index_en.htm

eMarketer. (2007). *User-generated content: Will Web 2.0 pay its way?* Retrieved from http://www.emarketer.com/Report.aspx?code=emarketer_2000421

Farchy, J. (2009). Economics of sharing platforms: What's wrong with cultural industries? In P. Snickars & P. Vonderau (Ed.), *The YouTube reader.* Stockholm, Sweden: National Library of Sweden.

Fox, S. (2009, October 6). *The patient is in.* Retrieved from http://www.pewinternet.org/Presentations/2009/30--The-Patient-is-In.aspx

Garfield, B. (2005, October 11). Inside the new world of listenomics: How the open source revolution impacts your brands. *Advertising Age.* Retrieved from http://adage.com/article?article_id=47020

Garfield, B. (2009). *The chaos scenario.* Nashville, TN: Stielstra.

Garfield, B. (2010). Bob Garfield's 'Chaos Scenario.' Retrieved from the National Public Radio website: http://www.npr.org/templates/story/story.php?storyId=111623614

Grossman, L. (2006, December 13). Time's Person of the Year: You. *Time.* Retrieved from http://www.time.com/time/magazine/article/0,9171,1569514,00.html#ixzz0fbKEXDZe

Hemmi, A., Bayne, S., & Land, R. (2009). The appropriation and repurposing of social technologies in higher education. *Journal of Computer Assisted Learning, 25*(1), 19-30.

Hemmungs Wirtén, E. (2008). *Terms of use: Negotiating the jungle of the intellectual commons.* Toronto, Ontario, Canada: University of Toronto Press.

Howe, J. (2006, June 16). The rise of crowdsourcing. *Wired.* Retrieved from http://www.wired.com/wired/archive/14.06/crowds.html

Hutton, G. (2009, November 30). *Dr Strangelove, or how I came to love UGC.* Retrieved from http://umwwblog.com/2009/11/30/dr-strangelove-or-how-i-came-to-love-ugc/

Hutton, G. (2010, March 8). *Yes, you can plan for word-of-mouth.* Retrieved from http://umwwblog.com/2010/03/08/yes-you-can-plan-for-word-of-mouth/

Jenkins, H. (2006a). *Convergence culture: Where old and new media collide.* New York, NY: New York University Press.

Jenkins, H. (2006b). *Confronting the challenges of participatory culture: Media education for the 21st century* [MacArthur Foundation Reports on Digital Media and Learning]. Boston, MA: MIT Press.

Kaplan, A. M., & Haenlein, M. (2010). Users of the world, unite! The challenges and opportunities of social media. *Business Horizons, 53,* 59-68.

Kozinets, R. V., Hemetsberger, A., & Schau, H. J. (2008). The wisdom of consumer crowds: Collective innovation in the age of networked marketing. *Journal of Macromarketing, 28*(4), 339-354.

Kucuka, U., & Krishnamurthy, S. (2007). An analysis of consumer power on the Internet. *Technovation, 27*(1-2),47-56.

Langenderfer, J., & Miyazaki A. D. (2009). Privacy in the information economy. *Journal of Consumer Affairs, 43*(3), 380-388.

Lenhart, A., Purcell, K., Smith, A., & Zickuhr, K. (2010). *Social media and mobile internet use among teens and young adults.* Retrieved from the Pew Internet & American Life Project website: http://www.pewinternet.org/Reports/2010/Social-Media-and-Young-Adults.aspx

McCracken, G. (2009). *Chief culture officer.* New York, NY: Basic Books.

McCracken, G. (2010. January 7). *How Ford got social marketing right.* Retrieved from http://blogs.hbr.org/cs/2010/01/ford_recently_wrapped_the_firs.html

Miller, T. (2009). Cybertarians of the world unite: You have nothing to loose but your tubes! In P. Snickars & P. Vonderau (Ed.), *The YouTube reader.* Stockholm, Sweden: National Library of Sweden.

Minocha, S. (2009). A case study-based investigation of students' experiences with social software tools. *New Review of Hypermedia & Multimedia, 15*(3), 245-265.

Muniz, A. M., Jr., & Schau, H. J. (2007). Vigilante marketing and consumer-created communications. *Journal of Advertising, 36*(3), 187-202.

O'Reilly, T. (2005). *What Is Web 2.0: Design patterns and business models for the next-generation of software.* Retrieved from http://www.oreillynet.com/lpt/a/6228

Pace, S. (2008). YouTube: An opportunity for consumer narrative analysis? *Qualitative Marketing Research: An International Journal, 11*(2), 213-226.

Poster, M. (2006). *Information please: Culture and Politics in the age of digital mechanics.* London, England: Duke University Press.

Postigo, H. (2008). Capturing Fair use for the YouTube generation: The digital rights movement, the Electronic Frontier Foundation and the user-centered framing of fair use. *Information, Communication & Society, 11*(7), 1008-1027.

Purcell, K., Lee, R., Mitchell, A., Rosenstiel, T., & Olmstead, K. (2010). Understanding the participatory news consumer. Retrieved from the Pew Internet & American Life Project website: http://www.pewinternet.org/Reports/2010/Online-News.aspx

Ray, A. (2010, April 20). *Peer influence analysis: What it is & how marketers use it.* Retrieved from http://blogs.forrester.com/augie_ray/10-04-20-peer_influence_analysis_what_it_how_marketers_use_it

Sandoval, G. (2009, January 27). YouTube users caught in Warner Music spat. *Cnet.* Retrieved from http://news.cnet.com/8301-1023_3-10150588-93.html?tag=mncol;txt

Sawyer, M. S. (2010). Filters, fair use, and feedback: User-generated content principles and the DMCA. *Berkeley Technology Law Journal*. Retrieved from http://ssrn.com/abstract=1369665

Shirky, C. (2008). *Here comes everybody: The power of organizing without organizations*. New York, NY: Penguin Press.

TACD. (2008). *Charter of consumer rights in the digital World*. Retrieved from http://tacd.org/index2.php?option=com_docman&task=doc_view&gid=43&Itemid=

Turner, B. S., & Rojek, C. (2001). *Society and culture: Principles of scarcity and solidarity*. London, England: Sage.

Universal McCann. (2008). *When did we start trusting strangers? How the Internet turned us all into influencers*. Retrieved from http://www.imaginar.org/docs/when_did_we_start_trusting_strangers.pdf

Urban, G. L. (2005): Customer advocacy: A new era in marketing? *Journal of Public Policy & Marketing, 24*(1), 155-159.

Vickery, G., & Wunsch-Vincent, S. (2007). *Participative web and user-created content*. Paris, France: Organisation for Economic Co-operation and Development.

vom Brocke, J., White, C., Walker C., & vom Brocke, C. (2010). Making user-generated content communities work in higher education—The importance of setting incentives. In U. D. Ehlers & D. Schneckenberg (Ed.), *Changing cultures in higher education: Moving ahead to future learning* (pp. 149-166). Berlin, Germany: Springer.

von Hippel, E. (2005). *Democratizing innovation*. Cambridge, MA: MIT Press. Retrieved from http://web.mit.edu/evhippel/www/books.htm

Wasko, J., & Erickson, M. (2009). The political economy of YouTube. In P. Snickars & P. Vonderau (Ed.), *The YouTube reader*. Stockholm, Sweden: National Library of Sweden.

Wesch, M. (2010). *Students helping students*. Retrieved from http://mediatedcultures.net/ksudigg/?p=249

Yar, M. (2005). The global 'epidemic' of movie 'piracy': Crimewave or social construction? *Media, Culture & Society, 27*(5), 677-696.

CHAPTER 7

FACEBOOK "FRIENDSHIP" AS EDUCATIONAL PRACTICE

Eva Ossiansson

For young people between 9-24 years of age, often called digital natives, Internet and new media has become a natural part of their lives. Recent studies have acknowledged this and researchers have increasingly become interested in how young people use social media. In this chapter I will share my experiences of using Facebook, a social network, in a pedagogical setting and how that affected my students, our interaction, norms and the way the master course was created together by us all. As autoethnography, this chapter details a journey that is both personal and professional. I offer a narrative, which is presented alongside my interpretive commentary. A retrospective reflection reveals that using Facebook leads to a major shift in my role becoming a mentor and facilitator, how I interacted with my students and became "friends" with them. The potential use of Facebook in pedagogical settings and important experiences are highlighted to extend current knowledge of how to use new media in higher education.

The emergence of Web 2.0 has created a host of new tools for online interaction. Accordingly, we are communicating with each other more than ever before and use new social media platforms to interact both privately and professionally. Examples of that are social networks and com-

Cutting-Edge Social Media Approaches to Business Education:
Teaching With LinkedIn, Facebook, Twitter, Second Life, and Blogs, pp. 117–140

munities like Facebook. The emergence of user-generated material, the boundary between materials that are created by amateurs and professionals, has become blurred. Especially, young people between 9-24 years of age are using social media and act as active senders of media messages (Hast & Ossiansson, 2010). For these digital natives, Internet and new media, has become a natural part of their lives. They communicate, interact, and create content online. They have become increasingly influential through their "clicking" and virtual communities.

Recent studies (Hast & Ossiansson, 2010; Subrahmanyam, Reich, Waechter, & Espinoza, 2008) have acknowledged this and researchers have increasingly become interested in how young people use social media. By studying usage of social networks such as Facebook or Ning in a pedagogical setting (Boostrom, Kurthakoti, & Summey, 2009), group dynamics, norms and interactions can be analyzed. For example, one study has found that there is a strong link between an individual's social identity, group norm, and subjective norm (Cheung & Lee, 2010). Thus, understanding norms are essential if social media is to be used in an educational setting. This is important given the current debate on whether social media is a suitable learning environment. Problems in this area that has been debated are often authority related; professor-student power relations, professor code of conduct and technical skills (Foulger, Ewbank, Kay, Popp, & Carter, 2009; Pempek, Yermolayeva, & Calvert, 2009; Vie, 2008).

According to Pempek et al. (2009), social network sites foster social interaction and communication. They found out that students use Facebook approximately 30 minutes throughout the day as part of their daily routine, using a one-to-many style when communicating. The popularity of social networking applications among contemporary young adults could make them a powerful cognitive tool if adapted for academic pursuits.

Still, higher education very seldom uses these new social media platforms for interaction and communication. Instead, course portals are often used to inform students about course syllabus, time schedules, exams, literature and results. My own experience is that administrators take care of these course portals and there is little or no direct interaction between the students and professors. It emphasizes a traditional sender—receiver relationship and not even the responsible professor is in control of the information put there, but rather administrators.

Being a marketing researcher within social media, consumption and branding, with an interest of pedagogic development, I felt a great need to test social media platforms in an educational setting. My aim was to see if the use of social media would affect us all—both me as a professor and my students—to become more social, interactive, and collaborative.

The researcher Kozinets (1999) has found that it is mainly two things that drive individuals when interacting in new media. First, they seek to strengthen their own self-image. Second, they are trying to strengthen social ties with others that are knowledgeable or passionate "fans" of a product or brand. Besides wanting to become "one of the gang" their aim can be to have just fun and mingle, or to be curious.

Accordingly, one reason for interacting in social media is to "boost" yourself or the group you want to belong to. You can engage in branding, thus, creating a personal brand in a world where everything revolves around brands, consumption, and to be heard and seen (Ossiansson, 2008). Social media also makes it possible to "bond," that is, build relationships with other like-minded people, which can help them build their brands and confirm their ego.

But, could it then be possible to test a social media platform like Facebook in higher education to see if this will lead us to boost, bond, or brand ourselves? I knew from my research that most of all social media is used by us as individuals to experiment with our identities. We can use social media to brand ourselves as a resource for the symbolic construction of the self—both social identity and self-identity (e.g., Elliot & Percy, 2007; Ossiansson, 2008). The social symbolic meanings of our personal brand can be used to communicate to other people the kind of person you wish to be seen as. Consequently, the self-symbolic meaning of your personal brand is what you say and do to communicate to others regarding who you are and want to be. Further, Cheung and Lee (2010) mean that social identity consists of three interrelated components in social networks; self-awareness of one's membership in a group, evaluative significance of one's membership in a group and emotional significance of one's membership in a group.

Would I change my identity toward my students and vice versa? Other critical aspects when using social media in education are related to authorities and power relations. The concept of power is an abstract—who is in power to act and who has the power to stop something. Just by being a professor gives me authorities to exercise power, but also to empower my students. Therefore, I was interested to know if the use of a social media platform in an educational setting, a master course, could affect the way my students would look upon me and how our power relationship might change.

Consequently, I will in this chapter share my experiences of using Facebook, a social network, in my master course about branding and social media, and how that affected my students, their communication, our interaction, norms and the way the master course was created together by us all. As autoethnography, this chapter details a journey that is both personal and professional. I offer a narrative, which is presented alongside my interpretive commentary. In the end, I hope that my experiences will encourage other professors to use social media in their education, since it is a fantastic platform for interaction. However, it is important to understand the drivers for interaction and beware of how they affect professor-student relationships.

TELLING MY STORY—THE USE OF AUTOETHNOGRAPHY

A Story of Action

Autoethnography refers to an autobiographical genre of research, where the researcher uses the cultural practices he or she performs and/or observes in the course of his or her everyday life—in my case education and teaching—to learn about particular cultural phenomena (Moisander & Valtonen, 2006). Since, the use of social media is an important part of our present cultural practices and the way we interact, this type of method may produce relevant insights into how social media can be used in education. The strength of this method according to Moisander and Valtonen is that it enables us to empirically display the multiple ways in which particular cultural discourses are played out and practiced in the course of everyday life. Mills (2000, p. 196) has expressed this in the following way:

> You must learn to use your life experience in your intellectual work: continually to examine and interpret it. In this sense craftsmanship is the center of yourself and you are personally involved in every intellectual product upon which you may work.

When applying an autoethnographic method you put yourself at the center of the research process and the researcher is simultaneously the subject and object of the research. You observe and interpret culture through your own reflections of personal life experiences (Mills, 2000; Moisander & Valtonen, 2006). Consequently, you are personally involved in the intellectual product you work with.

Since this methodology uses the personal position as a valuable means of investigating culture and in doing so, it challenges several conventional practices. The method challenges the division between the researcher and the researched. Moreover, by maintaining that personal accounts can be sources of insightful analysis, the autoethnographic tradition openly works against the ideology of detachment that has dominated academic research (Moisander & Valtonen, 2006). By problematizing the ways in which research may be written and represented, the tradition also reacts against the insularity of academic writing. In sum, autoethnographic research is thus based on making the most of the situated self as well as on writing from that situated position.

The introspective and retrospective nature of autoethnography can enhance the understanding of the link between the professor and the student/students. The reflexive nature of autoethnography allows me as a researcher to make that link. And the prime focus in this autoethnographic study is to illustrate the relationship between professor and student. Boyle and Parry (2007) call this form of autobiographical form of research a way to "connect to the cultural through a 'peeling back' of multiple layers of consciousness, thoughts, feelings and beliefs." However, by doing so, I will expose myself personally and professionally (e.g., Lee, 1995; Morse, 2000; Rose, 1990). Still, Boyle and Parry draw the conclusion that this form of research is suitable when studying new social media arenas for interaction.

Autoethnography is characterized by personal experience narratives—in this case I will tell my story as a professor using social media in an educational setting. I will lead myself via a story of action in a dialogue with the reader. That means guiding the reader when I interact and shape the desired context in which I am situated. I will highlight my lived experiences as a professor when making an experiment with my students regarding the use of social media. And when doing so I will weave the extant literature into the narrative that I present. Additionally, I will use the "friend" metaphor as an integrating theme when guiding the reader in my journey.

Does Sensemaking Make Sense?

What is then the major contribution using autoethnography? When you do large surveys your findings are generalizable compared to autoethnography where the findings are experiences of just one person. According to Boyle and Parry (2007), it is instead how the findings are reported that influences the impact of the research. One paper may impact due to its cognitive nature—another paper due to its emotional and evocative nature.

Instead, this methodology may advance our theoretical understanding of the complex ways in which social media in our consumer culture operates. We can empirically illustrate the repertoires of practices. The method provides us with personal texts that can be sources of insightful analysis. Using a reflexive narrative invites the reader to know the world from the position for the writer (Moisander & Valtonen, 2006). Additionally, it invites the reader to notice the multiple ways in which shortness becomes produced throughout social life and gives room for the reader's own self-reflection according to Moisander and Valtonen (2006).

One might criticize this methodological approach by arguing that there is a lack of control over the research process and the source of data in a positivist sense. And this is a challenge since there is no guarantee of a correlation between the degree of control a researcher exercises over the research process and the resultant impact on the reader (Boyle & Parry, 2007). However, the process of conducting autoethnography throws down a challenge to this notion of researcher as controller. Boyle and Parry argue that the process of creating an autoethnography account involves, in one sense, an acknowledgment that there is no guarantee of a correlation between the degree of control a researcher exercises over the research process, and the resultant impact on the reader. Instead, autoethnography expresses how we struggle to make sense of our experiences achieved via encouraging compassion and promoting dialogue (e.g., Ellis & Bochner, 2000). Therefore, autoethnography is about making sense of your experiences and communicate that (Boyle & Parry, 2007; Ellis & Bochner, 2000). By writing this story, I communicate that sensemaking to the "educational" audience. I try to help the reader to make sense of the phenomenon under investigation—in my case using Facebook in an educational setting.

Although I use my own body as primary data, the focus is not on my body as such, but on the ways in which cultural practices, in my case the use of social media in an educational setting, define and label certain bodies as short, and on the particular meanings inscribed in such label, and on the social and cultural consequences of these particular meanings (Moisander & Valtonen, 2006). These practices are not the property of me as the author or any other individual. Instead, they are shared, as cultural knowledge always is. And in that particular story, these public cultural events are drawn attention to, analyzed and displayed.

Consequently, this method can open the door to new fascinating knowledge about social media phenomena in educational settings. The story and narrative is an explanation of what has happened in the past and cannot predict the future. It is up to the reader to make up his or her mind about predictive validity. And the fact that this research has the emotive power makes it a more powerful explanation of phenomena.

The story is a creation contextualized as a narrative and presented with interpretive commentary. When doing this, I am sensemaking and reflecting in order to help the reader to understand my feelings, hopes, reactions and as well as conditions and context with reference to past, present and future. When sensemaking I will involve my identities, for example, private and professional identities (e.g., Weick, 1995). I will tell my story in experiential terms while contextualizing reflection and sensemaking interpretations (e.g. Vickers, 2007; van Manen, 1990). I want to share my story so that you as a reader can enter and feel that you are part of it. And most of all, I hope that I can evoke some feelings and thoughts that enable you to use social media in educational settings. With that said, I think it is time for the story to begin.

A STORY ABOUT "FRIENDSHIP"

Relationships That Counts

I have during my 20 years of working at the university as a professor often wondered how I could create mutually valuable relationship with my students and develop their skills for life. A relationship between professors and students can normally be characterized as an asymmetrical relationship, since there is an imbalance in power. A professor is in power to decide the content of the course, the literature to be used, forms for examination, how communicate with each other should be done and most of all a professor is the one setting the final grades. I am as a professor the one in power and my students look upon me as a person high up in the educational hierarchy.

Some of you might ask yourself if this is a problem. Being in power is good and you are controlling the situation. And like everybody else I like to be in control when I teach. However, I know that this is a "give-and-take"-situation. If I give away some control I might win something else—trust and more committed students.

I knew from my research that asymmetrical relationships can affect and reduce trust in a relationship (Ossiansson, 2006). Therefore, I wanted to reduce these types of imbalances in relation to my students. If I was to develop them and become more of a mentor and coach to my students, I really had to change and develop my relationship to the students. A good relationship is often long-term, personal and mutual, such as, a win-win relationship (Brodie, Coviello, Brookes, & Little, 1997; Morgan & Hunt, 1994). Is it then possible to extend that relationship beyond the time you spend in class?

Relationships characterized by commitment and trust are also the ones most valuable (O'Malley & Tynan, 1999). Being really committed, information transparency, trying to share as much information and knowledge as possible are all important aspects when developing mutually valuable relationships, according to O'Malley and Prothero (2004). Marketing is moving into a new paradigm regarding how to deal with customer relationships according to Vargo and Lusch (2004) and I realized that my relationships to students ought to follow the same principle. If it is possible to create mutually valuable relationships in business life—one ought to be able to do the same thing in the academy.

And it is the "soft issues" that are hard to grasp in relationships that counts. A feeling of being valuable, committed, seen, important and part of a group, are all things that count in our everyday life. Additionally, we emphasize coproduction and how customers have gotten the power to affect the power balance in relationships through the use of new media (Hast & Ossiansson, 2008a, 2008b, 2010). And the same is true for my students—they have new possibilities to interact, coproduce, and affect the relationship to me in educational settings.

I started to ask myself if it was possible to use the drivers for interaction found in social media and develop a mutually valuable relationship built on trust with committed students as well as professors?

Peltier, Drago, and Schibrowsky (2003) confirm that marketing education community is well suited to use technology in higher education, since it has been at the forefront developing curricula on such as, Internet marketing, interactive marketing and web-based interactions. It is according to them possible to employ an interactive marketing approach to the development and improvement of interactive and more web-based courses. Virtual communities, like social network sites, can play a role in enhancing student-professor relationships and student-to-student relationships. When using a social network platform the professor is not in the center of knowledge, nor is the student a passive recipient of interaction, according to Peltier et al. The professor can, thus, be seen as an instructor or facilitator. Or as Peltier et al. express it (p. 263); "The educator in an online environment is less of an actor and more of a director or producer of experience." Could I then become this producer of experiences and how would my students react?

CAN WE BECOME "FRIENDS"?

When being involved in social media, the concept of becoming "friends" is quite essential. According to Boyd (2006) friendship is often defined as an exceptionally strong relationship with emotional and practical support. On a social networking site like Facebook, the choice of "friends" could refer to workers, classmates, family members or just friends. Deresiewicz (2009) means that we live at a time when friendship has become both all and noting at all, since friendship is devolving from a relationship to a feeling. We have "friends" on Facebook that gives us a "sense" of connection.

The number of friends that you have indicates your popularity and social contacts that you are linked to. Pempek et al. (2009) found out that young adults in their study reported an average of 358 Facebook friends. However, "friendships" in social media is something complicated since these social networks can become rather large. Who should you add to your social network and who should you deny?

South Park has done a great film about becoming friends on Facebook, one of the most widely used social networks (YouTube.com, n.d.). In one dialogue Stan sits in front of his computer trying to do his home work when his dad confronts him with Facebook:

—Hey Stan, I was on my computer at work and saw that you had a Facebook page now.

—Ye dad, I was kind of forced to it.

—Well, so … are you going to add me as a friend?

—No dad, I really don't want to get more into it.

—Oh, ok … So, I am not your friend then?

—Dad, you are my friend!

—You just don't want to add me as a friend?

—Dad, it is just a stupid click on a button that takes two seconds!

—Right, but you don't have that two seconds or?

—I just want to do my home work.

—All right, fine … just to be clear … you and I are not friends?

—All right dad, I'll add you!

—Oh, cool … ok!

The scene with Stan and his father is rather interesting and could be compared with me as a professor in relation to my students. I knew that if I was going to use social media as a platform to enhance our relationship and drivers for interactions in an educational setting I had to take this complex "friendship-thing" into account. You simply do not add an authority into your network by a click. It does not matter if it is your parent or a professor—you have a specific power relationship that cannot be underestimated.

In an American study of how students use social network sites it was found that these networks functioned as a bridge between friends outside internet and on internet (Subrahmanyam et al., 2008). A majority of the students would just accept persons that they had met in real life as "new friends." A friend is someone you have met in real life (IRL).

And there are other dangers for professors who create their own profiles and add their students as "friends," since these forums undercut concepts of more conventional spaces and blur the line between acceptable communication and conduct as a professor (Maranto & Barton, 2009). In contrast, other researchers embrace technologies such as Facebook as inevitable for twenty-first century education (e.g., Kemp, 2007). Faculty should not avoid social networking spaces, but rather embrace them and realize that student initiative is the key in an interactive environment. Faculty should instead be the guide to learning.

In sum, I realized that I would have to deal with students that could be rather skeptical to use social media to communicate and interact with me as a professor. I would be more than two clicks away! Moreover, if I was going to use social media I had to show them that I could use that media and liked it. Having the knowledge about the media in itself is necessary in order to become trustworthy. On the other hand, the whole course was about branding and how social media has affected the way we communicate in business life. Therefore, the subject in itself could strengthen their interest to use social media. At least, that was my thought.

No—We are Not "Friends"

There exist a lot of social networks that can be used as a platform for interaction in an educational setting. However, I knew that I had to know the platform very well and be quite used to handle it. Another aspect to have in mind was that it should be a platform widely used. One platform that dominates social media is Facebook. It is a social network site functioning like a digital meeting place for new and old friends. Facebook started in 2004 and had in February 2010 approximately more than 400 million active users. And about 70 % of them are outside of the United States according to their own website (Facebook, n.d.). Facebook is one of the worldwide most used social networks. According to Fogel and Nehmad (2009), Facebook also has a perception of being a trustworthy social networking website and when using it in a higher educational setting that is of great importance.

Consequently, I decided to use a closed Facebook group named after my master course. Everyone can create a Facebook group and I categorized mine as an academic group. I wanted to have a closed group due to privacy and security reasons. My students should be able to feel comfortable that all the information we shared just reached the members of the group. A fan page would not have the same status and academic level. Accordingly, I wanted to use a group where I could be the administrator having the full control over invitations and the ones accepted to join the group. All members had to be accepted by me before they could join and I was the only one that could invite new members to join. Since, it was a closed group my students would be able to join this group without becoming a friend with me. And what we discussed in our group would stay in that forum.

I am quite familiar with Facebook and use it both professionally and privately as a communication platform. You can write messages on a wall where all "friends" and members can read and take part of the latest news. The wall is like a news site where you can write status updates about the things you want to share with your friends. You can write comments and discuss each other's status updates. But, you can also create forums for discussions, send personal messages, chat and add photos, films and links. Therefore, Facebook is a communication platform that can be used for many forms of communication.

According to Pempek et al. (2009) wall posts are the preferred way of interacting with friends on Facebook among students. Wall posts can be written quickly, illustrating the fast-paced nature of online information exchange. The information exchanged have a wide range of topics including content relevant to identity construction and users are presenting themselves following the postmodern logics of identity construction (Maranto & Barton, 2009; Subramanyam et al., 2004).

It seemed so simple and I was convinced that my students would realize that they had to join this Facebook group. The Facebook group was to be the only platform used for communication outside the class room, for example, about time schedules, changes in class, guest lecture information, booking supervision time etc.

My master class in marketing and consumption consisted of 23 students—12 men and 11 women. The students' average age was 24 years old, where the oldest was 33 years old and the youngest was 23 years old. We had 15 Swedish students and 8 foreign students from other countries (e.g., Mexico, China, Bangladesh, and Peru) and all teaching was done in English. The theme of the course was branding and how communication through new media has changed marketing conditions. The class had a real-life case project regarding the largest film festival in the Nordic countries, Göteborg International Film Festival (GIFF) and my aim was that my students would be able to share all information regarding the case in Facebook. The problem to be solved in the case was to find out how GIFF could strengthen their brand and communication through new media.

Problem-based learning was applied at the course and my students had to define the problem for the case company, form project groups, find applicable literature and they were examined through a home exam in form of an essay about their reflections about branding and social media linked to both theories and companies of today. My role as a responsible professor was to guide them through this new media landscape and develop them to become great marketers for the future. I held inspirational lectures, recommended articles, supervised them, had guest lecturers from outside the academy and we also visited one web agency.

During my introduction of their new course I explained that I had created a closed Facebook group for their class. I asked them to join our group and I told them that they would find all necessary information there. My students did not ask any questions about it and I noticed that they did not believe that this was true. A Facebook group—not a chance! I became aware of my doubts—they were afraid to join a group and become "friends" with me. Since, two of my students already were friends with me on Facebook I sent invitations to them. I put out information about interesting lectures coming up, for example:

> This evening I had an interesting conversation with a guy doing film production. And I mean really interesting stuff. I hope he will join our "team" and be part of the course. I will tell you more when we start.

Still, I heard nothing and few seemed interested to join my group. I waited a couple of days and reminded them in class that it was necessary to join our group. Finally, I realized that I had to give them a reason to join our Facebook group. I had to force them to join in order to follow our course. I put out a schedule for supervision. Put simply, they had to book a time for supervision through our Facebook group. Consequently, all project leaders joined and with them at least one third of my class.

Since the very basic idea of a social media platform is that its members want to socialize and interact with each other I still felt that it was not working as it should. Was my idea, that this type of platform in an educational setting would enhance our student-professor relationship, a bad idea? Was this a failure? How could I overcome this?

A Platform for Exhibitionism and Cocreation

It took me one more week after having introduced my class to our Facebook group before I understood what I had to do. If I was going to use a social media platform I had to emphasize things that would drive interaction and communication in that type of forum. According to Holbrook (2000) exhibitionism is important in "life with computers." We like to manipulate our social image and enhance it in different ways. It is a kind of impressions management. We communicate openly what we think, like and stand for.

I needed them to get a reason to boost themselves, their project groups, or class. I had to find something that would want them to build relationships and confirm their ego. Since, I had three other professors and eight practitioners, that is, well-known managers from advertising agencies, public relations agencies, information associations and social media companies giving lectures in class, there was an interest from my students to interact with them. Therefore, I invited them into our Facebook group and they could interact with, follow my students and participate in their discussions. Additionally, one administrator from the university joined the group and together we could solve administrative issues as well.

I started to give my students advice concerning literature and the case. I also boosted my ongoing research and interviews made with me in TV and radio. Out and proud—share everything with the class! Five of my guest lecturers and practitioners started to do the same and joined the group. They shared interesting films and links of interest to my students. The Facebook group became an important forum for students', professors', and practitioners' discussions about the case, literature, interesting news, films, as well as social interaction. Students also helped each other with technical issues regarding how to consume the material they found. One of the students wrote the following in one post:

> Another interesting link on the use of social media, this time in English. You can also subscribe to the podcast on iTunes, which I really recommend. It's both interesting and fun, about "the marketing trends that matter."

After 2 weeks all students except for one had joined my Facebook group. The man, who did not want to join, explained to me that he felt uncomfortable with Facebook and had his doubts about social media. However, after our course had ended he changed his mind and joined Facebook.

My students saw a meaning in sharing information in order to solve their case project. In the end of our course 40 links and films had been added to our Facebook group. Still, both students and practitioners, add interesting things about social media and branding at the Facebook wall after the course has ended.

I found myself part of a community—the class—coproducing a course in branding and social media. When my students were going to present their conclusions to the case company, one student wrote the following on the wall:

> Hi heroes and goddesses! We wonder if the other groups would like to meet and discuss how we should present our reports for GIFF?[1] Our suggestion is that one person from each group meets and figure out a good solution. What do you guys think?

My class was planning everything and the feeling was rather strange, because normally you want to feel that you are in control as a responsible professor for a university course. But, in this case I got a feeling of being proud of my students and how their relationships to each other, me and my guest lecturers developed.

Changing Norms by Sharing and Boosting

Social media has changed the way we communicate with each other, what we say and how (e.g. Hast & Ossiansson, 2010). The tone of voice mirrors the way we look upon authorities. Being a professor does not mean that your opinion will be the one that counts. Communication has become more democratic. Through argumentation and interaction a majority decides what will be the "truth." My students followed the same norm. Their decisions were based on consensus after having tried to convince each other who had the right opinion.

My students made jokes about the case company and how bad they thought that organization dealt with social media. The tone was open and it did not matter if it was a student, professor or practitioner who wrote on the wall. The discussion was open-minded and free of restrictions. I never took anything away from the wall and I think that it is important that everyone can feel free to write and share posts. That is how social media works and you must like what's up! If there would have been inappropriate postings it is necessary to comment on why it is inappropriate. That will also send a message to the rest of the group when someone has done something inappropriate. It never happened to me, but it is something you have to be aware of.

One might look upon the interaction that went on in the Facebook group as a form of democratic communication that lacked a link to authorities. As long as you had something of interest to share and could convince the rest of us that it was something worthwhile your posts got attention. I also gave them appetizers to create an interest for what was coming up, such as:

> Today, I got in contact with another "big boss" that will come and tell the class about the situation in his company. A hot case. I think it will be exciting.

The digital format is accessible and can be shared with many. My students boosted their knowledge and shared interesting films and links with me, the rest of the class and our guest lecturers. They wanted to make a good impression and you could easily notice which ones who were the greatest exhibitionists. Subsequently, another norm in the digital civilization is to share (Hast & Ossiansson, 2010). And you share in order to build trust with each other, make a good impression and visualize what you can (e.g., Muise, Christofides, & Desmarais, 2009). Through this type of social "consumption" value is created in terms of a social capital.

Social capital can be defined as the resources available to you when socially interacting (e.g., Mathwick, Wiertz, & De Ruyter, 2008; Valenzuela, Park, & Kee, 2009). It is like an intangible force that helps to bind together members of social networks. Therefore, social capital is a multidimensional construct that is based on individuals' social networks and their predicted effects (Valenzuela et al., 2009). Social capital creates value for members of a social network (Mathwick et al., 2008). When sharing and interacting in a social network the social capital can be enhanced for the members and this was clearly the case for my students. According to Chi, Chan, Seow, and Tam (2009), repeated interactions are the underlying mechanism for generating trust and shared norms that define social capital in social networks like Facebook.

By sharing and cocreation my students got confirmation that they were important and could contribute to the course content. Also, the act of sharing made it possible for them to build relationships and to bond with each other as well as to me. My students could "boost" their social capital or "brand" when sharing something valuable, especially if it was of emotional value, for example, a funny film or link. When sharing something that had a meaning for them—they would share something of themselves. And they really did share not only information, but also ideas, feelings and thoughts. The learning process was not a top-down knowledge delivery, but rather a collaborative learning environment that relied on peer-to-peer learning in the form of group discussions and team projects, which also has been confirmed by Eastman and Swift (2001).

Taking part of and being active in our Facebook group became an investment in my students' social capital. And the same thing was true for me. I tried to create a picture of me as knowledgeable, open-minded and media savvy with a large network of business friends. Being the only professor using social media and chatting with my students felt well and a way to live as you preach.

PROS AND CONS OF USING SOCIAL MEDIA

Relationships Toward "Friendship"—Conclusions

In the beginning of this chapter I asked myself if the drivers for interaction found in social media could be used to develop a mutually valuable relationship built on trust with committed students as well as professors. I tested a social media platform, Facebook, for interaction and communication in my master course. I found that Facebook was a good platform to build trust and engage students in their master course. It was a challenge in the beginning, since this situation was quite new to them and they had their doubts to become "friends" with me.

Since, the platform made it possible for us to share everything we were able to reduce information gaps and misunderstandings. We could communicate 24-7. I was always available for them and so were they. However, this was my own choice since I already use and check Facebook every day. You may check your Facebook group as much as you like and have time for. You decide the tone and level of communication. If you want to restrict your time on Facebook—you do that and if you want to have a formal relationship with your students, you communicate to them in that manner. But, in my case I wanted to communicate with them and build more mutual relationships without too many formal boundaries. Quick questions or just having a talk could be taken care of through the chat function. If one student wanted to contact me for a specific reason they could send me a message. When it was time for them to do their home exam they started a discussion in a forum for that in our Facebook group and the whole class could take part and participate.

It is important to show your students that you have faith in them, value them and trust that the things they do—in the same way as companies treat their customers in order to build long-lasting relationships (e.g., Casielles, Álvarez, & Martín, 2005). In this case I got the tools to show my appreciation and my praise. Through our social media platform I could comment, support and create a positive feed-back whenever I wanted to do so.

Facebook as a platform in an educational setting was time efficient, gave professors and students the opportunity to socially interact and helped us to build our identities in relation to each other. It took me less than ten minutes to start my group and it was easy to invite my guest lecturers and students since you can send an invitation using an e-mail function in Facebook. It was easy to check status updates and post information. Therefore, time for preparations was reduced and the speed of information was increased. Especially, when you compared the use of Facebook with normal course procedures, where all information should be sent to administrators in advance.

Previously passive students could become more active coproducers. Social media enabled them to collaborate and share information online. But, it also allowed them to build a social capital in relation to each other and to me as a professor (e.g., Valenzuela et al., 2009; Muise et al., 2009).

This was done by sharing, social interaction and a sense of belonging to a group that has something in common.

However, you expose yourself when being open-minded and sharing your thoughts and inner self. Still, in a study conducted by Mazer, Murphy, and Simonds (2007) it was found that students exposed to a high self-disclosing teacher on Facebook reported higher levels of motivation, affective learning and evaluated the climate of the teacher's classroom more positively than students who viewed a teacher's Facebook page featuring limited self-disclosures.

The use of social media changes the norms—for example, view of authorities, what to share, and how you communicate. The tone of voice can become tough, raw and very open. On the other hand, you may be able to create a fantastic atmosphere, where the class functions as a community. Selwyn (2009) mean that Facebook must be seen as being situated within the "identity politics" of being a student. It is a space for students for contesting and resisting the asymmetrical power relationships built into the institutional offline positions of student and university system. Additionally, 80% of my students thought it was a good and excellent platform for interaction when we evaluated the course[2] and asked them about their experiences. And if you as a professor want to build relationships characterized by trust—social media can enhance these social processes necessary to make these things happen. Trust will also be facilitated in student project groups when communication can be open and common goals can be shared (Huff, Cooper, & Jones, 2002).

My role as a professor was associated with mentoring, supporting and motivating (e.g., Peltier et al., 2003). McGrath (1997-1998) has come to the conclusion that web-based learning environments demand a transition from the instructor's role as an authority figure to that of one voice among many. Therefore, you cannot resist this transference of power from professor to students, but rather serve as an online mentor and moderator who can stimulate, guide and challenge your students (Kitchen & McDougall, 1998-1999; Peltier et al., 2003; Sherron & Boettcher, 1997; Sullivan, 2001). If you want to maintain a strong virtual community, the professor and instructor must get involved with motivating students to participate in interactive discussions. When doing so, the level of involvement is rather tricky. Insufficient management might lead to chaos and if you manage it too much it will affect the intangible level of trust, relational bonding and knowledge exchange associated with virtual communities negatively (Brown & Eisenhardt, 1998).

Vie (2008) argues that social networking sites are challenging because of their ability to be both threatening to the established order of things and at the same time protective of traditional ways of understanding the world. Facebook forces professors to confront and challenge the labels placed on individuals in academia, that is, student and professors. The behavior of individuals in network sites will instead force us to re-envision what it means to be an academic of today, what a classroom looks like, or what good writing entails. According to Vie, it is when we confront the traditional hierarchies of power in social network sites, we can take these as opportunities to reconsider which voices are allowed to speak with authority in the classroom.

In sum, my conclusions are that the usage of social media as a communication platform really changed the norms for interaction and enhanced all forms of communication. I really believe that it is necessary to confront and challenge our roles as professors and authorities. Thus, I see this as a promising research area with great potential for educational relevance. Facebook can definitely be used in educational settings when a problem-based learning approach is used. Still, a social media platform can be used in many different ways depending on the projects in focus of the education and the discipline in itself.

EPILOGUE—RETROSPECTIVE REFLECTIONS AND RECOMMENDATIONS

Using social media and Facebook in an educational setting was an exciting experience and I can really recommend others to test it. My role as a professor changed towards becoming more of a mentor, facilitator and coach. In some cases, I would say I have gotten friends for life. Still, my students contact me for guidance in their lives and careers. They listen to me and they have respect for me. Seven of my students became friends with me at Facebook, write on my wall, post things, send messages, and chat with me.

My students became active coproducers instead of passive listeners. As the course went on communication changed more towards communication "among equals." Students saw themselves as cocreators of the course, along with me responsible for the course. They really developed their communication skills. Even though students initially doubted whether they should take responsibility for their own learning and participation or not, this gradually changed when using Facebook. They lived according to the norms that exist in digital civilizations, that is, sharing and participating. They liked to build their social capital by boosting, bonding and branding themselves. And so I did.

The group and class functioned like a community. When presenting their final case reports, the students took charge over the planning and scheduling of their projects. In line with traditional Facebook usage the class members increasingly saw themselves as a group. They were not afraid of open-minded discussions and intense debates. They were all active participants. However, it became evident that some students were more exhibitionists than others.

Additionally, our Facebook group made it possible for us all to administrate the communication by ourselves and the administrator had a little role in the course. Still, he was part of our Facebook group and could follow what we were doing.

In sum, a social media platform made it possible for both me as a professor and my students to interact with people outside the academy. I invited important managers into our group and all guest lecturers could join the group if they wanted. Consequently, they became coproducers of the course content and part of our education. My students could get a scent of what was going on outside the walls of our university. And moreover, build relationships with people important for their future career.

And what advice can I give other professors about using a social network site like Facebook? I think it is very important that you have a positive attitude towards using social networks sites. First, you have to understand how Facebook works, use it actively, and most of all—love it. Otherwise, you will not be able to understand the norms of sharing, participating and interacting. You have to understand how it works. Most of my colleagues do not use Facebook and for them it is not a good platform of interaction. But, they are not negative—they simply do not understand social media and how to use it.

Second, you cannot have too many students or too few students when using this type of platform for interaction in education. I would recommend students groups consisting of approximately 20-40 students—not more and not less. Brown and Duguid (2000) have come to the conclusion that too many participants will limit the close-knit relationships of the group and Rothaermel and Sugiyama (2001) mean that too few will limit the number of valuable insights that can be generated.

Third, one negative aspect with Facebook is that you cannot add documents, just links, photos, and films. I used e-mail when I wanted to send documents, but it could have been good to have a homepage that could have supported my Facebook group with that type of information. Consequently, you have to use other instruments to inform your students about grading and results. The Facebook group was an important platform for interaction about projects, tasks, ongoing classes, but it is not suitable for all types of information, e.g. grades. Therefore, individual student-to-professor communication should be handled by e-mail or by using the message function in Facebook that makes it possible to send a personal message to each individual.

Fourth, keep track of time and beware of how much effort you put into your interaction and communication on Facebook. It is difficult to adjust time for professors, since students want them to be "on-call" all the time with easy-to-access instructions as well as quick feedback (e.g., Baily & Coltar, 1994; Bishop, 2000; Greco, 1999). Additionally, you have to tell your students what to expect when it comes to timing, feedback and response. And it is confirmed by Eastman and Swift (2001), that it is more likely your students will be more satisfied with the learning experience if you can meet these student-to-professor needs. Tell them what to expect.

Fifth, it is good to use a Facebook group in an educational setting when you have a course with projects and group work. A Facebook group can then enhance the interaction between the professor and students as well as between students. The possibilities to share, participate and communicate are strengths in many ways. Relationships can develop, trust can be built and the final results of the projects can be improved. It can also make course learning more fun and interactive, while not being just entertaining (Boostrom et al., 2009).

Still, I have just tested one type of social networking site—Facebook. Others might be applicable as well. My master students attending this university course had easy access to fast Internet connection and they were at least 24 years old. They might differ from other Internet users. However, social networking sites like Facebook can provide new venues for professors and students to express themselves and to interact with each other.

To end my story, I would like to give you all this final advice—if you never dare to test anything innovative—you will never be able to gain new experiences!

ACKNOWLEDGMENTS

I would like to acknowledge PhD candidate Lennart Hast at the School of Business, Economics and Law, Gothenburg University, for his contribution to this chapter in its early stages. Moreover, I would like to acknowledge all my master students (class 2009-2012) from the master of marketing and consumption at the School of Business, Economics and Law, Gothenburg University, who became "friends" with me and joined my Facebook group.

NOTES

1. Göteborg International Film Festival.
2. All students got a course evaluation survey to fill in. Their answers were anonymous and their result was analyzed statistically by administrators at the university.

REFERENCES

Baily, E. K., & Coltar, M. (1994). Teaching via the Internet. *Communication Education, 43,* 184-193.

Bishop, A. P. (2000). Communities for the new century. *Journal of Adolescent & Adult Literacy, 43*(5), 472-478.

Boostrom, R. E., Jr., Kurthakoti, R., & Summey, J. H. (2009). Enhancing class communication through segregated social networks. *Marketing Education Review,* 19(1), 37-41.

Boyd, D. (2006). Friends, friendsters, and top 8: Writing community into being on social network sites. *First Monday, 11*(12). Retrieved from http://www .firstmonday.org/issues/issue11_12/boyd/ (6/14/2010)

Boyle, M., & Parry, K. (2007). Telling the whole story: The case for organizational autoethnography. *Culture and Organization, 13*(3), 185-190.

Brodie, R. J., Coviello, N. E., Brookes, R. W., & Little, V. (1997). Towards a paradigm shift in marketing: an examination of current marketing practices. *Journal of Marketing Management, 13*(5), 383-406.

Brown, J. S., & Duguid, P. (2000). *The social life of information.* Boston, MA: Harvard Business School Press.

Brown, S. L., & Eisenhardt, K. M. (1998). *Competing on the edge: Strategy as structured chaos.* Boston, MA: Harvard Business School Press.

Casielles, R. V., Álvarez, L. S., & Martín, A. M. D. (2005). Trust as a key factor in successful relationships between consumers and retail service providers. *The Service Industries Journal,* 25(1), 83-101.

Cheung, C. M. K., & Lee, M. K. O. (2010). A theoretical model of intentional social action in online social networks. *Decision Support Systems, 49,* 24-30.

Chi, L., Chan, W. K., Seow, G., & Tam, K. (2009). Translating social capital to the online world: Insights from two experimental studies. *Journal of Organizational Computing and Electronic Commerce, 19,* 214-236.

Deresiewicz, W. (2009). Faux friendship. *Chronicle of Higher Education, 56*(16), pp. B6-B10.

Eastman, J. L., & Swift, C. O. (2001). New horizons in distance education: The online learner-centered marketing class? *Journal of Marketing Education, 23,* 25-34.

Ellis, C., & Bochner, A. P. (2000). Autoethnography, personal narrative, reflexivity: Researcher as subject. In N. K.Denzin & Y. S. Lincoln (Eds.), *Handbook of qualitative research* (pp. 733-768). London, England: Sage.

Elliot, R., & Percy, L. (2007). *Strategic brand management.* Oxford, England: Oxford University Press.

Ellis, C., & Bochner, A. (2000). Autoethnography, personal narrative, reflexivity: Researcher as subject. In N. Denzin & Y. Lincoln (Eds.), *Sage handbook of qualitative research* (pp. 733-768). Thousand Oaks, CA: Sage.

Facebook. (n.d.). *Press room.* Retrieved from http://www.facebook.com/press/info.php?factsheet

Fogel, J., & Nehmad, E. (2009) Internet social network communities: Risk taking, trust, and privacy concerns. *Computers in Human Behavior,* 25, 153-160.

Foulger, T. S., Ewbank, A. D., Kay, A., Popp, S. O., & Carter, H. L. (2009). Moral spaces in MySpace: Preservice teachers' perspectives about ethical issues in social networking. *Journal of Research on Technology in Education, 42*(1), 1-28.

Greco, J. A. (1999). Going the distance for MBA candidates. *Journal of Business Strategy, 20*(3), 30-34.

Hast, L., & Ossiansson, E. (2008a). Sociala medier ökar betydelsen av känslomässiga värden [Social media increases the importance of emotional values]. In L. -G. Mattson (Ed.), Marknadsorientering—Myter och möjligheter [*Market orientation—Myths and opportunities*] (pp. 187-203). Malmö, Sweden: Liber.

Hast, L., & Ossiansson, E. (2008b). Consumption power 2.0 (*Konsumtionsmakt 2.0*), Center for Consumer Science (CFK), School of Business, Economics and Law at Göteborg university.

Hast, L., & Ossiansson, E. (2010). Sociala Medier – Myter och Möjligheter [Social Media—Myths and Opportunities]. In U. Carlsson & U. Facht (Eds.), *Medie-Sverige 2010* [MediaSweden 2010] (pp. 187-204). Gothenburg, Sweden: Nordicom.

Huff, L. C., Cooper, J., & Wayne, J. (2002). The development and consequences of trust in student project groups. *Journal of Marketing Education, 24*(1), 24-34.

Holbrook, M. B. (2000). The millenial consumer in the texts of our times: Experience and entertainment. *Journal of Macromarketing, 20*(2), 178-192.

Kemp, F. (2007). Comment posted to "Death of Email" thread on techrhet listserv. Message posted to http://www.interversity.org/lists/techrhet/archives/Nov2007/msg00254.html

Kitchen, D., & McDougall, K. M. (1998-1999). Collaborative learning on the Internet. *Journal of Educational Technology Systems, 27*, 245-258.

Kozinets, R. V. (1999). E-tribalized marketing?: The strategic implications of virtual communities on consumption, *European Management Journal, 17*(3), 252-264.

Lee, R. M. (1995). *Dangerous fieldwork*. Newbury Park, CA: Sage.

Maranto, G., & Barton, M. (2009). Paradox and promise: MySpace, Facebook, and the sociopolitics of social networking in the writing classroom. *Computers and Compositions, 27*, 36-47.

Mathwick, C., Wiertz, C., & De Ruyter, K. (2008). Social capital production in a virtual P3 community. *Journal of Consumer Research, 34*, 832-849.

Mazer, J. P., Murphy, R. E., & Simonds, C. J. (2007). The effects of teacher self-disclosure via Facebook on teacher credibility. *Learning, Media and Technology, 34*(2), 175-183.

McGrath, C. (1997-1998). A new voice on Interchange: Is it talking or writing? Implications for the teaching of literature. *Journal of Educational Technology Systems, 26*, 291-297.

Mills, C. W. (2000). *The sociological imagination*. New York, NY: Oxford University Press.

Moisander, J., & Valtonen, A. (2006). *Qualitative marketing research—A cultural approach*. London, England: Sage Publications.

Morgan, R. M., & Hunt, S. D. (1994). The commitment-trust theory of relationship marketing, *Journal of Marketing, 58*, 20-38.

Morse, J. (2000). Editorial: My own experience, *Qualitative Health Research, 12*(9), 1159-1160.

Muise, A., Christofides, E., & Desmarais, S. (2009). More information than you ever wanted: Does Facebook bring out the green-eyed monster of jealousy? *CyberPsychology & Behavior, 12*(4), 441-444.

O'Malley, L. O., & Prothero, A. (2004). Beyond the frills of relationship marketing. *Journal of Business Research, 57,* 1286-1294.

O'Malley, L., & Tynan, C. (1999). The utility of the relationship metaphor in consumer markets: a critical evaluation. *Journal of Marketing Management, 15,* 587-602.

Ossiansson, E. (2006). Försök inte lura mig gosse—jag inga konster tål! [Don't try to fool me—I will not accept it!]. In I. -L. Johansson, S. Jönsson, & R. Solli (Eds.), *Värdet av förtroende* (pp. 135-170). Lund, Sweeden: Studentlitteratur.

Ossiansson, E. (2008). When the brand is a feeling [När varumärket är en känsla]. *Brand Manager, 2,* 36-41.

Rothaermel, F. T., & Sugiyama, S. (2001).Virtual Internet communities and commercial success: Individual and community-level theory grounded in the atypical case of TimeZone.com. *Journal of Management, 27*(3), 297-314.

Rose, D. (1990). *Living the ethnographic life*. Newbury Park, CA: Sage.

Peltier, J. W., Drago, W., & Schibrowsky, J. A. (2003). Virtual communities and the assessment of online marketing education. *Journal of Marketing Education, 25*(3), 260-276.

Pempek, T. A., Yermolayeva, Y. A., & Calvert, S. L. (2009). College students' social networking experiences on Facebook. *Journal of Applied Development Psychology, 30,* 227-238;

Selwyn, N. (2009). Faceworking: Exploring student' education-related use of Facebook. *Learning, Media and Technology, 34*(2), 154-174.

Sherron, G., & Boettcher, J. V. (1997). *Distance learning: The shift to interactivity*. Boulder, CO: Cause.

Subrahmanyam, K., Reich, S. M., Waechter, N., & Espinoza, G. (2008). Online and offline social networks: Use of social networking sites by emerging adults. *Journal of Applied Development Psychology, 29,* 420-433.

Sullivan, P. (2001). Gender differences and the online classroom: Male and female college students evaluate their experiences. *College Journal of Research & Practices, 25,* 805-818.

Valenzuela, S., Park, N., & Kee, K. F. (2009). Is there social capital in a social network site? Facebook use and college students' life satisfaction, trust and participation. *Journal of Computer-Mediated Communication, 14*(4), 875-901.

van Manen, M. (1990). *Researching lived experience: Human science for an action sensitive pedagogy*. Ontario, Canada: The University of Western Ontario.

Vargo, S. L., & Lusch, R. F. (2004). Evolving to a new dominant logic for marketing. *Journal of Marketing, 68,* 1-17.

Vickers, M. H. (2007). Autoethography as sensemaking: A story of bullying. *Culture and Organization, 13*(3), 223-237.

Vie, S. (2008). Digital divide 2.0: "Generation M" and online social networking sites in the composition classroom. *Computers and Compositions, 25,* 9-23.

Weick, K. E. (1995). *Sensemaking in organizations*. Thousand Oaks, CA: Sage Publications.

YouTube.com. (n.d.) *South Park Facebook scenes*. Retrieved from http://www.YouTube.com/watch?v=4SgkfghupFE

CHAPTER 8

USING SECOND LIFE FOR TEACHING MANAGEMENT OF CREATIVITY AND INNOVATION

Gary Coombs

Second Life and other virtual worlds provide a unique opportunity for teaching about the management of creativity and innovation in organizations. As an emergent technology, examination of Second Life as an innovation provides fertile ground for analysis and discussion of the process of adoption and dispersion of an innovation. Linden Lab is also an interesting example of an organization pursuing a strategy of innovation based on creative participation or consumer cocreation of valuable products, services, or experiences, which parallels other recent innovative offerings such as YouTube and Firefox. Additionally, Second Life is filled with examples of individual creativity as well as entrepreneurial and organizational innovation that can be examined and critiqued.

RICH IMMERSIVE ENVIRONMENTS

Virtual worlds or synthetic worlds were once the realm of science fiction but are now emerging on the Internet as new applications with real-world

Cutting-Edge Social Media Approaches to Business Education:
Teaching With LinkedIn, Facebook, Twitter, Second Life, and Blogs, pp. 141–157

crossover. Edward Castronova et al. define them as "persistent online 3D spaces that replicate many of the features of the real world" (Castronova et al., 2007, p. 174). This definition has been used to describe *rich immersive environments* ranging from on-line gaming worlds or massively multiplayer online games (MMOGs) such as World of Warcraft, to 3D social networking sites like Kaneva and Onverse, to *metaverses* that bring together social interaction, education and economic activity like Second Life, IMVU (instant messaging virtual universe), and ActiveWorlds. Many of the gaming environments have been extremely successful, attracting millions of users around the world. Social networking environments, like Kaneva, are a more recent variation attempting to cash in on the success of services like Facebook through avatar based interactivity. The focus of this chapter, however, will be on the metaverse, Second Life, as it offers the broadest range of business related applications, though the described projects could be equally applicable to ActiveWorlds. Virtual worlds can be an effective pedagogical tool for creating a constructivist learning environment (cf. Dede, 1996) and it is that aspect that the following projects attempts to utilize.

For instructors, examples are provided of two projects with which I have been involved. The first, used in an introduction to management setting, is an environmental analysis of Second Life and development of a rudimentary business plan for a virtual entrepreneurial start-up (Appendix A). The second, used in a course on managing creativity and innovation, is a value-creation project utilizing the ability to create, from scratch, virtual products or services with potential economic value or educational utility, and two variants of this project are shown (Appendix B).

SECOND LIFE OVERVIEW

The best known of the rich immersive environments, Second Life is a product of Linden Lab, a San Francisco-based company founded in 1999 by Philip Rosedale, the former chief technology officer of RealNetworks. Second Life launched in 2003 and by 2010 had approximately 18 million registered users, though average concurrent users is about 38,000 with a peak of under 90,000 users in-world at one time (Second Life Economic Statistics, 2010). To provide some context for the size of the in-world economy represented by Second Life, recent figures indicate that user-to-user transactions in the first quarter of 2010 reached $160 million U.S. dollars and $31 million USD were exchanged on the Lindex monetary exchange. Additionally, over 800,000 users logged multiple log-ins during that quarter with peak concurrent logins exceeding 81,000 users (Nino, 2010).

It has been most successful in attracting users in Europe and Asia but has started to move into the U.S. popular culture, appearing as a plot element in prime time television shows like CSI: NY (Carter, 2007) and as a site for virtual screenings for the Sundance Channel (Itzkoff, 2007). CBS went so far as to create an entire CSI interactive experience within Second Life where fans could use their avatars to solve virtual crimes using the techniques highlighted in the show.

Major corporations, including American Apparel, IBM, Dell, and Brookstone, have gotten involved, opening in-world retail experiences (leading to a new term "v-tail" for virtual retailing, cf. Rubel, 2007), consulting services (Shankland, 2006), and even establishing a monetary exchange between in-world Linden dollars and real-world currencies (Aronson, 2004). While not all companies who have dabbled in Second Life have retained their presences there, the full range of commercial activity is replicated, for good or ill, within the virtual world and virtual entrepreneurship is found everywhere. Through currency exchange, the virtual economy crosses over to the real world and Second Life has already produced its first real life millionaire, a German woman who profitably bought and sold virtual real estate on popular islands (Benner, 2006; Hof, 2006) even making a 2006 cover of *Business Week* in avatar form. The mainstreaming of this topic can be reflected by the fact that the *Journal of Electronic Commerce Research* has a special issue that focuses on e-commerce in virtual worlds like Second Life. Even McKinsey & Company has weighed in, warning companies not to ignore the possibilities of virtual worlds (Richards, 2008).

There are aspects to these virtual worlds that are like the "wild west." Rules of behavior are emergent and application of real-world law is a topic of debate (Associated Press, 2008) and litigation (Balkin, 2004; Berry, 2007; Bringardner, 2007; Davis, 2007), and is currently somewhat of a moving target as countries sort out whose laws apply and where in-world activity actually occurs. A current law suit is challenging changes in Linden Lab user agreement with respect to property ownership (Lazarus, 2010). The United States asserted its right to regulate in-world gambling, leading to the elimination of a highly profitable business model within Second Life, and demonstrating that what happens in Second Life doesn't necessarily stay there.

Universities are also getting their feet wet, creating virtual campuses where geographically dispersed students and faculty can interact in a setting that visually replicates a classroom environment but also provides opportunities for interaction with dynamic learning objects, three dimensional models, and role playing. As instructors, all of the technologies we are accustomed to using in the classroom can also be used in the Second Life virtual classroom along with other approaches that are not easily rep-

Figure 8.1.   The Ohio University Virtual Campus Gateway.

licable in the real world. Second Life has created an educational microsite and its educational directory, while incomplete, currently lists 86 institutions. While a full undeveloped region of land (an island) currently sells for $1,000 for set-up plus a $295 per month maintenance fee to regular users, educational institutions receive a 50% discount on these land prices. Ohio University currently owns multiple islands, including a main campus and several developmental areas for experimentation and student projects (see Figure 8.1 for a screen shot of the entrance to the Ohio University virtual campus.) Larry Johnson, CEO of the New Media Consortium has testified before Congress about the potential educational benefits of virtual learning environments like Second Life (Second Life Education, 2009).

CREATED ENVIRONMENTS

Though full engagement in the virtual world can require monthly premium membership fees, property maintenance fees, and other costs, basic Second Life access for individual users is free, providing a unique opportunity for students to observe, engage in, and interpret creativity and organizational behavior in a compelling and novel way at no cost. Users create their own identity, choose a new name, and even design their own appearance. They can create objects with full intellectual property rights and then have the option of selling those objects to others to generate in-world currency or even giving them away as a public service. They can observe and evaluate the commercial and social activities that are occurring in-world in order to apply business, management, and organizational behavior concepts in a unique context, all through their computer. Communication with others can occur through typing (chat), in-world instant messaging, or vocally using a microphone/headset. Users are also able to use avatar gestures to simulate real-world nonverbal communications.

Users with the interest and the funds can upgrade to premium membership and can then purchase plots of land or even entire "islands." Those who own islands are able to establish localized rules for their spaces, including restrictions on access, limitations on some aspects of movement and behavior of avatars, and the appearance of their land, limited only by their imagination and ability to construct or purchase objects and create scripts. They may also sell or rent virtual land on their island to other users. Many users acquire and dispose of land through online auctions, using either in-world Linden dollars or actual U.S. dollars.

It must be acknowledged that Second Life imposes a relatively steep learning curve on both students and faculty to fully take advantage of all of its functions, particularly when it comes to creating objects and scripts beyond the most rudimentary level of sophistication. However, simple movement and communication is not too difficult to master, allowing students to quickly enter Second Life as observers.

PARTICIPANT OBSERVATION IN SECOND LIFE

These immersive environments truly bring a new meaning to the idea of participant-observation. Participant-observation is a methodology drawn from cultural anthropology and sociology whereby an individual can gain a deep understanding of a social group through intensive engagement with members of that group in their own environment over an extended period of time. Author Tom Boellstorff, in his 2008 book *Coming of Age in Second Life: An Anthropologist Explores the Virtually Human*, applies the full range of ethnographic approaches to the Second Life experience. From a management perspective, in Second Life students are able to enter into created (and creative) social environments to interact with others and observe the behaviors of those around them and, more importantly, to observe the creative output of the island owners and other inhabitants. They can experience and reflect on the ways in which the builders of these different social environments attempt to structure social interaction and interaction with the objects placed in their environments through manipulation of space, movement, localized rules/restrictions, media, and imagery.

APPLICATION TO COURSES IN MANAGEMENT

I have been involved with projects involving Second Life in two distinct course settings and will provide descriptions of the projects and ways that they could be adapted to other settings. In the first, I was the instructor of an Introduction to Management course within our integrated cluster of core business courses using a team-taught, problem-based methodology. The second was a management of creativity and innovation course, a required course within our management and strategic leadership major. In each case, all of my students were completely naïve with respect to Second Life at the launch of the project described, beyond a few who had heard or read something about it.

Business Evaluation and Value Creation Project

In Ohio University's Integrated Business Cluster, students enroll in four business core courses concurrently and complete three team projects in addition to the content of the courses in management, marketing, professional communications, and management information systems. (Since the project using Second Life, finance has replaced professional communications as the fourth course in the cluster.) Our projects are developed and delivered using a problem-based learning (PBL) methodology, an approach that utilizes authentic, ambiguous problems to create situated learning opportunities for students (cf. Perotti, Gunn, Day, & Coombs, 1998 for more on the use of PBL in the Integrated Business Cluster). For their first project, the students were asked to examine Second Life as a business and to identify two possible new applications within SL, one educational and one for-profit (see Appendix A for the full project charge). Working in five person teams, they were asked to assess the business potential of synthetic worlds by conducting research into the business operations of Linden Lab, as well as of companies who had chosen, at the time, to pursue business opportunities within Second Life. The project charge required them to do secondary research into Second Life and to enter the virtual world only to observe and get a sense of what types of business were being conducted in-world at that time. Their initial reaction was that "they didn't get it"; they didn't see any particular appeal to Second Life as an experience nor did they see how there could be economic potential in an immersive environment that wasn't a game.

The learning outcomes associated with this project fell into different disciplinary areas. From the management perspective, students learned how to conduct a basic environmental and industry level analysis. Applying such typical business tools as a PEST analysis (Political, Economic, Social, and Technological), a SWOT analysis (Strengths, Weaknesses, Opportunities and Threats), and Porter's Five Forces, students evaluated the competitive environment faced by Linden and the value proposition of Second Life as a product/service. They discovered the business model pursued by Linden and its revenue streams from recurrent premium membership fees, sale of server space in the form of islands and other virtual real estate, and sale of in-world Linden dollars. They were also exposed to the lifecycles of innovation from development through introduction to adoption and dispersion. As with any industry-level analysis, this learning outcome is easily transferable to application in projects in other business classes. The communications outcomes focused on development of a professional written report and oral presentation of findings and recommendations, important skills for all business students.

The result of the industry analysis set the context for the other components of the project. The project also required examination of Second Life as a novel, self-contained business environment for the companies conducting business within it. The students were able to examine the rationale for conducting business in Second Life, legitimate questions about viability of corporate engagement with Second Life, and the expected opportunities and unexpected challenges faced by companies that were early entrants into this generally unproven business model. Competition and competitive strategies employed to generate income, the role of entrepreneurship, and forecasting of demand had to be understood in determining what types of new user-created businesses concepts would be viable. This addressed learning outcomes in management (entrepreneurship, strategic planning, competitive analysis) and marketing (consumer behavior, four Ps), as well as application of their prior knowledge from accounting in analyzing and communicating projected costs and revenues.

At the time that the project was running, in addition to the numerous individuals selling Second Life products, a variety of real-life companies were selling their virtual products to users for their avatars and providing the option for immediate ordering of the equivalent real products online. In effect, users were able to virtually experience the product before purchasing it for their "first life." Other companies allowed virtual exploration of their product lines as a means of familiarizing potential customers and encouraging them to seek out the real-life product at a retail location. While the majority of real-world businesses that have experimented with Second Life have since exited after brief sojourns there, a few well known businesses still have a presence in Second Life. CISCO Systems, for example, has an entire island dedicated to their connected home product line and Dell sells computers through a Second Life island.

Based on their analyses of the Second Life business environment, students were then challenged to propose their own for-profit business concept that they believed had the potential to be successful if implemented in Second Life. This business could be a pure Second Life based business or a hybrid Second Life to real-life business. As with any entrepreneurial plan, they had to come to an understanding of the size and character of the target market, existing competition, and means to attract potential customers. They were able to conduct primary research by interviewing avatars they encountered to supplement their secondary research. This element of the project took them further from their comfort zones, as many of their existing understandings of how businesses operate, how consumers behave, how products are marketed, etc were severely challenged in the unique environment of a metaverse (cf. Au, 2007). This forced them to consider the application of business concepts creatively to a new situation, building their problem solving capabilities. While they remained skeptical of the long term viability of Second Life businesses, they demonstrated a strong understanding of core business concepts and approaches and reported a much enhanced ability to apply business theories and concepts to their analysis of an ambiguous business situation, to develop creative solutions and to present strong arguments in support of their conclusions.

Additionally, they were also required to develop a concept for an educational experience that would take advantage of Second Life's unique characteristics. The students felt that this is, perhaps, the area that offers the most promise for long term viability. Second Life offers a unique opportunity for creating engaging learning experiences, particularly for distance learning. By combining the visual impact of the simulated environment with the ability to deliver video content, PowerPoint presentations, and audio, Second Life can be used to create turn-key modularized content delivery. Learners can visit the location asynchronously to engage with the learning object and can revisit it as often as they wish. If synchronous content delivery is desired, by using voice over Internet protocol (VOIP), the instructor can deliver real-time lectures to geographically dispersed students, hold team meetings, or virtual office hours.

Challenging students to conceptualize effective learning modules integrating the different delivery modes that Second Life permits allows them to utilize their creativity in an arena with which they are intimately familiar. It also gives them a new appreciation of the effort that goes into a well constructed course.

This project was conceptual in nature, focusing the students on understanding the industry within which Linden Lab operates Second Life, the potential of the business model represented, and how to create value in a synthetic world. While students created avatars and explored Second Life to understand what types of business opportunities and educational experiences existed, they did not engage in creation of objects or scripts themselves. In that sense, they were much more observers than participants. This type of project has the lowest "cost" to the instructor in terms of set-up, the lowest learning curve for the students to become engaged, and is easily adaptable to various courses and project timeframes. However, it must be understood that the "synthetic" nature of business within Second Life creates a limitation on the transferability of some learning to Real Life business environments. While it simulates the real world, Second Life is, in many ways, simply another tool that savvy companies might use to reach customers and students are quick to point out those limitations. The largest business component remains user-to-user sale of virtual products, driving traffic to online advertising and spam generation sites, and various entertainment options including live performance venues (often with a cover charge) and adult oriented islands. Universities, on the other hand, have expanded their presence in Second Life and are still experimenting with the possibilities that a virtual teaching environment offers. The changing nature of the Second Life business environment offers a renewable set of opportunities for future projects of this type as the environment continues to evolve.

Application in Creativity

In my management of creativity and innovation course, the project was more hands-on and application oriented. Teams of students were challenged to conceptualize and then to implement environments within Second Life. Ohio University owns multiple islands in Second Life, with a publicly available main campus and several others set aside for research and learning object development. In two offerings of the course across two years, I was able to get permission to use an area of one of the private islands on a temporary basis for my students to be able to build their own projects and leave them in place until the end of the course. I also had access to one of the university's technical experts on scripting in Second Life, who provided my students with training sessions, basic scripts, and consulting assistance as they built their projects.

The first version of the project was an extension of the educational concept included in the project used for the business cluster. Students were tasked with creating an educational experience in Second Life with the specific purpose of helping other students prepare for study abroad. This required them to identify learning outcomes, conceptualize how to deliver those outcomes as a turn-key experience, design and build (or otherwise acquire) the needed objects to create the learning environment, and to do whatever scripting was necessary to deliver the content to visitors to their site. Each team was assigned a different country that matched locations to which our College of Business would be sending students during the summer to do consulting projects. These included China, Denmark, Germany, Greece, France, Italy, and Hungary.

Intermediate deliverables were required that served as milestones in the development of their projects and a mechanism to keep them on track and making progress at a steady rate over the quarter. These formed some of the grading components for the course and represented some of the creativity tools that I wanted the students to master. This project had a much steeper learning curve for the students as they were not simply observing Second Life, but actually participating in the creation of intellectual property from primitive objects (or "prims") and developing scripts to trigger actions within their environment. Those actions could be giving the visiting avatar a notecard with information or displaying a video or connecting the visitor, through their web browser, to an out-of-Second Life website. Many groups integrated YouTube language training videos into their environments. While all groups built some objects from prims, they all became adept at acquiring free objects that they could repurpose for their environments. A few found ways to earn Linden dollars to buy objects that exceeded their abilities to build. They all also discovered the multinational aspect of Second Life, visiting islands where the dominant language was of the country for which they were preparing students, chatting with nationals of those countries about traveling there, and so forth. Presentations were simply walk-throughs of the student created environments by my avatar projected on the classroom screen, with the students explaining as I experienced their learning environment. See Figure 8.2 for a screen capture of my avatar visiting one of the student-created activities.

The second variation was an extension of the entrepreneurial component of the cluster project. The student teams were required to conceptualize, construct, and demonstrate a business start up within Second Life. As with the first variant, the engagement with Second Life was far more hands-on, requiring building with prims and scripting. The same intermediate deliverables were required as progress checks and the final project deliverables were the same with two significant additions. They had to interview Second Life users to get a sense of the desirability of their business concepts. Also, in this version, all team members had to be in Second Life in avatar form from a different classroom location to present their

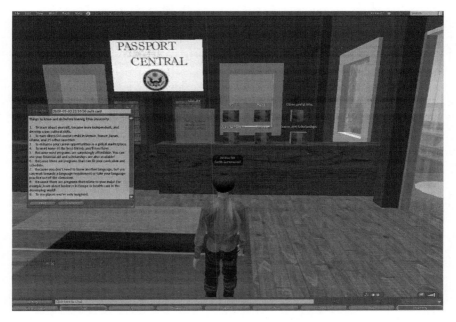

Figure 8.2.   Example of a student-constructed in-world learning space.

projects virtually to the class. Again, my avatar served as the proxy for the class and was projected on the main classroom screen with full two-way audio. The teams were required to guide me through their presentation, including the use of a PowerPoint presentation delivered within their environment (see Figure 8.3 for a screen shot of one such presentation) and to engage in a question-and-answer session with the class at the conclusion of the formal presentation. Once again, student environments were a mixture of team-built and acquired objects, and some teams utilized other islands as "locations" for segments of their presentation, sending my avatar teleport coordinates to guide me from place to place, ultimately ending up back at their home location. I maintained a "home office" near their work spaces and would frequently visit their work sites to observe their construction efforts and to hold virtual office hours.

Students were more directly exposed to the role of entrepreneurial activity through their examination of user created businesses in Second Life during this project. They were amazed by some of the creative concepts that users had developed and, admittedly, puzzled by others. Many comments focused on the "coolness" of some of the things that were being sold but few could conceive of actually paying for them.

Figure 8.3.   In-world student team presentation.

These projects provided a much different experience for the students from the previously described cluster project. The level of engagement with Second Life was much deeper (and in some ways more frustrating) as they struggled with building and scripting. At the same time, they developed a more thorough appreciation of the possibilities and limitations of Second Life as a platform for commercial and educational activity and engaged much more with others within the Second Life environment. Ultimately, it also engaged them in direct creative efforts in bringing their concepts to virtual life. In terms of my learning objectives for the project, this was highly successful in engaging students in direct creative effort as well as in exposing them to an emerging creative business model.

CONCLUSION

The learning curve for both the instructor and the students engaging with rich immersive environments like Second Life can be steep, but many of our students are already familiar with some aspects of these types of experiences from interactive gaming and massively multiuser online role playing. However, while they fully engaged with the environment for the purposes of the project, many of my students did not find Second Life to be of interest to them beyond the project requirements and all indicated that they would be highly unlikely to ever return to Second Life after the end of the class. A small number went above and beyond the project requirements, developing strong scripting skills, extensively customizing their avatars, and visiting "welfare islands" to earn small amounts of Linden dollars to buy some clothing and special effects. One student even experimented briefly with "griefing" (engaging in virtual harassing behaviors) and had to be reprimanded and threatened with expulsion from the Ohio University Second Life environment. These few students did end up being good resources for their classmates, as they developed greater proficiency with creating objects and scripting actions and were able to assist their classmates in their work.

Examination of the typical Second Life user makes the common decision not to pursue further, nonclass related experience with the technology unsurprising. In that way, they are like the 90% or more of users who sign up for a free account, explore for a short time, and never or very rarely return after their initial experimentation. Perhaps because of their experience with video games and MMOGs, traditionally aged American college students find the more passive experience within Second Life to be less appealing. It must be noted, however, that it was not a goal of any of the projects described that the students should become aficionados of Second Life any more than it would be the objective of doing a case study on IBM to have students choose to seek employment there. Second Life provided an effective and novel learning opportunity through which to accomplish specific learning outcomes that are not as readily addressed in other, more traditional ways. Perhaps as Linden Lab continues to upgrade the functionality and appearance of Second Life and other competitors enter the market with expectations of higher quality graphics and easier navigation, these metaverses may become more attractive to our student demographic. As a learning experience, however, these projects offered unique opportunities for student interaction with Second Life as an immersion in creative and innovative activity on a different scale than could be as easily experienced in a typical classroom setting.

APPENDIX A:
INTEGRATED BUSINESS CLUSTER PROJECT DESCRIPTION

Your team is to conduct extensive research on the functioning, uses, and potential impact of Second Life. As we will discuss, Second Life is a "synthetic world" accessed via the Internet in which participants create an identity, interact with others, and lead a "synthetic" existence. While this environment is still very new, possible applications exist in education, business, and other settings. You are expected to make extensive use of library as well as internet resources for this study. PLEASE REMEMBER:

It is always our expectation that you back up your findings with the data found in your research, and that you make EXPLICIT REFERENCE to numbers where necessary.

This study will have three elements:

1. A discussion of the pros and cons of Second Life as an interactive environment,
2. An analysis of the possible educational and business uses of Second Life, and
3. Suggestions of the two most promising ideas your team has for new spaces in Second Life, with an explanation of why you feel each would succeed. These two proposed spaces must meet the following criteria:

    (a) They should be "suitable for family viewing."
    (b) One of your suggestions must be for an educational application of Second Life.
    (c) One of your suggestions must be for a business application of Second Life.

Each observation or recommendation you make must be substantiated by the research you conduct, with clear justifications provided in all cases.

APPENDIX B: MANAGEMENT OF CREATIVITY AND INNOVATION PROJECT DESCRIPTION

Variant 1

The group project will require you to work with teammates to develop a proposal for an educational experience within Second Life aimed at preparing students to study abroad. The proposal will consist of a market analysis (that is, a description of who you believe will be interested in your experience and how they like to learn/interact/experience things, competitive products in that same market space, etc.), a full description dealing with educational strategy, types of experiences, et cetera, and a storyboard to show visually how you think the experience would progress. In addition, you will work with your team to construct as many aspects of that experience as you can in space provided by the Ohio University Second Life Campus. You will present the proposal as a written proposal and also do a presentation to the class and, possibly, guest experts, walking us through the experience where you will try to sell us on your idea.

Variant 2

The group project will require you to work with teammates to develop the concept for a new, innovative product or service that must be able to be marketed and sold from within Second Life. The deliverables will be a paper describing your product concept and target market, and a final presentation to me, as the CEO of the company, which will have to be given in Second Life. You will need to use the 3D capabilities of Second Life in the presentation for this new product. You will be limited to a certain number of Second Life building objects or *"prims"* and should use SL to demonstrate concepts as opposed to simply building structures or product replicas. You will also need to include in your presentation the reaction from interviews conducted **about the marketability of your product** with 2 to 3 Second Life residents who are not members of the class.

Project interim assignments are milestones along the way to completion of your final project for the course. Each is described below and will represent an activity critical to the creative process and will help keep you on track to completing the project on time. You will be required to submit, individually, an individual brainstorm list, a decision criteria list, and a variations brainstorm list. As a team, you will submit a group brainstorm list, a final decision criteria list, a reduced alternatives list, an alternatives evaluation, and a final selection. The final project will include other elements as described under the Group Project description.

- **Individual Brainstorm list**—Your individually generated list of possible ideas.
- **Individual Decision Criteria list**—How you think a good idea should be judged.
- **Individual Object Creation**—You must create an object in Second Life to demonstrate that you are learning the skills you will need for the project.
- *Group Decision Criteria list*—Your group's agreed upon criteria.
- *Group Reduced Alternatives list*—after applying your criteria, what ideas remained from your original brainstorm list that are still worth considering for final selection (one typewritten copy to me per group).
- *Group Final Concept Selection*—Which idea are you going to carry forward to completion for the project? (one typewritten copy to me per group)

REFERENCES

Aronson, S. (2004, November 11). 'Second Life' lessons from a virtual world. *E-Commerce Times*. Retrieved from http://www.ecommercetimes.com/story/38074.html

Associated Press. (2008). *House Committee explores commerce, safety in virtual worlds*. Retrieved from http://www.linuxinsider.com/story/62393.html

Au, W. J. (2007). Marketing in Second Life doesn't work … here's why! Retrieved from http://gigaom.com/2007/04/04/3-reasons-why-marketing-in-second-life-doesnt-work/

Balkin, J. M. (2004). Virtual liberty: Freedom to design and freedom to play in virtual worlds. *Virginia Law Review, 90*(8), 2043-2098.

Benner, K. (2006). Investing in the online property boom. *CNN Money.com* Retrieved from http://money.cnn.com/2006/10/20/technology/second_life_money/index.htm

Berry, A. (2007). Lawyers find real revenue in virtual world. *Legal Technology*. Retrieved from http://www.law.com/jsp/legaltechnology/PubArticleFriendlyLT.jsp?id=1185820702695

Boellstorff, T. (2008). *Coming of age in Second Life: An anthropologist explores the virtually human*. Princeton, NJ: Princeton University Press.

Brindgardner, J. (2007). IP's brave new world. *Law.com*. Retrieved from http://www.law.com/jsp/law/LawArticleFriendly.jsp?id=1170237755271

Carter, B. (2007). Fictional characters get virtual lives, too. *The New York Times*. Retrieved from http://www.nytimes.com/2007/10/04/arts/television/04CSI.html

Castronova, E., Cummings, J., Emigh, W., Fatten, M., Mishler, N., Ross, T., et al. (2007). What is a synthetic world? In F. von Borries, S. P. Walz, & M. Bottger (Eds.), *Space time play—Computer games, architecture and urbanism: The next level* (pp. 174-177). Basel, Switzerland: Birkhäuser Verlag AG.

Davis, P. (2007). 'Second Life' virtual sex devise spawns a real-life lawsuit. *The Boston Globe*. Retrieved from http://www.boston.com/news/globe/living/articles/2007/08/11/second_life_virtual_sex_device_spawns_a_real_life_lawsuit/

Dede, C. (1996). The evolution of constructivist learning environments: Immersion in distributed, virtual worlds. *Educational Technology, 35*(5), 46-52.

Hof, R. (2006, November 26). Second Life's first millionaire. *Business Week*. Retrieved from http://www.businessweek.com/the_thread/techbeat/archives/2006/11/second_lifes_fi.html

Itzkoff, D. (2007, June 24). A brave new world for TV? Virtually. *The New York Times*. Retrieved from http://www.nytimes.com/2007/06/24/arts/television/24itzk.html

Lazarus, D. (2010, April 30). A real-world battle over virtual-property rights. *The Los Angeles Times*. Retrieved from http://articles.latimes.com/2010/apr/30/business/la-fi-lazarus-20100430

Nino, T. (2010, April 28). *Linden Lab hands down Second Life metrics for Q1 2010*. Retrieved April 30, 2010 from http://www.massively.com/category/second-life/

Perrotti, V., Gunn, P., Day, J., & Coombs, G. (1998). Business 2020: Ohio University's integrated business core. In R.Milter, J.Stinson, & W. Gijselaers (Eds.),

Educational innovation in economics and business III: Innovative practices in business education (pp. 169-188). Boston, MA: Kluwer Academic Press.

Richards, J. (2008, April 23). McKinsey: Ignore 'Second Life' at your peril. *Times Online*. Retrieved from http://technology.timesonline.co.uk/tol/news/tech_ and_web/article3803056.ece

Rubel, S. (2007, January 8). *V-tail: Where virtual words meet e-commerce*. Retrieved from http://www.micropersuasion.com/2007/01/vtail_where_vir.html

Second Life Economic Statistics. (2010). Retrieved from http://Second Life.com /statistics/economy-data.php

Second Life Education. (2009). *Developing new learning and collaboration environments for educators: The new media consortium (NMC) in Second Life*. Retrieved from http://education.secondlife.com/successstories/case/nmc

Shankland, S. (2006, December 12). IBM to give birth to 'Second Life' business group. *CNET News.com*. Retrieved from http://earthlink.com.com/IBM+to +give+birth+to+Second+Life+business+group/2100-1014_3-6143175 .html

CHAPTER 9

SOCIAL MEDIA ENGAGES ONLINE ENTREPRENEURSHIP STUDENTS

Geoffrey R. Archer and Jo Axe

Royal Roads University in Victoria, British Columbia, Canada delivers a bachelor of commerce degree in entrepreneurial management in both online and on-campus formats. While the curriculum for each delivery method is nearly identical, the course assignments had diverged over the past decade. In the entrepreneurial expertise course, on-campus students gave a traditional elevator pitch (a concise individual presentation that summarizes a new business concept for a potential investor) and they excelled in an experiential learning exercise called the Venture Challenge. Alternatively, online students worked on a higher number of cases and analyzed more business plans. In response to the online students' feedback, and in recognition of the near ubiquity of so many powerful social media tools, an assignment revision was undertaken in the winter of 2010. As a result, online students videorecorded a 2-minute elevator pitch which was posted on YouTube. In addition, this newly invigorated cohort utilized social media in a team-based experiential learning exercise called the Online Venture Challenge. Using a wiki, such as Wetpaint, each four-person team brainstormed, designed, and created a mission-driven e-commerce website. This chapter documents the paths trodden by the students as they worked

Cutting-Edge Social Media Approaches to Business Education:
Teaching With LinkedIn, Facebook, Twitter, Second Life, and Blogs, pp. 159–177

through the course deliverables. Assignment structure and expected outcomes, as well as unexpected outcomes, are included. The experiences documented in these pages will allow other educators to adapt the exercises for use in their own courses.

TWO PATHS DIVERGED

Royal Roads University in Victoria, British Columbia, Canada delivers a bachelor of commerce degree in entrepreneurial management in both online and on-campus formats. The bibliography and curriculum for each delivery method is similar; however, the specific assignments in the Entrepreneurial Expertise course had diverged over time. On-campus students gave a traditional elevator pitch (a concise individual presentation that summarizes a new business concept for a potential investor) and they excelled in an experiential learning exercise called the Venture Challenge. Seemingly constrained by the online delivery medium, students taking the same course online had neither of those experiences. Instead, these students worked on a higher number of cases and analyzed more business plans. The online students loaded up on the type of vicarious experience that came through case analysis, but without a social-media-based solution, they were denied the first person benefits of real experiential learning. The feedback received from online students indicated that it was time to rethink the pedagogical approach.

In the online learning environment, where individuals are separated in both space and time, instructors may be challenged to find solutions that allow students to apply theory to practice. Recalling that in their paper discussing isolation in online education McInnerney and Roberts (2004) made the argument that social context is a key factor in the success of the student, it could be expected that injecting social media into an online entrepreneurial course would increase the potential for an enhanced classroom experience. With this in mind, and in recognition of the near ubiquity of so many powerful social media tools, a two-part course revision was undertaken in the winter of 2010.

The first part of the course revision involved each student making a videorecording and posting it to YouTube for class discussion and feedback. This allowed students to actively participate in assessment of, and dialogue with, classmates. The second part of the revision directed students to use a wiki to prepare a mission-driven e-commerce website. Both exercises engaged class members in activities that were previously reserved exclusively for their on-campus contemporaries.

In the pages that follow, we discuss the design and implementation of this revision, as well as some of the contributions made by students who worked on the assignments. The impact these new deliverables had on the students' ability to develop community and increase the sense of context will be explored. Also examined are the practical implications of using social media tools in online courses, thereby allowing the reader to assess the value of this type of activity for online students.

THE VIDEO ELEVATOR PITCH

Online students videorecorded a 2-minute elevator pitch. Also known as an elevator speech (Barringer, 2009), this short talk about a new business opportunity (Baron & Shane, 2008) is a typical assignment at the beginning of an introductory entrepreneurship course. This video clip was then uploaded to (1) YouTube, (2) Vimeo for those who wanted password protection (which seemed to be a self-confidence issue), or (3) FTP'd directly to the instructor (with permission, if a student's employer insisted). Starring in movies about themselves and their ideas was humanizing and provided the opportunity to build trusting relationships with classmates. In e-learning situations that are individualistic, problems of isolation can create a negative learning environment (McConnell, 2006); conversely, in a classroom where students are encouraged to share video recordings they have made and interaction is applauded, isolation is reduced and strong student-to-student bonds are established.

When students build trusting relationships, in addition to minimizing isolation, benefits such as risk-taking are experienced (Jarvenpaa, Knoll, & Leidner, 1998). Although online trust building can be challenging, it is a key ingredient for individuals working in online teams (Hasler-Waters & Napier, 2002). Some of the students overcame the challenges associated with online work as they completed the video recording exercise; this was evident when they took the risk to post hilarious out-takes like those pictured in Figure 9.1.

Even though online learning environments can change student and faculty communication patterns (Aggarwal, 2000), the students in the entrepreneurial expertise class were able to capture some elements of traditional relationship-building by taking part in multidimensional exchanges that relied on more than text messages and email. This latter benefit was catalyzed by the peer feedback requirement seen in the assignment below:

Assignment#1: The Video Elevator Pitch
An elevator pitch is industry jargon for a short presentation of your new business concept. It is called an elevator pitch, because the idea is that you imagine you are working on a start-up company, and

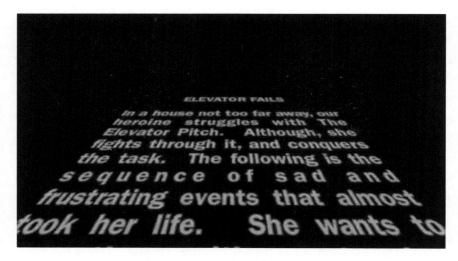

Figure 9.1.   Blooper reels humanize students who live thousands of miles apart.

you accidentally end up in an elevator with a wealthy potential investor. In order to earn a follow-up appointment, get a business card, or hear the proverbial "have your people call my people," your pitch better be good: You should be able to quickly and clearly communicate a general overview of the opportunity you are pursuing. Of course, if this happened to you in real life, you would not have any time to prepare a script, you would probably be more than a little nervous, and soon enough the elevator would reach its destination and your time would be up. Thus elevator pitch assignments involve well-rehearsed public speaking under a strict time limit.

If you are good at an elevator pitch in the classroom, you will be very well prepared to pitch your business convincingly at a moment's notice. With practice you would probably also do well in a business plan competition (which is one way that collegiate entrepreneurs find seed capital to get started.) In fact, the elevator pitch is so well accepted by entrepreneurship educators that several schools hold elevator pitch competitions (i.e., Princeton University, Purdue University, Wake Forest University).

If you have watched the BBC's Dragon's Den (UK) TV show (http://www.bbc.co.uk/dragonsden/), the Canadian CBC's Dragon's Den (http://www.cbc.ca/dragonsden/) or the American ABC's Shark Tank (http://abc.go.com/shows/shark-tank/), you will know that these are really exciting programs. This enthusiasm has even carried into the Web 2.0 world through the development of start-up fundraising websites. Take a few minutes to check out the finalists in startup.com's elevator pitch competition from last year (http://www.startupnation.com/elevator-pitch-2009). Think about how short, impactful video would enhance the listings found on www.raisecapital.com.

Given that you are online for this part of the course, we cannot just have you stand up and give your pitch at the front of the class-room. (Does that remind you of that old saw, "If a tree falls in the forest and nobody is around to hear it ...?") So, like the real entre-preneurs on www.vator.tv, you are going to video record your indi-vidual elevator pitch and share them online with the whole class.

With two exceptions, the video elevator pitch grading rubric is very similar to the schematic used in marking the traditional elevator pitches given by on-campus students in the same course. We must admit as educators that it is very satisfying to organize face-to-face and distance versions of the same assignment with such a high degree of over-lap. One imagines that homogeneity of learning experience would increase the odds that alumni from the two different cohorts are deriving very similar lessons and benefits. That vision is inspiring to course design. Still, there are some nuances that separate the groups: (1) given classroom time constraints, on campus students have less time (only 30 seconds ver-sus 2 minutes) to blurt their idea before the gong sounds for the next con-testant, and (2) on-campus students are not formally evaluated on their feedback to their peers (because it is verbal and therefore evanescent not semi-permanent like words typed into a chat forum). We will strive to re-center this swinging pendulum in future terms, perhaps augmenting the on-campus course with a Video elevator pitch assignment as well.

We wish to note also the trade-offs inherent in editable assignments. From the students' perspective the ability to redo a portion of their talk probably feels like a benefit (once they have developed some basic facility with video editing). The instructor, however, laments the obvious diminu-tion of public speaking practice. This omission is particularly poignant unless the course or the curriculum as a whole can somehow compensate with face-to-face training and practice in this critical business skill.

Assessment

You will be graded on your pitch and on your (150 word +/-) posting that offers positive, constructive, and specific feedback to one or more of your peers.

Here are the guidelines that will be used to grade this assignment (the following line items do not need to be covered in any specific order—common sense prevails). This assignment is out of 20 points—up to 2 points each for:

1. What is it? (What is the product/service?)
2. Who will buy it?
3. Where will they buy it?
4. Why will they buy it? (What problem does it solve for them?)
5. Who is on your team? (Who would you have working with you in an ideal world?)
6. Your offer in one sentence (How much money do you need? What are you willing to give up for that in terms of owner-ship and control? Do you seek a loan? At what interest rate?
7. Use of a powerful statistic (be sure to give credit here, for example, "a survey by XYZ demonstrated that so many mil-lions of people want blah blah blah ...")
8. Presentation quality (Poise, creativity, etc.)
9. Max. length is 2 minutes (go longer than 2 minutes and you lose these points)
10. The quality of your feedback to others

Additional direction was provided to the students regarding how to make a video and post it online. These directions have been included in Appendix A.

As can be seen in the above description, students examined critical entrepreneurial business concerns such as market strategy, competition and financing issues, then applied their knowledge in an experiential exercise by creating a videorecording of an elevator pitch that could be made to potential investors. This type of experiential learning is aligned with Kolb's (1984) premise that theory and application are both critical to effective learning.

The video elevator pitch assignment brings context. Video produc-tion requires attention to several elements that, when considered care-fully, enhance the challenge and the final product. While the wardrobe and the script are probably top of mind and a fairly straightforward affair, we found that the set was also important. Whether they were at home or on a business trip, in a hallway, in their living room, at their desk, in an office park or in a parking garage, many of these 30 stu-dents used the video aspect to their advantage by setting a more appro-priate scene than they would have been able to in a traditional classroom. The parking garage backdrop drove home the obvious nature of the opportunity to wash people's cars while they are parked in a con-

Figure 9.2.   Video enables two-person dialogue.

centrated urban area. Two videos that presented gift giving ideas (home-baked cookies and high octane experiences) were set in living rooms decorated for the holidays. Two of the clips were actually shot in elevators. One of these included a realistic two person dialogue (see Figure 9.2) that helped illustrate how scraping ice and snow off one's windshield can be such a hassle in colder climates. Including the role play in that scene leveraged the very nature of video recording; its dramatic interactions emphasized that people need a solution to windshield ice in a creative and impactful way that likely would have been awkward in a live classroom event. Together the role play and the various settings described here evidence that the video aspect of the elevator pitch assignment brings context to the deliverable, context that can increase the presentation's impact.

The video elevator pitch assignment encourages creativity. Entrepreneurship professors typically struggle with measuring creativity, one of those nebulous but essential elements to the start-up phenomenon (Baron & Shane, 2008; Hisrich, Peters, & Shepherd, 2008; Katz & Green 2007; Morris, Kuratko, & Covin, 2008). A short video can demonstrate a great deal of creativity without forcing the issue (Zelazny, 2006). Simply put, one can do more with video. One student pitched a GPS-enabled child's watch that would help parents find a lost kid quickly. The video opens with an excerpt from an old episode of *Lassie*. As he describes the device called "Lass-E" still photos of the product scroll by, providing the perfect segue to a "demo" (Gallo, 2010) in which the viewer is led through the

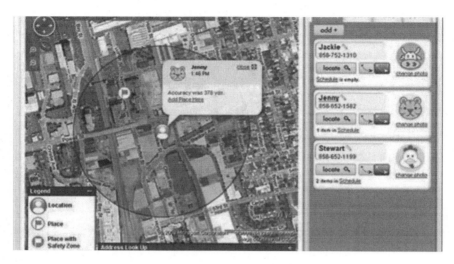

Figure 9.3.   Video elevator pitch seamlessly integrating a product demo.

screenshots and maps that a parent would see when tracking their child online (see Figure 9.3). This complete picture would have been very hard to paint in a classroom.

The video elevator pitch assignment trains students in the use of new technologies. Students in Royal Roads online bachelor's of commerce program hail from all over the world. Although most of them live in Canada—the second largest country in the world—many of them are on virtual teams with classmates who live thousands of miles away. Travel costs impede get-togethers outside of the half dozen on-campus residency weeks during the two year program. Inconvenient, maybe. Realistic, definitely. Working in virtual teams that are separated by time zones and vast distances encourages the use of Skype videoconferencing and Google Docs to mimic the way business is done in the "real world" these days. While some students (like the Lass-E inventor) handled the technical aspects of the video elevator pitch assignment with aplomb, others stayed up all night cursing their hardware and software. These struggles, though unfortunate, come in the relatively safe environment of university where failure might mean lower marks or mild embarrassment but makes no threat to one's livelihood. Furthermore, when a student masters these new communication mediums in class, the result can be very powerful. This is well illustrated in Figure 9.4 where one student recaps the funding request for his chicken wings restaurant franchise across the bottom of the screen in a firm yet subtle way (that would have seemed anything

Figure 9.4.   One student recaps his funding request in a powerful yet subtle way.

but subtle if he had been holding up a chunk of posterboard at the head of the class.)

THE VENTURE CHALLENGE

For 11 years, teams of five on-campus entrepreneurship students have been dreaming up, refining, launching, and operating a small business with only $5 seed capital. While the nature of these businesses varies, they do have one thing in common; the goal is to raise as much money as possible for charity within a 5-week period. For example, some students baked healthy dog biscuits which they then retailed to benefit the SPCA. Others held a silent auction to benefit Haiti earthquake relief. A few of the more epicurean held an iron chef competition wherein local restaurateurs prepare gourmet meals using only a microwave, a hotplate and ingredients found at the food bank. Similar learning-by-doing exercises are deployed by other universities (e.g. Bucknell University) and encouraged by educators such as Michael Morris at Oklahoma State (http://entrepreneurship.okstate.edu/classroom). In 2010, fourteen teams of four or five on-campus students earned more than $41,000 for charity through Royal Roads' Venture Challenge. Until this year, our online students, taking the same entrepreneurship course in a different format, might have read about the Venture Challenge in the local paper but they had no way of participating in this type of exercise.

Enter the *Online* Venture Challenge

As the name would imply the inaugural Online Venture Challenge endeavored to bring this same valuable learning experience to students taking their degree through distance education. In the Online Venture Challenge each four-person team brainstormed, designed, and actually created a mission-driven e-commerce website. They used a wiki (e.g. Wetpaint) to create everything-but-the-online-checkout. For tax reasons, these websites did not "go live" this first time around, but they were expected to be as turn-key as possible in all other respects. The assignment instructions can be found below:

Assignment #2: Online Venture Challenge

This assignment is comprised of two components that together will be 30% of your final grade:

1.   Mission-driven e-commerce website/wiki (15%)
2.   Investment presentation (15%).

Venture Challenge History

Royal Roads University launched the Venture Challenge more than a decade ago. In what has become a tradition of social entrepreneurship, on-campus ENMN 313 students have dreamed up, refined, launched and operated small businesses that "make a difference while making a dollar." Each team starts with only $5 seed capital and has 5 weeks to generate revenue, all of which goes to charity. Last year's on-campus cohort raised more than $30,000 while having all kinds of fun, and learning about start-ups in a very hands-on way.

Introducing The Online Venture Challenge

Your online cohort will pioneer the venture challenge experience, customized for online participation; The Online Venture Challenge. In the latter part of this course your team will brainstorm, design, and actually create a mission-driven e-commerce website. You will not have $5, because you don't need it. You will use a wiki to create everything-but-the-online-checkout. For tax purposes, we do not want your websites to "go live," but we do want them to be as turn-key as possible in all other respects.

During your on-campus residency in February, your team will give a presentation about your website to a live audience who will judge your concept using the Venture Intelligence Quotient framework

(Mainprize et al., 2007). After this class is over, the websites that hold the most promise may be taken "live" under the auspices of the student group SIFE (Students in Free Enterprise). They might also form an excellent basis for the business plan you will write in your ENMN 420 Entrepreneurial Projects course.

Your Mission

To encourage maximum creativity the rules of the game are few: In the simplest of terms, you are to build a mission-driven, e-commerce website that is ready to launch in all respects *except* payment processing.

Mission

The "mission" you adopt is up to you. Check out these two very different reasons to purchase livestock online. Heifer International (http://www.heifer.org) would have you buy a goat to help a (human) family in need. Contrastingly, the WWF (World Wildlife Fund) wants you to buy a goat to help a leopard (http://wwf.panda.org/how_you_can_help/gifts/products/goat/).

Business Model

A business model is a description of how you make money. You and your team will brainstorm the business model that you will implement in this assignment. Many different business models might support the same mission. For example, Kashless.org relies on the support of advertisers to maintain the support of their site which keeps used items (sofas, baby toys, flower pots, etc.) out of the landfill by connecting them with new owners. Babyplays.com keeps toys out of the landfill by offering a rental service.

Profit Orientation

Yours may be either a for-profit or a nonprofit venture. Notably, www.microplace.com and www.kiva.org do roughly the same thing—connecting microfinance lenders and borrowers. Kiva is a nonprofit, whereas microplace is owned by eBay (and is obviously not a nonprofit!).

Because this course is a fundamental element of a bachelor of commerce degree that is offered exclusively to working professionals who each have several years of full-time work experience, we expected this assignment to produce the opposite of a circus. For the most part, that is what we got. Whereas trapeze artists are typically described by carnival barkers as performing, "live without a net," these seven websites could be best described inversely as, "on the net without going live." There were two graded aspects of this assignment; (1) the website itself; and (2) the in-person presentation of the associated investment opportunity (during exam week, on-site.)

Without real sales figures to measure performance, we enlisted the help of two groups of experts; scholars of teaching technologies and the venture capital investment process. Royal Roads University's Centre for Teaching and Educational Technologies (CTET) supports professors in online course design and further aids instructors in the mechanics of course delivery. As specialists in using the internet to convey new information clearly they were the perfect partners we needed to help generate the first part of the grading rubric below. It is also worth mentioning that including them in the discussion around the creation of both of these assignments greatly increased interdepartmental goodwill.

Evaluating the second part of this assignment required a different expertise. The appeal of each of these business concepts as a potential investment was evaluated through the use of a tool created by Brent Mainprize, a scholar of the venture capital process, and a well-regarded entrepreneurship expert in the community at large. Notably, these same 15 VIQ (Venture Intelligence Quotient) criteria are used to judge final presentations made by on-campus students in this course.

To enhance networking and learning opportunities for both student cohorts, a special event was coordinated wherein the on-campus students graded the presentations made by the online students. Given the last minute nature of planning for this event, and the different cohorts' schedules, this evaluation was unfortunately only made one way. In other words, the online students were not afforded the opportunity to watch and analyze presentations made by the on-campus students. The instructors explained how and why this decision was made, but nevertheless suffered (justifiably) in some parts of the course evaluations. Next year this inter-cohort exchange will be better scheduled to allow reciprocal constructive criticism.

Assessment Criteria

Part 1—Mission-Driven e-Commerce Website (Wiki)

Site Design/Layout—3 points

- general layout & use of space: clarity + simplicity over complexity + density. Remember: white space helps people read ;

- ease of use—users can easily navigate the site and find information; and
- visual appeal (design does not detract from message/content). Aim for professional appearance (clean lines and simple color schemes are better than being overly "busy."

Content—9 points

- specific mission or goals clear (3 points);
- clarity of grammar and use of language—spelling, punctuation , et cetera. No spelling or usage errors (2 points);
- absence of duplication and repetition (2 points); and
- write for the web, not for an academic paper (2 points). You might be interested in how users read on the web (hint: they don't, they scan). Usability guru Jacob Neilson (1997) has lots to say about this stuff here http://www.useit.com/alertbox/9710a.html

Site Functionality (connected to goals)—3 points

- contact info—how can they get in touch? Information should exist on the site and be easy to find;
- e-biz element—how can they give you money? (mockup only, not functional, but it should be visually placed on the site as though it were real); and
- it all works—absence of dead ends, dead links, and outdated pages—everything on the site works (except the shopping cart).

Part 2—Presentation (in class, during residency week)

- Each team will have 15 minutes (+ 5 minutes for Q&A) to present their business concept to a live audience during the last week of class (which is also the start of your second residency); and
- Your investment presentation will be graded on the basis of how well your proposed venture scores along the 15 Venture Intelligence Quotient (VIQ) criteria (see Appendix B) delineated in your Unit 4 reading by Mainprize et. al. (2007). Simply addressing each criterion will not earn you the point for that line item; your business concept needs to score well (5 or higher) on each 9-point scale to get full credit.

Wiki

- For this assignment, you are to use a wiki to develop your team project. We recommend: WetPaint Wiki available at www.wetpaint.com

Your task:

- assign one team member to create your team wiki;
- be sure to add your team members as editors/administrators;
- also, please add your instructor (geoff.archer@royalroads.ca) as editor/administrator; and
- consider naming your wiki something that relates to your topic (i.e., something other than "Team # wiki").

NOTE: If you want to use wiki other than WetPaint, you are free to do so—here is a list of free wiki tools http://c4lpt.co.uk/Directory/Tools/web.html.

The Online Venture Challenge assignment generated viable businesses. Seven teams created mission driven e-commerce websites. Many of those appeared viable, and scored well according to the grading criteria outlined above. The most promising business concepts developed for this assignment included; an organic T-shirt business that offered unique designs to support various causes, an organic seed and plant vending system that helped parents raise money for their local elementary schools, a nonprofit organization that received and redistributes quality used baby related items to low income mothers (Figure 9.5), and a socially oriented travel business (Figure 9.6).

Watch this space. Notably two teams had more advanced web development expertise and chose not to use the wetpaint wiki. One of those teams (whose work is shown in Figure 9.6) created quite a stir during the last few days of class. Their presentation was so effective that at least two classmates offered to invest five figure sums. While the equity structure behind the business is private, and unknown to your authors, we can tell you that the protagonist behind www.govoluntouring.com has begun the process of phasing out his day job in order to pursue this opportunity full-time. This social media project is an example of the high quality of the businesses created in the spring of 2010. Buoyed by the success of this pilot, we plan on raising the bar next time around: The Online Venture Challenge will include check-out functionality so that student teams can compete on a revenue basis. Unleashing social capitalism in this way should also greatly increase the learning experience. Students will have to work

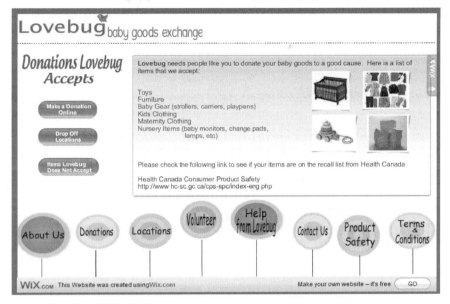

Figure 9.5.   A mission-driven e-commerce website built with a free Wetpaint template.

Figure 9.6.   GoVoluntouring.com did not use the Wetpaint wiki.

out answers to critical questions like, "how do we efficiently collect and redistribute used baby goods through the Internet? How can we greatly increase awareness with no budget and severe time constraints? What are the obstacles to increased usage of our service?" Quickly it will be apparent that talking about a business concept and actually building that business concept are very different.

SUMMARY: SOCIAL MEDIA ENGAGES ONLINE ENTREPRENEURSHIP STUDENTS

These two new assignments have improved Royal Roads University's Entrepreneurial Expertise course. Course evaluations were positive overall, a step up from earlier terms. They included telling comments such as "great job adding more practical content." Several students mentioned "the practical elevator pitch and the online venture challenge" as the most positive aspects of the course. In our observations the Video Elevator Pitch facilitated bonding among far flung cohort members while affording students new ways to integrate context and creativity into a professional looking (though do-it-yourself) asynchronous presentation. Just as Mosey and Wright (2007) theorized that the ability to develop social capital reduced barriers to venture development for academic entrepreneurs, we propose that exercises for online students, which take advantage of social media, could greatly reduce barriers to learning. The implications of embedding social media, such as wikis and websites, into courses for online students are manifold. As evidenced in the entrepreneurial expertise course, students were able to develop relationships, build trust and take risks when provided with exercises that made use of multi-media, as opposed to purely text-based assignments. They engaged in the exercises with enthusiasm, provided meaningful feedback to each other, and found creative and thought provoking solutions.

The Online Venture Challenge pilot created several promising business concepts, one of which will soon be coming to fruition. Acknowledging the great difference between building a compelling website and setting up a process to make sales and satisfy customers, we consider this first run a resounding success. This fall we look forward to adding real check-out functionality that will test just how good these socially responsible start-ups really are. Perhaps next year we will invite you and your students to build your own sites and join us in a friendly competition, and experience for yourselves how injecting social-media into online courses makes all the difference.

APPENDIX A

How to Make a Video

Technically, these are the essential steps:

1. record the video;
2. put it online (upload it somewhere); and
3. provide a link so others can see it.

Recording the Video

Your approach will depend on what equipment you have (e.g., web cam, digital camera (with sound recording), digital video camera, phone, etc) but here are some general resources to help.

YouTube: How to make a video (http://www.YouTube.com/t/howto_makevideo)

- general advice on getting started; and
- some advice on file formats.

Putting it Online

How to upload to YouTube (http://www.ehow.com/video_2201763 _uploading-videos-YouTube.html)

- a tutorial on how to upload an existing file;
- advice on size (max: 100mb) and file types (mov, wmv, avi, mpg are most common);
- advice on how to make your video easy to find (or not!);
- advice on how to make your video private or public ("broadcast options"); and
- a series about how to make a video if you want to see more.

How to make a video: using Quick Capture on YouTube (http://www.YouTube.com/watch?v=exFI7NlFqNc)

- explains how to use a web cam + the "quick capture" feature on YouTube (i.e. you record right in to YouTube); and

- blends step 1 (recording) and step 2 (putting it online). This might be the easiest way to go.

Flickr.com is another storage option (handy if you already use Flickr)—you can upload 90 sec./150mb files there.

There are lots of other places you can put your video: http://www.c4lpt.co.uk/Directory/Tools/media.html

NOTE: If you believe that you cannot post your video elevator pitch (and have a really good/entertaining/believable excuse) please contact your instructor at least 48 hours before the deadline to make alternate arrangements (which may involve pitching the class live via Elluminate online meeting software.)"

APPENDIX B

VIQ Criteria

1. Innovation;
2. Intellectual property protection;
3. Market receptiveness;
4. Industry attractiveness;
5. Personal aspirations;
6. Social capital;
7. Revenue model;
8. Margins;
9. Cash cycle;
10. Value proposition;
11. Target market;
12. Sustainable advantage;
13. Ability to execute;
14. Sales break-even; and
15. Cash break-even (Mainprize et al., 2007).

REFERENCES

Aggarwal, A. (2000). *Web-based learning and teaching technologies: Opportunities and challenges*. London, England: Idea Group.

Baron, R. A., & Shane, S. A. (2008). *Entrepreneurship: A process perspective* (2nd ed.). Mason, OH: Thomson.

Barringer, B. R. (2009). *Preparing effective business plans.* New York, NY: McGraw Hill.

Gallo, C. (2010). *The presentation secrets of Steve Jobs: How to be insanely great in front of any audience.* New York, NY: McGraw Hill.

Hasler-Waters, L., & Napier, W. (2002). Building & supporting student team collaboration in the virtual classroom. *Quarterly Review of Distance Education, 3*(3), 345-352.

Hisrich, R. D., Peters, M. P., & Shepherd, D. A. (2008). *Entrepreneurship* (7th ed.). New York, NY: McGraw Hill.

Jarvenpaa, S. L., Knoll, K., & Leidner, D. E. (1998). Is anybody out there? *Journal of Management Information Systems, 14*(4), 29-64.

Katz, J. A., & Green, R. P. (2007). *Entrepreneurial small business.* New York, NY: McGraw Hill.

Kolb, D. A. (1984). *Experiential learning: Experience as the source of learning and development.* Englewood Cliffs, NJ: Prentice-Hall.

Mainprize, B., Dorofeeva, K., & Hindle, N. (2007) *Venture intelligence: How smart investors and entrepreneurs evaluate new ventures.* Vancouver, British Columbia, Canada: Venture Intelligence.

McConnell, D. (2006). *E-learning groups and communities* (1st ed.). Maidenhead, England: Open University Press.

McInnerney, J. M., & Roberts, T. S. (2004). Online learning: Social interaction and the creation of a sense of community. *Educational Technology & Society, 7*(3), 73-81.

Morris, M. H., Kuratko, D. F., & Covin, J. G. (2008). *Corporate entrepreneurship & innovation* (2nd ed.). Mason, OH: Thomson.

Mosey, S., & Wright, M. (2007). From human capital to social capital: A Longitudinal study of technology-based academic entrepreneurs. *Entrepreneurship: Theory & Practice, 31*(6), 909-935.

Neilson, J. (1997) *How users read on the web.* Retrieved from http://www.useit.com/alertbox/9710a.html

Zelazny, G. (2006). *Say it with presentations.* New York, NY: McGraw Hill.

CHAPTER 10

INTERSECTION OF REGULATIONS, FACULTY DEVELOPMENT, AND SOCIAL MEDIA

Limitations of Social Media in For-Profit Online Classes

Hamid H. Kazeroony

In for-profit higher education (HE) institutions, the intersection of regulatory environment, faculty development requirements for improving performance online, and effectiveness and utility of social media in creation and transfer of knowledge, in accordance with accrediting agencies, determines the degree that social media can be used. Recent regulatory upheavals in the United States, challenges in faculty development to meet the appropriate outcomes in virtual environment while meeting institutional missions, measuring learning outcomes by students using social media, particularly, in for-profit institutions in online teaching where innovation is frowned on by regulators, utilization of social media for teaching presents formidable limitations. Despite the limitations, I will review the extant literature and

Cutting-Edge Social Media Approaches to Business Education:
Teaching With LinkedIn, Facebook, Twitter, Second Life, and Blogs, pp. 179–193
Copyright © 2010 by Information Age Publishing
All rights of reproduction in any form reserved.

regulatory sources and discuss when, where, and to what extent social media may be used.

This chapter will first present the current regulatory landscape and how it is constraining new approaches to teaching such as use of social media. Second, it will discuss challenges of faculty development in using social media in for-profit online environment to produce the necessary competencies and skills for each learner as required by regulations. Finally, in light of regulations and faculty development challenges, this chapter determines the extent that social media can be used to teach in online environment. Based on these findings, the chapter will explicate some of the regulatory and educational ramification of social media in for-profit online teaching.

TERMINOLOGY

Regulations implies any action by governments, regulatory agencies, accrediting bodies, peer and/or professional bodies constraining or requiring for-profit institutions to abide by a particular rule for conducting their business in HE. Faculty development in the context of our discussions connotes continuous professional activities in enabling faculty members in online environment to become: (a) student centered through understanding learners' needs (educationally) and (b) learning centered by applying the appropriate andragogical methods in facilitating learning and transferring knowledge by helping students to analyze theories and practice their application. Social media includes: (1) blogs, wikis, organized networks, applications, RSS Reader, social bookmarking, and any other website pages which provide opportunity for individual interactions with others, and (2) interaction of individuals with individuals or individuals and groups using the internet as the medium of communication globally. Online learning refers to courses or institutions that use internet based learning management systems (LMS) in conducting all facets of class work asynchronously. Currently 53% (795) of for-profit institutions offer courses and/or degrees in online format (U.S. Department of Education, Institute for Educational Sciences, 2006-2007). Web 2 refers to new web structure where the content initiators can collaborate with participants in the discussions, blogs, social bookmarking, and other web venues to generate a new stream of information, synthesis them, and create knowledge.

REGULATORY LANDSCAPE

Regulatory landscape encompasses three levels: Public interest and governmental approach, HE accrediting associations/agencies (which could be used by institutions as a tool for self-regulation), and specific requirements by various entities for particular requirements to be met by institutions in conducting their classes or meeting number of instructional hours. Each level provides a particular perspective on online, for profit institutions and the requirements which must be met in every online course. Therefore, addressing the most general view of regulatory landscape would be most appropriate as a starting point for the purpose of our discussions.

Public Interest

In the United States, although the Department of Education uses the recommendations of independent bodies for accrediting higher learning institutions, it requires each accrediting body to ensure that faculty operates within his/her respective institutional mission, assists with retention, adheres to appropriate licensing criteria as set by various professional associations, and provides the means for students' gainful employment after graduation (U.S. Department of Education, Financial Aid for Post Secondary Education, 2010). The U.S. Department of Education, Center for Technology in Learning (2009) in a recent meta-analysis suggested that online or combination of online and face-to-face learning offers slight advantage over the purely face-to-face learning in HE, setting the stage for how regional accrediting bodies conduct their review of many for-profit educational establishments who essentially rely on online coursework for conducting their teaching activities. In the United States, an elaborate maze of bureaucracy oversees the enforcement of higher education rules:

- The Office of Postsecondary Education (OPE) formulates federal postsecondary education policy and administers programs that address critical national needs in support of our mission to increase access to quality postsecondary education.
- Policy, Planning, and Innovation (PPI) develops postsecondary education policy and legislative proposals and is responsible for budget formulation and forecasting for programs administered by OPE.
- PPI leads OPE strategic planning and is responsible for developing program performance measures. The Program Oversight Staff is

responsible for overseeing program monitoring throughout OPE. PPI is responsible for a number of data collections and for developing the Secretary's Annual Report on Teacher Quality (U.S. Department of Education, OPE, 2010).

However, the U.S. Department of Education defers the actual accreditation to regional accrediting bodies as the law mandates. Each of the six accrediting bodies view professional development and pedagogical training as one of the important pillars of the accreditation as explained by their charter (U.S. Department of Education, Financial Aid for Post Secondary Education, 2010). More specifically, faculty development is driven by different factors across the Atlantic: In the United States, it is the result of the policies apropos competition and cost effectiveness whereas in Europe, it is the result of competitiveness in excellence and public good versus faculty power (Organization of Economic Co-operation and Development report, Meeting of OECD Education Ministers, 2006a). Europe focuses on factors such as: (a) internal quality assurance, (b) external quality assurance, and (c) external quality assurance agencies in addressing faculty developmental needs (European Commission on Education and Training, 2010). Higher education is attracting unprecedented public attention across the OECD. In Germany a competition to create universities of excellence is fuelling debate; in France discussions continue about struggling mainstream universities versus more well-endowed grandes écoles; in the United Kingdom there is a debate about education as a public good versus faculties as market-oriented enterprises; and in the United States public focus continues on accessibility, competition, and costs (OECD Insights, Higher Education for a Changing World, 2006b). Additionally, various international HE associations such as the Association to Advance Collegiate Schools of Business take a more stringent view of the process requirements (Romero, 2008).

HE Accreditation Requirements

Accrediting agencies' rules usually covers various topics. For the purpose of our discussion, we will confine our discussions to those areas with most relevance to faculty development, student learning and needs, online courses, and for-profit institutions. As the first decade of the twenty-first century was underway, one proposal suggested that accrediting community should seek out collective approach to rigor and student learning outcome, conceptual framework, and resources to address students' needs as consumers of higher education to provide quality education supported by explicit evidence and learning outcome assessments

(Ewell, 2001). In reality, accrediting bodies have determined that each institution must provide administrative infrastructure to support students' needs as consumers outside the class and create rigorous audit process to ensure quality education. Additionally, accrediting bodies have continued to require faculty development to enhance teaching and learning necessary to provide expected outcomes to address the future professional needs of employers and create value for students. Currently, each regional accrediting body, as evidenced by their standards, adheres to the proposed criteria by Ewell (2001).

For Profit Online Requirements

On January 11, 2010 (the assistant secretary for Office of Post Secondary Education), in a letter to the Council for Higher Education Accreditation executive board, provided heightened level of clarity in distinctions for distance educational institutions (where online for profit institutions operate) from traditional universities and asked for all member accrediting bodies to comply with new requirements. Accrediting bodies were asked to establish clear rigorous standards for (a) educational quality, (b) substantive interaction between student and faculty, and (c) systems and process for securing student data and verification of activities are met.

CHALLENGES OF FACULTY DEVELOPMENT IN FOR-PROFIT ONLINE ENVIRONMENT

Within the last 5 years, faculty development has been facing unique challenges. Online technology has changed the role of faculty, the rules of engagement in the online forums, and the way each faculty interacts and communicates ideas to transfer knowledge apropos the influences of social, psychological, and affective factors on learners' learning (Ali et al., 2005; Shaffer, Lackey, & Bolling, 2006; Zheng, Perez, Williamson, Flygare, 2008). New faculty members who have been exposed to wide use of social media prior to their arrival at the teaching scene had to learn the teaching and researching methods from colleagues who are about to retire and have had little exposure to digital world (Diaz et al., 2009). The evolving nature of online higher education has led to changes in relationship and roles of faculty and learners where faculty should become designers and learners become information gatherers and analyzers (McIsaac & Craft, 2003). In online environment, where learning replaces teaching, faculty development includes instructional approach and technology utilization (Barker, 2003).

There is a general perception that anyone with a graduate degree from an accredited institution is capable of teaching in HE (Minter, 2009). In the twenty-first century where old industrial models of teaching should be abandoned and replaced with collaborative learning and collaborative knowledge production (Tapscott & Williams, 2010) examination of social media as a part of collaboration becomes imperative. In addition, to effectively support faculty development in online environment, two conditions must exist. First, (a) faculty must have prior knowledge of basic tools such as document manipulation and understanding of internet functionality, (b) institutions should offer formal training frequently, (c) online communities must be created to enable faculty share ideas with colleagues and mediate feedback by peers, (d) course designs should correspond to faculty learning in formal training, (e) and continuing institutional assessment for faculty developments' effects on teaching and students' learning (Fang, 2007). Second, the online class requires: (a) social presence of each participant, (b) cognitive and constructivist approach, and (c) faculty presence and effective interaction (Arbaugh, 2007; Arbaugh & Hwang, 2005). Such efforts should be complemented with integration of curriculum design, teaching method, and, available technology (Kinuthia, 2005).

Faculty development, in general, requires addressing several factors. First, learning self-efficacy must be addressed through furthering individual faculty's capacity to positively affect learning outcome for each learner (Burton, Bamberry, & Harris-Boundy, 2005). Second, learning, as a part of faculty development and by students, must be contextualized within the existing learning theories. Learning theories are not necessarily exclusive domains at a philosophical level. Among such theories are:

- Experiential learning: Where learning can be described as a process (versus outcome), drawing on student's innate beliefs about the world, resolving the conflicts in perceiving the same world from different learners' perspectives and creating a holistic view, and allowing learners construct knowledge (versus transmitting the knowledge) (Kolb & Kolb, 2005).
- Faculty as independent worker (with no supervisor), when trained, can decide on when, how, and to what extent transfer learning to apply to teaching (Yelon, Sheppard, Sleight, & Ford, 2004).

To help learners become engaged in the process of knowledge acquisition, faculty should be trained in transforming learning by incorporating technology in teaching (Morales & Roig, 2002). One study suggested that online faculty in particular require training on the nature of participation and feedback, quantitatively and qualitatively (Blignaut & Trollip, 2003).

In general, faculty development is only a small component, yet powerful part of the equation which should be addressed in relating to social needs at large (Ischinger, 2006). The U.S. Office of Post Secondary Education (2010) issued a *Dear Colleague Letter* to the regional accrediting agencies, explaining faculty development and support requirements for granting any distance education accreditation. A longitudinal study confirmed that it is possible to provide training in transfer of knowledge for application of concepts by professors who are essentially independent workers in online environment (Yelon et al., 2004). There are several challenges in faculty development that deserve particular attention apropos regulatory environment, developmental needs, and opportunities presented by social media utility: (a) engagement and responsiveness in online environment as the first step in facilitating learning (Blignaut & Trollip, 2003), (b) assuring quality for longevity, prestige, fulfilling requirements, continuous improvement, adding value to the process and remaining student-centered, and addressing new skill acquisition requirements by learners (Clovey & Oladipo, 2008; Dew, 2009; Lavoie & Rosman, 2007; Marek, 2009; McLean, Cilliers, & Van Wyk, 2008; Stigmar, 2008), (c) responding to the requirements by accrediting agencies for specialized degree programs to provide comprehensive training for online teaching (Barker, 2003; Dyrbye, Cumyn, Day, & Heflin, 2009; Steinert et al., 2009), and (d) helping the faculty to become a resource for students learning online (McIsaac & Craft, 2003). The training provided for online faculty will support their activities, create a community of practitioners, provides guidance on performance focused teaching, and develops their skills for knowledge transfer (Fang, 2007; Santovec, 2005). Studies of professors have confirmed these challenges and training needs (Shea, 2007; Shea, Pickett, & Chun Sau, 2005).

SOCIAL MEDIA OPPORTUNITIES AND LIMITATIONS

In the twenty-first century where old industrial models of teaching should be abandoned and replaced with collaborative learning and collaborative knowledge production (Tapscott & Williams, 2010) review of social media as a part of collaboration becomes imperative. There are two opposing camps when addressing social media: the educators who believe social media is inherently counterproductive to learning and those educators who view it as a method of pollinating information in creating individual knowledge (Walling, 2009). In a recent international conference, some educators defended the role of social media in opening various channels for global research while others saw social media as a way of diluting the value of elite research by true scholars (Labi, 2010). In addressing self-direct andragogical approach in HE social media presents a unique opportunity (Dale & Pymm, 2009; Väljataga & Fiedler, 2009).

There is a rapid expansion of social media utility among corporations (Barnes & Mattson, 2008). Social media as a platform allowing individuals to have their own voice is here to stay (Bailey, 2010). Social media allows text to be supplemented with images and sound in enhancing learning (Alvermann, 2008). Social media has democratized content creation ("Revolutionizing Knowledge Work," 2008). Social media can be effectively explored to design new self-directed learning approaches (Pata, 2009). Higher education, by building a two-way bridge between formal learning in classrooms and informal learning taking place using the social media can enhance and elevate the learning outcome for the more complex twenty-first century learner (Gibson, 2008).

Social media remains subject to defining is etiquette (Armstrong, 2009), its content generating capability and human interactivity remains primitive despite Web 2 developments (Swongwoon et al., 2010), inefficient in identifying and tagging texts in complex cases where human cognition in recognizing meanings become important (Savage, 2010), difficult to connect to a fixed syllabus and hence pre-determined learning outcome (Taylor, 2009). Although learners work with social media, they should learn the strategy behind working with it (Pasquinucci, 2009). Social media use pattern by initiators of conversations and followers indicates that the top 10% of Twitter users produced over 90% of the content (Schonfeld, 2009) which suggests a small group dominate content creation and any possible knowledge that is created. Social media conversation threads recently have suggested that such enterprise may be a growing concern with plagiarism rather than creating knowledge and deeper understanding of a subject (Young, 2010).

Various indicators suggest a strong influence by social media in training the next generation of professionals ("Training Professionals," 2009). Social media despite its shortcomings allow new forms of interconnectivity through exchanges of audio and visual content in addition to text creating new learning possibilities (Sweeny, 2009). Despite skeptics' view of social media, it provides meaningful utility for construction of shared knowledge (Pachler & Daly, 2009). For example, social media through search engines can provide a powerful tool to understanding the way content seekers are searching for particular information and determine demographic characteristics to better connect the learner and the source (Social Website Analyzer, 2008).

In general, social media presents a unique opportunity to open source material. One argument in favor of social media use is that epistemologically, provides a community based collaborative pathway to acquisition and application of knowledge enabling novice learners become proficient in grasping and using knowledge (Eijkman, 2008), providing divergent social learning ecosystems through integration of technology (Brooks, 2009), offering an effective tool for knowledge management based on theories of communities of practice, transactive memory, boundary spanning, and social capital (Parise, 2009). One argument against using social media is possible structural organization and inadequate security to prevent spam and protect data (Finin et al., 2008).

THE INTERSECTION POINT

The intersection of regulations, faculty development to enhance professional performance, and utilization of social media to enhance learning styles of the twenty-first century in online for-profit institutions is a difficult point and a moving target at best under current conditions. Regulatory environment requires security-protected LMS where students can learn and faculty through engagement can help students construct knowledge, arrive at an understanding of the subject matter, and earn their degree as outlined by institutional mission and accredited by regional accrediting bodies and other licensing officials. In for-profit online universities, the requirements dictate the appropriate infrastructure to provide faculty support services such as developmental plans to familiarize them for working with relevant LMS technologies and the nature of engagement. Additionally, faculty performance requires monitoring and training follow-ups to ensure regulatory requirements are met quantitatively and qualitatively. For example, as a starting point, University of Phoenix (n.d., FAQs to Become a Faculty Member) states that each prospective faculty must take an online certification course which requires 4 weeks of training and 5 days of active participation to become eligible for hire. Other universities, such as South and Argosy Universities, as explained by their respective online faculty expectation documents (South University, n.d.), presents additional training requirements and follow-up mentoring for each faculty. Other for-profit online universities require similar certification as a condition of employment with additional professional developmental courses as required by each college within their universities. These stringent initial and subsequent developmental trainings are established to (a) make sure each faculty knows the specific expectation for engagement in courses and (b) to establish guidelines for faculty presence in each course within a given LMS to validate the nature and rigor of teaching and learning as required by accrediting bodies. Therefore, the adherence to regulations and the need for faculty development in for profit online environment make the point of intersection with utilization of social media as a teaching and learning tool extremely difficult to attain.

In physical classrooms where instructors attend and verify their presence in a particular location, social media is used as an additional tool to help learners with quick access to their instructors and for faculty to communicate developing relevant information that become available to learners. However, in virtual environment where a secured record of interaction and engagement of each faculty is required to prove intellectual interactivity and engagement by the faculty and the learners, social media can only be used to the extent that can be incorporated within a given LMS while directing all communications through an specific course within that LMS. In addition, many social media are open source without appropriate security and in online environment would e technically challenging at this time to verify each student's input and provide credit for them as they complete their assignments.

Retrospectively, examining the usefulness of social media as addressed in this chapter, one should admit that social media is a viable and democratic tool which can virtually liberate individuals from the traditional confine of university walls to create knowledge. Also, current LMS used by for-profit online universities are a form of social media that allow for sharing, communicating, and disseminating information where faculty through rigorous training and development learns to work, engage, and interact with students to create knowledge. Nonetheless, the intersection of the three elements in for-profit online universities: Regulations, faculty development, and social media (Facebook, Twitter, etc.) is difficult to attain unless regulatory environment or LMS technology can change to accommodate new realities of twenty-first century education.

Further research is required to provide the community of administrators, publishers, and peer reviewers (who perform accrediting functions for various accrediting bodies) in higher education more details about the intersection point. Additional qualitative research is needed to establish a common ground for what should be the intersection point. Once an in depth understanding of the perceptions is established, empirical studies should be conducted to examine the possibility of convergence of perceptions among regulators, accrediting bodies, administrators, faculty, technologists, and publishers to establish a point of intersection for implementing social media in for-profit institutions' online courses.

REFERENCES

Ali, N., Hodson-Carlton, K., Ryan, M., Flowers, J., Rose, M., & Wayda, V. (2005). Online education: needs assessment for faculty development. *Journal of Con-*

tinuing Education in Nursing, 36(1), 32-38. Retrieved from CINAHL Plus with Full Text database.

Alvermann, D. (2008). Why bother theorizing adolescents' online literacies for classroom practice and research? *Journal of Adolescent & Adult Literacy, 52*(1), 8-19. Retrieved from Education Research Complete database.

Arbaugh, J. (2007). Does the community of inquiry framework predict outcomes in online MBA courses? *Academy of Management Proceedings*, 1-6. Retrieved from AOM Archive database.

Arbaugh, J., & Hwang, A. (2005). A confirmatory study of "teaching presence" in online MBA courses. *Academy of Management Proceedings*, A1-A6. Retrieved from AOM Archive database.

Argosy University, Online Faculty Expectations. (n.d.). Retrieved from http://online.argosy.edu/documents/auo_faculty_hr_packet.pdf

Armstrong, L. (2009). Think before you talk, tweet or text: The need for technology etiquette guidelines. *Public Relations Tactics, 16*(8), 10. Retrieved from Business Source Complete database.

Bailey, H. (2010). Gadgets. *Legacy (National Association for Interpretation), 21*(1), 32-35. Retrieved from Education Research Complete database.

Barnes, N., & Mattson, E. (2008). Social media in the Inc. 500: The first longitudinal study. *Journal of New Communications Research, 3*(1), 74-78. Retrieved from Communication & Mass Media Complete database.

Barker, A. (2003). Faculty development for teaching online: Educational and technological issues. *Journal of Continuing Education in Nursing, 34*(6), 273-278. Retrieved from Education Research Complete database.

Blignaut, S. A., & Trollip, S. R. (2003). Measuring faculty participation in asynchronous discussion forums. *Journal of Education for Business, 78*(6), 347-353.

Brooks, L. (2009). Social learning-by-design: The role of social media. *Knowledge Quest, 37*(5), 58-60. Retrieved May 3, 2010, from ProQuest Education Journals.

Burton, J. P., Bamberry, N., & Harris-Boundy, J. (2005). Developing personal teaching efficacy in new teachers in university settings. *Academy of Management Learning & Education*, 4(2), 160-173. Retrieved from ABI/INFORM Global.

Clovey, R., & Oladipo, O. (2008). The VITA Program: A catalyst for improving accounting education. *The CPA Journal, 78*(12), 60-65.

Dale, S., & Pymm, J. M. (2009). Podagogy: The iPod as a learning technology. *Active Learning in Higher Education, 10*(1), 84-96. doi: 10.1177/1469787408100197

Dew, J. (2009). Quality issues in higher education. *The Journal for Quality and Participation, 32*(1), 4-9

Diaz, V., Garrett, P., Kinley, E., Moore, J., Schwartz, C., & Kohrman, P. (2009). Development for the 21st century. *EDUCAUSE Review, 44*(3), 46. Retrieved from ABI/INFORM Global.

Dyrbye, L., Cumyn, A., Day, H., & Heflin, M. (2009). A qualitative study of physicians' experiences with online learning in a masters degree program: benefits, challenges, and proposed solutions. *Medical Teacher, 31*(2), e40-6. Retrieved from CINAHL Plus with Full Text database.

Eijkman, H. (2008). Web 2.0 as a non-foundational network-centric learning spacer. *Campus - Wide Information Systems, 25*(2), 93-104. Retrieved from ABI/ INFORM Global.

Ewell, P. T. (2001). *Accreditation and student learning outcomes: A proposed point of departure.* Paper presented by National Center for Higher Education Management Systems. Council for Higher Education Accreditation. Retrieved from CHEA website: http://www.chea.org/chea_dev/pdf/EwellSLO_Sept2001.pdf

European Commission on Education and Training (2010). Retrieved from: http:// ec.europa.eu/education/study-in-europe/overview_en.html

Fang, B. (2007). A performance-based development model for online Faculty. *Performance Improvement, 46*(5), 17-24. Retrieved from ABI/INFORM Global.

Finin, T., Joshi, A., Kolari, P., Java, A., Kale, A., & Karandikar, A. (2008). The information ecology of social media and online communities. *AI Magazine, 29*(3), 77-92. Retrieved from ABI/INFORM Global.

Gibson, D. (2008, October). Editorial: Make it a two-way connection: A response to "Connecting informal and formal learning experiences in the age of participatory media." *Contemporary Issues in Technology & Teacher Education*, 305-309. Retrieved from Education Research Complete database.

Ischinger, B. (2006). Higher education for a changing world. *OECD Observer* (No. 255). Retrieved from http://www.oecdobserver.org/news/fullstory.php/aid/1868 /Higher _education_for_a_changing_world.html

Kinuthia, W. (2005). Planning faculty development for successful implementation of web-based instruction. *Campus - Wide Information Systems, 22*(4), 189-200. Retrieved from ABI/INFORM Global.

Kolb, A. Y., & Kolb, D. A. (2005). Learning styles and learning spaces: Enhancing experiential learning in higher education. *Academy of Management Learning & Education*, 4(2), 193-212. Retrieved from ABI/INFORM Global.

Labi, A. (2010, March 25). Education leaders gather in London to imagine the new global university. *The Chronicle of Higher Education*. Retrieved from http:// chronicle. com/article/Education-Leaders-Gather-in/64843/

Lavoie, D., & Rosman A. J. (2007). Using active student-centered learning-based instructional design to develop faculty and improve course design, delivery, and evaluation. *Issues in Accounting Education, 22*(1), 105-118.

Marek, K. (2009). Learning to teach online: Creating a culture of support for faculty. *Journal of Education for Library and Information Science, 50*(4), 275-292. Retrieved from Research Library.

McIsaac, M., & Craft, E. (2003). Faculty development: Using distance education effectively in the classroom. *Computers in the Schools, 20*(3), 41-49. Retrieved from Education Research Complete database.

McLean, M., Cilliers, F., & Van Wyk, J. M. (2008). Faculty development: Yesterday, today and tomorrow. *Medical Teacher, 30*(6), 555-584. doi: 10.1080/ 01421590802109834

Minter, R. (2009). The paradox of faculty development. *Contemporary Issues in Education Research, 2*(4), 65-70. Retrieved from ABI/INFORM Global.

Morales, L., & Roig, G. (2002). Connecting a technology faculty development program with student learning. *Campus - Wide Information Systems, 19*(2), 67-72. Retrieved from ABI/INFORM Global.

Organization of Economic Co-operation and Development report, Meeting of OECD Education Ministers. (2006a). Retrieved from http://www.oecd.org/ document/24/0,3343,en_21571361_36507471_36507480_1_1_1_1,00.html

Organization of Economic Co-operation and Development Insights, Higher Education for a Changing World. (2006b). Retrieved from http://www .oecdobserver.org/news/fullstory.php/aid/1868/ Higher_education_for_a_changing_world.html

Pachler, N., & Daly, C. (2009). Narrative and learning with Web 2.0 technologies: towards a research agenda. *Journal of Computer Assisted Learning*, *25*(1), 6-18. doi:10.1111/j.1365-2729.2008.00303.x

Parise, S. (2009). Social media networks: What do they mean for knowledge management? *Journal of Information Technology Case and Application Research, 11*(2), 1-11. Retrieved from ABI/INFORM Global. .

Pasquinucci, R. (2009). Social studies: Teaching students the strategy behind social media tools. *Public Relations Tactics*, *16*(10), 15. Retrieved from Business Source Complete database.

Pata, K. (2009). Modeling spaces for self-directed learning at university courses. *Journal of Educational Technology & Society, 12*(3), 23-43. Retrieved from Academic Search Complete database.

Revolutionizing knowledge work. (2008). *Leader to Leader, 49*, 55-56. Retrieved from Academic Search Complete database.

Romero, E. (2008). AACSB accreditation: Addressing faculty concerns. *Academy of Management, 7*(2), 245-255. Retrieved from AOM Archive database.

Santovec, M. (2005). Defining, supporting faculty excellence. *Distance Education Report, 9*(21), 1-6. Retrieved from Education Research Complete database.

Savage, N. (2010). New search challenges and opportunities. *Communications of the ACM, 53*(1), 27-28. Retrieved from Academic Search Complete database.

Schonfeld, E. (2009, June 6). Re: On Twitter, most people are Sheep: 80 percent of accounts have fewer than 10 followers [Online forum comment]. Retrieved from http://techcrunch.com/2009/2009/06/06/on-twitter-most-people-are-sheep-80-percent-of-accounts-have-fewer-than-10-follower/

Shaffer, S., Lackey, S., & Bolling, G. (2006). Quick reads. Blogging as a venue for nurse faculty development. *Nursing Education Perspectives, 27*(3), 126-128. Retrieved from CINAHL Plus with Full Text database.

Shea, P. (2007). Bridges and barriers to teaching online college courses: A study of experienced online faculty in thirty six colleges. *Journal of Asynchronous Learning Networks, 11*(2), 73-128. Retrieved from Education Research Complete database.

Shea, P., Pickett, A., & Chun Sau, L. (2005). Increasing access to higher education: A study of the diffusion of online teaching among 913 college faculty. *International Review of Research in Open & Distance Learning, 6*(2), 1-18. Retrieved from Education Research Complete database.

Social Website Analyzer. (2008). Retrieved from http://www.socialwebsiteanalyzer .com

Steinert, Y., McLeod, P., Boillat, M., Meterissian, S., Elizov, M., & Macdonald, M. (2009). Faculty development: A 'field of dreams'? *Medical Education, 43*(1), 42-49. Retrieved from CINAHL Plus with Full Text database.

Stigmar, M. (2008). Faculty development through an educational action programme. *Higher Education Research & Development*, 27(2), 107-120. doi: 10.1080/07294360701805242

South University, Online Faculty Expectation. (n.d.). Retrieved from http://online.southuniversity.edu/docs/SUO_Faculty_HR_Packet.pdf

Sweeny, R. (2009). There's no "I" in YouTube: Social media, networked identity and art education. *International Journal of Education through Art*, 5(2/3), 201-212. doi:10.1386/eta.5.2and3.201/1

Swongwoon, K., Inseong, L., Kiho, L., Seungki, J., Joonah, P., Yeun Bae, K., et al. (2010). Mobile Web 2.0 with multi-display buttons. *Communications of the ACM*, 53(1), 136-141. Retrieved from Academic Search Complete database.

Training professionals must embrace social learning. (2009). *Professional Safety*, 54(12), 1. Retrieved from Academic Search Complete database.

Tapscott, D., & Williams, A. (2010). Innovating the 21st-century university: It's time! *EDUCAUSE Review*, 45(1), 16. Retrieved , from ABI/INFORM Global.

Taylor, A. (2009). The problem with teaching social media: "It moves faster than a syllabus." *Public Relations Tactics*, 16(10), 14. Retrieved from Business Source Complete database.

University of Phoenix, FAQs to Become a Faculty Member. (n.d.). Retrieved from http://www.phoenix.edu/faculty/become_a_faculty_member/faculty-faq.html

U.S. Department of Education, Institute for Educational Sciences. (2006-2007). Retrieved from http://nces.ed.gov/fastfacts/display.asp?id=80

U.S. Department of Education, Financial Aid for Post Secondary Education. (2010). Retrieved from http://www2.ed.gov/admins/finaid/accred/accreditation_pg14.html

U.S. Department of Education, OPE, (2010). Retrieved from http://www2.ed.gov/about/offices/list/ope/index.html

U.S. Department of Education, Financial Aid for Post Secondary Education. (2010). Retrieved from http://ed.gov/admins/finaid/accred/accreditation_pg7.html

U.S. Department of Education, Office of Post Secondary Education. (2010). *Dear colleague letter* (dcl-01-11-2010.doc). Retrieved from http://www2.ed.gov/about/offices/list/ ope/policy.html

U.S. Department of Education, Office of Planning, Evaluation, and Policy Development Policy and Program Studies Service, Center for Technology in Learning. (2009). *Evaluation of evidence-based practices in online learning: A meta-analysis and review of online learning studies*. Retrieved from www2.ed.gov/rschstat/eval/tech/evidence-based-practices/finalreport.pdf - 2009-05-28

U.S. Department of Education, Office of Postsecondary Education, The Assistant Secretary Letter to the Executive Board of CHEA. (2010). Retrieved from http://www.chea.org/pdf/ltr%20to%20Exec%20Dir%20HEOA%20011110.pdf

Väljataga, T., & Fiedler, S. (2009). Supporting students to self-direct intentional learning projects with social. *Journal of Educational Technology & Society*, 12(3), 58-69. Retrieved from Academic Search Complete database.

Walling, D. (2009). Idea networking and creative sharing. *TechTrends: Linking Research & Practice to Improve Learning*, 53(6), 22-23. doi: 10.1007/s11528-009-0339-x.

Yelon, S., Sheppard, L., Sleight, D., & Ford, J. K. (2004). Intention to transfer: How do autonomous professionals become motivated to use new ideas? *Performance Improvement Quarterly, 17*(2), 82-103.

Young, J. R. (2010, March 28). High-tech cheating abounds, and professors bear some blame. *The Chronicle of Higher Education*. Retrieved from http://chronicle .com/article/High-Tech-Cheating-on-Homework/64857/

Zheng R., Perez, J., Williamson, J., & Flygare, J. (2008). WebQuests as perceived by teachers: Implications for online teaching and learning. *Journal of Computer Assisted Learning, 24*(4), 295-304.

CHAPTER 11

REAL LESSONS
IN VIRTUAL WORLDS

Using Virtual World Technology
to Educate and Train Business Students

Natalie T. Wood

The emergence of new information and communication technologies has significantly influenced the way we learn, and the way we teach. To meet the needs and learning styles of today's (and tomorrow's) students educators are exploring the use of virtual worlds for instructional purposes. Despite the less than favorable reviews that worlds such as Second Life have received from the corporate world (specifically marketing) these environments hold great promise for those in the educational field. It is unlikely that they will entirely replace traditional in-person techniques in the foreseeable future. But when utilized correctly they offer a variety of educational experiences that can enhance student learning. This chapter explores the characteristics of virtual worlds that make them unique to other popular forms of social media. It discusses why educators and their students are attracted to these environments and the potential hurdles that need to be overcome to achieve success in an educational setting.

Cutting-Edge Social Media Approaches to Business Education:
Teaching With LinkedIn, Facebook, Twitter, Second Life, and Blogs, pp. 195–216
Copyright © 2010 by Information Age Publishing
All rights of reproduction in any form reserved.

INTRODUCTION

The May 1, 2006 cover of the popular business insights magazine *BusinessWeek* prominently displayed a picture of an avatar (digital persona) with the headline, "Virtual World, Real Money" ("Virtual World," 2006). In the months that followed virtual worlds became a hot topic in both the corporate world and among educators. Major news outlets reported on the opportunities that virtual worlds had to offer the business community (e.g., "A Virtual World, but Real Money"—*The New York Times*, October 19, 2006, Siklos, 2006). They also discussed the potential of this technology as a successor to traditional classroom instruction (e.g., "Educators Explore Second Life Online"—CNN, November 14, 2006, Wong, 2006). What followed was a virtual land rush with numerous corporations and educational institutions eager to get a early start with this new technology.

Fast forward a couple of years and it appeared, at least based on media reports, that the virtual world bubble had burst. Encouraging headlines were replaced with less than enthusiastic ones (e.g., "Is Marketing in Second Life a Dud?"—BusinessWeek, April 6, 2007, Hof, 2007; "Will the Last Corporation Leaving Second Life Please Turn Off the Light" —Tech Crunch, July 14, 2007, Riley, 2007). For those who have little to no knowledge or experience with virtual worlds it may appear that these environments were nothing more than a passing fad. However, reality is quite the opposite. The virtual world market is alive and thriving. As of the end of 2009 the number of total registered accounts in the virtual worlds sector had reached 803 million—almost a 100% growth rate in 12 months ("Virtual World," 2010). Twenty-four percent of these accounts are owned by people aged 15-25. Researchers predict that the number of active users will increase to 1,899 million by 2013 ("Active VW," 2010).

In this chapter we explore the evolution of virtual worlds and the characteristics that makes them so appealing for educational purposes. The chapter then explores the benefits and challenges of working in these environments and those factors that need to be taken into consideration when selecting a virtual world. It concludes with some general suggestions on how educators can use these environments to supplement classroom instruction.

THE EVOLUTION OF VIRTUAL WORLDS

Virtual environments have existed in one form or another since the launch of the Internet. However, it was not until the introduction of multi-user dungeons (MUDs) in the mid seventies (circa 1975) that their popularity began to rise. A MUD is a text-based online role-playing game in which players participate in a story-based challenge set in a fantasy or science fiction based world. Over the following decade MUDs were quickly replaced with Massively Multi User Online Role Playing Games (MMORPG). As a successor to MUDs MMORPGs not only permitted larger numbers (tens of thousands) of people to play simultaneously but it also replaced the text based environments with visual rich 2D or 3D spaces (Wood, 2010).

Avid players of MMORPGs will advocate that there is more to these environments than simple entertainment. Virtual worlds offer many other benefits that are useful in the real world. For instance, they encourage role playing and experimentation; they promote problem solving, risk taking and team work. However, in order to realize the opportunities and benefits the individual must be willing to play the "game." Unfortunately, a public 2D or 3D virtual environment that simply allowed individuals to experiment, create and interact with others around the world did not exist. That changed in the mid 1990s with the introduction of multi user virtual environments (MUVEs), otherwise known as virtual worlds (Wood, 2010).

CHARACTERISTICS OF VIRTUAL WORLDS

A virtual world is an online representation of real world people, places, companies and products (Wood, 2010). All virtual worlds share six common characteristics (Wood, 2010; "What is," n.d.).

1. Graphical user interface: Virtual worlds use 2D or 3D digital imagery to create realistic environments and user *avatars*. An avatar is an online digital persona that allows the user to navigate the virtual environment and interact with other virtual world participants (Wood, Solomon & Allan, 2008) (see Figure 11.1).

2. Shared space: Virtual worlds have the ability accommodate tens of thousands of people in-world, at the same time. Each world is composed of scores of small regions—parcels of virtual real estate, similar to plots of land. Each region can usually host 40-60 avatars simultaneously. This allows individuals to log in from any location around the world to interact with others. Similar to any real world location (e.g., park, store), a virtual world location (e.g., virtual park, virtual store) will contain a number of people, some of whom may be known to the user and others who are complete strangers, but all are visible to each other.

Figure 11.1.   An avatar: Digital persona of a real person.

3. Interactivity: In a virtual world, the user can alter, develop, build, or even submit customized content to the environment. The platform can be easily calibrated to reflect real world environments such as a retail store, a corporate boardroom, or the trading floor of the New York Stock Exchange (see Figure 11.2).

4. Immediacy: In a virtual world, all interactions take place in real time. Communication via text messaging or voice chat is instantaneous. Individuals (through their avatars) are able to "individually and/or collaboratively create and use in-world artifacts such as text, images, and three-dimensional models" (Davis, Murphy, Owens, Khazanchi, & Zigurs, 2009, p. 99).

5. Persistence: Similar to the real world a virtual world continues regardless of whether an individual user is logged in or not.

6. Socialization/community: A virtual world is essentially a virtual community—a group of individuals that connect and interact online for the purpose of personal and shared goals (Dholakia, Bagozzi, & Pearo, 2004).

Figure 11.2.   A board room in the virtual world of Second Life.

While it is true to say that other popular forms of social media (e.g., social networking, blogs and wikis) do present a number of these characteristics they may do not offer <u>all</u> of them. When all six characteristics are combined into one platform, as they are in virtual worlds, they may provide a more compelling and engaging experience than many of other social media tools do on their own.

A CASE FOR TECHNOLOGY BASED EDUCATION AND TRAINING

The purpose of education is to increase insight and understanding; it teaches the "why." Training on the other hand increases skills and competence; it teaches the "how" (Stack & Lovern, 1995). The challenge for many educators is how to successfully instill and integrate both the "why" and the "how" in the confines of a semester long (distant or campus based) course. Over the years educators has adopted many creative techniques to achieve this goal. One popular technique is to have students complete projects for real world companies. Whereas this offers great opportunities for students to hone a variety of skills, the challenge is finding companies that are willing to work with students. A further issue is the amount of time that the instructor has to dedicate to supervising these real world projects that may have real world consequences. As a result many instructors turn to other traditional classroom techniques (e.g., case studies) and those that incorporate technology either in or outside of the classroom (e.g., E-learning)

E-learning

E-learning incorporates computer-assisted learning tools such as stand-alone computer-based training programs, materials, and exercises, as well those that are accessed through the Internet or an intranet (Womble, 2008). It offers many advantages for students including a more flexible studying schedule, access to archived and recorded materials and exercises for completion and reexamination at a time and place that is convenient to them. E-learning is particularly popular with distant learning/online courses, or those that adopt a hybrid approach (part online, part classroom). Two popular forms of e-learning are game-based systems and virtual learning communities.

Game-Based Systems/Simulations

Game-based systems are customizable, individually (or instructor) paced, interactive computer games (Wood, Solomon, Marshall & Lincoln, 2010). They are useful for helping to bridge the gap between classroom theories and the real world. Reports from the corporate world suggest that use of game-based systems results in a knowledge transfer four times greater, and in knowledge retention ten times greater, than traditional methods ("Total Learning," 2008). An example of game-based systems used in higher education is simulations. In these computer games students (often working in teams) assume the role of a specific company and compete against other teams in a business strategy simulation. Students typically meet in person and/or use popular communication tools such as email, blogs, and wikis and Internet phones services such as Skype to analyze and strategize. The selection of, and the degree to which they use these communication tools is at the discretion of the team. Once a strategy has been formulated the team either forwards it to the instructor who inputs it into the simulation, or they enter it directly themselves. The team waits for feedback on the success of their strategy and then proceeds to the next round of decision making or stage of the game. This approach is often considered a good compromise to working with a real company. However, in many cases students are simply working with data to make decisions and there is very little interaction with others participants (outside of their own team) as would be customary in the real world (e.g., customers, competitors). Whereas this form of e-learning may help to improve analytical skills it may not be very successful in improving other skills that are important for real world success (e.g., interpersonal, communication, presentation, negotiation skills).

Virtual Learning Communities

Another popular option is the creation of virtual learning communities. At the basic level virtual communities encourage communication and the sharing of knowledge and information among students. There are more comprehensive instruments that can include tools such as videos, podcasts and other course materials which are posted online. Instructors attempt to create virtual communities using many of the tools (e.g., wikis, blogs) that can be found on popular course management sites such as Blackboard and WebCT, or by employing popular social networking platforms such as Facebook or Ning. The aim is to encourage students to collaborate on the project thereby enhancing both their understanding of a particular subject matter and relevant skills. Whereas in game-based systems the use of these communication and collaboration tools is "optional" in virtual learning communities the use of them is often "required." However, success relies heavily on both the quality and quantity of information provided by community members ("Learning Communities," 2009). Furthermore, a high reliance on email or text chat can leave students with a feeling of being "out there" on their own (Wood et al., 2010). Simulations often pose similar problems when students are unable to observe or interact with other teams participating in the game, or even see physical representations of the industry, product or scenario they are working on. One solution to this problem is to use a virtual world.

Virtual Worlds

Virtual worlds offer a unique opportunity to combine (in one environment/platform) the benefits commonly associated with business simulations with the opportunities for collaboration offered by virtual communities. Not only does this technology combine the advantages of both forms of e-learning but it also eliminates some of the problems that students and instructors encounter when using simulations or virtual communities. As previously mentioned, a common problem with simulations is that students are simply working with data (figures, statistics, etc). They do not have the opportunity to see the product or examine the industry first hand. Furthermore, they are unable to interact with others outside of the simulation (such as potential competitors, customers etc). In the case of virtual learning communities students sometimes never get to see their fellow students which may create a sense of isolation resulting in limited interaction or contribution to discussion/projects. In a 3D virtual environment where products, companies and places can be recreated and where individuals are represented by their avatars these problems are largely eliminated. Students can now see what they are working on and who they are working with thereby creating a greater sense of community and encouraging greater levels of engagement. The following section elaborates on these benefits

THE ATTRACTION WITH VIRTUAL WORLDS

Educators are attracted to virtual worlds for four reasons:

1. They appeal to undergraduate students;
2. They have the ability to enhance experiential learning;
3. Virtual worlds foster an increased sense of community between students; and
4. They enhance collaboration between students, other universities and the business community.

Appeal to Undergraduate Students

Today's undergraduate student population are members of Generation Y (those born after 1982), often referred to as the Millenial Generation. A generation raised on technology it infiltrates every aspect of their live, from how they locate information, access entertainment, to how they purchase products and communicate with others. This insatiable appetite for all things electronic has strongly influenced the way in which they learn. Characteristics of Millennials' learning styles include "fluency in multiple media and in simulation-based virtual settings, communal learning, a balance among experiential learning, guided mentoring and collection reflection" (Dede, 2005, p. 1). This generation (and those that will follow them) are highly receptive to technology-based pedagogical experiences, and they thrive in online environments (Ferrell & Ferrell, 2002). Exposure to technology happens early in their education—in K-12 schools virtual and online learning is growing at an estimated 30% annually (North American Council for Online Learning, 2006), and an estimated 20% of tweens have indicated an interest in taking a virtual class before they graduate high school ("Tweens," 2007).

Experiential Learning

Virtual worlds also offer potentially greater opportunities than traditional classroom based and online courses to employ experiential learning techniques in a timely and cost efficient manner (Wood et al., 2008). Experiential learning is a process whereby knowledge is created through transformation of experiences (Kolb, 1994). It is a nondirect teaching style in which the "instructor delegates, consults, and facilitates (Shields, 1997). The process positions students as active collaborators in their learning, as opposed to passive recipients of knowledge (Bobbitt, Inks, Kemp, and Mayo, 2000; Saunders, 1997). Whereas passive learning techniques offer limited opportunities to facilitate learning (Shakarian, 1995) active learning techniques encourage application of theory to real-life situations with the opportunity for reflection, increased level of student involvement and higher-order thinking (Anderson, 1997; Horwood, 1995; Shakarian, 1995). Experiential learning is believed to be more effective as it leads to better internalization of content (Lamont & Friedman, 1997). Whereas game-based systems/simulations are a form of experiential learning—they encourage collaboration, reflection, and higher-order thinking, the high reliance on textual data may result in low levels of engagement. Lack of engagement can lead to social loafing where some team members exert minimal levels of effort to complete the project.Whereas as it is true to say that social loafing can (and does) occur in all kinds of team projects it is also true to say that the more engaged the student the less likely it is to happen. By immersing students (via their avatars) into visually rich 3D environment, the experiental process is enhanced as students are now provided with more stimuli—they can see the product/company/person etc, and they have a greater opportunity to interact with others—team members, customers et cetera, thereby providing a greater sense of "realness." Furthermore students are challenged to be creative in their problem solving and take risks that they may not be comfortable doing in a classroom environment (Wood et al., 2008).

Sense of Community

In contrast to popular e-learning tools, virtual worlds offer rich visual interfaces and real-time text and audio communication. Students are no longer simply a name or a user ID rather each individual is represented by his own avatar and has the ability to see others (represented by their avatars) and communicate with them via voice chat or text. Students interact within the simulated world and the avatars they encounter as if they are actually there, thus suspending their attention to the real world and transferring that attention to the virtual world. This sense of immersion allows students to engage with content in the first person (Bricken, 1991). The sense of community created helps to replace the feeling of isolation common to other forms of e-learning (Childress & Braswell, 2006; Wong, 2006). We can attribute this sense of community to the ability of virtual worlds (compared to other forms of e-learning) to not only create *telepresence* (the feeling of being there via an avatar), but even more powerfully a feeling of *copresence* (the sense of being there with others—I can see you and you can see me) (Wood, et al., 2008).

Collaboration

The illusion of being physically present with other students (via their avatar) is a positive development for teaching and learning as it facilitates collaboration, promotes greater reflection and encourages conversation much like one would experience face to face (Cheal, 2007; Kirkup, 2001, Wagner, 2007). Collaboration is not just limited to those in the same physical (on-campus) classroom but also between those that are geographically removed from one another (e.g., students enrolled in distance education classes). In virtual worlds people from all corners of the globe can come together for personal, professional and educational reasons to collaborate and create.

In an educational context the benefits of in-world exercises which require collaboration with others include prolonged interaction and engagement with course material; the opportunity to challenge students to create and be creative; the opportunity to test market their ideas and to apply their newly acquired skills and knowledge (Wood, 2010). If the project/activity is completed in conjunction with another (national or international) school, they will also learn valuable skills such as project management, effective communication and cultural awareness. A recent report on emerging education technologies suggests that virtual collaboration—working with people who are not physically with you is likely to enter mainstream within the near future ("The Horizon Report," 2008).

Furthermore, virtual worlds may offer the opportunity for students to work with real companies on projects. For instance, the Chicago School of Public Health CADE worked with BP to develop a prototype counseling site in the virtual world of Second Life. The site allows employees to report anonymously on ethical issues to upper management (Monahan, Harvey, & Ullberg, 2007). Johnson & Wales University partnered with the Ministry of Tourism of Morocco to create a Virtual Morocco that would help educate people about Moroccan culture and encourage them to consider it as a vacation destination. Students had to create a plan and develop a technical prototype that required them to communicate with partners on another continent and across language barriers. Students studying entrepreneurship were given the opportunity to write business plans and prototype business concepts (Mason, 2007).

Virtual worlds allow educators and students to experiment, interact, and experience the unimaginable. Nevertheless some will argue that no matter how well designed the virtual experience it cannot offer the same benefits as a real life experience. They may be correct. But some things are impossible or impractical to replicate in the real world, particularly within the confines of one semester. In these cases virtual environments offer the next best thing. Moreover, it is not necessary to replace all traditional methods of instruction with virtual worlds. Instead instructors should adopt a hybrid approach that matches learning objectives with the best delivery system to achieve those objectives (Wood et al., 2010).

THE CHALLENGES OF TEACHING WITH VIRTUAL WORLDS

Despite the positive aspects of teaching with virtual worlds there are some challenges. The top three are

1. Overcoming the game stigma;
2. Conquering the learning curve; and
3. Dealing with privacy and security issues.

The Game Stigma

One of the major misconceptions about virtual worlds is that they are games. Many people will look at these environments and make the assessment that because it looks like a game and perhaps feels like a game, it must be a game. However, virtual environments have been used for years as training tool in many professions. For instance, pilots spend many hours enhancing their skills in flight simulators and the medical profession uses simulators to practice critical clinical skills (e.g., surgical and neurological). Up until recently a cost effective highly realistic 3D virtual environment that allows business students to apply the skills they learn in the classroom did not exist. With the introduction of virtual worlds the opportunity is now available to those who are willing to invest a small amount of resources.

It fair to say that legitimacy of this technology is more likely to be questioned by non traditional students—those that are perhaps part of an earlier generation. For these students the idea of virtual world learning will be viewed as "unusual" and they may be apprehensive about using it. This is to be expected. The best way to legitimize the technology is through detailed explanation of what these environments are and who uses them, demonstration of how they work, and careful selection of in-world activities that highlight the contribution they make to the class and student learning (Wood, 2010).

The Learning Curve

As with any new technology there is always a learning curve. The slope of the curve varies depending upon the virtual world chosen. But as time passes even the more challenging worlds are being more user-friendly. An increasing number of worlds are now web-based which negates the need for software downloads. The degree of the learning curve also depends on the characteristics of the student, with nontraditional students and those who are uncomfortable with technology or a willingness to try new things being challenged the most (Wood et al., 2010). The instructor needs to carefully assess the skill and comfort level of his students and then identify what resources are needed to speed up the adoptions process (Schiller, 2009). Most virtual worlds offer a variety of resources (e.g., tutorials, virtual guides and in some cases online videos) to help new users learn how to utilize the world.

Privacy and Security

For educators there are a number of virtual worlds offering varying degrees of privacy and security that can be utilized to enhance student learning. These worlds can be classified into two groups—public worlds and private worlds.

Public Worlds

A public world is, as the title suggests, a virtual world that is open to the general public—anyone can join. All that is required is for the user to create an account (basic membership is free) and access the world via the web. One of the primary benefits of a public world is the ability for students to interact with students from other universities around the world, non students (the general public), national and international companies, and entrepreneurs and not-for-profit groups. This can allow for some interesting class assignments. The down side to utilizing a public world is that it is public. The lack of privacy and security may be an issue for some educators (Johnson, 2008). Moreover, public worlds (much like the Web in general) are a haven for various controversial activities (Wood et al., 2008). Members of the academic community have voiced concern about the legal and ethical responsibilities of educational institutions to their students (Bugeja, 2007). This problem may be overcome by (1) Carefully screening virtual worlds for student use, (2) Preparing an orientation session that addresses these issues and how to deal with them, (3) Creating a hyperlink that will take students directly to the site and/or the classroom, thereby minimizing the chance that they will encounter such activities, (4) Restricting the use of class facilities to registered students only, and, (5) Presenting students with a disclaimer when they enter the world. Examples of public virtual worlds include Second Life (www.Second Life.com), Whyville (www.whyville.com), Entropia Universe (www.entropiauniverse.com), and Habbo Hotel (www.habbohotel.com).

Private Worlds

Another way to avoid this problem is to choose a private world. A private world is a virtual environment that can be housed on your own network, behind your firewall. Membership and access to the environment is thereby restricted to approved individuals. These worlds offer the highest degree of security. A number of these worlds have been created by educators. Some examples include OpenSimulator (www.opensimulator.org) and Open Cobalt (www.opencobalt.org). There is also a number of companies that are actively courting the education market with web-based virtual platforms at various price points (e.g., 3DXplorer www.3dxplorer .com; ProtonMedia www.protonmedia.com; Designing Digitally www .designingdigitally.com).

The downside to private virtual worlds is that they may provide limited opportunity to interact with others outside the class. For example, if a university decides to create their own custom built private virtual world, housed on the university server, then students will only be able to interact with other students. Instead of creating a custom world, some institutions may choose to use a private educational world such as OpenSimulaor and Open Cobalt. These worlds are strictly for educational purposes. Whereas these worlds may permit students to interact with other students from other universities, they do not provide students with the opportunity to interact with the general public and business community. In addition, whereas it is possible to use public worlds without any financial outlay (basic membership is free), there is a cost associated with using private worlds. The least expensive option is OpenSimulator and Open Cobalt where instructors can utilize the technology for as little as $100 per month. Other off-the-shelf virtual platforms and those that are custom built can cost thousands of dollars.

In the face of growing competition from private worlds Linden Lab, the creators of Second Life (a public world) recently launched a new product—Second Life Enterprise (a private world). This standalone environment allows institutions to run Second Life on their own network, behind their firewall. One of the early adopters is Case Western Reserve University. However, at a starting price of $55,000 this is not viable product for the casual user. For those interested in using virtual world technology so students can interact with others (public, businesses etc) but on a limited basis, the best option (at the time of writing) is to use the public grid of Second Life. Whereas other virtual worlds have come and gone (e.g., There.com) Second Life has a steady following, attracts a variety of groups (profit, not-for-profit, entrepreneurs, educational institutions, etc.) and is free to use.

SECOND LIFE

In 2003, Internet company Linden Lab launched the virtual world of Second Life. Although Second Life was not the first public world to launch it is perhaps the one that has received the most media attention, primarily for the number and variety of users it attracts.

There are five primary users of Second Life:

1. Individuals who enter these worlds to interact and socialize with others.

2. Entrepreneurs who use Second Life to test-market real world products, or to create and sell (for a profit) virtual items to other Second Life residents. For example designers (e.g., fashion, furniture, jewelry, home), artists (e.g., painters, musicians) and consultants (e.g., virtual world, web, advertising, IT).

3. Educational institutions that use these environments to enhance traditional classroom teaching or for distance learning.

4. Corporations that employ Second Life as a promotional tool, an alternative product, and service delivery system, or as a platform to conduct training.

5. Not-for-profit organizations (e.g., Global Kids, American Cancer Society, and The Center for Disease Control) that use Second Life for community outreach and education (Wood, 2010).

As of April 1, 2010 the public grid of Second Life boasted over 1 million residents—real life people who have Second Life accounts. More than 1,400 corporations, universities, government agencies and the U.S. military own virtual property in Second Life (Vollmer, 2010).

The characteristics of members of Second Life's public grid make it an appealing environment for teaching experiences that focus on experiential learning, collaboration, and community. On any given day there are hundreds if not thousands of students in Second Life working on a variety of projects. For instance, Students at California University, Fresno use Second Life to explore the legal and ethical issues that face businesses that choose to operate in new/alternative market places. Students begin by immersing themselves in Second Life to develop an understanding of how virtual worlds work and to identify potential legal issues. They then meet in-world to participate in a series of group discussions on how these legal issues can best be addressed by the courts. While some graduate students are resistant to using the technology (for a variety of reasons) most feel that they learn a great deal by participating in the experience. To overcome resistance it is important for the instructor to be well prepared, flexible and encouraging (Wood, 2010).

At Swinburne University of Technology in Australia students explore alternative business models for e-commerce. Working in teams, students select two businesses that have a presence both on the web and in Second Life. Over the course of the semester they compare and contrast the business models adopted by each of these businesses. Through this exercise students have the opportunity to complete real hands-on analysis, rather than working from the examples offered in their textbook. The 3D technology is very successful at increasing student engagement and enjoyment for the exercise. It also helps students develop an appreciation for real business operations while preparing them for the workforce. Once again planning is an important factor in determining success. At the beginning of the exercise students need to be provided with support materials (e.g., instructions, help resources) and enough time to become conversant with the technology (Wood, 2010).

At North Carolina State University students collaborate to develop in-world marketing communication strategies. The purpose of the exercise is to introduce students to a new and growing way of doing business. Virtual worlds are also used in their distance learning program. Virtual worlds such as Second Life are usefully for allowing students to meet in real time to work together on projects. Even though they are miles apart in the real world, this technology helps students to feel like they are really there in the same space (telepresence) with their fellow students (copresence) (Wood, 2010).

Finally, students at Saint Joseph's University in Philadelphia meet with a representative of IBM (who is based in North Carolina) in IBM's Second Life faculties to discuss ways in which the company uses new technology to enhance productivity, train and educate employees and understand customer needs. Students log into Second Life from a variety of locations both on and off campus and meet as a group on IBM Island. They listen to a formal presentation, participate in a group discussion and are taken on a virtual tour of IBM facilities. The entire exercise lasts approximately

90 minutes. Although skeptical at first students find the experience to be informative, engaging and inspiring.

ADOPTING VIRTUAL WORLDS

In March 2010 the 3rd Annual Virtual Worlds Best Practices in Education conference brought together 170 conference presenters and attracted over 5000 attendees. The size of this conference alone suggests that instructors are intrigued with the idea of incorporating virtual worlds into their curriculum, but many require guidance on where to begin and how to be successful. The following section addresses some of the major decisions that need to be made and answers some common questions.

Public or Private?

The first decision is whether to use a public or private world. If the instructor's goal is to have students interact with non students (adults) or businesses then he will need to select a public world. The most popular, and at this time most appropriate world is Second Life. If interaction is not important then a private world may be more suitable. In this case instructors should consider OpenSimulator (www.opensimulator.org) and Open Cobalt (www.opencobalt.org).

Level of Investment

Many instructors are concerned about the cost of using virtual worlds. All public virtual worlds offer a basic (free membership). The only time an instructor would need to allocate funds for teaching in a public virtual world is if he wants to own his own piece of the world to create a virtual classroom or other environment. However, purchasing virtual real estate for occasional use is not necessary. Instead instructors should consider renting or borrowing facilities from other universities or groups. Another option is to take advantage of the Second Life Land Grant. Second Life offers temporary—semester long, land grants for educators interested in trying out Second Life for the first time (see the "Educators" section of the Second Life website).

The only other real investment required is that of time—time to learn how to use the world and to teach students how to use it. As previously mentioned degree of difficulty is a function of the world selected. Historically Second Life was viewed as one of the most challenging worlds to master (Wood et al., 2008). However, with the recent introduction of a new improved viewer (interface) this environment is a significantly easier to use.

Training and Support

In preparation for the virtual experience instructors should introduce the topic of virtual worlds slowly, systematically and well in advance of the assigned exercise. An introductory lecture and demonstration is important, as well as providing students with the opportunity to explore and learn how to use the technology. Beyond the introductory lecture it will be necessary to provide students with some additional resources. These resources can be posted online for easy reference. Some important items to consider include a code of conduct and help resources.

Code of Conduct

All virtual worlds have a participant code of conduct which is normally accessible from the home page. Students should be provided with a copy of this. Instructors may also want to impose additional guidelines. Some of these may relate to the planned exercise/experience, others may be more general in nature. For example, instructors may want to impress on students the importance of behaving in a professional and courtesy manner when representing their institution in-world, or the procedures for collecting data in-world.

Help Resources

For some students an introductory lecture and demonstration will provide all the information they need to utilize the virtual world. Others may require further training or support. If the instructor is using Second Life there are a variety of online resources that can help build skill level and provide help when needed. These resources include, a quick start guide, a Second Life for Beginners wiki and an assortment of video tutorials.

Second Life also boasts a very active and responsive community of educators (see: http://education.Second Life.com/resources/community/). This community is very supportive and offers many valuable insights and best practices to teaching in virtual environments. They provide great opportunities for project collaboration.

VIRTUAL WORLD EXPERIENCES/EXERCISES

To ensure success instructors need to carefully select their virtual world exercises. They should begin by identifying goals that are difficult to achieve using existing technologies or tools. From here they can begin to examine the suitability of virtual worlds. Regardless of what this exercise is, the golden rule is that virtual worlds should be adding value to the exercise that existing means and tools cannot.

The first virtual world exercise should be a very simple one—one that requires the student to have mastered only the basic navigation (e.g., walking) and communication (e.g., voice and text chat) skills. Instructors should use this exercise as an opportunity to showcase the potential of the technology, build interest in and improve skill level. More advanced exercises and experiences may be introduced later in the semester or reserved for another class.

One appropriate introductory exercise is to identify a real world business that currently uses virtual worlds and contact their in-world representative to arrange a virtual presentation and tour of their facilities. Another option is to have students attend a scheduled in-world public presentation or event that may apply to the content of the class. Observation is another activity that is easy to undertake in virtual environments. Students can examine, compare and contrast the virtual world activities of business with their real world activities.

As previously discussed, virtual worlds are a valuable tool for skill training. In each discipline there are a set of skills that graduating students should possess. A number of these skills may involve interpersonal interactions. For example, a human resource specialist needs to be able to conduct interviews, or counsel others on a variety of issues; a sales representative needs to be proficient at delivering a sales presentation to a prospective customer; and a lawyer or business professional needs to be able to negotiate. It can be difficult to find time in-class to practice these skills. Virtual worlds allow students to apply these skills outside of the classroom without the need to be physically present with other students (or the instructor). Furthermore, at first some students may be apprehensive about participating in a practical exercise. This can hinder their performance and result in the need for further training and practice. Performing these exercises in a virtual world allows students to focus on the task at hand without having the pressure of classmates observing their performance. As confidence and skill increases they can move from virtual role plays to real world ones.

To illustrate, students enrolled in a pharmaceutical sales training course at Saint Joseph's University participated in a series of virtual world role plays. In this role play the pharmaceutical representative (student) meets with a doctor (instructor/former pharmaceutical executive) in a virtual doctor's office. The objective of the role play is to gain the doctor's support to adopt a new medical device. Both the student and instructor are in different (private) locations in the real world and only interact with each other through the virtual environment. Students, particularly those who are apprehensive about completing the exercise, find the experience to be a positive one. They claim that by completing the role play in a virtual environment they are able focus on the sales process and their sales pitch without being distracted by other factors, such as other people in the room. The exercise helps to increase their confidence to both complete and perform well in their subsequent real world role plays. Furthermore, the instructor points out that the exercise allows her to focus on student understanding and execution of the sales pitch (product knowledge, delivery and tone) without her being distracted by non verbal communication cues (e.g., dress). This allows her to provide swift accurate recommendations for improvement.

The use of virtual worlds for such exercises is not confined to the formal education environments, many business are beginning to use virtual worlds for education, training and as a more efficient way of conducting meetings. For example virtual developers ProtonMedia have worked with Johnson & Johnson, Merck Inc., BP, Chevron and Lockheed-Martin. Designing Digitally has created virtual worlds for TD Ameritrade and The Brooks Group. It is highly likely that once students enter the workforce they are going to encounter these environments.

CONCLUSION

Technology has infiltrated every aspect of our lives. Whether this is viewed as something positive or negative is a matter of personal opinion. But one cannot dispute the fact that technology has enabled us to achieve more in a more effective and efficient manner. Virtual simulations have been used for many years to train professionals. Historically the high cost of developing these environments was a barrier to entry for many sectors of the business and educational communities. Today that barrier has been removed opening up many exciting possibilities for those who dare to explore. These virtual environments may never completely replace traditional classroom based teaching, but they do offer an exciting opportunity to enhance learning. More specifically they allow instructors and students the opportunity to experience and achieve those things that are difficult or impossible to achieve in a classroom and/or through the use of other technologies. As illustrated by the examples presented in this chapter it is possible to learn real lessons in virtual worlds.

REFERENCES

Active VW user forecast: 2009–2013. (2010). Retrieved from http://www.kzero.co.uk/blog/?p=3836

Anderson, E. J. (1997). Active learning in the lecture hall. *Journal of College Science Teaching, 26*, 428-429.

Bobbitt, L. M., Inks, S. A., Kemp, K. J., & Mayo, D. T. (2000). Integrating marketing courses to enhance team-based experiential learning. *Journal of Marketing Education, 22*(1), 15-24.

Bugeja, M. J. (2007). Second thoughts about Second Life. *The Chronicle of Higher Education.* Retrieved from http://www.chronicle.com.

Bricken, W. (1991). A formal foundation for cyberspace. In S. K. Helsel (Ed.), *Beyond the vision: The technology, research, and business of virtual reality. Proceedings of the second annual conference of virtual reality, artificial reality, and cyberspace.* Westport, CT: Meckler.

Cheal, C. (2007). Second Life: Hype or hyperlearning. *On The Horizon, 15*(4), 204-210.

Childress, M. D., & Braswell, R. (2006). Using massively muliplayer online role-playing games for online learning. *Distance Education, 27*(2),187-196.

Davis, A., Murphy, J., Owens, D., Khazanchi, D., & Zigurs, I. (2009) "Avatars, people, and virtual worlds: Foundations for research in metaverses," *Journal of the Association for Information Systems, 10*(2), 90-117.

Dede, C. (2005, November 1). *Planning for neomillennial learning-styles,* Retrieved from http://www.educase.edu

Dholakia, U. M., Bagozzi, R. P., & Pearo, L. K. (2004). A social influence model of consumer participation in network- and small-group-based virtual communities. *International Journal of Research in Marketing, 21*(3), 241-264.

Ferrell, O., & Ferrell, L. (2002). Assessing instructional technology in the classroom. *Marketing Education Review, 12*(3), 19-24.

Hof, R. (2007, April 6). Is marketing in Second Life a dud? Message posted to http://www.businessweek.com/the_thread/techbeat/archives/2007/04/is_marketing_in.html

The Horizon Report. (2008). Retrieved from http://connect.educause.edu/Library/ELI/2008HorizonReport/45926

Horwood, B. (1995). Experiential learning: A teacher's perspective. In R. J. Kraft & J. Kielsmeier (Eds.), *Experiential learning in schools and higher education* (pp. 201-211). Dubuque, IA: Kendall-Hunt.

Johnson, C. (2008). Drawing a roadmap: Barriers and challenges to designing the ideal virtual world for higher education. *EDUCAUSE Review, 43*(5), 64.

Kirkup, G. (2001). Teacher or avatar? Identity issues in computer-mediated contexts. In E. J. Haughey & M. Burge (Eds.), *Using learning technologies: International perspectives on practice* (pp. 72-81). London, England: Routledge Falmer.

Kolb, D. A. (1994). *Experiential learning: Experience as the source of learning and development.* Englewood Cliffs, NJ: Prentice Hall.

Lamont, L. M., & Friedman, K. (1997). Meeting the challenges to undergraduate marketing education. *Journal of Marketing Education, 9*(3), 17-30.

Learning communities in the workplace: The virtues of going virtual. (2007). *Development and Learning in Organizations, 21*(6), 28.   Retrieved from ABI/INFORM Global database.

Mason, H. (2007). Experiential education in Second Life. *Proceedings of the Second Life Education Workshop 2007* (pp. 14-19). Retrieved from http://www.simteach.com/slccedu07proceedings.pdf

Monahan, C., Harvey, K., & Ullberg, L. (2007). BP tries Second Life for employee ethics and compliance. *Proceedings of the Second Life Education Workshop 2007:* (pp. 93-96). Retrieved from: http://www.simteach.com/slccedu07proceedings .pdf

North American Council for Online Learning and the Partnetnship for 21st Century Skills. (2006, November). *Virtual schools and 21st century skills.* Retrieved from http://www.inacol.org/research/docs/NACOL_21CenturySkills.pdf

Riley, D. (2007, July 14). *Will the last corporation leaving Second Life please turn off the light.* Retrieved from http://techcrunch.com/2007/07/14/will-the-last-corporation-leaving-second-life-please-turn-off-the-light/

Saunders, P. M. (1997). Experiential learning, cases and simulations in business. *Business Communication Quarterly, 60*(1), 97-114.

Schiller, S. (2009). Practicing learner-centered teaching: Pedagogical design and assessment of a Second Life project. *Journal of Information Systems Education, 20*(3), 369-381.

Shakarian, D. C. (1995, May-June). Beyond lecture: Active learning strategies that work. *Journal of Physcial Education, Recreation and Dance,* 21-24.

Shields, P. (1997). Teaching techniques for contemporary marketing issues. In Varble, Young, & Maliche (Ed.), *Marketing Management Association,* 1-5.

Siklos, R. (2006, October 19). *A virtual world but real money.* Retrieved from http://www.nytimes.com/2006/10/19/technology/19virtual.html

Stack, R. T., & Lovern, E. R. (1995). A lively learning agenda. *The Healthcare Forum Journal, 38*(5). Retrieved from http://www.proquest.umi.com.

Total learning concepts develops interactive game-based learning system to train sales force for leading specialty company. (2008, September 3). *Business Wire,* Retrieved from ABI/INFORM Dateline database.

Tweens eager for virtual learning. (2007, November 2). Retrieved from http:// www.emarketer.com

Virtual world registered accounts reach 800m. (2010). Retrieved from http:// www.kzero.co.uk/blog/?p=3943

Virtual world, real money. (2006, May 1). *BusinessWeek.*

Vollmer, S. (2010, April 4). *How much life is there in Second Life?* Retrieved from http://scienceinthetriangle.org/2010/04/how-much-life-is-there-in-second-life

Wagner, M. (2007, September 21). *The future of virtual worlds.* Retrieved from http:/ /www.informationweek.com

What is a virtual world? (n.d.). Retrieved from http://www.virtualworldsreview.com/ info/whatis.shtml

Womble, J. (2008). E-learning: The relationship among learner satisfaction, self-efficacy, and usefulness. *The Business Review, Cambridge, 10*(1), 182.

Wong, G. (2006, November 14). *Educators explore 'Second Life' online.* Retrieved from http://www.cnn.com

Wood, N. T. (2010). *Marketing in virtual worlds.* Upper Saddle River, NJ: Pearson.

Wood, N. T., Solomon, M. R., & Allan, D. (2008). Welcome to the matrix: E-learning gets a Second Life. *Marketing Education Review, 18*(2) 45-53.

Wood, N. T., Solomon, M. R., Marshall, G. W., & Lincoln, S. (2010). Corporate training goes virtual: A hybrid approach to experiential learning. In W. Ritke-

Jones (Ed.), *Virtual environments for corporate education: Employee learning and solutions* (pp. 284-301). Hershey, PA: IGI Global.

CHAPTER 12

USES, CHALLENGES, AND POTENTIAL OF SOCIAL MEDIA IN HIGHER EDUCATION

Evidence From a Case Study

Suling Zhang, Caroline Flammer, and Xiaolong Yang

INTRODUCTION

Higher education institutions are on a constant quest for creating knowledge and educating students. The development of the Internet and its latest social media tools such as YouTube, Facebook, and Twitter, that facilitate interactive information sharing and collaboration on the World Wide Web, has significantly influenced this quest in many ways. While many discussions have ensued around social media used in educational institutions, very limited academic research has been conducted on open access interactive tools in learning design (Bonk, 2009a, 2009b; Craig, 2007). Social media have been used for networking and information gathering for 3 decades since the Bulletin Board System was created in the 1970s. However, only recently has it become part of mainstream culture

Cutting-Edge Social Media Approaches to Business Education:
Teaching With LinkedIn, Facebook, Twitter, Second Life, and Blogs, pp. 217–240
Copyright © 2010 by Information Age Publishing
All rights of reproduction in any form reserved.

and the business world. The exponential growth of social media communities and the fast innovations of social media technologies in recent years outpaced the advancement of academic research on social media. This paper aims to address the emerging phenomenon of social media and focuses on the challenges and opportunities that social media cause for the education of students. It also examines how higher educational institutions can exploit the potential of social media in a constructive way.

Social media are rapidly changing the way people interact with each other and provide organizations with new ways to reach target groups. Higher education institutions serve largely digital natives who are a quick adopter of social media. Social media provide higher education institutions unique opportunities and challenges for connecting with their student community and for innovative teaching and learning. Their use is facilitated by the common availability of computer devices and Internet on campus. Recently, educational magazines and educators' associations have experienced a substantial increase in reports and discussions on existing and potential applications of social media in higher education learning and teaching. A casual search on the Internet shows that many universities and colleges have created official accounts on social media websites, especially on Facebook and Twitter. Research on the impact of social media in higher education, however, is still in its infancy stage. Faculty and schools urgently need guidance on how to efficiently use social media for teaching and learning.

This paper is an attempt to address this gap. We conduct a case study at a medium-sized public university on the usage of social media and take a comprehensive approach by looking from the perspectives of various stakeholders. This study investigates how social media are used officially and unofficially at the university. It focuses on the effects and challenges of using social media for teaching and learning. Particular attention is paid to identifying the differences of adopters and nonadopters and exploring how the university can make constructive use of social media. The study provides insights into the phenomenon of social media in higher education institutions and offers guidelines on how to enhance the instrumental value of social media for learning and teaching.

The rest of this paper is organized as follows. In the next section, a brief literature review is presented focusing on scholarly work on social media in the educational context. The third section introduces the research methodology and the fourth section discusses the case study findings. The fifth section summarizes the results and suggests strategies for constructively using social media in higher education institutions. Finally, the last section discusses future research questions related to social media in higher education.

LITERATURE REVIEW

Many discussions have been held on social media in educational magazines and educators' forums and meetings. It is widely acknowledged that social media are embedded into the everyday life of students (Alexander, 2006; Hoffman, 2009; Maloney, 2007). Proponents claim that social media hold great potential for improving teaching and learning, for example, by creating a student-centered learning, promoting collaboration among students, supporting individualized learning, providing an enjoyable learning experience, and enabling flexible learning schedules (Alexander, 2006; Hoffman, 2010; Horizon Report, 2010). Critics of social media argue that reliance on social media technologies which are controlled by commercial companies may align educational methods with corporate motives (see, e.g., "Economist," 2008).

With the growing interest for social media in educators' circles, an increasing yet still small number of academic studies on social media in higher education institutions have been conducted. One major theme in the existing research is learning through social interaction. As Meltzoff, Kuhl, Movellan, and Sejnowski (2009) point out, new insights from the fields of neuroscience, psychology, machine learning and education are converging and give rise to a new science of learning. These findings may lead to a transformation of educational practices. In their experimental studies, Meltzoff et al. (2009), Meltzoff (1995, 2007), and Meltzoff and Moore (1977) show that social interactions are essential for learning. It is the inherent nature of human beings to have an intense interest in other people and their behavior, and to interact with them. These authors show that humans possess powerful implicit learning mechanisms that are affected by social interaction.

These findings from research in development psychology and neuroscience are consistent with insights from research in pedagogy and sociology. Specifically, Bloom (1984) finds that interactive forms of in-class instruction (e.g., face-to-face tutoring) enhance learning. In addition, Johnson and Johnson (1986) show that collaborative learning helps students retain information better than students working individually. Learning also occurs outside of the formal setting during natural social interaction (see, e.g., Bell, Lewenstein, Shouse, & Feder, 2009; Brunner, 1996; Lee, 2008). Informal learning is based on the idea that informal settings are venues for a significant amount of learning. They are often very social and offer a form of mentoring, apprenticeship, and participation that increases motivation.

A theoretical backbone to the above findings is provided in Bandura's *Social Learning Theory* (Bandura, 1977) and Vygotsky's (1978) "Social Development Theory." These two constructivist theories posit that learning is a social process and occurs through interactions, collaboration, and sharing information with each other. Furthermore, Rogoff's concept of "guided participation" regards guided active participation as an important component of effective learning environments (Rogoff, 1990). To conclude, research from different fields suggests that social interaction enhances lifelong learning.

This social learning traditionally took place in person. Nowadays, however, other forms of interaction have evolved and have greatly increased the desire to communicate with others. New social technologies, such as Facebook, MySpace, text messaging, and Twitter, have emerged and play a predominant role in the life of especially the younger generations. The importance of social interaction in the learning process and the general trend to virtual communication calls for a change in educational practices to enhance student learning.

Educational technology (such as intelligent tutoring systems[1]) is increasingly incorporating principles of social interaction into the learning process, and a growing number of experimental studies are supporting the learning benefits of interactive learning technology (e.g., Koedinger & Aleven, 2007; VanLehn, 2006). So far, however, this technology and research have focused on the one-to-one interaction between professor and students.

In contrast, the Internet and the latest development of social media, allow several people to interact with each other in an informal setting. Thus, this technology has significant potential to support and enhance teaching and learning through increased interactive information sharing, reflection, sense of community, and collaboration. Social media play a vital role in nowadays society. They are influencing the way people interact and provide new learning opportunities and challenges. Despite the extraordinary effect of social media on social interaction, very limited research has been done in this area. The emerging research suggests that social media actively engage students and have the potential to enhance students' learning experience. For example, Halic, Lee, Paulus and Spence (in press) study the effectiveness of blogs in perceived learning. Mazer, Murphy, and Simonds (2007) study the effects of teacher self-disclosure via Facebook on student motivation, affective learning, and classroom climate. Both studies find a positive relationship. These results are in line with Hamann and Wilson (2002) who find that students participating in a web-enhanced class outperform students in a traditional lecture format.

The large majority of existing studies investigated how a small group, for example, a class and a project team, used social media or how a particular social medium is used for learning. For example, Gunawardena et al. (2009) examine the process of a team of six students engaged in online community; Dennen (2008) study the lurking behaviors of a group of students in online discussion forum. The narrow focus of the existing studies yielded in-depth detailed findings regarding the utility of a particular technology or the impact of social media on a small group. However, the big picture of institution-wide pedagogical landscape is seldom studied. It is not clear how social media overall impact multiple stakeholders involved in higher education including the school, faculty and students. Little guidance is given on how institutional policy, processes and infrastructure can be coordinated along with the efforts of individual faculty and students to make constructive use of social media.

Some other existing studies are comparative and focus primarily on social networking tools such as Facebook and MySpace. Jones, Blackey, Fitzgibbon, and Chew (2010), Cole (2009), and Tams (2006) investigate the pattern of students' usage and attitudes toward social software for learning. Their results suggest that there is a distinct separation between the learning space and personal space—students are reluctant to use social media for educational purposes and let their professional life infiltrate their social life. Furthermore, Roblyer, McDaniel, Webb, Herman, and Witty (in press) compare students and faculty in their use of Facebook and email technologies. This comparison simply indicates that students are more likely to use Facebook than faculty. The study, however, doesn't address the above-mentioned key issue regarding how and why social media is used and what institutional efforts can be taken to use social media for teaching and learning. The study of Ajjan and Hartshorne (2008) provides a preliminary insight into these questions. They find that some faculty members are aware of the potential pedagogical benefits of social media applications but that only few decide to use them in their teaching. The authors point out that important questions still need to be investigated.

In the following, we attempt to find answers to these questions. Specifically, we explore how social media are used officially and unofficially by multiple stakeholders at higher education institutions. The focus is laid on the reasons and effects of social media usage in the areas of teaching and learning. We pay particular attention to identifying the differences of adopters and non-adopters, and explore how the university can support and effectively use social media for teaching and learning.

RESEARCH METHODOLOGY

This paper adopts a case study approach. Benbasat, Goldstein, and Mead (1987) suggest three reasons for using a case study method. All three reasons apply to this research project and further justify the research method of this paper.

First, case study methods can be used when it is hard to study the phenomenon of interest outside of its natural setting. The purpose of this paper is to identify the impact of social media in higher education institutions and the strategies for using it in a constructive way. It requires examination of teaching processes and organizational factors. It explores the questions "why" and "how" by going beyond merely describing specific outcome variables. It aims to investigate the use of social media in the real settings of higher education to gain deep understanding of the complexity of this issue. It is almost impossible to study the plethora of issues, which might exist in real university settings, through a controlled study. Second, the study should focus on contemporary events and learn about the state of the art. Third, the case study is appropriate for a field in which there is no established theoretical base. Social media in higher education context are an emerging phenomenon. Few studies have been conducted to explore this issue and no well-accepted theory has been developed yet. This research area is still in its formative stage and, accordingly, a case study method can be used to induce more generalizable knowledge from the myriads of complex facts.

The Research Site

The case study is conducted at a medium-sized public university in the northeastern United States (referred to as the University hereafter). The University is a comprehensive teaching institution covering a wide range of disciplines and offers both undergraduate and graduate programs. It serves some 13,000 students with an average class size of 20. The student body at the University is very diverse with students of different cultural and ethnical background.

Data Collection

To "triangulate" the data and gain comprehensive understanding of the research topic, data were collected through multiple sources as follows:

Method One: Survey

A survey is conducted with189 students including 126 undergraduates (67.7%) and 60 graduates (32.3%). Age of the survey participants varied. One hundred thirty-two were between 18 and 25 years of age, 27 (14.3%) were between 26 and 30 years of age, 16 (8.5%) were between 31 and 40 years of age, 7 (3.7%) were between 41-50, and 2 (1.1%) were above 50.

Sixty (34.4%) of the survey participants were art and humanities majors, 48 (25.4%) were business and management majors, seven (3.7%) were education majors and 59 (31.2%) were science and technology majors.[2]

The survey instrument consists of demographics questions and five questions on social media including:

- Which social media do you use?
- How long have you been using social media?
- How often do you use social media?
- What do you use social media for?
- What do you like or dislike about social media?

Except for the last question which is open-ended, multiple choices including a special choice (other: please specify) are given for the first four questions.

Method Two: In-Depth Interview

Semistructured interviews were conducted with 28 people including 16 faculty members, 2 administrators, and 10 students. The interviews explore how the interviewees use social media, why or why not they use social media, and what they suggest the university do for constructively using social media in teaching and learning. A sample question is "what social media do you use?" The interview questions were broad but detailed follow-up questions were asked to explore the examples and incidents mentioned by the interviewees in order to collect a rich body of information. The interviews were recorded with the interviewees' consent and transcribed.

Method Three: Observations

As the project was ongoing, the authors observed on-campus events, activities, classroom teaching and the daily happenings on campus to collect relevant information. These observations provided contextual information to corroborate and complement the survey and interview findings.

Method Four: Documents

The authors also collected relevant documents including university, departmental, faculty members' and students' social media Web pages, course outlines, program flyers, technology training announcements, teaching evaluation standards, and so on. These documents enrich the information regarding how social media are used and promoted and provide understanding regarding university policies on pedagogical technologies.

Data Analysis

Chi-square tests and ANOVA tests were used to analyze the quantitative data from the survey and compare the use of social media among different groups. Detailed analyses will be presented in the next section. Interview data and the other qualitative data including observations and documents were analyzed using the iterative hypothesis generation method. The authors listened to one interview, read the interview transcripts and generated a list of new hypotheses related to the research questions of interest in this study. Next, a different interview was analyzed with special attention paid to confirming, or rejecting the initially listed hypotheses. As a result of this second interview, the hypothesis list was revised and a third interview was analyzed. This process continued until all the interviews were analyzed. During the analysis of each interview, the hypotheses were also modified and refined based on the observations, the collected documents and the survey results.

RESULTS

In this section, the study findings are presented on how social media have been used at the University by different stakeholders, the perceived benefits and challenges, the reasons for social media adoption and non-adoption, and what the University has done to promote the adoption of social media for teaching and learning.

Overview of Social Media Usage

Social Media Usage Among the Students

The survey identified the adoption of several social media among the students. Social media are widely adopted by the students and none of the students reported not using any social media. A variety of social media are adopted. Facebook is the most popular social medium. Ninety-two percent of the students use Facebook. YouTube is the second most popular and 60% of the students use it. MySpace, Wikipedia, LinkedIn, and Twitter are also popular, used by respectively 18%, 18%, 15% and 13% of the students. Blogs, Yahoo! Answers, Friendster, and Flicker are also used by the students but are not popular. None of the students reported using Second Life. A few other social media are reported used by one or two

Table 12.1. Adoption of Social Media Among the Students

Technology	Percentage	Frequency
Facebook	92	173
YouTube	60	114
MySpace	18	34
Wikipedia	18	34
LinkedIn	15	29
Twitter	13	24
Blog	7	13
Yahoo! Answers	7	13
Friendster	2	3
Flicker	1	2
Second Life	0	0

Table 12.2. Purposes of Using Social Media

Technology	Frequency	Percentage
Social networking	150	79%
Entertainment	142	75%
Learning	82	43%
Professional networking	57	30%

individual student including ClassMates, Podcasts, Vlog, Orkut, DailyMotion, and QQ.

Despite the overall variety of social media used among the student population at the University, each individual student uses only one or two social media tools. Fifty-five percent of the surveyed students reported using only one social medium and 25% reported using two social media.

Table 12.2 shows the purposes for which the students use social media. Social media are primarily a social tool at the University. Seventy-nine percent of the students reported using it for social networking and 75% use it for entertainment. Only 43% of the students reported using it for learning. Thirty percent of the students also use social media for professional networking. Two students commented on using it for job search.

The primary way that the students use social media for learning purposes is to pull information from social media including Wikipedia and

Table 12.3.   History of Social Media Usage

History	Frequency	Percentage
Under 1 year	13	7
1-3years	62	33
3-5 years	51	27
More than 5 years	60	32

Table 12.4.   Frequency of Social Media Usage

Frequency of Usage	Frequency	Percentage
Once a week	25	13
3-5 times a week	35	19
Once per day	43	23
More than 3 times a day	82	44

YouTube to complete course assignments. Another way of using social media for learning is the use of social networking websites for team collaboration. Two students described that they had discussions about course projects with their team members on Facebook. One faculty also observed that the students in her class posted brief reminders about project deadlines on their project team members' Facebook. Another faculty reported that the students in his class were required to keep a log of project activities in a blogging website so the faculty and the project teams can monitor the project progress.

Table 12.3 shows that social media are not new among the students. 32% of the students have been using social media for more than 5 years; only 13% have been using social media for less than 1 year.

The survey found that social media have become part of the students' daily life. As shown in Table 12.4, 67% of the students use social media at least once per day.

Social Media Usage Among Faculty

Similar to the students, none of the faculty reported that he or she doesn't use social media at all. Faculty members who use social media fall into two groups. The major difference between these two groups is whether one uses social media to create participatory or interactive learning.

The first group is the majority. Eleven out of the 15 faculty members interviewed are in this group. They take social media as just another media type and view it primarily as a source of information. Using video clips from YouTube to enrich lecture contents is a common behavior among this group. However, the frequency of such behavior varies. Some faculty members use YouTube Video once or twice a semester while some use it in every class. This group does not incorporate into teaching the social interaction potential which differentiates social media and the traditional media. For example, in the interview, a faculty laughed at the idea of allowing the students to use Facebook in class and said she could not imagine what good it could do.

The second group adopts social media not only to take in information from social media but also to embed social interaction in course delivery. This group believes that social media can bring large positive change to education and promote the use of social media for teaching and learning. For example, one of the professors introduced to her class the discussion groups on LinkedIn related to course topics and encouraged the students to join the discussion groups. Another professor is designing a distant learning course which requires students to create collaborative work using Wiki and VoiceThread. In this group, the extent of social media usage also varies. Two professors use social media as a small component in their courses and design one or two interactive and collaborative assignment involving the use of social media in a course. Two other professors use social media throughout their courses and require their students to extensively use social media in almost all assignments. For example, one professor asked his student in a Hindi language program to network with Indian students on Orkut and to learn Hindi through ongoing interactions with their Indian Orkut friends.

Using social media for social networking and entertainment occurs in both groups. However, three of the professors in the first group do not use social media for leisure purposes.

Usage of Social Media at the Departmental and University Level

The University has been maintaining official accounts of Facebook and Twitter for 14 months and 9 months, respectively. One administrative office collects information about events and activities on campus and posts announcements on the University's Facebook and Twitter pages. There are more than 5,000 student followers associated with the University Facebook and 500 followers with the University Twitter. A recent survey of 11,000 students found that 40% of the students check University Facebook for information, e.g. whether a class is cancelled due to snowstorm. Except for one travel learn study announcement, there are no other posts on the University Facebook or Twitter related to courses and research. None of the professors interviewed in this study check the University Facebook and Twitter for information. Three professors were not even aware that the University is present on Facebook and Twitter.

In addition to the University, more than 10 departments, 5 university offices and 2 student groups created their Social Media web pages through tools such as Blog, Twitter and Facebook. These social media Web pages mainly serve as an electronic bulletin board for posting announcements and little interactive communication happens in these social media. None of the faculty members and students interviewed in this study visited these Web pages frequently.

The university library has an online presence on multiple social media including Facebook, Twitter, MySpace, LibraryBlog, as well as Second Life, and can be contacted through four different instant messaging tools. The library posts research guides such as reference styles and event announcements on these social media tools. However, despite multiple online presences, faculty's and students' interaction with the library online is very limited. There are only 149 followers on the Library Facebook account and the large majority of the University faculty or students do not even know that the library is reachable through social media. The library does not post frequently on the social media Web page. On average, there is one post per month.

In summary, social media are not a new phenomenon at the University. The students extensively use social media. However, students' usage is primarily related to social purposes and limited to a very small number of popular social media. There is a divide among faculty members on how social media is used for teaching. The majority of professors deploy social media as source of information while the other small percentage of professors uses social media to create interactive learning. At the university and departmental level, social media are mainly used for spreading administrative information to the campus communities. Social media adoption is still a decision made on an individual basis by faculty, students or offices. There has been no coordination across the student body, the faculty body and the university offices. No prominent institution-wide efforts have been taken to promote the use of social media.

Benefits and Challenges of Using Social Media

Benefits and Challenges Perceived by the Students

The benefit of social media most frequently mentioned by the students is *connectivity*. Social media enables the students to remain in touch with their professional acquaintances, classmates, family members and friends, no matter where they are. One student participant in this study has more than 1,000 friends on his Facebook account including the business and professional contacts he met from various campus events. He hopes this broad network will benefit him in his long-term career development. However, according to the survey results, 70% of the students do not use social media for professional networking. The relationship web the students build through social media is currently rather for social networking.

The second major benefit of social media for the students is *convenience*. Social Media tools such as YouTube and Wikipedia are free and do not require any special software or access code. When asked why he used Wikipedia instead of library resources for course projects, a student said simply "I prefer online." The simplicity of interface and the easy accessibility through Web browser make social media more attractive to the students than the traditional library.

The third benefit frequently mentioned by the students is the vast amount of *information* available through social media. The abundance of information also comes with a wide range of perspectives which are not available through a traditional textbook. Exposing students to different perspectives and developing their ability of independent thinking is an important part of higher education. Social media provide an easily accessible venue for educators to perform this task.

The other side of the two above-mentioned benefits is a significant challenge that is *filtering and selecting quality information from social media sources*. As to be introduced in later sections, many professors do not trust the quality of information published in social media and question the ability of students to critique the credibility of information from social media. It is not rare that professors explicitly ask the students not to use information from social media for academic projects. Despite the warning from the professors, students still introduce information from social media into their project reports through the back door. As one student puts it, "I still use Wikipedia but I don't reference it anymore." None of the students reported receiving guidance from the school or the faculty how to judge the quality of information from social media. Traditional metrics for evaluating scholarly work such as citation index cannot be applied to information in social media. Therefore, the lack of guidance of sense making and critiquing information from social media is a key challenge. This challenge hinders the students' ability of effectively using social media for acquiring knowledge.

In addition to the difficulty of critiquing and sense making, there are four other challenges associated with social media which are found in this study. First, social media *privacy* is a concern from all surveyed and interviewed students. They expressed a sense of insecurity and lack of control in protecting their privacy online. Second, social media can *consume significant amount of time and distract the students* from studying and working. Several interviewees use the word "addiction" to describe some students' constant engagement with social media. One student said, "You get sucked in (social media)." An example of such distraction is that during the interviews, two students checked every 2 minutes what their friends posted on their Facebook and posted replies using their cell phones. Third, *inappropriate exposure* in social media may be detrimental to a student's professional outlook. One incident revealed in the interview is that an undergraduate student was found by her fellow students and the school post "flashing" pictures on her Facebook. Such online behavior leaves a marred record. One student commented on this incident: "I don't understand. How could these students expect to be hired?" Fourth, over-reliance on online social networking may result in reduced ability of interacting face-to-face. For example, one student complained that social networking websites "take away from true human interaction."

The above four challenges do not directly relate to classroom teaching. However, they do relate to an important educating role higher education institutions play as a whole, that is, to prepare the students for life and career in a digital age.

Benefits and Challenges Perceived by the Faculty

Reflecting on their own experience with social media and observing the students' interactions on social media, faculty members perceive the benefits and challenges differently from the students.

Social media provide faculty members with *an easy and flexible way* to deliver the information to the students. The professors commented that, in order to play YouTube video clips, they do not need to set up any device and carry a disc and that the students can review the video after class. Compared to traditional classroom technologies, social media are easier to deliver and distribute information. The professors do not need to use the pedagogical technologies centrally managed by the university which is cookie cut for all. They will have the flexibility to choose from a great variety of social media and choose a technology which fits their needs better. For example, a sign language professor can create videos through vLog tools and share the vLog with her students.

Another benefit is that playing videos from social media *makes class lively.* For example, a geography professor plays videos from YouTube, showing the natural and cultural environments of different geographies. The videos introduce a different rhythm of course content delivery and engage the students more.

However, only four faculty members discussed the benefits of social media in creating the interactive, enjoyable and innovative learning experience. First, they believe social media such as social networking websites connect the students with professionals and resources outside the school.

Such connection persists after a course is completed and will help the students achieve *life-long learning*. Second, they found that social media provide a convenient and low-cost venue for *international collaboration*. Students can reach to students from international universities and collaborate on school projects and research projects. An example of such international collaboration is when students learning a foreign language reach out to foreign students in social networking websites to interact online and practice that language. Another example is when a faculty invited a leading international scholar to give a free seminar through Skype to her students in the classroom. Third, social media create opportunities for *innovative ways of teaching*. For example, a professor discussed a course assignment which requires the students to look for inadequacies and inaccuracies in the Wikipedia contents related to the topics covered in the course. Another assignment he designed required his students to interview politicians and to create podcasts of the interview. These assignments are more participatory and engaging, which changes the students' role from passive knowledge receiver to active knowledge constructor. Fourth, the *participatory learning style* will benefit those students who otherwise cannot be engaged in a traditional classroom lecture format of course delivery.

Beside the benefits, the professors are also concerned with three challenges of using social media for teaching: First, how to *draw the boundary* between professional and social relationship? Social media blend professional and social connections and the line between professional and social relationship is blurred. Several professors viewed the teacher-student relationship as a professional type and expressed the need to maintain a clear boundary to separate the students from their social life. They were not sure how the online social relationship with the students may interfere with the professional activities of teaching students in class. Second, using social media in teaching may *increase complexity of communication* and result in more workload. All professors say they already have a busy schedule. The majority of them say they do not have time to toggle between different social media and prefer to use a single communication tool. Several were afraid that they do not have time to handle the *extra workload of tracking students' activities in social media* in addition to classroom teaching. One faculty member gave the example that a professor may not have time to read and analyze the students' posts in online discussion forum if he/she is teaching a big class.

Benefits and Challenges Perceived by the University

At the university level, the main benefit is that more distant learning classes can be offered if social media are used as the course delivery platform. The university will *reach to more prospective students in a larger geographic area*.

The main challenge will be how to *ensure the security, privacy and intellectual property* of information generated in teaching through social media, which are controlled by external organizations. Currently the University information technology department centrally manages the Blackboard system through which Web enhanced courses are offered. The IT department is yet to acquire experience in managing dispersed diversified technology platforms which are not controlled internally and in *providing assistance* with the social media technologies and platforms when faculty and students need help.

The other challenge is that the University needs to design ways to *coach the students' behaviors with social media usage and to prepare them for career in the digital age*. Currently the University has done little in this aspect. The only relevant policy found in this study is that the University reserves the right to fire student workers if they post inappropriate information in social media which could taint the University's reputation and image.

In summary, the benefits and challenges of social media need to be examined at two levels. The first one relates to curriculum teaching and learning. At this level, potential benefits of social media for learners are easy access to information and connectivity with outside-school human and information resources. The challenge for learners mainly associates with the difficulty of assessing and sensing-making information in social media. For educators, social media provide more flexibility for delivering course contents and may lead to innovative way of teaching and engaging students in the learning process. For the university, social media improve its ability of reaching more students. However, it requires new ways of providing pedagogical technology support.

The second level concerns the role of higher education in preparing the students for life and career. Social media benefit the students in providing opportunities for professional networking while they also require them to understand the professional implication of their behaviors when using social media. They also require efforts from the higher education institutions on coaching students to appropriately use social media for both social and professional purposes.

Differences Between Adopters and Nonadopters

To understand how higher education institutions can constructively use social media for teaching and learning, it is imperative to find who have adopted social media in their learning or teaching and who haven't or use social media in a minimal way. Finding the reasons of adoption and nonadoption will shed light on what can be done to convert non-adoption into adoption. For that purposes, this study compared adopters and non-adopters among the students and faculty.[3]

Adoption and Nonadoption Among Students

The survey found that using social media for social networking and entertainment is common among all age groups or in both graduate and undergraduate groups. However, using social media for learning and professional networking occurs more frequently among the graduate students. Chi-square test found that the graduate students use social media for learning significantly more than the undergraduate students ($p <$ 0.01). 65% of graduate students reported using social media for learning while only 33% reported so. The graduate students also adopt social media for professional networking more than the undergraduate students ($p < 0.01$). 50% of the graduate students use social media for professional networking while only 21% of the undergraduate students do so. This difference is reflected in the difference between how graduate and undergraduate students adopt LinkedIn which is a professional networking website. The graduate students use LinkedIn more than the undergraduate students (32% versus 8%, $p < 0.01$). Overall, graduate students use a broader variety of social media than undergraduate students ($p < 0.01$). On average the graduate students use 2.5 types of social media while the undergraduates use 1.4 types of social media. During the interviews, none of the undergraduates knew LinkedIn.

The frequency and history of using social media do not vary among the students of different majors. However, the business and management students use social media for learning more than the other majors ($p <$ 0.01). 60% of the business and management majors use social media for leaning while 39% of the other majors do so. Also the business and management students use social media for professional networking more than the other majors ($p < 0.01$). 48% of the business and management majors use social media for professional networking while 22% of the other majors do so. The Science and Technology majors use social media for professional networking. None of the 60 science and technology majors in this study reported using LinkedIn.

Finally, the study did not find evidence that the age group affects the differences among the students in using social media for learning and professional networking.

Adoption and Nonadoption Among the Faculty

In previous sections, two groups of faculty members use social media differently—one group uses social media for pulling information only and the other uses social media more in-depth for creating innovative teaching. The interviews found the following key difference among these two groups.

Professors in the first group are less *social media literate* than those in the second group. They know the names of different social media. However, their experience of using social media is often limited to a very small number of popular social media such as Facebook, YouTube and Wikipedia. They were not aware of the detailed functions of other social media which could be used for pedagogical purposes. Therefore it is hard for them to envision how social media can be blend into teaching. The professors in the second group have more exposure to a broader variety of social media. One example is that a faculty is familiar with and frequently uses more than 10 social media including PodCast, VoiceThread, ICQ, Second Life, PodCast, Wikipedia, et cetera.

The second difference is that many professors in the first group view social media as a social tool. They do not think that this social tool fits into the venues of traditional learning activities, such as listening to the professor's lectures, studying in the library, or participating in classroom discussion. Their perspective of teaching is more faculty-centered and classroom-bounded. However, the professors in the second group are more inclined to view teaching and learning from the students' perspective and take rather *a student-centered approach*. They see the extensive use of social media among the students as an opportunity to extend the learning and teaching outside the classroom. As one faculty puts it, "wherever my students are, I want to be there."

The third difference is that the professors in the first group have more inertia of sticking to the pedagogical technologies they have been using than the second group. Frequently mentioned by the professors in the first group is that "I can do what I want to do with email and BlackBoard." They are less willing to take time to learn new technologies and switch from current technologies to new ones. The second group is *more experimental* and has less adherence to the existing technologies. For example, a professor in the second group is very interested in learning how social media technologies are used in different countries and finding how these social media can be applied in his teaching.

In summary, among the students, graduate students and business majors use social media for learning and professional networking more than the other students. To explain this difference, the authors speculate that the graduate students are more mature than the undergraduates and the extensive use of social media in industry and among business professionals exposes business majors relatively more to social media. Among faculty members, social media are more frequently adopted for teaching by those who have higher social media literacy and are more experimental and student centered.

The Environment for Social Media Usage at the University

This study also investigated what has been done by the University to promote the use of social media for teaching and learning by students and faculty members.

The University provides typical technology support such as Wi-Fi access on campus, computer facilities, computer labs and a computer helpdesk. However, as previously mentioned, the University IT department is used to a centrally planned way of managing information technologies and has no experience in supporting the diverse dispersed social media technologies, which are housed outside the University.

The faculty members, when newly hired, are required to go through an orientation which includes BlackBoard training. No trainings or seminars are centrally coordinated on social media. One university office ran a series of workshops on Social media technologies in the year before the study. However, the workshops were not widely marketed and received little attention and support from the school administrators. The attendance at these workshops was very low and 50% of the workshops were cancelled due to low attendance.

The teaching evaluation process and policy implemented by the University emphasize the cognitive aspect of learning, that is, *what* the students learned, instead of the attitudinal aspect of learning, that is, *how* the students learned. Faculty members are not rewarded for creating enjoyable participatory learning. Also the current teaching evaluation focuses on the learning inside a course. It does not take into account the after-course learning induced by innovative course delivery and enabled by the connections made through social media which are built in the course. Overall the teaching evaluation process and policy do not provide adequate incentive for the faculty to overcome inertia of sticking to old pedagogical technologies and innovate in the teaching and learning process.

Except for the language department where the chair instructs the faculty to use social media for teaching, the professors in all other departments use their discretion to decide whether and how social media should be incorporated into teaching. There has been no universitywide dialogue on how social media bring opportunities and challenges for teaching and learning.

In summary, the University provides little support and incentive for teaching innovation through social media. How much the University can benefit from social media in delivering quality education largely depends on the voluntary individual efforts of faculty members.

DISCUSSION AND RECOMMENDED STRATEGIES

This study found that social media has embedded into the daily life of students and faculty members and an increasing number of students intertwine learning with relationship on social media. However, using social media for teaching is an emerging phenomenon and a small percentage of professors are innovating the way they teach through social media.

Social media present both benefits and challenges to learners and educators. From the students' perspective, social media provide abundance of information and a wide range of perspectives at their fingertips but also challenge their ability of sense making and assessing the information quality; social media provide easy connectivity but also bring the risk of reduced privacy, reduced face-to-face interaction and addiction; social media make information sharing easy but require students to understand the professional implication of their online behaviors.

From the faculty perspective, social media have the potential of enabling innovative teaching including creating flexible ways of course delivery, engaging the students more, creating participatory learning and fostering life-long learning by connecting students to external resources and through international collaborations. However, social media may create considerable workload as they increase communication and interaction complexity. They blur the boundary between professional (teaching) and social activities and require the faculty to adjust their role as educators and become more student-centered.

From the University perspective, social media further detaches teaching from physical classroom settings and improves the distance learning option. This, in turn, helps the university reach more prospective students at a broader geographical scale. However, it challenges the traditional centrally managed IT support of classroom teaching and requires new wisdom of dispersed pedagogical technology management.

To take advantage of the benefits social media may bring to higher education and to overcome the challenges social media create, institute-wide efforts are needed. The practice of relying on individual students and professors to learn and teach through social media is not effective. It depends on one's personal experience and attitude which may be limited or biased. The study found that the students, especially the undergraduate students, who are less mature or goal-oriented, mainly use social media for social networking. The faculty-centered educators, who are less "social media-literate" and have high inertia of continued use of traditional technologies, use social media at a minimal level in teaching.

Therefore, for constructive use of social media in teaching and learning, efforts have to come from all stakeholders: university, faculty and students, and should be coordinated through university policies and processes.

At the university level, institution-wide dialogue should take place. A permanent program should be in place to provide a venue for faculty, students, IT staff, and school administrators to share developments on social media, exchange ideas on innovative teaching and learning, provide feedbacks and plan for future technology support. An example of such effort is the annual Program on Teaching and learning with Technology forum at Harvard University. Also training and workshops can be held to improve professors' and students' social media literacy. Such training for faculty should focus on the evaluation of various social media tools and the pedagogical applications of social media. The training for students should emphasize coaching online behaviors and assessing information. More importantly, the university teaching evaluation should provide incentive for the professors to innovate teaching with social media. The evaluation should not only assess the cognitive factors but also collect attitudinal feedback on the learning process. The evaluation should reward the professors for inspiring and facilitating after-course learning through social media.

The IT department of the University should be actively involved as well. They can provide support such as evaluating social media technologies, assisting on using the technologies and integrating social media with the existing technology platform. Therefore a central management portal of all educational technologies and a central support point should be established in order to greatly reduce the overhead costs of using social media by faculty and students.

The school administrators should publicly voice support for social media-related teaching and learning. Champion programs or courses which innovatively use social media should be widely publicized. The top-down support is critical in creating an atmosphere of teaching innovation.

At the faculty level, creativity is needed for professors to innovate teaching through social media. To foster the creativity, professors need to improve their social media literacy and keep up to date with the pedagogical technology innovation through attending trainings, going to meetings and networking with peer educators. Experimentations can be taken first with individual assignments and then be extended to an entire course.

At the student level, individual efforts should also be taken to improve one's social media literacy, not only the literacy on what the technology is but also how to use the technology for learning. The students need to actively seek ways to use social media to improve their learning experience and share their findings with the professors.

FUTURE RESEARCH

This study is conducted at only one public teaching-oriented university. More empirical studies at various types of higher education institutions are needed to corroborate and generalize the findings of this study.

This study raises several research issues which could be further explored in future research, including: What institutionwide efforts on using social media for teaching and learning should be taken? How should IT departments of higher education institutions adapt to the dispersed diverse social media used in teaching and learning? How can faculty members improve pedagogical creativity by using social media? This study provides preliminary insights into these issues. However, each of these questions is important and complex and warrants more focused scholarly investigation. The authors call for a cross-disciplinary approach in studying these questions. Scholars from multiple disciplines including education, business and information technology can bring in insights from different perspectives so to develop comprehensive understanding of social media in high education context and to develop guidelines of using social media for faculty and students from different background.

Intelligent tutoring systems are based on cognitive psychology and provide an interactive environment embodying key elements of individual human tutoring while avoiding its extraordinary financial cost.

These numbers do not add up to 189 as there were missing answers to some of the demographics questions.

In this study, all students and faculty members adopted social media in a certain way. However, for specific teaching or learning functions, some adopted social media while some did not.

REFERENCES

Alexander, B. (2006). A new way of innovation for teaching and learning. *Educause Review, 41,* 32-44

Ajjan, H., & Hartshorne, R. (2008). Investigating faculty decisions to adopt web 2.0 Technologies: Theory and empirical tests. *The Internet and Higher Education, 11,* 71-80.

Bandura, A. (1977). *Social learning theory.* Englewood Cliffs, NJ: Prentice Hall.

Bell, P., Lewenstein, B., Shouse, A. W., & Feder, M. A. (2009). *Leaning science in informal environments.* Washington, DC: National Academy Press.

Benbasat, I., Goldstein, D. K., & Mead, M. (1987). The case research strategy in studies of information systems. *MIS Quarterly, 11*(3), 369-386.

Bloom, B. S. (1984). The 2-sigma problem: The search for methods of group instruction as effective as one-to-one tutoring. *Educational Researcher, 13,* 4-16.

Bonk, C. J. (2009a). The wide open learning world: Sea, land, and ice views. *Association for Learning Technology (ALT) Online Newsletter, 17*. Retrieved from http://newsletter.alt.ac.uk/g57hhv01ses15pbvrjm4bf

Bonk, C. (2009b). *The world is open: How Web technology is revolutionizing education*. San Francisco, CA: Jossey-Bass.

Bruner, J. (1996). *Culture of education*. Cambridge, MA: Harvard University Press.

Cole, M. (2009). Using Wiki technology to support student engagement: Lessons from the trenches. *Computers & Education, 52*, 141-146.

Craig, E. M. (2007). Changing paradigms: Managed learning environments and web 2.0. *Campus-Wide Information Systems, 24*, 152-161.

Dennen, V. P. (2008). Pedagogical lurking: Student engagement in non-posting discussion behavior. *Computers in Human Behavior, 24*(4), 1624-1633.

Economist debates: Social networking. (2008). *Economist.com* Retrieved from http://www.economist.com/debate/overview/123

Gunawardena, C. N., Hermans, M. B., Sanchez, D., Richmond, C., Bohley, M., & Tuttle, R. (2009). A theoretical framework for building online communities of practice with social networking tools. *Educational Media International, 46*, 3-16.

Halic, O., Lee, D., Paulus, T., & Spence, M. (in press). To blog or not to blog: Student perceptions of blog effectiveness for learning in a college-level course. *The Internet and Higher Education*.

Hamann, K., & Wilson, B. M. (2002). Beyond search engines: Enhancing active learning using the Internet. *Politics & Policy, 31*, 533-553.

Hoffman, E. (2009). Evaluating social networking tools for distance learning. *Proceedings of Technology, Colleges & Community Worldwide Online Conference, Volume 2009* (Vol. 1, pp. 92-100). Retrieved from http://etec.hawaii.edu/proceedings/2009/hoffman.pdf

Hoffman, E. (2010). Social media and learning environments: Shifting perspectives on the locus of control. *Education, 15*(2). Retrieved from http://www.ineducation.ca/article/social-media-and-learning-environments-shifting-perspectives-locus-control

Horizon report. (2010). *The new media consortium*. Retrieved from http://wp.nmc.org/horizon2010/

Johnson, R. T., & Johnson, D. W. (1986). Action research: Cooperative learning in the science classroom. *Science and Children, 24*, 31-32.

Jones N., Blackey, H., Fitzgibbon, K., & Chew, E. (2010). Get out of MySpace! *Computers & Education, 54*, 776-782.

Koedinger, K. R., & Aleven, V. (2007). Exploring the assistance dilemma in experiments with cognitive tutors. *Educational Psychology Review, 19*, 239-264.

Lee, C. D. (2008). 2008 Wallace Foundation distinguished lecture—The centrality of culture to the scientific study of learning and development: How an ecological framework in education research facilitates civic responsibility. *Educational Researcher, 37*(5), 267-279.

Mazer, J. P., Murphy, R. E., & Simonds, C. S. (2007). I'll see you on "Facebook": The effects of computer-mediated teacher self-disclosure on student motivation, affective learning, and classroom climate. *Communication Education, 56*(1), 1-17.

Maloney, E. (2007). What web 2.0 can teach us about learning. *Chronicle of Higher Education, 25*(18), B26.

Meltzoff, A. N. (1995). Understanding the intentions of others: Re-enactment of intended acts by 18-month-old children. *Developmental Psychology, 31*, 838-850.

Meltzoff, A. N. (2007). The 'like me' framework for recognizing and becoming an intentional agent. *Acta Psychologica, 124*, 26-43.

Meltzoff, A. N., Kuhl, P. K., Movellan, J., & Sejnowski, T. J. (2009). Foundations for a new science of learning. *Science, 325*, 284-288.

Meltzoff, A. N., & Moore, M. K. (1977). Imitation of facial and manual gestures by human neonates. *Science, 198*, 75-78.

Roblyer, M. D., McDaniel, M., Webb, M., Herman, J. & Witty, J. V. (in press). Findings on Facebook in higher education: A comparison of college faculty and student uses and perceptions of social networking sites. *The Internet and Higher Education.*

Rogoff, B. (1990). *Apprenticeship in thinking: Cognitive development in social context.* New York, NY: Oxford University Press.

Tams, S. (2006). Self-directed social learning: The role of individual differences. *Journal of Management Development, 27*(2), 196-213.

VanLehn, K. (2006). The behavior of tutoring systems. *International Journal of Artificial Intelligence in Education, 16*, 227-265.

Vygotsky, L. S. (1978). *Mind in society: The development of higher mental processes.* Cambridge, MA: Harvard University Press.

CHAPTER 13

THE USE OF SOCIAL MEDIA AND NETWORKS IN TEACHING PUBLIC ADMINISTRATION

Perceptions, Practices, and Concerns

Thomas A. Bryer and Baiyun Chen

An exploratory study was conducted on the use of social media and networking technologies in teaching public administration courses. After reviewing literature on technology adoption in higher education and learning through technology, we present findings from a survey and interview conducted. We also present an analysis of the first author's use of social media and networking technologies in teaching an undergraduate course in civic engagement. In closing we address future directions related to the following topics: (1) social learning assessment, (2) distinct cultural orientations that define the relationship between one's personal/private and public identities, (3) cyberbullying, (4) student-faculty relations outside a traditional or closed classroom environment, (5) Family Educational Rights and Privacy Act requirements and institutional policies, and (6) innovation diffusion through academia.

Cutting-Edge Social Media Approaches to Business Education:
Teaching With LinkedIn, Facebook, Twitter, Second Life, and Blogs, pp. 241–267
Copyright © 2010 by Information Age Publishing
241

INTRODUCTION

Public administration is a social enterprise. Degrees are granted to students in a plethora of fields under the umbrella of or in relation to public administration. These include graduate and undergraduate degrees and certificates in public administration, public management, nonprofit management, urban and regional planning, emergency management and homeland security, and health services administration. Public administration programs are sometimes housed in their own schools or colleges, or they are found under the auspices of political science departments or business schools. Public administration can essentially be defined as the intersection of multiple disciplines and sub-disciplines, joined together in the common interest of supporting or developing community, region, state, country, or world. Increasingly, public administration is recognized as a field well suited to forge collaboration across businesses, nonprofit organization, government agencies, faith organizations, and active citizens.

Given the social and collaborative nature of the public administration field, it is appropriate to consider the use of social networking and media tools. Broadly speaking, public administrators (or individuals working for the public good, as opposed to working for a private good or interest) are increasingly using social media and networking tools for intraorganizational and interorganizational communication. Yet, it is unclear the extent to which students preparing for careers as public administrators are taught to use these tools, nor is it clear what the benefit of the tools are for teaching (or practice). This chapter reports on qualitative research that examines how public administration faculty in the United States are using social media and networking tools for instructional purposes. For the purposes of this study, social media and Web 2.0 are defined as: "activities that integrate technology, social interaction, and content creation. Social media tools use the "wisdom of crowds" (or crowdsourcing) to collaboratively connect online information. Through social media, people or groups can create, organize, edit, comment on, combine, and share content. Social media and Web 2.0 use many technologies and form, including RSS and other syndicated web feeds, blogs, wikis, photo-sharing, video-sharing, podcasts, social networking, social bookmarking, mashups, widgets, virtual worlds, microblogs, and more" (Federal Web Managers Council, 2010).

The guiding questions for this study: How are public administration faculty using social media and networking tools to teach public administration courses? What tools are being used? What concerns do faculty have regarding the use of social media and networking tools for teaching? What strategies are available to overcome perceived concerns?

Data are drawn from a survey of faculty from universities with accredited masters in public administration degree programs, semi-structured interviews with volunteer survey respondents, and a case analysis of the first author's use of social media and networking tools in teaching an interdisciplinary undergraduate and online course on civic engagement. The chapter closes with a discussion of implications and future directions for research and pedagogical experimentation.

LITERATURE REVIEW

Two streams of literature are considered here. First is literature on technology adoption in higher education. These sources suggest potential barriers to and facilitators of adoption of new technologies in teaching; they also suggest a path that might be followed in future adoption. Second is literature on use of social media in learning, with particular attention on existing research and commentary regarding the efficacy of social media and networking tools for teaching and learning.

Technology Adoption in Higher Education

New technology adoption in organizations, including higher education, is driven by perceived costs. The more information an individual has, the lower the costs and uncertainty of adoption. Lower adoption costs can lead to early adoption (Wozniak, 1987). For faculty in higher education, "the extent and rate of technology adoption is related to availability of resources and acceptance of innovations by faculty" (Groves & Zemel, 2000, p. 58). Early adopters are considered innovators and represent, typically, a small minority of a subject population. Most in a subject population are late adopters and laggards (Groves & Zemel, 2000). As such, and in particular relating to higher education, there are populations of innovators and populations of slow adopters; the latter group represents mainstream faculty (Jacobsen, 1998).

Rogers (2000) identifies three levels of information technology adoption in higher education: (1) personal productivity aids that allow for more efficient task performance, (2) enrichment add-ins allow for additions to standard teaching, such as e-mail and course websites, and (3) paradigm shifts that require faculty to reconfigure teaching methods to best utilize technological capacity. Social media and networking technologies are, at a minimum, enrichment add-ins but have the potential, for some innovators with a supportive institutional framework, to cause a paradigm shift. Teaching can be supplemented with social media and networking tools, or they can be used to create new teaching methods entirely. If faculty innovators use these technologies as paradigm shifting tools, they represent disruptive innovations, which are "technological innovations, products, services, processes, or concepts that disrupt the status quo" (Meyer, 2010, p. 1). Maddux and Johnson (2005) offer a further category for social media and networking tools as paradigm shifting mechanisms: Type II technologies allow new relationships between student and teacher to emerge that did not exist before.

The beginnings of a paradigm shift may be occurring in higher education, but the costs of individual and widespread adoption still need to be reduced. As data reviewed below suggest, faculty in public administration programs have begun, to varying degrees, to proceed through the first three states of an organizational change and information technology implementation process. Faculty have started to unfreeze and change (Lewin, 1952), but institutional barriers prevent change beyond individual faculty members at this point. Change has been initiated, as individual faculty members have recognized opportunities for teaching and learning with social media and networking technologies. Individual faculty have adopted technologies with backing from immediate departmental or college supervisors, and certain training has occurred within limited university settings on social networking and media technologies (Cooper & Zmud, 1990). The next stage, not yet broached, is a general acceptance of technologies by mainstream faculty (Jacobsen, 1998). These and other findings are addressed below, following a review of teaching and learning through technology.

Use of Social Media in Learning

The use of social media and networking services has surged globally in the recent years. Based on individual companies' statistics in February 2010, Facebook passed 400 million users; LinkedIn added its 60th million member (Rao, 2010); Twitter hit over 50 million tweets per day; and YouTube, in October 2009, reached 1 billion views per day (Grove, 2010). In January 2010, Facebook surpassed Google and become the number-one time sink on the Web. According to the Nielsen Company, the average U.S. Internet user spends 7 hours per month on Facebook, which is more time than on Google, YouTube, Microsoft, Yahoo, Amazon, and Wikipedia combined (Nielsen, 2010). Social media is part of our daily life.

While personal social communication is the biggest reason for people to stay on Facebook every day, data has suggested that few people use social media and networking services for educational purposes. The EDUCAUSE Center for Applied Research (ECAR) has collected 4-year comparison data on student use of information technologies from 39 undergraduate institutions in the United States (2006-2009). Based on the 2009 ECAR data, 90% of students responded that they used social networking services, such as Facebook, MySpace, Bebo, and LinkedIn. Despite the high percentage of personal use of social networks, only 28% of respondents reported using them in a course during the quarter or semester of the survey (Caruso, Smith, & Salaway, 2009). The use of social media in teaching by instructors is even scarcer.

Many educators see the potential benefits of using social media (Hughes, 2009; Nellison, 2007) because they are integrated into students' daily life. Possibly, social media could be used to engage students to facilitate student-centered social learning activities. Should educators want to take advantage of social media and networking services as part of learning spaces, they should consider how they can encourage and engage students and instructors in use of these technologies and infuse social networking practices into learning activities using sound pedagogical practices (Caruso et al., 2009). Unfortunately, there are few studies on the pedagogy of how to use social media to facilitate learning.

The literature identified concerns for using social media and networking services as a teaching and learning tool. One of the concerns is that the technology is reshaping the instructor-student relationship. "Friending" between instructors and students on Facebook is a new territory. Some people think it is awkward and problematic. For instance, Beckenham (2008) discusses her concerns about perceived preferential treatment or inappropriate or too informal relations between instructors and students due to familiarity on online social networks. Instructor-student relationship varies from person to person in face-to-face classrooms.

There is much discussion in the literature regarding ethical concerns of using social networks in academic environments. Students' privacy and security issues are the priority concern (Foulger et al., 2009). The Family Educational Rights & Privacy Act (FERPA) requires that students' education records be protected. However, a class discussion on open social media might reveal student class list to be public. Moreover, some students are not aware that their posted information on the Internet is publicly available. A piece of personal information or a picture on the web might lead to issues of identity theft or prevent them from future career opportunities. It is a long way for students to fully understand the social, economical and legal consequences resulting from their online social networking activities.

METHOD

The study was designed as an exploratory analysis of current practices, concerns, and perceptions of public administration faculty regarding the use of social media and networking tools in teaching. Requests for participation in a survey were emailed to the chairs/directors of all public administration departments or degree programs at institutions with accredited masters in public administration degrees. A total of 57 faculty members from 28 universities across the United States completed the survey. Figure 13.1 represents the academic rankings of the respondents. The two respondents who chose "Others" in academic rankings are respectively the program director and the associate dean of academic affairs.

The survey was followed up with semistructured interviews. Participants were drawn from the survey respondents who had expressed willingness to sit for an extended discussion. A total of eight interviews were conducted. The interviewees were from six universities and held six academic rankings from department chair, professor, associate professor, assistant professor, to instructor. Last, an analysis of the first author's use of social media and networking tools was conducted.

RESULTS

Findings are presented from all data sources below. Specifically, the findings are reported with respect to the following questions: (1) What social

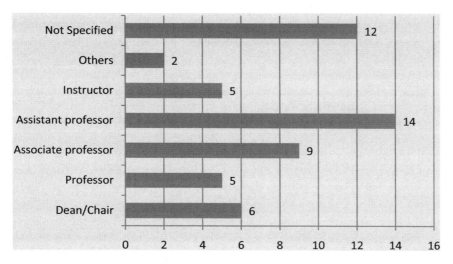

Figure 13.1.   Academic ranking of respondents.

media tools do public administration faculty use? (2) What activities do faculty use with social media? (3) How are social media activities assessed? (4) Would social media help improve students' learning outcomes? (5) What are the benefits of using social media in education? (6) What are the concerns of using social media in education? (7) What are identified best practices and suggestions for improvement? The results section is closed with analysis of the first author's use of social media and networking tools.

What Social Media Tools
Do Public Administration Faculty Use?

In the survey, 53 out of 56 respondents report their uses of social media, either for personal, academic, research and/or professional purposes. Table 13.1 illustrates the types of social media the respondents used. The most popular services are Facebook and LinkedIn. The majority of them use Facebook for personal communication and LinkedIn for professional connections. Some other services mentioned in the survey and interviews include course management systems (CMS) (e.g., Blackboard), wiki services (e.g., PBWorks), blog services (e.g., Blogger.com), social videos (e.g., YouTube), audio/video conferencing tools (e.g., Illuminate), and screencast tools (e.g., Jing).

In the interviews, seven out of eight respondents reported that they use CMS, such as Blackboard, as the major platform to post course contents

**Table 13.1.   Self-Reported Social Media Usage
by Public Administration Faculty (2009)**

Academic Position	Social Media Services (N=53)						
	Facebook	MySpace	Ning	LinkedIn	Second Life	Twitter	Others
Dean/chair	2		1	2	1	2	
Professor	2		1	2	1	1	
Associate professor	5			3	1	1	1
Assistant professor	10		1	5	1	2	3
Instructor	3			3			1
Others	2			1			1
Not specified	5	1	1	7	1	2	4
Total	29	1	4	23	5	8	10

and facilitate online interactions. They are happy with the discussion and mail tools inside their CMS system for interacting with their students. Most respondents are more or less exposed to external social media services, and have used these services as supplemental resources beyond CMS activities.

What Activities Do Faculty Use With Social Media?

The survey respondents report that they use social networks to connect with friends and coworkers, interact with students, and teach classes. Social media serve as alternative avenues for them to reach students. While almost half of the respondents encourage their students to participate in social networking activities, only 7 out of 41 require them to do so.

Posting media and mailing have been the most frequently used social media teaching features. These respondents take advantage of the Web 2.0 technologies to interact with students, help them with job seeking, facilitate group projects, organize student association networks, and promote their courses, programs, and conferences. They facilitate a strong sense of community and encourage collective intelligence by creating social networks around academic topics or connecting students with alumni, outside communities and experts around the world.

In the interviews, besides using social media to communicate with family and friends, respondents report that they use media as a platform for their students to discuss, collaborate, learn and network. Figure 13.2 shows nine categories of activities respondents report in the interviews. Most frequently, they use discussion tools in CMS to facilitate student interactions. Students also collaborate with each other via discussions, blogs, wikis and social networks. One of the common uses of social media is to provide students with extra learning contents. Respondents integrate YouTube videos, online cases, and news articles as part of their curriculum.

Moreover, online social networks are convenient ways for faculty and students to keep up with their professional connections. Five out of eight interviewees maintained an active LinkedIn profile to connect with friends and former students in the profession, discuss career development, maintain their professional organization membership, and expand their consulting businesses. They also encourage their students to do the same. One respondent indicated that registering with LinkedIn is one of their program entry requirements for freshman students. All of her students use LinkedIn to connect with classmates and alumni. In classes, students are required to post questions for alumni and keep an active dialogue. Such activities help students to link their classroom study with

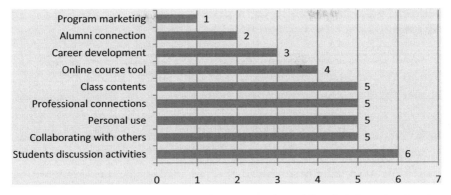

Figure 13.2.   Self-reported social media activities by public administration faculty (2010).

real world practices, enrich their learning experience, and prepare them for better career opportunities.

How are Social Media Activities Assessed?

The interviewees were probed about their assessment strategies regarding their social media activities. Most respondents do not have an assessment strategy specifically designed for social learning. They feel that social learning should be optional, not required in classes. If some students choose not to complete the activities on social media due to personal reasons, they should not be punished for nonparticipation.

However, two interviewees list their social media assignments in the course syllabi. Students are informed in the syllabi that they will need to use blogs, wikis, or online social networks in the classes as part of the course assignments. Both respondents review students' postings. One interviewee awards participation credits based on students' blog postings. The other interviewee requires students to summarize and reflect their assigned LinkedIn activities and then post their reflections as discussion postings inside their university CMS. She does not grade students' social media activities directly due to FERPA requirements and school policies, which do not allow any grading outside university systems. Instead, she grades students' reflections on their LinkedIn activities in the CMS based on her rubrics for online discussion posts. The rubric criteria include clarity, comprehension, original thinking, and writing. None of the criteria are designed to directly guide students on their LinkedIn activities.

Would Social Media Help to Improve Students' Learning Outcomes?

When we ask if respondents thought social media improves students' learning outcomes, there 21 "Yes," 23 "No," and 9 respondents did not answer the question. As Table 13.2 below shows, more associate, full professors and instructors select No, and more assistant professors answer Yes. The majority of the assistant professors are relatively young. Most likely, they use social media in their personal life, so it is easier for them to adopt these technologies as tools for teaching.

The Yes respondents suggest that social media have positive learning outcomes because they enhance social interactions and sharing. Learning is rather a social event than a simple acquisition activity (Mott & Wiley, 2009). Social networks present learners with multiple worldviews and opportunities to experience alternatives, hear different stories, and ask meaningful questions. Social interactions, formal or informal, are a less threatening discourse to add depth, meaning and value to the learning contents. They also comment that social media is an alternative method to engage students in learning. Students are familiar with this alternative. It is a reasonable assumption that a college student only logs into his/her CMS once or twice a day, at most, to engage in formal learning activities. However, they spend way more time on Facebook or MySpace. When the instructor sends them a message or posts an article on Facebook, it is more likely to get their attention and interests immediately.

The No respondents give various reasons why they see social media would have negative learning outcomes. Like the literature has suggested,

Table 13.2.   Self-Reported Attitudes on Social Media Impacts on Learning by Public Administration Faculty (2009)

Academic Position	Do you think social media improves students' learning outcomes? ($N = 44$)	
	Yes	No
Dean/chair	3	3
Professor	2	3
Associate professor	3	6
Assistant professor	9	5
Instructor	2	3
Others		2
Not Specified	2	1
Total	21	23

the biggest concern for using social media is students' and faculty's security and privacy concerns. They also mentioned that there are too many noises and distractions on the web, such as advertisements and entertainment news. It is almost impossible for learners to focus on in-depth learning and discussions in such an open environment. The No respondents are suspicious because they are not aware of any teaching strategies for social media. They have heard that social media are popular among their students, but they are not familiar with these tools. They simply have no ideas on how to implement them in classes.

In the interviews, four out of eight respondents think that social media have huge potentials for learning. So far, they are not sure if social media could improve students' learning outcomes. The open web brings learning, research and job opportunities for all users. However, to achieve in-depth and quality learning, students' activities need to be structured and facilitated carefully in an un-structured Web environment. Social media can be useful, if they are used properly. If they are misused, they can be very distracting, especially for undergraduate students who are still inexperienced with juggling between learning and playing.

Benefits of Using Social Media in Education

In the interviews, seven out of eight respondents discussed the benefits of using social media in education. One of the biggest benefits is the ease of use. Students are familiar with social media technologies. Checking out Facebook and reading blogs are part of their daily life. These tools also make social connections at the ease of our finger tips. A number of interviewees strongly encourage their students to setup social connections with alumni and community professionals via LinkedIn or other social networks.

Social media also provide added learning benefits, according to our respondents. Students can exercise their creativity with image, audio and video mashups. These visual and interactive learning materials engage students both inside and outside of classroom. Social media is a platform for informal learning. It is not only a place for students to reinforce what they have learned in class but also to explore new knowledge.

Concerns of Using Social Media in Education

Despite the benefits of communication and collaboration, concerns are raised on cybersecurity, privacy and student-instructor relationship issues. Table 13.3 illustrates concerns that our respondents from diverse aca-

Table 13.3.   Self-Reported Concerns of Using Social Media by Public Administration Faculty (2009)

	Concerns of Using Social Media in Education (N = 53)					
Academic Position	*Not Enough Time*	*Technology too Complex*	*Ethical Issues*	*Student Privacy Issue*	*Faculty Privacy Issue*	*Others*
Dean/chair	1	2		5	3	
Professor	1	2	2	3	2	3
Associate professor	2		2	2	3	6
Assistant professor		1	2	8	9	4
Instructor	1	1	2	4	3	2
Others						2
Not specified			1	1	2	2
Total	5	6	9	23	5	19

demic rankings reported in the survey. Obviously, privacy issue is the top concern to all respondents. Faculty are concerned about their professional identity. Two respondents mention RateMyProfessor.com in the interviews and fear that the web presence might damage their professional reputation. The Internet is such an open environment that nobody can control what others might post about you. At the same time, respondents are also concerned about students posting inappropriate contents online which might pose danger to their future career development.

Ethical issues are the next concern for respondents who are not in a leadership position. Such issues include cyber bully, marginalizing students, and being unfair because of befriending one student over another. A number of the interviewees claim that, to avoid potential student-instructor relationship issues, they don't friend their students until they graduate. Time constraints and technology barriers are big concerns among senior faculty. Junior faculty are interested in learning new technologies, but work load and productivity also prevent them from exploring new tools for teaching.

In the interviews, many respondents mentioned that they are not allowed or encouraged to adopt new technologies in teaching in their university environment. In most universities, there are a number of authorized delivery systems, such as CMS, school e-mail, and human resources system. Interviewees feel that university policies do not appreciate innovations due to privacy requirements (FERPA) or security concerns. They are not able to install any new software on school computers, unless they are assisted by the technical staff.

Best Practices and Suggestions From Faculty

Student and faculty support is the key to success of using social media for education, according to the interviewees. One respondent stated that all students in her program have joined LinkedIn. Her students have been benefited enormously from social networking activities. Her program provides students with strong support services, such as free training sessions from the IT unit, library and digital media specialists. The IT staff coach students if they have any difficulties using technologies for learning. The librarians also regularly deliver sessions on what should or should not be revealed on social media. Since students are using online social networks extensively in their program study, other instructors in the program start to adopt this technology more willingly. Other respondents also mention the importance of student training. Not all students are comfortable with new technologies. Even if they know how to use technologies for entertainment, the majority of them need guidance on how these technologies can assist their learning process.

Interviewees expressed a strong need for faculty support in terms of adopting new technologies. They would like to have access to technologies and learn more about new ways of using them, such as best practices and pitfalls. They look forward to their institutions embracing innovations. There is a need for crafting and implementing clearly-stated institutional policies on the use of social media in educational environment.

CASE ANALYSIS

Presented here is an analysis of the first author's use of social networking and media tools for teaching an undergraduate online course in civic engagement. The course is interdisciplinary and open to students in public administration, political science, and other majors. Before describing the course and how tools are used in teaching the course, a few words regarding the instructor's general orientation towards the use of social media and networking will establish a context.

The instructor established a Facebook profile (http://www.facebook.com/dr.bryer) primarily to interact with students but naturally extended the reach of his network to include long lost friends/associates, family, colleagues, and other somewhat random people. Early on in the development of his network, a decision was made to not request "friendship" with students. The logic of the decision was to avoid placing students in an awkward position of choosing to "friend" or "not friend" their instructor. However, if students requested "friendship," it would be accepted. Recognizing the potential for embarrassing situations, the instructor largely maintains content on his Facebook profile that is relevant to his broad interest in government and civic engagement. By posting news articles, he seeks to facilitate conversation amongst current and former students, as well as the network of friends, associates, colleagues, family, and other random people. He posts personal information, such as news related to family, but he avoids novelty "games" such as the application developed to determine one's stripper name.

In order to specifically encourage networking amongst his current and former students, he established a Facebook Group for that purpose: Dr. Bryer's Current and Former Students (http://www.facebook.com/#!/group.php?gid=32342856166&ref=ts). He defined the general purpose of the group in response to students who joined: " I would love to get as many from your class on here as possible ... over time, this can be a great networking tool, job finding tool, happy hour buddy finding tool, social movement tool, or whatever."

The civic engagement course presented an opportunity to more intensively integrate social media and networking tools within a particular class. As an online course, it seemed a good opportunity to teach civic engagement theory and skills using the very tools that are increasingly used in civic action and activism. The official home for the course was the Webcourses/Blackboard system, which is a closed classroom environment. Within this closed environment, the instructor delivered lecture-style course content through modules but also directed students, through modules, to external social media/networking sites.

The primary external home for the course was a Wiki located at the following address: http://centralfloridacivicengagementprojectspaces.wikispaces.com. Figure 13.3 presents a screen shot of the front page of the wiki.

The design was intended to encourage individuals (citizens) outside of the class to engage with students regarding student civic projects. Each student was given their own page on the wiki, which they developed on their own. Outside community members were invited to give feedback to students and otherwise give ideas or support as students sought to address a community or neighborhood problem. Issues identified included limited parking on campus, limited street lighting in neighborhoods, litter in apartment complexes, and children playing unsupervised on the street.

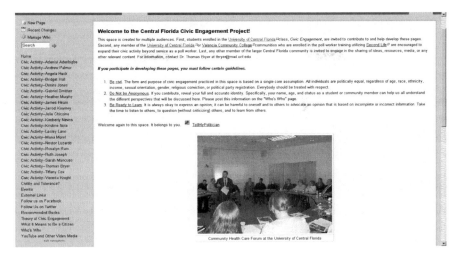

Figure 13.3.   Screen shot of civic engagement course wiki.

Given the public nature of the wiki, proactive steps were taken to mitigate against "outsiders" entering dialogue with students in a hostile or negative manner. Three rules or norms were established for participation on the wiki: (1) be civil, (2) do not be anonymous, and (3) be ready to learn/listen to others without prejudging. Otherwise, all students and non-students were invited to contribute to the civic projects, as well as to the list of external links, video and other media, recommended books, and general discussion on topics related to civic engagement.

A complementary fan page was created on Facebook for the course, located at the following address: http://www.facebook.com/pages/Central-Florida-Civic-Engagement-Project/140691059343. Figure 13.4 presents a screen shot of the front page of this site.

Like the Wiki page, the Facebook fan page was open to the public. The purpose of the Facebook page was to allow students to explore civic opportunities within the Facebook and other social media environments. The instructor initiated that process with a video uploaded to ScreenCast: http://www.screencast.com/t/OTUxNWEzM. Ultimately, students contributed dozens of new links and resources; they became aware of the potential use and power of social networking tools for civic action.

The last social media and networking tool used in the class was Second Life. The tool was used here with the specific purpose of training students to serve as poll workers during elections. Second Life is a simulated world in which users create avatars to interact with other individuals from anywhere in the world. The tool is used by governments for simulated train-

Figure 13.4.   Facebook page for civic engagement course.

ing exercises, such as emergency response. In this case, students participated in three structured Second Life activities: (1) an orientation to learn how the program works, (2) a lecture on poll working, and (3) a simulated election. Students were required to write essays reflecting on their experiences in Second Life; most expressed satisfaction with the training exercise and saw much opportunity for such trainings in other fields. At the same time, students expressed hesitancy regarding the likely use of the tool for social networking outside of formal structured processes. Figures 13.5 and 13.6 show images of first, the lecture, and second, the election simulation:

Lessons Learned

Based on experiences teaching with the social media and networking tools identified above, five lessons have been learned for future pedagogical practice. These lessons are: (1) use technology, don't force technology, (2) respect privacy, but encourage transparency, (3) promote civility and reduce timidity, (4) teach the technologies but be open to learn about the technologies, and (5) facilitate learning through social engagement and interaction.

Several different social networking and media tools were used in the class. Each had a specific function, and none were treated as comprehensive teaching or course management tools. This is the first lesson: use

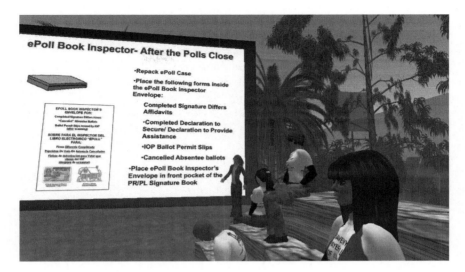

Figure 13.5.   Lecture in Second Life.

Figure 13.6.   Election simulation in Second Life.

technology, don't force the technology. Facebook is used to introduce students to civic resources online and to allow students to comment on current events relevant to subjects of study. Wiki is used for student creation and cocreation of content related to the course. Second Life is used for structured, synchronous professional training and lecture. Each technology is well suited for the designated purpose and introduces students to the diversity of networking tools available.

In a course on civic engagement, it is particularly important for students to stand behind their ideas and efforts to enhance community and qualities of life. However, some students desire privacy, particularly with elements of their life or personality that are not directly relevant to the subject of the course or their civic efforts. In using the various social media and networking tools, students are encouraged to be fully open, to make clear their biases and experiences that shape their civic attitudes and opinions, but they are not required to reveal any information if they wish to not do so.

Given the open nature of social networking and media tools, efforts are required to ensure civility and supportive communication. Efforts taken to do this are described above. Also, in using these technologies, the instructor needs to recognize his or her own limitations. Students may be more conversant with the capacity of the different tools, and instructors ought to be prepared to learn along with their students.

Last, a benefit of using these tools is the opportunity to facilitate learning through social engagement and interaction. One of the central questions of interest in this study and for public administration faculty is whether the use of social media for teaching enhances student learning. Some respondents considered that learning may be harmed, given the vast amount of unfiltered information, and the other stimulants in the social media environment that might distract from core content. The experience of the instructor in this case aligns with the perceptions of other respondents. If student content is facilitated and agenda-driven in the social media and networking world, learning can be achieved. Is the learning superior to face to face? Future research needs to be conducted on this question. It seems safe to suggest, though, that the publicly open social media and networking sites provide students with access to more information and experiences than they would get in a closed environment alone. If properly facilitated and framed, such expanded exposures can benefit student learning. There are other questions for future research, however. These are explored in the final section.

FUTURE DIRECTIONS AND IMPLICATIONS

Findings suggest a variety of areas for follow up research and experimentation. Topics discussed below are not exhaustive but reflect the ideas and concerns raised by participants in this study. In no particular order, we briefly address future directions related to the following topics: (1) social learning assessment, (2) distinct cultural orientations that define the relationship between one's personal/private and public identities, (3) cyberbullying, (4) student-faculty relations outside a traditional or closed classroom environment, (5) FERPA requirements and institutional policies, and (6) innovation diffusion through academia.

Social Learning Assessment

There are two types of assessment: summative assessment and formative assessment. Summative assessment has been used extensively in traditional classroom education. It is generally carried out by the instructor at the end of a course or a project to determine what students have learned for grading and accountability purposes in forms of standardized testing (U.S. Department of Education, 2010). However, social learning, many times, is student-centered and happens outside classrooms. It is difficult to use fixed criteria, such as tests or quizzes, to evaluate learning outcomes that happen on social media. Many of our respondents raise the question on what is the best strategy to measure students' learning on LinkedIn, blogs or wikis. Formative assessment could be an appropriate method.

Formative assessment is normally carried out by either the instructor or the students throughout the learning process to diagnose and aid the condition of learning and instruction in forms of feedbacks and reflections (U.S. Department of Education, 2010). Formative assessment is generally conducted to facilitate learning, not necessarily for grading purposes. For example, a student can post questions on personal career goals in the discussions area on LinkedIn. He might get feedbacks from not just the instructor, but also peers, alumni, and professionals in the community. The feedback information is not evaluative but diagnostic. It might augment, concur or conflict with the student's ideas and facilitate him on subsequent learning.

Learning on social media is informal, open and self-regulated. Instructors could integrate social media to supplement and reinforce classroom teaching using formative assessment strategies, such as rubrics, portfolios and reflections. Nicol and Macfarlane-Dick (2006) suggest seven principles of good feedback practice to facilitate self-regulations. These seven principles can be transferred to facilitation of effective social learning:

1. helps clarify what good performance is (goals, criteria, expected standards);

2. facilitates the development of self-assessment (reflection) in learning;

3. delivers high quality information to students about their learning;

4. encourages teacher and peer dialogue around learning;

5. encourages positive motivational beliefs and self-esteem;

6. provides opportunities to close the gap between current and desired performance;

7. provides information to teachers that can be used to help shape the teaching.

If educators make use of the informal learning that occurs on social media and networking services, the authors assume that the achievement gap between marginalized students and mainstream students can be reduced. The assumption needs to be tested in subsequent studies. Future research can also explore the effects of using rubrics and feedback on learning outcomes using social media and experiment with the best facilitation and assessment strategies for social learning.

Distinct Cultural Orientations

How much should faculty (and students) be expected to share about their "personal" life within the "public" spaces created through social media and networking tools? Some research participants expressed significant hesitation about such openness. For instance, one respondent offered that she would not post pictures of her children on Facebook for her students to see; another offered that she would not friend any active students on Facebook to avoid having them see her off-work interactions. This orientation is a distinctly Western cultural norm. Rather than treat the self as a single, cohesive identity, the tendency is to treat the self as multiple selves: a work identity, a family identity, a church identity, et cetera. To bridge these roles and let the "personal" or "private" into the work or "public" space would be to integrate roles.

Palmer (2000, p. 17) captured well the dominant cultural norm in Western society:

> To reduce our vulnerability, we disconnect from students, from subjects, and even from ourselves. We build a wall between inner truth and outer performance, and we play-act the teacher's part. Our words, spoken at remove from our hearts, become "the balloon speech in cartoons," and we become caricatures of ourselves. We distance ourselves from students and subject to minimize the danger—forgetting that distance makes like more dangerous still be isolating the self.

The alternative, suggested Palmer, is an integration of roles (2000, p. 17):

But a good teacher must stand where personal and public meet, dealing with the thundering flow of traffic at an intersection where "weaving a web of connectedness" feels more like crossing a freeway on foot. As we try to connect ourselves and our subjects with our students, we make ourselves, as well as our subjects, vulnerable to indifference, judgment, ridicule.

In the space available here, we will not fully dissect this issue. However, it is necessary to observe that role fragmentation as a dominant way of interacting with parts of our individual world may limit the potential benefits in using social media and networking tools for teaching. The tools are developed as a means to achieve transparency of self and process; to conceal parts of our individual identities as some teachers do in the face-to-face world may be limiting. Future research can explore these implications further, as well as explore cultural connections with willingness to integrate roles, thus eliminating any distinction between the "private" or "personal" and "public."

Cyberbullying

Some respondents expressed concern regarding bullying in the social media and networking environment, particularly bullying of students by other students or bullying of students by non-class members who have access to the public social media or network site. Bullying in higher education environments is not a new concern (Keashly & Neuman, 2010). Indeed, social networking sites have been created to address the very issue, at least in the face-to-face environment. See for instance:

- http://bulliedacademics.blogspot.com,
- http://www.mobbingportal.com, and
- http://www.facebook.com/group.php?v=info&gid=295040946478

Bullying has been defined as the following (Einarsen, Hoel, Zapf, & Cooper, 2002, p. 15):

Bullying at work means harassing, offending, socially excluding someone or negatively affecting someone's work tasks.... It has to occur repeatedly and regularly (e.g., weekly) and over a period of time (e.g., at least six months). Bullying is an escalating process in the course of which the person confronted end up in an inferior position and become the target of systematic negative social acts.

In the context of social media or networking sites, bullying might take the form of harassing or offending written or video comments, or imagery, directed to a particular student or set of students. In the closed classroom environment, such as in a Blackboard or Webcourses environment, such behavior can be controlled relatively easily by the instructor. If the course is taken into a more public domain, instructor control is reduced. In the case example presented previously, the instructor identified norms for behavior for any individual wishing to participate on the Wiki. Specifically, the instructor asked that users:

1. Be civil. The form and purpose of civic engagement practiced in this space is based on a single core assumption. All individuals are politically equal, regardless of age, race, ethnicity, income, sexual orientation, gender, religious conviction, or political party registration. Everybody should be treated with respect.

2. Do Not be Anonymous. If you contribute, reveal your full and accurate identity. Specifically, your name, age, and status as a student or community member can help us all understand the different perspectives that will be discussed here. Please post this information on the "Who's Who" page.

3. Be Ready to Learn. It is always okay to express an opinion; it can be harmful to oneself and to others to advocate an opinion that is based on incomplete or incorrect information. Take the time to listen to others, to question (without criticizing) others, and to learn from others.

It remains possible, however, for an outsider to enter as a bully and to disrupt the learning environment. Any such comments can be deleted by the instructor or another administrator, but there may be other strategies for facilitating online discourse to prevent or reduce the influence of bullying. Further study can be conducted in this area to determine available social and technological strategies for achieving this end.

Student-Faculty Relations

Some respondents raised ethical concerns regarding relations with students outside of class. For instance, one respondent offered that she will not friend students on Facebook, given the fear of perceived preferential treatment. How could she defend being "friends" with some students but not all? She will, however, link with students on Linked-In, which is perceived as more of a professional development and career focused networking tool. These are noteworthy concerns but perhaps easily overcome. For instance, faculty can "friend" students who request such friendship but can avoid asking students, without prompt, to become friends. Of course, the issue raised previously regarding the division of "personal" and "public" may interfere with this strategy. Faculty can also use their personal social networking sites as an extension of their professional work, thus potentially integrating their "personal" and "public," potentially leading to online discussions between faculty friends (actual, real life friends) and students, or even between family of a faculty member and students. Future research can explore the drawbacks or benefits of this kind of approach.

FERPA Rules and Institutional Policies

The Family Educational Rights and Privacy Act (FERPA) is a federal law that protects students' privacy by prohibiting disclosure of education records without consent from adult students or their parents, if students are younger than 18 (U.S. Department of Education, 2008). Some respondents feared that using an open blog, wiki or social networks in class would break FERPA requirements and relevant institutional policies. It is important for educators to be aware of the FERPA regulations and know the difference between directory information and education records. Directory information which includes name and contact information, may be disclosed, unless the student requests otherwise. Education records, on the other hand, such as grades/GPA, may not be disclosed. Therefore, it is okay for instructors to integrate social media in classes and have students participate in blogs and social networks outside the school system. However, instructors need to avoid discussing any grade-related issues on any external systems, including any third-party social media tools.

The U.S. Department of Education released an 80-page draft of National Educational Technology Plan entitled Transforming Education: Learning Powered by Technology on March 5, 2010. The plan lays out an ambitious agenda for transforming teaching and learning through technology, and proposes changes to FERPA to open access to student data (U.S. Department of Education, 2010). The plan is bold and still debatable. However, this indicates that the U.S. government is embracing and promoting a collaborative and open learning environment, where technologies will provide access to the most effective teaching and learning resources, and provide more options for all learners at all levels. Social media will be part of the formal and informal teaching and learning arena.

There is a need for universities to craft and implement their own institutional policies on the educational use of social media. The institutional policies may repeat federal and state laws, and include contents, such as a security plan to protect sensitive data, a data recovery plan in the event of server failure, records retention rules, content permission rules, and a plan to communicate the security so that faculty and students can help safeguard sensitive data while enjoying the free collaboration and networks (Wilkins, 2010). This will help faculty better understand the benefits and limitations of the technologies. Future research can explore how institutional policies can be customized to best supplement their infrastructure and meet faculty and students' needs.

Innovation Diffusion: Future Use and Development

The beginnings of a paradigm shift may be occurring in higher education, but the costs of individual and widespread adoption still need to be reduced. As data reviewed below suggest, faculty in public administration programs have begun, to varying degrees, to proceed through the first three states of an organizational change and information technology implementation process. Faculty have started to unfreeze and change (Lewin, 1952), but institutional barriers prevent change beyond individual faculty members at this point. Change has been initiated, as individual faculty members have recognized opportunities for teaching and learning with social media and networking technologies. Individual faculty have adopted technologies with backing from immediate departmental or college supervisors, and certain training has occurred within limited university settings on social networking and media technologies (Cooper & Zmud, 1990). The next stage, not yet broached, is a general acceptance of technologies by mainstream faculty (Jacobsen, 1998).

Research on innovation diffusion suggests that later adopters may not be as successful as early adopters in applying social media and networking technologies. Late adopters are more likely to adopt given organizational and legitimacy pressures, rather than for well understood pedagogical purposes. Future research can track adoption and implementation.

That said, adoption may be more than simple decisions to apply technological innovation for teaching and learning. By the time a laggard adopts Facebook or Twitter, for instance, in teaching, those specific tools may be nonexistent, or they may be so dramatically different that simple mimicry may not be possible. In considering adoption and implementation evolution, it may be more important to understand the evolution of organizational culture in universities and departments. The question over time may not be whether and how specific tools and technologies are adopted but rather how adaptable faculties are to adopting emergent and continually evolving tools and technologies.

CONCLUSION

The use of social networking and media technologies in higher education teaching is an emergent area for study. As the discussion on future directions and implications makes clear, much scholarly research needs to be conducted, and, perhaps more importantly, individual experimentation is needed to understand what works, how, and in what circumstances. We close, then, with a call in the public administration discipline but also in other areas, for study and experimentation. Importantly, we call for institutional changes that can facilitate and indeed encourage experimentation by faculty members who wish to determine the efficacy of social media and networking tools for teaching. Institutional changes might include resources for training, as well as for technology acquisition. They might include opportunities for controlled experimental research to test different tools and technologies and their efficacy in teaching and learning. Last, they might include the granting of flexibility to faculty members who wish to test new tools and technologies on their office computers and for interacting with students in new, boundary-spanning ways. This is an exciting time to be a teacher; our task is to take advantage of opportunities without remaining frozen given fears and concerns.

REFERENCES

Beckenham, A. (2008). Face off online: Pedagogy and engagement in social network sites. *HERDSA 2008 Conference proceedings*. Retrieved from http://www.herdsa.org.au/wp-content/uploads/conference/2008/media/Beckenham.pdf

Caruso, J., Smith, S., & Salaway, G. (2009). *The ECAR study of undergraduate students and information technology, 2009*. Retrieved from http://www.educause.edu/ers0906

Cooper, R. B., & Zmud, R. W. (1990). Information technology implementation research: a technological diffusion approach. *Management Science, 36*(2), 123-139.

Einarsen, S., Hoel, H., Zapf, D., & Cooper, C. L. (2002). The concept of bullying at work: The European tradition. In S. Einarsen, H. Hoel, & C. Cooper (Eds.), *Bullying and emotional abuse in the workplace: International perspectives in research and practice* (pp. 1-30). London, England: Taylor & Francis.

Federal Web Managers Council. (2010, April 15). Social media and web 2.0 in government. *WebContent.gov: Better websites. Better government.* Retrieved from http://www.usa.gov/webcontent/technology/other_tech.shtml

Foulger, T. S., Ewbank, A. D., Kay, A., Popp, S. O., & Carter, H. L. (2009). Moral spaces in MySpace: Preservice teachers' perspectives about ethical issues in social networking. *Journal of Research on Technology in Education, 42*(1), 1-28.

Grove, J. (2010, February 26). Remarkable stats on the state of the Internet [Video]. *Mashable.* Retrieved from http://mashable.com/2010/02/26/state-of-internet/

Groves, M. M., & Zemel, P. C. (2000). Instructional technology adoption in higher education: An action research case study. *International Journal of Instructional Media, 27*(1), 57-65.

Hughes, G. (2009). Social software: New opportunities for challenging social inequalities in learning? *Learning, media and technology, 34*(4), 291-305.

Jacobsen, D. (1998, June). *Adoption patterns of faculty who integrate computer technology for teaching and learning in higher education.* Paper presented at the ED-MEDIA/ED-TELECOM 98 World Conference on Educational Multimedia and Hypermedia & World Conference on Educational Telecommunications, Freiburg, Germany.

Keashly, L., & Neuman, J. H. (2010). Faculty experiences with bullying in higher education. *Administrative Theory & Praxis, 32*(1), 48-70.

Lewin, K. (1952). Group decision and social change. In G. E. Swanson, T. Hartley (eds.), *Readings in social psychology* (pp. 459-473). New York, NY: Holt.

Maddux, C. D., & LaMont, J. (2005). Type II applications of technology in education. *Computers in the Schools, 22*(1&2): 1-5.

Meyer, K. (2010). The role of disruptive technology in the future of higher education. *EDUCAUSE Quarterly, 33*(1).

Mott, J., & Wiley, D. (2009). Open for learning: The CMS and the open learning network in education. *Education, 15*(2). Retrieved from http://www.ineducation.ca/article/open-learning-cms-and-open-learning-network

Nellison. (2007, December 11). The blog of nellison: ECAR: Facebook as a teaching tool? [Web log message]. Retrieved from http://nellison.blogspot.com/2007/12/ecar-facebook-as-teaching-tool.html

Nicol, D. J., & Macfarlane-Dick, D. (2006). Formative assessment and self-regulated learning: A model and seven principles of good feedback practice. *Studies in Higher Education, 31*(2), 199-218.

Nielsen. (2010, February 16). Facebook users average 7 hrs a month in January as digital universe expands. *Nielsen Wire.* Retrieved from http://blog.nielsen.com/nielsenwire/online_mobile/facebook-users-average-7-hrs-a-month-in-january-as-digital-universe-expands/

Palmer, P. J., & Neuenschwander, D. E. (2000). The courage to teach: Exploring the inner landscape of a teacher's life. *American Journal of Physics, 68*, 93.

Rao, L. (2010, February 11). LinkedIn now 60 million strong. Retrieved from http://techcrunch.com/2010/02/11/LinkedIn-now-60-million-strong/

Rogers, D. L. (2000). A paradigm shift: Technology integration for higher education in the new millennium. *Educational Technology Review, 33*(13), 19-27.

U.S. Department of Education. (2008). *Family Educational Rights and Privacy Act (FERPA)*. Retrieved from http://www2.ed.gov/policy/gen/guid/fpco/ferpa/index.html

U.S. Department of Education. (2010, March 5). National education technology plan 2010. *U.S. Department of Education Website*. Retrieved March from http://www.ed.gov/technology/netp-2010/executive-summary

Wilkins, D. (2010, January 12). Social learning strategies checklist. *Social Enterprise Blog*. Retrieved from http://dwilkinsnh.WordPress.com/2010/01/12/social-learning-strategies-checklist/

Wozniak, G. D. (1987). Human capital, information, and the early adoption of new technology. *Journal of Human Resources, 22*(1), 101-112.

CHAPTER 14

SOCIAL MEDIA STRATEGIES FOR THE ACADEMIC DEPARTMENT

A Three-Phase Framework

Irvine Clarke III and Theresa B. Flaherty

This chapter provides managerial guidance about how academic departments in higher education can successfully deploy and manage communications via social media applications. Based on the unique characteristics and potential benefits of different forms of social media, a 3-phase framework is presented to assist in the initial creation, implementation, and management of a social media strategic plan. The 3 phases are divided into prelaunch, launch, and postlaunch activities and each phase considers best practices from an integrated marketing communications perspective. The strategic framework should assist faculty members charged with developing social communication endeavors with internal and external stakeholders.

Cutting-Edge Social Media Approaches to Business Education:
Teaching With LinkedIn, Facebook, Twitter, Second Life, and Blogs, pp. 269–287
Copyright © 2010 by Information Age Publishing
269

INTRODUCTION

Despite its widespread use, there is limited understanding of what "social media" exactly means (Kaplan & Haenlein, 2009). Social media is generally defined as media that is designed to be shared and disseminated through social interactions. Social media has experienced widespread use (Hathi, 2010) and has brought great changes in the way that people communicate, meet others, learn about products, and seek entertainment. It requires new processes and a unique orientation for effective communications (Saperstein & Hastings, 2010). Over 80% of Americans use social media monthly (McCollum, 2009) and 73% use social media at least once per week (Morrissey, 2010). Social networking and blogs are considered to be more popular than personal e-mail (Nielsen Online, 2009). What makes social media so powerful in comparison to traditional communications is its power to engage and collaborate through two-way conversations. Mangold and Faulds (2009) argue that social media has become a hybrid element of the promotional mix because it allows companies to talk to customers in the traditional sense, but in the non-traditional sense it enables customers to talk with one another.

Today's college students are "digital natives" (Prensky, 2001a, 2001b; Wankel, 2009) and are less reliant upon traditional forms of media such as radio, newspapers, and television to get information. Technologies such as computers and smart phones are used to engage in instant messaging, online communities, and networking to access information, provide entertainment, and help in making educational decisions. The Participatory Marketing Network (PMN) and Pace University's Lubin School of Business' IDM Lab third Gen Y behavior study found that 59% of college students spend more than 20 hours per month using social media (eMarketer, 2009). Because of this fundamental shift in the way that college students are communicating, a corresponding shift may be required for academic departments to most effectively reach and communicate with students and associated departmental stakeholders. Further, the benefits associated with social media may be useful for an academic department in higher education. Unlike the traditional methods of communication which often have long lead times prior to publication and dissemination, social media messages can be deployed quickly and easily (Dewhurst, 2010). Such messages have the potential to be spread in a viral manner quite rapidly as well. Once spread through electronic means, search engines have easier access to find and index the content for their databases, ultimately yielding better results for search engine marketing.

However, the potential challenges associated with social media may cause some academic departments to question the transition from purely traditional forms of communication into the fast-paced world of social media. The greater level of transparency is one factor that may deter academic departments from delving into social media. Social media requires a much greater level of exposure, accountability, and immediacy in communication situations (Postman, 2009). Another common fear is the handling of complaints, problems, and other unanticipated issues that may arise from two-way, public online communication. Social media has some unique jargon that requires getting up to speed (e.g., fan pages, retweets, hashtags, etc.). Some faculty may lack the online experience, technological skills, and understanding of social media etiquette to engage online in meaningful ways. A final issue is commitment, as some may not believe that engagement in social media is a wise use of faculty time and expertise in relation to research, teaching, and service responsibilities and expectations. While some faculty will embrace, and have embraced, social media, others may be resistant.

There is value to having well-connected faculty members who are able to enhance the reputation of the Department through interaction and engagement in social media. The purpose of this chapter is to provide managerial guidance that assists in developing effective social media processes, strategies, and policies for use at the departmental-level within higher education. Key opportunities are presented to assist departmental leaders charged with implementing a social media strategy while simultaneously addressing some of the common challenges that may arise within an academic department.

Drawing on first-hand experience, a three-phase framework is presented to assist academic departments in synthesizing the major steps involved before, during, and after a social media launch. The authors used various forms of social media for departmental communications during a 2-year period of time. One of the authors served as department head; the other as a lead faculty member for social media initiatives for their department. The lessons learned from this experience, as well as a literature review, serve as the basis for the three-phase framework and corresponding social media recommendations.

FRAMEWORK FOR INCORPORATING SOCIAL MEDIA INTO AN ACADEMIC DEPARTMENT

Figure 14.1 illustrates a three-phase framework which may be used to assist academic departments in developing a social media presence. The three phases of prelaunch, launch, and postlaunch indicate the recommended activities and general time frames associated with each main phase.

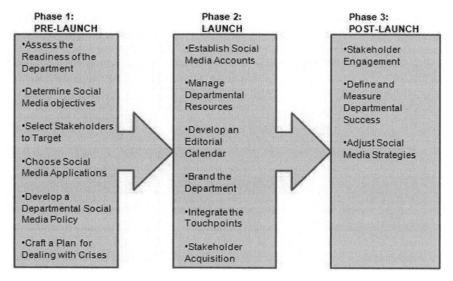

Figure 14.1.   A three-phase framework for incorporating social media into an academic department.

Phase 1:   Prelaunch

The first phase, prelaunch, involves the preparatory activities that must be undertaken before any type of social media initiative goes live. The six proposed areas within the prelaunch phase set the strategic foundation for implementation and engagement. By devoting the necessary time to prelaunch, activities, the academic department will be more prepared to manage the subsequent launch activities that follow. Below is a discussion of each area within this first phase.

Assess the Readiness of the Department

To integrate social media into a department's marketing communication efforts, there may be a requisite shift in the internal culture and method of past communication. Social media changes the balance of power and may feel like a loss of control over external communications. Departmental leadership, such as department chair, academic unit heads, and area coordinators, should lead the discussions about the shift from "talking to departmental stakeholders" to "listening to and engaging with stakeholders" via social media. Because academia is founded on the concept of collaboration, it is important to get the appropriate "buy in" from constituents within the department before moving forward with any other effort. Without internal collaboration and contact, the development of a strong social media presence will be virtually impossible. In order to successfully integrate social media into departmental communications, it is imperative to listen to faculty ideas. Expect there to be a strong fear of change from some internal constituents who want to maintain the status quo. Departmental leaders must help faculty understand how social media initiatives can benefit the department as a whole and the faculty individually. The true value of social media is undermined if it is viewed as an initiative that only affects a few people.

Determine Social Media Objectives

It is important to establish social media objectives to provide focus for the strategy. Below is a sampling of various social media objectives that may be fitting for an academic department.

- To generate awareness of benefits associated with being a potential student in the academic department;
- To educate current students about career opportunities, guest speakers, and other events;
- To highlight career success stories of alumni of the academic department;
- To integrate communications between student organizations within the academic department;
- To showcase achievements of faculty, students, and alumni of the academic department;
- To improve communications and provide opportunities for professional networking between students, alumni, and prospective employers;
- To answer questions from various stakeholder groups;
- To drive traffic to the departmental website for answers to frequently asked questions; and
- To develop and maintain a positive and lifelong association with the academic department.

It may be advantageous to establish *acquisition* and *interaction* objectives. Acquisition goals develop the initial base of social media users (e.g., acquiring Facebook fans, acquiring Twitter followers, acquiring subscribers to a blog, etc.). Interaction goals quantify the minimum, and possibly the maximum, levels of engagement through social media applications (e.g., number of Facebook wall posts per week, number of tweets per day, number of blog posts per month, etc.). In establishing objectives, consider adding a realistic target and a measurable time frame based on academic calendars such as academic year and semester. Examples of acquisition and interaction objectives for an academic department are presented below:

- To increase the LinkedIn group page to 250 members by the end of the academic year with seven discussions per semester; and
- To establish a Facebook fan page with 100 fans during the current semester with two wall posts and four comments per week.

Select Stakeholders to Target

There are number of different groups that can be reached via social media efforts. In crafting the social media strategy, it is important to identify and prioritize which stakeholders should be targeted. Table 14.1 below provides a number of different internal and external stakeholder groups that might be associated with an academic department. To prioritize which audiences to target, it is imperative to understand where they are currently engaging online, the size of each group, their interest in the department's content, their degree of involvement in the social community, and the forms of social media they are most and least likely to use. A short survey sent to select stakeholder groups can provide insights about these issues. Additionally, it would be helpful to analyze social media usage by other academic departments within and outside of the institution to gain meaningful insights.

Table 14.1.   Stakeholder Groups Internal and External to the Academic Department

Internal to the Academic Department	*External to the Academic Department*

• Current students
• Faculty
• Staff
• Other areas within the institution closely associated with the academic department
  o the university
  o the college
  o related departments
  o departments offering minors
  o student organizations
  o advising services
  o career management services
  o study abroad
  o service learning centers
	• Prospective students
	• Guidance counselors
	• Parents
	• Alumni
	• Prospective employers
	• Donors
	• Media
	• The community at-large
	• Individuals with the ability to create hypertext links back to the department or influence links of others
	  o influential bloggers o
	  o heavy social media users

Choose Social Media Applications

The main social media categories and applications should be carefully evaluated in relation to opportunities before diving into use. Proper evaluation can help the department determine what best meets objectives and reaches the targeted stakeholder groups. Table 14.2 provides a number of different media categories, applications, and opportunities.

Develop a Departmental Social Media Policy

Barnes and Barnes (2009) recommend that organizations engaging in social media should design a comprehensive social media policy. Recent updates to the Federal Trade Commission's "Guides Concerning the Use of Endorsements and Testimonials in Advertising" now make social media ethics a matter of law rather than personal preference. Sernovitz (2009) suggests that creating a social media policy can help to limit liability within the FTC guides. In addition to avoiding legal entanglements, social media policies can help faculty understand their unique role for engagement, protect the institutional voice, and safeguard the departmental reputation.

Begin by checking if a social media policy exists for the university and/ or college. Such a policy can serve as a guide for crafting subsequent departmental policy. In some institutions, permission may be needed before any type of social media program is launched. Be mindful of the Terms of Service, Privacy Policies, and Promotion Polices, such as Facebook Promotion Policies (Facebook, 2009), of any social media platform employed. Second, provide guidelines regarding applicable federal requirements such as the Federal Educational Rights and Privacy Act (FERPA) to protect confidential and proprietary information of students. Include policies regarding copyright and fair use to protect the intellectual property of others, especially, images and photographs.

Third, discuss issues pertaining to professional tone, accuracy, respect for the audiences targeted, and privacy. Clarify what should and should not be discussed in social media by setting guidelines regarding commentary about other entities (e.g., other departments, colleges, etc), controversial topics, the use of humor, and other areas where questions may arise regarding proper conduct. Finally, specify the parameters regarding connections with others based on selected social media type (e.g., Twitter follows, Facebook friends, etc.). It is important to integrate with and support other aspects of the college and university. Yet, departments must carefully consider with whom they will be "connected" in social media. It is important to avoid creating an impression that the department favors and/or endorses certain individuals, groups, and causes. Ball (2010) discourages making connections that may be too personal.

Table 14.2. Examples of Social Media Applications and Key Opportunities for Main Social Media Categories

Main Social Media Categories	Examples of Social Media Applications	Key Opportunities
Blogging	• Blogger, LiveJournal, Moveable Type, TypePad, WordPress, Xanga • RSS buttons can signal to users that blog content is available.	• Showcase scholarly work of faculty • Engage stakeholders through blog commentary opportunities • Post departmental announcements that require a strong degree of elaboration
Bookmarking and social news	• *Bookmarking*: AddThis, Delicious, Google Reader, StumbleUpon • *Social News*: Digg, Mixx, Reddit, Sphinn	• Tag relevant departmental content to drive site traffic • Collect reviews and comments from others interested in departmental content
Community building	• CrowdVine, KickApps, and Ning	• Organize conversations based on topic or forum, rather than the chronological sequence presented in most blogs and social networking sites
Microblogging	• Jaiku, Pownce, Plurk, Posterous, Tumblr, Twitter, Yammer	• Promote other social networking activities. • Integrated with other forms of social media with ease • Directly engage with stakeholders. • Listen to and track conversations of stakeholders
Online video and photo sharing	• *Online Video*: Seesmic, UStream, Viddler, Vimeo, YouTube • *Photo Sharing*: Flickr, Photobucket, Picasa	• Encourage stakeholders to share video and photos of relevant experiences associated with the department • Create instructional materials such as lectures, review sessions, guest speakers, and student presentations • Tag photos and videos to link back to departmental website or other online location of choice

Category	Tools	Uses
Podcasting	Podcasts are typically distributed on websites where users can download audio and/or video content.	• Create online lectures to assist students with the "hard to grasp" concepts within the curriculum • Showcase the talents of faculty and students
Presentation sharing	Prezi, Slideshare, Scribd	• Share slide presentations from select course content • Share slides from faculty research presentations
Social and professional networking	Bebo, Facebook, Friendster, LinkedIn, MySpace, Nexopia, Orkut, Plaxo Pulse	• Engage stakeholders through announcements, questions, discussions, and other forms of online social interaction • Share current content such as text, photos, links, and video • Provide a means for potential recruiters and alums to reach out to current students • Possibly purchase ads to reach a desired audience (e.g., Facebook Advertising and Social Recommendation Ads)
Virtual worlds	Second Life, Teleplace, Whyville	• Produce sample classes to help students explore and understand the type of content in the discipline • Create a virtual meeting place for formal and informal teaching and learning opportunities in an immersive environment
Wikis	Jotspot, PBwiki, PBworks, Wet Paint, Wikipedia	• Provide relevant and accurate information to people searching for insights and archival information about the department. Wikis provide collaboration opportunities and assist in departmental search engine optimization efforts • Post departmental policies and procedures

Once the social media policy has been established, publish the social media policy in a public location, such as a departmental website or wiki, to show the department's commitment to ethics and transparent communications. For further information about establishing a departmental social media policy, the Word of Mouth Marketing Association (2010) provides an excellent ethics code as well as guidelines for prudent social media practices. Examples of social media policies from a wide variety of organizations is available at 123Media (2009).

Craft a Plan for Dealing With Crises

Ideally, all stakeholders become champions of the departmental brand, but that is not always the case. Fortunately, in most forms of social media, objectionable content can be removed from departmental-controlled social media platforms. For example, negative comments and wall posts can be removed from a departmental Facebook fan page. Beyond the department-controlled venues, this same level of control is not available, but monitoring tools can be helpful. For instance, Google Analytics can be easily installed on a departmental website to help understand which social networks are providing site traffic. The Social Medial Analyzer tool (http://www.socialwebsiteanalyzer.com/) provides a quick snapshot of the department's social media presence across the top 20 social media sites. Google Alerts (http://www.google.com/alerts) can be established for key terms such as "Department of _____" to get up-to-date reports e-mailed about recent updates within the Google Search Network.

A communication crisis plan should be crafted to prepare internally for addressing complaints and negative feedback on social media sites. One or more of the following actions can be used to respond in these situations: (a) update social media with correct information, (b) outreach publicly by responding on nondepartmental social media platforms, (c) respond privately by making an offer to discuss the matter via phone, e-mail, or in person, or (d) do not respond at all. There are a number of excellent resources that provide more detailed guidance on how to handle social media crises. For example Solis (2008) compares crisis communications for traditional versus the social web, Sherman (2009) proposed an eight-point blueprint of planning how to handle a fallout, and Owyang (2010) describes how to practice a crises response in social media. In addition to monitoring the departmental-controlled social media, it is wise to track when the departmental name is mentioned in other outlets. Tools such as Google Alerts (http://www.google.com/alerts) or Twilert (http://www.Twilert.com) can provide timely brand monitoring service capabilities at no cost.

Phase 2:   Launch

The second phase, launch, involves making accounts active, putting the right faculty in charge, managing the content on a macro-level, branding the department, and acquiring stakeholders within selected social media applications. This phase is when the social media finally "goes live" in real time. Launch is highly focused on management- and marketing-oriented activities.

Establish Social Media Accounts

In setting up accounts, one faculty member should be responsible for setting up the selected social media accounts. Ideally this faculty member serves in a key leadership position such as a department head or committee chair. Another plausible approach is for at least two people in the department be granted access to the user ID, password, and other security credentials necessary. When possible, accounts should be set up using a common account (e.g., departmentname@schoolname.edu) rather than a personal, individual account (e.g., professor@gmail.com). A suggested tool to manage multiple social media accounts is HootSuite (http:www.hootsuite.com). This tool is designed for groups of people that manage multiple social network accounts. HootSuite provides team collaboration tools and a designated "owner" who "holds the keys" to that account. The owner can add others to the social network accounts without compromising password security. Different levels of access can be set (e.g., basic to advanced) depending on the roles of various team members.

Manage Departmental Resources

Although most social media tools do not cost significant fees to create or use, they require a different set of valuable faculty resources: time and expertise. Departmental leaders are concerned with maximizing efficiency and effectiveness of their faculty in order to meet institutional goals. If social media initiatives are to be adopted, faculty must be given time and other types of support/rewards to successfully share their expertise. *Do not* have a graduate assistant, teaching assistant, or other type of student assistant run the social media. While it is tempting to hand this off to a college student from the Facebook generation, they lack the "authentic voice" of the department. Although assigning this to a student may provide a short term convenience, it is likely to dilute the long-term success, especially given the high rate of turnover of student workers. Instead, it may be fruitful to assign students as "participants" within the various networks where they can be charged with starting discussions, providing comments, and reporting any suspicious or negative activity taking place online. Before a departmental representative is assigned, or asked to volunteer, in a social media capacity ensure that they understand the medium, have some experience working in the select media through a personal account, and are properly authorized to utilize the account. Departmental leaders may wish to create a committee that consists of a team of faculty interested in leading and participating in the social media efforts. Appropriate reward structures, such as recognition of social media involvement on annual evaluations, should be established to acknowledge departmental contributions of this type. Most likely this would fall into the service duties, but could also fall under teaching or research depending on the institution type.

Develop an Editorial Calendar

There is a need for both spontaneity and frequency in social media conversations so that the department can directly respond to what others are discussing. Yet, there is a corresponding need for regularly updated content that is delivered at planned intervals. To stay on track with social media objectives and keep content up to date once the social media has been launched, develop an editorial calendar of outgoing engagement. A simple Excel spreadsheet can work quite well for scheduling planned social media activity. Hazlett (2009) offers a simple editorial calendar template at http://onehalfamazing.com/blogging/social-media-calendar-template/. The editorial calendar should include a listing of social media tasks, due dates, person(s) responsible, and a place to show that the task was accomplished. Remember to include plans for vacations and semester breaks. For example, five Twitter tweets per week during the semester and one tweet during an academic break.

Brand the Department

In order to convey a consistent theme across a variety media, including social media, a unique departmental brand mark is needed. Departmental branding should be distinct from any branding of the associated university and college. In Facebook, it is possible to create a profile image as large as 200 × 600 pixels (similar to a skyscraper banner ad) but from a practical standpoint, it is advised to use a very simple brand mark that looks good within a 50 × 50 pixel space. This is a commonly used size across many forms of social media.

Some academic departments may have complete freedom in creating and using brandmarks. In this "unrestricted" brand mark scenario, any combination of colors and images may be used. Other academic departments may be "restricted" due to their institution's policies on

**Table 14.3. Sample 50 x 50 Pixel Brand Marks
for Unrestricted and Restricted Scenarios**

Unrestricted Departmental Brand Mark	*Restricted Departmental Brand Mark*
ATU Dept. of Sociology	XYZ College **Chemistry**

branding/identity. In this case, it is advised to consult with the institution's internal policies on developing or preparing communications to ensure compliance. In highly restricted scenarios, it is recommended that a straightforward brand mark that has the university/college name (or university/college acronym) and the name of the department, in plain font on a white background. Table 14.3 below provides examples of unrestricted and restricted brand marks for an academic department.

Integrate the Touchpoints

To assist in recruiting participants, regardless of the media applications selected, it is important to integrate each unique touchpoint. A touchpoint is considered to be any type of interaction that a consumer has with a brand. Touchpoints may include everything from class meetings to a departmental brochure. In the case of an academic department using electronic and social means, touchpoints could include a Facebook fan page, a departmental blog, a departmental website, and many others. To integrate the touchpoints, connections should be made between one touchpoint and another. For example, if the academic department uses Myspace, provide links from the social networking pages to other touchpoints, such as a departmental website. Likewise, the departmental website should include reciprocal links back to the MySpace page. To further develop the integration of touchpoints, encourage faculty members to use their business personnas for departmental marketing purposes. As an example, include links to social network platforms within faculty e-mail signature line. Request that faculty members update their personal social media platforms, as they deem appropriate, to include links to departmental social media. For example, a personal profile in LinkedIn may need to include a link to a departmental "group" page in LinkedIn. A personal Twitter account could be used to RT (retweet) post from the departmental Twitter account.

Stakeholder Acquisition

As a starting point, contact officers of student organizations associated with the academic department. There is a high probability that they will already have some type of social media presence, especially in Facebook. Specific tactics at this stage involve a mutual following (e.g., becoming fans, following, etc.). Within Facebook, include the student organizations in the "Favorite Pages" section of the departmental Facebook fan page. Visit the student organization pages, and add comments, likes, and so on, to their activities to show support of their efforts. Ask faculty to make class announcements about the new forms of social media being utilized by the department.

Phase 3:   Postlaunch

Activities in the postlaunch phase entail keeping the departmental stakeholders engaged, determining what is working and what is not, and adjusting the strategies accordingly.

Stakeholder Engagement

A common concern is keeping the content updated, relevant, and current across all forms of social media. Due to the nature of social media, content strategies will involve both internal and external groups. A key concern is how to creatively informative, educational, and meaningful content in the selected social media tools. Social media obviously provides the opportunity for user generated content (UCG) which can come in a number of different forms. There is also likely a pool of content from other traditional sources that could be incorporated into social channels (e.g., photos, videos, articles, flyers, etc.).

Messages must be created based on the audiences targeted. For example, if a department is targeting current students and alumni, messages need to be crafted for both groups. Because engagement is an integral part of most social media campaigns, interesting questions should be posed to stakeholders as part of the content strategy. Prepare a list of engaging questions that have good potential to generate positive responses and meaningful dialog. Example questions aimed at departmental alumni: "Who will be coming back to campus for homecoming this fall?" and " Can you share some job hunting advice to help our current students?" Social media provides unique opportunities to capitalize on user generated content (UGC) or content created by others. Table 14.4 below provides several ideas for engaging departmental stakeholders to facilitate creation of UGC.

**Table 14.4.   Suggested Ways to Engage Departmental
Stakeholders Through User Generated Content**

- Ask students to showcase course outcomes or class projects through photos and video;
- Embed polls or short surveys to get user engagement on any number of departmental issues such as "Which elective courses should be offered online this summer?";
- Request faculty members to create short blog posts that summarize research endeavors or abbreviated abstracts of recently published works;
- Involve student organization officers by requesting regular announcements about upcoming recruiting events, fundraisers, guest speakers, community service projects, and other activities associated with their organization;
- Ask student-services such as advising and career services centers to regularly provide job tips, advising information, seminar/workshop information, career fair information, etc.;
- Encourage faculty to take pictures of guest speakers and write short stories about the speakers; and
- Interview alumni about career experiences and opportunities.

Define and Measure Departmental Success

Adding social media into a department's communication mix involves a long-term commitment, a willingness to change, and patience to see results. It also requires frequent monitoring of acquisition and engagement levels with the online community to determine if the social media objectives are being met. To ensure that the department is on track with social media objectives, periodic measurements of success should be undertaken. Table 14.5 illustrates a sampling of various success metrics to monitor various social applications and understand what resonates with stakeholders. Fortunately, many social media have built-in analytical tools to measure interaction within an online community.

When including hypertext links within social media communications, as much as possible, include links back to departmental websites rather than university/college websites. There may be built-in features that provide link tracking services within some applications. When a link-tracking option is not available, the bit.ly utility (http://bit.ly) is recommended to easily shorten a long URL, share it, and then track the resulting usage. For example, a very long URL from a Facebook note page (http://www.facebook.com/note.php?note_id=1707448291021707448291021707448829102] could be shortened to bit.ly/42rdsp for easy posting in another social media platform, such as Twitter. Bit.ly also allows for tracking of each link such as number of clicks, number of referrers (e.g., those who shared your link within their own social networks), and geographical location of those who clicked the link. Additional useful tools worth further exploration include Social Oomph, HootSuite, and Tweet-Deck.

**Table 14.5.   Examples of Success Metrics
for Main Social Media Categories**

Main Social Media Categories	Example Success Metrics
Blogging	• Number of blog posts • Number of subscribers and growth in subscribers over time • Number of inbound links • Listings in well-known directories such as Technorati and Alltop • Number and quality of comments and questions in response to blog posts
Bookmarking and social News	• Referrals from bookmarking sites to other sites • Page rankings on bookmarked sites • Number of referrers who have "tagged" or voted positively on content
Microblogging	• Number of followers and growth of followers over time • Level of influence (e.g., retweets) and degree that the messages reach others • Degree of social capital such as the influence of other followers
Online video and photo sharing	• Number of videos shared • Referrals from other websites • Number of views • Page ranking
Podcasting	• Podcast views • Referrals from podcast directories
Presentation sharing	• Presentation views • Presentation referrals to other social media
Social and professional networking	• Number of friends, connections, etc. acquired and growth of such over time • Number of "likes," "comments," and other forms of user interaction with the department • Tracking number of conversations about select topics
Virtual worlds	• Unique visitors • Time spent in virtual worlds • Type and number of interactions
Wikis	• Referrals from wiki sites • Number of web pages ranking on key terms in wiki sites

Adjust Social Media Strategies

By defining and measuring success metrics, the academic department will be in a better position to adjust social media strategies based on the targeted audience's online behaviors. Unless there are serious performance deviations from the targeted objectives, strategies can be adjusted once per "semester" or "quarter." This level of frequency provides sufficient balance between faculty obligations in research, teaching, and service, and the need to regularly adjust social media strategy.

CONCLUSION

Social media reflect a new and dynamic method of communicating online. An overarching goal of social media is to provide opportunities for the targeted stakeholder groups to spread positive messages that enhance the academic department's brand to others in their own networks. Social media opens new communication channels to these valued stakeholders with the potential of extending the relationships critical to brand development. The academic department could therefore engage in meaningful individual conversations, or mass dialogs, with limited resource outlays. In addition, social media allows the academic department to leverage modern electronic technologies to circulate information to groups, in personally relevant configurations, nearly instantly. Real-time feedback becomes a more plausible prospect.

Before diving into social media, academic departments are advised to (a) develop a process, and (b) be prepared to change technologies and strategies over time. By following the framework presented in this chapter, typical challenges faced by academic departments can be minimized. For example, the framework prepares the department for the greater level of transparency, accountability, and immediacy in online communication situations. Through the development of social media policies and a crisis plan, the handling of complaints, problems, and other unanticipated issues is more manageable. By encouraging faculty to engage in social media through personal accounts, they develop the requisite experience and skills to engage with departmental stakeholders. Appropriate reward structures provide evidence of commitment to faculty who engage in social media on behalf of the academic department.

Please recognize that social media will not reach everyone. Even though many people report having social media accounts, do not assume that everyone utilizes the technologies at the same rates. The individual relationships and levels of involvement with social media can vary greatly across individuals. Expect the relationships to also change dependent on time or situation. A stakeholder that responds well to social media in one occasion may respond differently given different circumstances. Therefore, it is important to approach social media as part of an integrated communications strategy for the department. academic departments may be disappointed if social media is used as a replacement for other communication tools.

It is acknowledged that the three-phase framework in this chapter is not the only way to successfully incorporate social media into academic departments. Certainly, needs of academic departments and resource constraints will vary across institutions. However, this framework can be easily adapted to suit the needs of a wide variety of departments based on size of the department, institution type, resources, and faculty experience. Further research is recommended to explore additional challenges and experiences of academic departments as they develop, implement, and manage social media presences.

REFERENCES

123Media. (2009). *Social media policy examples.* Retrieved from http://123socialmedia.com/2009/01/23/social-media-policy-examples/.

Ball, S. (2010). *Facebook do's and don'ts for recruiting students.* Retrieved from http://educationtechnews.com/facebook-dos-and-donts-for-recruiting-college-students/

Barnes, N., & Barnes, F. (2009). Equipping your organization for the social networking game. *Information Management Journal, 43*(6), 28-29, 31-33, 47.

Dewhurst, S. (2010). Making the call: How and when to use social media. *Strategic Communication Management, 14*(2), 14.

eMarketer. (2009). *Average number of hours US college students spend on social networks per month, October 2009 (% of respondents).* Retrieved from http://totalaccess.emarketer.com/GetFile.aspx?type=chp&code=107971&sub=107001-108000&xsrc=icon_pdf_chartx

Facebook.com. (2009). Facebook promotion guidelines. Retrieved from http://www.facebook.com/promotions_guidelines.php

Hathi, S. (2010). Communicators remain unclear on business case for social media. *Strategic Communication Management, 14*(1), 9.

Hazlett, B. (2009). *Social media calendar template.* Retrieved from http://onehalfamazing.com/blogging/social-media-calendar-template/

Kaplan, A. M., & Haenlein, M. (2009). Users of the world, unite! The challenges and opportunities of social media. *Business Horizons, 53*(1), 59-68.

Mangold, W. G., & Faulds, D. J. (2009). Social media: The new hybrid element of the promotion mix. *Business Horizons, 52*(4), 357-65.

McCollum, J. (2009). *Over 80% of Americans use social media monthly.* Retrieved from http://www.marketingpilgrim.com/2009/08/over-80-of-americans-use-social-media-monthly.html.

Morrissey, B. (2010.) *Social media use becomes pervasive.* Retrieved from http://www.brandweek.com/bw/content_display/news-and-features/digital/e3iceae27f23a68f24b0b69f4508940e229

Nielsen Online. (2009). *Global faces and networked places.* Retrieved from http://server-uk.imrworldwide.com/pdcimages/Global_Faces_and_Networked_Places-A_Nielsen_Report_on_Social_Networkings_New_Global_Footprint.pdf

Owyang, J. (2010). *Crisis planning: Prepare your company for social media Attacks.* Retrieved from http://www.web-strategist.com/blog/2010/03/22/prepare -your-company-now-for-social-attacks/

Postman, J. (2009). *SocialCorp. Social media goes corporate.* Berkeley, CA: New Riders.

Prenksy, M. (2001a). Digital natives, digital immigrants. *On the Horizon, 9*(5), 1-6.

Prenksy, M. (2001b). Digital natives, digital immigrants, part II. Do they really think differently? *On the Horizon, 9*(6) 1–6.

Saperstein, J., & Hastings, H. (2010). How social media can be used to dialog with the customer. *Ivey Business Journal Online.* Retrieved from http://proquest. umi.com/pqdweb?did=2011797781&sid=1&Fmt=3&clientId= 50078&RQT=309&VName=PQD

Sernovitz, A. (2009). *What do the 'FTC Guides re: The use of endorsements and testimonials' mean for social media marketers?* Retrieved from http://www.damniwish .com/2009/10/what-do-the-ftc-guides-re-the-use-of-endorsements-and -testimonials-mean-for-social-media-marketers.html

Sherman, A. (2009). *Crisis communications for the social media age.* Retrieved from http://webworkerdaily.com/2009/06/01/crisis-communications-for-the -social-media-age/

Solis, B. (2008). Reinventing crisis communications for the social web. Retrieved http://www.briansolis.com/2008/11/reinventing-crisis-communications-for/

Wankel, C. (2009). Management education using social media. *Organization Management Journal, 6,* 251–262.

Word of Mouth Marketing Association. (2010). *WOMMA ethics code.* Retrieved from http://www.womma.org/ethics

CHAPTER 15

SOCIAL MEDIA OVERLOAD

What Works Best?

Walkyria Goode and Guido Caicedo

The chapter presents a critical analysis of social media tools in the context of graduate education. The influence of social media on learning and teaching environments is investigated. Social media applications reinforce class material and positively influence discussions, collaborative work, and authoring. Features such as file sharing, content delivery and creation, discussion forums, and evaluation are compared. The analysis is based on data gathered from an on-site MBA program through a series of 3 courses. The motivations and underlying assumptions behind the inclusion of specific social media within the teaching methodology are described. The online services used range from content creation and sharing sites like WordPress, YouTube, and MixedInk; group-oriented sites like Google Groups and Wiggio; and the increasingly ubiquitous social networking website Facebook. Based on this research, the chapter presents a set of guidelines to effectively pair social media tools with specific teaching approaches.

Educators and researchers have been experimenting with social media technologies to stimulate critical thinking, collaboration, and knowledge construction. Social media technologies include blogs, wikis, file sharing,

Cutting-Edge Social Media Approaches to Business Education:
Teaching With LinkedIn, Facebook, Twitter, Second Life, and Blogs, pp. 289–313
Copyright © 2010 by Information Age Publishing
All rights of reproduction in any form reserved.

video casting, and social networks, among others. These technologies offer the capability to both receive and create content under the assumption that through collaboration, a collective intelligence will emerge. Students will improve their learning experiences and will be prepared to enter a workforce that is not geographically constrained and expects them to have online collaboration skills. Social media promotes knowledge construction by putting an emphasis on collaboration and student-centered interaction. Students actively participate in learning through dialogue and connections within social media communities by exchanging information, creating content and collaborating in new ways (Duffy, 2008). The pursuit of such benefits drives academics to incorporate new technological approaches within their teaching methodology. Such approaches include content delivery, content creation, collaboration, critical assessment and evaluation. The popularity of social networks among students and their exposure to social computing suggest that the introduction of these tools in the classroom will enhance rather than hinder coursework. The wide availability of social media—with its vast list of tools with different offerings and functionalities—can turn into a dilemma for the practitioner when designing a course. The selection of one or more depends on concrete pedagogical objectives. This chapter presents a critical analysis of tools offered by social media in business graduate education and will propose a set of guidelines that will successfully pair social media tools with specific teaching objectives.

The term social media technologies will be used to encompass all Web 2.0 technologies. Web 2.0 refers to web applications that allow user-centered content creation and control, interactive information sharing and collaboration through social and idea networks. For a detailed comparison between traditional web applications versus Web 2.0 applications see O'Reilly (2005).

Academic institutions regularly use course management systems (CMS) to design and deliver course material and activities through the Internet. The leading commercial CMS are WebCT and Blackboard Learning System (both now owned by Blackboard), and the leading open-source CMS is Moodle (http://moodle.org/). These web-based CMS offer collaborative and communication tools, content creation and delivery tools, administrative tools and assessment tools (Dabbagh & Kitsantas, 2005). Social media technology provides features that are cost efficient and attractive for educational establishments that do not have the technical infrastructure to provide CMS or for instructors that may want to forsake the hegemony of an institutionalized CMS. Students can learn within a social network and through collaborative discussions and authoring using wikis, blogs and other collaborative software. More people are using social media technologies in the classroom (Harris & Rea, 2009) to learn, communicate and build knowledge.

Duffy (2008) suggests that educational institutions should shift from archetypical course management systems toward "user-centric, user-content generated and user-guided" systems, such as those provided by social media technologies. Their ubiquity makes them interesting and self-perpetuating.

BACKGROUND

The evaluation was performed with part-time MBA students, the majority of which have full-time jobs. The sample had an average age of 30 years (see Table 15.1). The analysis is based on data gathered from a series of three courses that employed social media.

Leadership Communication

Leadership communication (LC) is an introductory course designed to improve professional communication and to acquire leadership principles. The course met nightly for 3 hours for 10 days within a 3-week period.

Management Communication

Management communication (MC) prepares students to communicate effectively in a variety of managerial-level situations. The course met for 3 hours 1 night per week for 8 weeks.

Table 15.1. Student Demographics

	Leadership Communication	Management Communication	Entrepreneurship and New Businesses
N	21	21	19
Males	10	10	8
Females	11	11	11
Age (years)	$M = 29.10$ $SD = 4.19$	$M = 30.68$ $SD = 4.89$	$M = 29.99$ $SD = 5.08$
Full-time jobs	16	16	15

Note: Eighteen students were enrolled in all three classes, one student was enrolled in two classes.

Entrepreneurship and New Businesses

Entrepreneurship and new business (ENB) helps students gain an understanding of the primary principles necessary to start new ventures. The course met for 3 hours 1 night per week for 12 weeks.

Practical and flexible devices to perform work outside the classroom are essential due to the format and schedule of the program. Social media technologies provide such functionality. With the exception of social networking, most students did not have previous experience with social media (see Table 15.2). Different learning environments were used to directly involve and engage students. The Motivated Strategies for Learning Questionnaire (MSLQ: Pintrich, Smith, Garcia & McKeachie, 1993) was used to determine if students differed in their motivation and learning strategies across the courses. Students felt they were equally motivated and approached learning in a similar manner. In general, the students did not have significantly different perceptions for any of the courses. They considered the difficulty for all courses to be according to their expectations and dedicated—on average—6 to 9 hours per week to each course. The different tools are compared without concern that a particular course or instructor may influence student perception.

The tasks students and instructors perform in a course require different social media features. The selection of a specific platform is a function of such tasks. The instructors surveyed the social media market in order to

Table 15.2.   Previous Experience With Social Media

	N
Blogs	
Blogger	2
WordPress	0
Social Networking	
Facebook	20
Hi5	16
MySpace	4
Orkut	0
LinkedIn	4
Groupware	
Google Groups	1
Wiggio	0
Google Docs	4
Wikis	0

select the tool that best met the needs of a course. Table 15.3 compares the features offered by social media tools in a framework of educational tasks. LC and MC used single platforms for all tasks, while ENB used four complementary platforms for all tasks. This chapter is a first step in studying the effectiveness of social media in education. A comparison will be made based on the perceptions of instructors and students and experiences with six social platforms. The next sections will present a description of the main features each platform uses. The authors will report the instructional approach used and how the features matched the required tasks. The platforms will be reviewed in an exploratory context where student and instructor observations will be noted. Feedback was obtained from the students as an end-of-semester survey.[1] The chapter will conclude with a discussion that compares the platforms used and what works best. The positive aspects and troublesome issues will be recounted. The reader can discern which social media tool to select based on specific educational needs.

GOOGLE GROUPS

Google Groups (http://groups.google.com) is a social media tool that supports communication, discussion forums, content creation and file sharing. A group is configured to have public or private memberships. In the

Table 15.3.   Social Media Platforms and Features

	Leadership Communication	*Management Communication*	*Entrepreneurship and New Businesses*			
	Google Groups	*WordPress*	*Facebook*	*Wiggio*	*MixedInk*	*YouTube*
Collaborative content creation	Yes[a]	Yes	No	Yes[a]	Yes	No
Content/feedback delivery	Yes	Yes	Yes	No	No	Yes
Communication	Yes	Yes	Yes	Yes[a]	Yes[a]	Yes[a]
Discussion forums	Yes	Yes	Yes	No	No	No
Calendar	No	No	No	Yes	No	No
File sharing	Yes	Yes[a]	No	Yes	No	No
Notifications	Yes	Yes	Yes[b]	Yes	No	No
Personalization[c]	Yes	Yes	Yes	Yes	No	No

Note: [a]Feature available in platform but not used in course. [b]Facebook has specific rules on how notifications work. See Facebook section for more detail. [c]Personalization refers to whether a platform can be customized to display a particular look and present explicit features.

private forums, members are invited to join via email. The owner controls who can join the group, view the group and members, create and edit pages, upload files, post messages and invite new members (Lindoo, 2009). A group owner can also customize the group's appearance to better reflect its identity by changing color, style or pictures. The discussion forum is configured with listserv functionality so notices regarding posts are sent automatically to email inboxes (Rienzo & Han, 2009). Users can comment through a web interface or by email. Google Groups (GG) allows members to create and collaborate on shared web pages in a way similar to a wiki site. Wiki is a website where users can create and edit content (Wagner, 2004). Wikis use simple text syntax and support hyperlinks. In GG, pages are hosted within the group and any type of files can be shared. GG users can also publish and share profile pictures and general information. As of April 27, 2010, the Google Groups directory (http://groups.google.com/groups/dir) reports over 4.5 million groups.

Instructional Approach

Google Groups was chosen for its ability to easily manage content and solicit feedback from students. A private group was created for leadership communication (LC); with membership restricted to enrolled students. Custom colors and a group image were used to customize the appearance of the LC Google Group. The pages section was used for content delivery. In pages, the instructor published relevant newsworthy articles and partial grades. The course did not have a collaborative authoring assignment. The wiki capability of GG was not used. The files section was used for file sharing. In files, students could access the syllabus, readings, assignments and class notes. The Discussions section was used to discuss assigned readings.

Discussion forums present a venue for the review, discussion and reinforcement of class material. Students construe knowledge through online asynchronous dialogue (Goode, 2009). Online discussions are considered more approachable for students who have public speaking apprehension (Lam, 2004). The instructor engaged students in articulation and reflection by directing the discussion and dialogue. Introductory questions for each topic started the discussion. Expectations and ground rules on how to participate in an online discussion were provided. Students were required to post at least one "original comment" and one "extension comment." The extension comment was a response to a classmate's contribution. Students were informed on the appropriate tone and language for postings, to respect each other's opinions and to challenge an issue and not a person.

Application Review

Since the group was private, students required Google accounts in order to become a member. The majority of the students did not previously have Google accounts and had to register. Students were able to access course files and discussions without problems. Most students configured GG to send immediate announcements of all postings to their emails, as opposed to emails that digested or abridged postings. A digest email sends new messages bundled in a single email every day. An abridged email sends a summary of all new activity every day. Students valued instant notifications because they kept them updated on how the discussion developed.

Students showed a positive attitude towards online discussions of assigned readings and most participated in non-mandatory assignments. Students were able to post comments by either accessing the GG site or through their personal emails. Participation requirements promoted dialogue among course members. Original comments included answers to the introductory questions. Extension comments created a positive interaction among students and helped develop higher level of critical thinking. Students complained about peer participation, specifically in how they wanted more and earlier contributions from their classmates. During class, the instructor briefly synthesized the discussion and touched upon specific points mentioned online by the students. Students whose postings were mentioned seemed pleased that the instructor considered their points worth discussing and the rest of the class was aware that the instructor kept track of their online postings.

Student-initiated communication is achieved in GG by creating new discussion topics. Students created two topics to ask questions related to class assignments. It is the instructor's perception that creating a new discussion topic inhibited communication in GG. Students emailed the instructor directly for questions. The instructor would then post these questions on GG. For direct communication, the instructor could create a Q&A discussion topic within the group. Students suggested creating a nonacademic area within the LC Google Group. Lam (2004) mentions that informal areas provide a sense of community by designating a space for online socialization. To promote socialization, the instructor could create a discussion topic that specifically states that students can use it for casual communication.

The pages section was used to publish partial grades and relevant information. Student ids were linked to a grade to ensure privacy. Before the first posting, the instructor asked the class whether they were comfortable with this method. After a couple of posts, the instructor asked once more if there were any inconveniences or reservations. All students accepted this scheme. News and course-relevant information were published in the pages section and were accessed without difficulty by students.

In general, students felt comfortable using the tool and believed that it promoted a rich debate with their peers. They also found GG helpful for interacting with the instructor and amongst themselves. Many students mentioned they appreciated having a permanent record of their discussions.

WORDPRESS

WordPress (WP) is an open source web development framework, usually used for publishing blogs. A "web log," or blog, is a webpage that presents a personal commentary in reverse chronological order. Blogs incorporate features as links, comments, tags, archives, permanent links, and more. Blogs allow readers to leave comments in an interactive format (Duffy, 2008; Farmer & Bartlett-Bragg, 2005). WP can be deployed on a private or commercial hosting environment (by using the open source software provided in WordPress.org) or on a free hosting environment (such as WordPress.com). As of February 2010, there are 10.6 million blogs hosted on WordPress.com and 11.4 million installations of WordPress.org software. Around 250 million people visit WP blogs every month (WordPress Stats, n.d.).

WP blogs can include links, images, videos and audio files. There is a file sharing capability and a blog entry can include links to download PDF, MS Word, and PowerPoint documents. Members can tag and categorize entries and tag cloud and category cloud widgets serve as indexes for blog readers to access specific entries. WP has a wide variety of additional widgets that include other social media features such as access to del.icio.us bookmarks, a display of recent Flickr uploads, RSS and Twitter feeds. Blog readers can create their own RSS feeds or subscribe to receive notifications of all new posts. The blog owner has the capability to moderate comments and blog readers can rate them. Polls—with one multiple-choice question—can be included in an entry to get instant feedback from readers.

WP allows several authors to add and edit content, making it an effective tool for collaborative content creation. WP distinguishes three user roles: Editor, Author and Contributor. An Editor can publish, edit, and delete any posts, moderate comments, upload files/images and manage categories, tags and links. An Author can edit, publish and delete posts, as well as upload files/images. A Contributor can edit posts but cannot publish them.

Instructional Approach

WP was used as a blog on the free hosting environment for management communication (MC). The blog was personalized with a theme and images related to the course; instructor and students selected avatars or uploaded pictures to represent themselves within WP. The entire blog served as a content delivery medium. Separate entries included course-related information such as assignments, resources, due dates and grades. Tag and category clouds were created for easy navigation. Blog entries tagged "News" and "Info" were determined informal areas. Blog entries tagged "Score" presented an ongoing tally of a team contest and links to view student grades. As in LC, student ids were used instead of names. The instructor suggested that the MC blogs be public blogs—to share the experience and knowledge acquired within the course. Students willingly agreed. Due to the public nature of the course blog and to respect copyrights, files were not shared within WP. The school's course management system was used instead. Polls were used to obtain feedback on MC policy changes. All blog entries permitted commenting and students could post questions or remarks related to those particular topics. Blog entries tagged "Forums" were used to discuss assigned readings. Using the same scheme presented in LC, students were required to post original and extension comments that added value to the discussion.

A classical argument in favor of constructivist learning was proposed by Dewey (1916), who states that education does not result from presentations or lectures performed by an instructor. It is rather the product of an active and constructivist process. An instructor's role is to mentor students as they build knowledge. Student teams were required to create a weekly entry in a team blog that highlighted material covered in class. To promote creative and associational thinking, each entry had to include a minimum of three references to relevant articles or websites—with accompanying links when applicable. Initially, all team members were assigned Author roles. Teams had to nominate a tech savvy member to be appointed Editor. All members were expected to contribute in their weekly posts. Group blogs served as digital portfolios of course assignments.

Application Review

Students were unfamiliar with blogging, with only two having previously created a Blogger account. Blogger is a blog storage server that belongs to Google. However, all understood the concept of blogs and had some experience reading blogs. Students were able to access content and participate in discussion forums without any problems and voluntarily subscribed to the MC blog to receive automatic emails of all new posts. Students preferred receiving automatic notifications, as opposed to checking the blog for new activity. Again, some students mentioned they wanted classmates to contribute earlier to the discussions. Students believed WP facilitated class discussion to a greater extent than Google Groups. Unlike GG—where comments were permitted only in the discussions section—WP allows comments in any entry. They commented that WP was more visually appealing than GG.

Students experienced difficulty learning how to use WP for content creation. However, this did not influence their perception of how useful WP was for team collaboration. Unlike Farmer and Bartlett-Bragg (2005), students did not show signs of discomfort when writing publicly. In fact, some groups posted links to their blogs on Facebook to attract a larger audience. Teams enjoyed seeing each other's weekly posts and were quite creative—including videos, slide shares and images in their posts. All teams personalized their blogs to incorporate symbols of their team identity— including names, colors, and logos. As the class progressed, blog references improved in quality. The instructor motivated teams to be more discerning in their selections. Each entry required one academic and two non-academic references. Initially, students relied on Wikipedia for their non-academic references. Later entries incorporated references to management and communication publications. This ability to link and reference cultivates learning communities.

Several students commented that WP was difficult to use at the beginning, but they considered the advantages of having a blog and the flexibility and functionality of WP outweighed its complexity. In general, students considered that WP was useful for record keeping and self-monitoring. It served as a central repository of class material and notes. Feedback and grades were frequently updated.

FACEBOOK

Facebook (http://www.facebook.com) is an online social networking site. According to Wellman (1997), "a social network is a set of people (or organizations or other social entities) connected by a set of socially meaningful relationships" (p. 179). The leading social networking sites are Facebook (FB) and MySpace (Nazir, Raza, & Chuah, 2008). As of April 2010, FB reports having over 70 translations available for its 400 million active users, 70% of which are outside the United States (Facebook Statistics, n.d.). FB members are able to create personal profiles, find people and socially connect with other members. FB's popularity among college students enables communication (Cloete, De Villiers, & Roodt, 2009) and connections. A social network allows students to interact and share information through their profile.

FB users can publish and share profile pictures and general information. They can communicate by posting short messages, which can include links, photos or videos. Members can create events and groups. Users can publish, share and tag photographs and chat with FB friends who are online. Groups have the standard features as user profiles with the addition of discussion forums.

Facebook distinguishes among four types of general relationships among users: friends, friends of friends, networks, and other users. Privacy settings can limit viewable information based on relationship type. Additional privacy settings permit users to categorize their friends on user-defined lists and grant access privileges accordingly.

Instructional Approach

Online social networking communities are an integral part of a student's daily life (Cloete et al., 2009; Harris & Rea, 2009). A plausible guess before starting a course is that a significant number of students already have a Facebook account. When incorporating a social media technology into a course, the instructor can take into advantage students' familiarity with FB standard features and FB's networking and communication capabilities.

Facebook supports third-party applications that can be integrated to its framework. A list of education-related applications is found in the FB Application Directory, with examples including "Courses 2.0" and "CourseFeed." However, third-party applications were not incorporated into the Entrepreneurship and New Businesses (ENB) course for a number of reasons. First, ENB in Facebook was set to be a private group and some applications are open to all FB users. Second, some applications have features that are not applicable for the course and add complexity to the user experience. Third, some applications require a separate registration process and it was decided to reduce the number of registrations (since three other social media tools were going to be used in ENB).

A FB Group was created for ENB with features such as a FB "Wall" (akin to a bulletin board) for short messages, a general information section, photo and video sharing sections and discussion forums. The FB Group was personalized by including tabs for photographs, videos and relevant information. The Info section was used for content delivery. It displayed the course description and links to resources, including the syllabus, course project requirements and other documents and websites. The Discussions section was used to talk about class assignments, whether it be assigned readings or course activities. The Wall was used as a general communication platform where messages from the instructor and students were published. Postings included course logistics and questions and answers related to course topics or content. Postings could include links, photos or videos. Facebook sends Notifications for actions that involve its users. Actions related to this FB Group include messages, tags, comments and posts. However, there are specific rules that determine when a Notification is sent. See the following section for more details. The Photos section was used as a roll call. Pictures of students in the classroom were considered to promote course identity. Students could share, tag or comment on the photos. A potential risk related to student privacy, appearing on a photo meant that other class members had access to it and not appearing was a public testimony of being late or missing a class.

Application Review

All students had previous FB accounts and no account registration or basic familiarization with the tool was needed. The personalized FB Group and the personalized student profiles gave a sense of course identity to this platform. Students were able to access course documentation through the information section without any problem. Links were posted that directed students to the respective files stored on Wiggio (see next section).

Discussions were used for comments or questions on specific class assignments or topics. The Wall was used for general questions. A disadvantage was apparent immediately as posts in the Discussions section or group Wall are not announced by email or in the Notification section. Instead, they are occasionally published in a user's personal News Feed. Students had to explicitly check the group Wall and Discussions pages for new postings. As of publication, there is no configuration option to set up notifications for group Wall or Discussions postings. To circumvent this problem, the instructor created a mailing list and sent FB messages when new assignments were posted. FB messages are announced by email and in the Messages section. However, students were still not notified of postings from fellow classmates unless they had previously posted in that particular discussion.

The group Wall was used to request appointments with the instructor, to ask questions related to the class project, to request sources for topics discussed in class or related to the class project, to comment or ask a question referent to course logistics, class discussions or material published by the instructor or their classmates. An interesting assignment included posting a video from YouTube in the group Wall. The YouTube section describes this assignment in further detail.

In general, students felt comfortable using the tool to collaborate with their classmates and perceived that it eased discussions with the instructor and other students. They also found FB helpful for requesting comments, feedback or help. Many students made positive comments observing that FB was convenient as a platform for combining personal social interaction and class communication and collaboration.

The Photos section of the group was used as a roll call, with a picture taken at the beginning of class and after the break. In the first class, only two students showed up on time after the break. Once the photo was shared, classmates posted comments congratulating the two students and calling for the group to be punctual. As the course progressed, students developed a greater sense of punctuality. Initially, some students were surprised to have their picture taken. After the first couple of weeks, they felt more comfortable and started tagging themselves and posing when photographed. A note of caution should be considered regarding students' privacy. The instructor requested permission before photographing students the first time and assured students that only group members could see the photos. For those students who did not want their picture taken, the instructor would take note of their assistance in the traditional way. All students accepted participating in this activity.

WIGGIO

Wiggio (http://wiggio.com/) is a web-based collaborative software. Collaborative software supports interdependent and independent work, such as file sharing, decisionmaking, collaborative authoring, and asynchronous communication (Townsend, DeMarie, & Hendrickson, 1998). Other web-based collaborative software providers are WizeHive, Yammer, and Basecamp. Wiggio is becoming popular among college students. In October 2009, Wiggio had over 200,000 users and is said to incorporate over 1,500 new members every day (Rao, 2009).

Wiggio users can edit documents and spreadsheets and share any type of files. They can post short messages, which can include links. Members can poll each other with multiple-choice or short open-ended questions. Users can create events with reminders sent by email and/or text messages. They can communicate through a chat room, conference call or a virtual conference. Messages can be sent by email, text or as a voice note. Members can create to-do lists with assigned and prioritized tasks. A Wiggio user can coordinate and belong to several groups.

Instructional Approach

Wiggio was chosen for ENB because of its collaborative features and its usability as its interface is simple and straightforward. The instructor considered that it provided the necessary features without burdening the student with complexity or sophisticated functionalities. Several Wiggio groups were created, one for the entire class and the rest for each team. Wiggio offers very limited customization: groups can be assigned different colors. ENB has a course team project assignment. The instructor believed that each team would use Wiggio as a tool for team collaboration.

The course Folder section was used for file sharing. The instructor shared the course syllabus, grading policies and course assignments. Students can access files directly within Wiggio or from a generated URL (which can be published on FB or any other platform). The Folder section was also used to collect course assignments. Students can upload files into specified drop folders. The teams Folder sections were used to share files among team members.

The Calendar section was used to notify students of class events. Once an appointment was requested through the course Wall in FB, the instructor set it up in the Calendar section for all students to see. Notifications of upcoming events were sent to all invitees. Polls were used to obtain feedback on students' perception of their evaluations and to organize the scheduling of a makeup session. The instructor decided to select FB as the single communication platform because of its ubiquity. Wiggio's communication features were not used. MixedInk (see next section) was selected as the single collaborative content creation platform due to its specialized features. Wiggio's collaborative authoring feature was not used.

Application Review

Wiggio was setup initially to serve as a web-based file sharing application for the class. From the instructor's perspective, the file sharing component worked and integrated well with the other social media tools. Students did not report problems learning how to use the tool. The calendar feature was used to publish the class schedule and group meetings during the instructor's office hours. Wiggio was configured to send email alerts (notifications) 30 minutes before the time of the event, which facilitated punctuality.

Except for the uses designed by the instructor, most students did not rely on Wiggio as a collaboration tool for their own team projects. Except for file sharing, teams did not use the calendar, to-do or communication features. However, students believed the tool had useful features and would recommend it for team collaboration. Students highlighted the file sharing capability and valued having a common storage repository.

MIXEDINK

MixedInk (http://mixedink.com) is collaborative authoring tool. Collaborative authoring or writing involves the creation of a document by two or more authors. The creation process involves both independent writing and interdependent discussions on the editing of the final document (Dillon, 1993). Group dynamics play an important role for time-sensitive, collaborative-writing tasks. Authors need to define rules for document editing and manage conflict. MixedInk takes collaborative writing a step towards autonomous editing by introducing a rating system. Authors contribute ideas by writing, rating, commenting and using what other users have written. As authors write their contributions, MixedInk suggests text that matches what is being written. An author can decide whether to use a fellow author's previously written text. Authors can resubmit newer versions of their contributions. The top-rated version represents the collective contribution of all participating authors. This tool works best for short and focused documents, such as opinion editorials, petitions and mission statements. MixedInk is a young company, launched in January 2009 with about 7,250 registered users. It has been used in United States government initiatives for promoting active collaborative discussions among citizens and other stakeholders (for an example see Ginsberg, 2009).

In MixedInk, a collaborative authoring project starts when a user defines the title and type of the document to be created. Deadlines for submissions and ratings are set afterward. The project is shared with a specific set of authors or can be made public. Registered users can start contributing and rating. The system will not accept more contributions after the submission deadline has passed. Users can continue rating submissions until the project ends. The top-rated submission is considered the final document.

Instructional Approach

Collaborative learning is based on the idea that it is possible to build knowledge when a group of people perform specific activities and share their experience. This methodology requires intellectual and social involvement from students to collaboratively work in problem solutions, search for meaning and understanding or creating a product (Smith &

MacGregor, 1992). MixedInk was used to review, discuss and reinforce class material. Students were assigned readings, cases and short research topics. Instead of having students separately answer specific questions, the instructor required students to collaborative prepare a single answer for each assigned question. The answer would represent the collective knowledge of all course members.

The required protocol for collaborative answer assignments started with an "original" submission. Students had to provide individual answers to the questions posed. After they submitted their personal contributions, students were asked to rate their classmates' contributions. In addition to rating, students could comment on each other's contributions. Finally, they were required to submit a "combined" contribution incorporating content from their peers. The collective final answer was selected by the system based on the highest rating.

Application Review

All students submitted the two requested contributions—original answer and integrated answer. Students did not comment on other submissions. Student procrastination was apparent in this assignment. Contributions were scarce at the beginning even though students were advised that starting a collaborative writing assignment early would result in a higher quality product. Submission frequency increased as the submission deadline approached. A couple of students started their participation on the eve of this deadline. Combined submissions did not fully exploit the collective nature of this assignment. A true combined submission—one that would integrate content of a group of contributors—was never created. Instead, combined submissions included only incremental changes. A student would use a peer's contribution and edit it. Students kept rating new contributions until the rating deadline. The submission deadline was one day prior to the rating deadline. The top-rated contribution was submitted as the final answer. Usually, this answer did not represent the collective. It was a contribution that included the ideas of two or three students. Quality was similar to the answers students would have produced individually. Not only was the quality of the final answer reduced, so was motivation. Students that participated early complained that they had to wait for others in order to write their combined submissions.

Most students commented that the tool allowed them to work collaboratively. However, half mentioned they would not recommend the tool. They considered the collaboration ineffective because the result was substandard. The instructor was pleasantly surprised that students were metacognitively aware of the quality of their work. Some mentioned they preferred discussion forums to collaborative content creation.

In addition to procrastination, timing also influenced these assignments. Each collaborative writing project lasted a week. This does not allow for more than one cycle of writing-rating-combining (and perhaps even discouraged commenting). Introducing two or more cycles and requiring students to provide commentary may truly transform the assignments into effective collaborative authoring projects.

YOUTUBE

YouTube (http://www.YouTube.com) is a video sharing website where users can upload, view, and share video clips (Duffy, 2008). YouTube (YT) users have the capability to annotate videos they have uploaded. Captions can be created manually as commentary or through speech recognition technology as subtitles. The speech recognition feature allows same language and translation subtitles and is available in 51 languages. YouTube has 1.2 billion streams daily worldwide, placing it well above all the major competitors (Arrington, 2009).

YouTube offers several interactive social features. Users can rate or flag videos and comment through embedded communication tools such as personal bulletin boards and video and textual comments (Rotman, Golbeck, & Preece, 2009). Videos can be shared on social networks sites or embedded in personal blogs or websites. Johnson (2010) reports that 24 hours of videos were uploaded to YouTube each minute in March 2009.

Instructional Approach

Educational approaches for YT include in-class and online discussions of video relevant to the course and students created videos instead of traditional essays. For a detailed list of other educational approaches see Duffy (2008). In ENB, YouTube was used for feedback and exploratory tasks. Student mid-term presentations were videotaped and then edited to include PowerPoint slides. The instructor uploaded video clips and used YT's annotation tool to provide a running commentary. It was considered that students would better assimilate this evaluation method. Feedback provided during the presentation or immediately after may not be entirely processed due to the nerves of public speaking. Captioned video presentations on YT allow students to interpret comments at their own pace, have a permanent record of the evaluation and learn from feedback provided to their peers. In addition, it is highly recommended to see a videotape of one giving a presentation to improve oral presentation skills. The exploratory task assignment involved posting a video from YouTube in the FB group Wall. Students were required to share a video of an entrepreneur they admired with a short explanation of their selection. They were also required to comment on a classmate's choice. Commentary was performed in FB rather than YT to restrict participation to class members.

Application Review

Students used the evaluation videos to improve their subsequent presentations. They understood and incorporated feedback. The videos were observed several times—an average of 9.6 views per video until the end of the course. Students mentioned that they valued this approach. Viewing each other's evaluation videos strengthens their comprehension of the instructor's commentary. Editing and annotating a video though is time consuming. The ENB instructor spent on average 1.5 hours preparing each four-minute YT feedback video. Another issue to consider is privacy. Students may feel uncomfortable having a public video indicating their mistakes. The instructor polled the class on whether they preferred their videos to have restricted access. The entire class requested public access and wanted to be able to share the videos with family and friends.

The exploratory task assignment—sharing a YT video of an admired entrepreneur—was successful. Students gathered a variety of entrepreneurs and had very different opinions regarding entrepreneurial traits. Interesting discussions ensued both within the FB group Wall and during class. Students considered YT a rich repository of visual content that could complement topics discussed in class.

DISCUSSION

Social media provides a variety of approaches in education. However, single technologies that fit all educational needs of a course are not yet available. Some excel in simple communication, others in collaborative authoring and others in promoting a course's identity. The approaches presented in this chapter confirm this observation. Both the instructors and students considered certain features to work well with certain technologies, while others did not. A comparison between platforms is presented (see Table 15.4 for an overview). This comparison is based on perceptions and experiences within the context of particular course requirements. We believe this critical analysis can aid instructors in their selection of social media tools for learning. Their choice will depend on specific educational tasks.

Table 15.4. Comparison of Social Media Platforms and Features[a]

	Leadership Communication	Management Communication		Entrepreneurship and New Businesses		
	Google Groups	WordPress	Facebook	Wiggio	MixedInk	YouTube
Collaborative content creation	—	Okay	—	—	Okay	—
Content/feedback delivery	Okay Navigation, search	Okay Navigation, search	Okay	—	—	Okay Search[b]
Communication	Okay Text	Okay Text, links, html formatting	Okay Text, links, media	—	—	—
Discussion forums	Okay Text	Okay Text, links, html formatting, avatars	Okay Text, links, avatars	—	—	—
Calendar	—	—	—	Okay	—	—
File sharing	Okay	—	—	Okay	—	—
Notifications	Okay Configurable	Okay Configurable	Limited	Okay Automatic	—	—
Personalization[c]	Okay	Flexible	Okay	Limited	—	—

Note: [a]Features not used by students or unavailable features are not compared. [b]Videos in YouTube can be searched by title name, description or tags. Annotations within videos are not searchable. [c]Personalization refers to whether a platform can be customized to display a particular look and present explicit features.

Personalization-Course Identity

Google Groups (GG), WordPress (WP), Facebook (FB), and Wiggio allow personalization in different degrees. In GG, the group owner can change colors, styles and pictures. In FB, the group owner can include tabs for photographs, videos or applications. Students have personalized profiles with pictures. FB promotes course identity by linking the course to its members. Wiggio has limited personalization, a color and name represents group identity. Personalization in WP is quite flexible. The blog owner can select the layout, look and feel of the blog, in addition to including photographs, videos or widgets. Students can select a picture or an avatar to represent them. A personalized blog and the exchange of commentary among students within the blog create a higher sense of course identity.

Content/Feedback Delivery

Students had no problems accessing content through GG, WP, FB, or YouTube (YT). Announcements in GG are made through the Pages section and can include images and links. In WP, any announcement is a new entry in the blog and can include images, videos, audio files, documents and polls. In FB, the Wall permits short announcements with photos, videos or links. In addition, specific tabs for photos, videos or links can be configured as redundant repositories of content. A navigation problem may arise if numerous announcements are created within a course. In FB, announcements can only be ordered chronologically or categorized into tabs, where they are displayed in chronological order. Students need to remember when the announcement was made to access it within the Wall or within a tab. In GG, announcements can be arranged in a hierarchical order that the instructor designs. Students follow the hierarchy to navigate. In WP, all entries are ordered chronologically and can be tagged or categorized. Multiple tags and categories are allowed. Tag and category clouds permit navigation to specific announcements. In addition, GG and WP have search capability for any published content within the course. Content was delivered in YouTube as commentary within an evaluation video. Student presentations were recorded and the feedback was annotated. Students observe in real time the pointers provided by the instructor. In YT, videos can be accessed by a search for the video name, description or tags. However, a search for specific content within a video's annotations is not yet possible.

Communication

In GG, the instructor can communicate creating new Pages or responding to comments students have made. Students communicate by commenting on specific discussion topics or Pages and by creating new discussion topics. Comments in GG are text only. In WP, the instructor can communicate creating blog entries or responding to comments students have made; students communicate by commenting on specific blog entries. Comments in WP are textual; html formatting and links are permitted. Communication in FB is performed through the Wall. Students and instructor can post comments with photos, videos or links. Although Wiggio was not used for communication purposes (FB took this role in ENB), it has a sophisticated communication platform. Students can communicate through a chat room, conference call or a virtual conference and can send messages by email, text or as a voice note. In MixedInk, comments on contributions are permitted. Students did not take advantage of this feature. Comments in YT are in the form of text or as a video response. In ENB, YT videos were embedded in FB; YT comments were not used. The ability to include richer comments made WP and FB the preferred communication platforms among students. It is recommended to introduce students to (or remind them of) *netiquette* rules—such as not typing in all caps, asking for clarification, using proper language and writing with a positive tone.

Discussion Forums

Discussion forums in GG, WP and FB were effective. GG allows text-only comments. WP allows text, links and html formatting. Most students only used text in their responses. Discussions in FB are textual; links are permitted. The use of avatars and pictures in WP and FB, gave the discussions a graphic semblance of dialogue. Students could also upload photographs into their GG profiles. However, in order to see them, you had to click on each user name. Instructors can initiate a discussion by including a couple of preliminary topic-related questions. Instructors should establish ground rules and requirements for participation. For example, students can attack ideas but not the person. Instructors can promote dialogue by requiring students to include comments on contributions of their fellow classmates. It is recommended to allow some leeway when evaluating student contributions. Peterson and Caverly (2006) suggest toleration of keyboard and spelling mistakes. Students preferred WP—comments could be formatted, individual pictures were included and notifications were sent for any new entry (see Notifications section below).

Collaborative Content Creation

For the MC course, small groups of students created team blogs collaboratively. A WP setting assigns editing and author roles to users. Students initially considered WP as difficult to use. Perhaps its many features and flexibility daze non-technological users. As the course progressed, students shifted from mainly textual blogs to blogs with embedded media.

Team blogs developed into tailored blogs that reflected each team's identity. GG were not used for collaborative authoring.

In ENB, the entire class was to create a collaborative answer to a teacher imposed question. MixedInk allows students to contribute ideas by writing, rating, commenting and using what other users have written. The product of this collaborative writing project is the top-rated contribution. The concept under which MixedInk operates is compelling. Unfortunately, due to both timing and process issues, outcomes did not reflect collaboration. Assignments resulted in contributions from a couple students and not the entire class. It is recommended to carefully design an assignment to ensure full collaboration before using this tool.

Notifications

Students favored tools that sent notifications of all new activity. GG, WP, and Wiggio have this capability. GG and WP can be configured to send email notifications of all new announcements. Wiggio automatically sends notifications of all activity within its site. Students complained that they were not receiving up-to-date news on FB. Notifications in FB for general announcements in the group Wall are sporadically published in the News Feed. Notifications in FB for Discussions postings are sent once a user has commented in a particular discussion. Students had to actively check their FB group for new activity.

File Sharing

Wiggio and GG were used to share files. Both tools performed flawlessly. WP also offers this feature, caution should be taken with public access to these files.

Calendar

Students had no problems using Wiggio's calendar feature. The class—instructor and students—valued the automated event reminders that assisted punctuality. FB has an event feature but no calendar view. A calendar is an important element for a course. The instructors had to create 'calendars' with deadlines and class information in table formats in the other social media platforms.

Learning

Social media contributed to an enhanced learning experience. Contributions in discussion forums and collaborative content creation were richer and more methodical than in-class contributions. Students behaved as active agents responsible for the construction of knowledge. Students showed a positive attitude towards social media. They participated in both mandatory and non-mandatory assignments. Students voluntarily shared information that they considered related to course material. Negative comments were directed towards what they perceived to be poor peer participation. Students wanted their classmates to contribute more and at an earlier time—not right before the deadline. Both instructors and students positively perceived these shared learning experiences.

Final Thoughts

An instructor should take into account the hard and soft skills students need to develop in order to use these tools. The learning objective is the course itself and not the technology. Fortunately, the pervasiveness of social media in the life of current students reduces the time and difficulty to become familiar with these tools. An instructor may be tempted to use different social media technologies that complement each other. However, before doing so, the issue of overload should be analyzed. The technological choice should contemplate the number of tools, type of features and tool integration. A larger set of tools increases flexibility, but may hinder productivity. Another consideration is usability. For familiar tools, such as FB, this is not an issue. For newer tools, perceived usability influences perceived usefulness. One last consideration relates to technological service failures. Even the most widely-used social media platforms are not immune (Hesse, 2009; Schonfeld, 2009). An instructor should be flexible if such failures occur near deadlines.

Two interesting observations relate to privacy and intrusiveness. Students did not express concerns relating to privacy and favored open access. They wanted to share their videos, photos, assignments and course related information with friends and family. Students wanted email notifications of all course-related activity. They expressed frustration when a tool would not provide this feature. They did not consider email notifications to be intrusive (the MC blog sent close to 600 notifications to each student). These two behaviors may be culturally related.

Social media approaches for graduate education are feasible and positive. Educators should take advantage of their availability at little to no cost. Students are already involved in many social media activities. Both instructors and students can gain by directing those activities into learning. Instructors have willing and active participants in the classroom and students apply their social media knowledge in novel learning environments. It is hoped that the review of which features and which technologies worked in our experience will assist educators in the implementation of social media in their curricula.

Limitations

This is an exploratory analysis of social media in education. The tools were compared against each other but not against a standard course management system. Most of the educational tasks were used with all tools, but not all. In some cases, the platforms did not offer a particular feature. A systematic analysis, that consistently uses the same features with a set number of tools and a control group, should be considered for future research.

NOTE

1.   See Goode (2009), or email the authors, for detailed survey results.

REFERENCES

Arrington, M. (2009, June 9). YouTube Video Streams Top 1.2 Billion/Day. *Tech-Crunch*. Retrieved from http://techcrunch.com

Cloete, S., De Villiers, C., & Roodt, S. (2009). Facebook as an academic tool for ICT lecturers. *Proceedings of the 2009 Annual Conference of the Southern African Computer Lecturers' Association* (pp. 16-22). Eastern Cape, South Africa: ACM.

Dabbagh, N., & Kitsantas, A. (2005). Using web-based pedagogical tools as scaffolds for self-regulated learning. *Instructional Science, 33*, 513-540.

Dillon, A. (1993). How collaborative is collaborative writing? An analysis of the production of two technical reports. In M. Sharples (Ed.), *Computer-supported collaborative writing* (pp. 69-86). London, England: Springer-Verlag.

Dewey, J. (1916). *Democracy and education*. New York, NY: Macmillan.

Duffy, P. (2008). Engaging the YouTube Google-eyed generation: Strategies for using Web 2.0 in teaching and learning. *The Electronic Journal of e-Learning, 6*(2), 22.

Farmer, J., & Bartlett-Bragg, A. (2005). Blogs @ anywhere: High fidelity online communication. *Proceedings of ASCILITE,* 197-203.

Facebook Statistics. (n.d.). Retrieved April 17, 2010, from http://www.facebook.com/press/info.php?statistics

Ginsberg, W. R. (2009). *Freedom of Information Act (FOIA): Issues for the 111th Congress*. Washington, DC: Congressional Research Service, Library of Congress.

Goode, A. W. (2009, October). Implementation of online forums in graduate education. *II ACE Seminar: Knowledge construction in online collaborative learning communities*, XVII ISTEC General Assembly. Albuquerque, New Mexico.

Harris, A. L., & Rea, A. (2009). Web 2.0 and virtual world technologies: A growing impact on IS education. *Journal of Information Systems Education, 20*(2), 12.

Hesse, M. (2009, August 7). At a loss for words: The day Facebook, Twitter crashed. *The Washington Post.* Retrieved from http://www.washingtonpost.com/wp-dyn/content/article/2009/08/06/AR2009080602341.html

Lam, W. (2004). Encouraging online participation. *Journal of Information Systems Education, 15*(4), 345-348.

Johnson, S. (2010, April 22). *YouTube turns 5.* Retrieved from http://www.chicagotribune.com

Lindoo, E. (2009). Using Google Sites, Google Groups and Google Documents to enhance your course. *Journal of Computing in Sciences in Colleges, 25*(2), 46-51.

Nazir, A., Raza, S., & Chuah, C. N. (2008). Unveiling Facebook: a measurement study of social network based applications. *Proceedings of the 8th ACM SIG-COMM Conference on Internet Measurement* (pp. 43-56). New York, NY: ACM.

Peterson, C. L., & Caverly, D. C. (2006). Techtalk: What students need to know about online discussion forums. *Journal of Developmental Education, 20*(3), 40-41.

Pintrich, P.R., Smith, D. A. F., Garcia, T., & McKeachie, W. J. (1993). Reliability and predictive validity of the motivated strategies for learning questionnaire (MSLQ). *Educational and Psychological Measurement, 53,* 801-813.

O'Reilly, T. (2005). *What is Web 2.0: Design patterns and business models for the next generation of software.* Retrieved from http://oreilly.com/web2/archive/what-is-web-20.html

Rao, L. (2009, October 1). Wiggio adds Facebook Integration, video conferencing and more. *TechCrunch.* Retrieved from http://techcrunch.com

Rienzo, T., & Han, B. (2009). Microsoft or Google Web 2.0 tools for course management. *Journal of Information Systems Education, 20*(2), 123-127.

Rotman, D., Golbeck, J., & Preece, J. (2009). The community is where the rapport is—On sense and structure in the YouTube community. *Proceedings of the 4th International conference on communities and technologies* (pp. 41-49). University Park, PA: ACM.

Schonfeld, E. (2009, May 14). Google gets its own fail whale. *TechCrunch.* Retrieved from http://techcrunch.com

Smith, B. L., & MacGregor, J. T. (1992). What is collaborative learning? In A. Goodsell, M. Maher, V. Tinto, B. Smith, & J. MacGregor (Eds.), *Collaborative learning: A sourcebook for higher education.* University Park, PA: National Center on Postsecondary Teaching, Learning, and Assessment at Pennsylvania State University.

Townsend, A. M., DeMarie, S. M., & Hendrickson, A. R. (1998). Technology and the workplace of the future. *The Academy of Management Executive, 12*(3), 17-29.

Wagner, C. (2004). Wiki: A technology for conversational knowledge management and group collaboration. *Communications of the Association for Information Systems, 13,* 265-289.

Wellman, B. (1997). An electronic group is virtually a social network. In S. Kiesler (Ed.), *The culture of the Internet* (pp. 179-206). Hillsdale, NJ: Erlbaum.

WordPress Stats. (n.d.) Retrieved April 25, 2010 from http://en.WordPress.com/stats/

CHAPTER 16

CURRICULUM REDESIGN

Engaging Net Generation Students Through Integration of Social Media in Business Education

Jeanny Liu and Deborah Olson

This chapter focuses on how to integrate social media into class assignments and redesign curriculum to provide business students with meaningful learning experiences that will engage them in the concepts. Making changes to course delivery facilitates the development of skills that students need to be effective in today's evolving organizations. As with all business courses, it is the role of the faculty to assist students in understanding the power of new technologies and how these tools can be used to optimize (as well as derail) the effectiveness of organizations, teams, and individuals. This chapter offers some suggested approaches faculty can use when planning their courses and developing assignments which (further) integrate social media and technology to engage the hearts and minds of net generation students. A key element of our approach to course design focuses on assisting students in thinking about how these social media tools can be useful to expand their professional network, to achieve their targeted career goals, to understand the power of shared knowledge, and to experience a

Cutting-Edge Social Media Approaches to Business Education:
Teaching With LinkedIn, Facebook, Twitter, Second Life, and Blogs, pp. 315–335

rich learning environment that is enhanced by integrating social media technologies.

OUR CHALLENGE AS EDUCATORS: AN ISSUE, AN OPPORTUNITY

David is sitting in class, listening to the professor lecture on macroenvironmental influences and their impact in the global economy. He seems a bit restless as a red light starts to blink on his phone indicating an incoming message. Discretely, he glides his fingers across to unlock his iPhone and starts discussing with friends on Facebook about which restaurants have the best pepperoni pizza in town. According to Facebook statistics, David is not alone. There are more than 200 million active users that log on to Facebook in any given day and an average user spends more than 55 minutes per day updating their own information and writing on their "friends' walls" (Facebook.com, 2010). Social media networks have transformed the way students interact with each other and have also made a direct impact on what they think about and do in class. While engaging students in the learning process and keeping their attention during class is not a new issue, the influence of social technologies have created new tools and approaches for faculty to engage students who grew up with the advent of Internet and social media networks.

Students like David are prevalent and have developed an almost addictive need to immediately respond to every incoming message received. Many educators are intrigued by the success and the wide use of social media, especially its impact on the younger (net) generation (those born after 1980). As educators, we often spent a lot of time developing our curriculum and identifying creative strategies to engage students in the learning process. Thus, rather than address the challenges of students' texting behavior, we would like to explore its potential and embrace the possibilities it offers us as business educators as we design class assignments and facilitate learning.

We wrote this chapter to explore the possibilities and share ideas that would assist business educators in using social media and other technologies in curriculum design to engage net generation students. Our approach in this chapter is to share ideas about how to create a net generation student centered teaching approach to curriculum design by integrating social media and technology throughout the learning process. We start with a brief overview of the impact of social media in business education and its implications for student learning. Next, we discuss the social learning paradigm observed in net generation students and describe four prominent behavioral themes. We provide ideas and strategies for developing a process to redesign the current curriculum to meet the needs of net generation students. The chapter concludes with some examples of how social technologies were adopted in our business courses so that the framework provides practical ideas and approaches that can be used in a variety of business courses.

Individual experiences and skills can vary greatly among business students, therefore, not all of the studies and examples shared in this chapter may not directly apply to every student from the net generation. One of our assumptions as we wrote this chapter was that young people are highly influenced by peers and respond to peer pressure. Given the widespread use of social media across all age groups, students entering college have undoubtedly had some prior exposure to their peers who use social media networks and other technologies throughout middle and high school. As such, while some students do not possess these skills and interests, many do and it has a direct impact on what captures their attention and helps them learn (and retain) concepts and ideas.

THE ROLE OF SOCIAL MEDIA IN BUSINESS EDUCATION AND STUDENT LEARNING

Students of the net generation have revolutionized and shaped a new culture of learning and made a significant impact on how social media are used in organizations of all sizes and in all industries. Rapid changes in technology place new demands on faculty to design courses that incorporate multimedia and social technologies that will engage net generation students by using skills that these students already possess, but also raising students' skills to a new level of sophistication and relevance to business and organizational success. We hear about examples daily of how savvy businesses are actively using social media to expand their markets (be a Facebook friend), recruiting applicants through LinkedIn, and conducting background checks on potential new hires through Googling those individuals before job offers are extended. The reality is that social media and technology are embedded in how net generation students engage the world and how organizations have evolved to tap the power of social technology to sustain and grow their organizations and improve their business processes (marketing, operations, human resources, etc.) on many levels.

Within the context of education and learning, Goodfellow and Hewling (2005) state that technology has evolved from being a mere "mental prosthetic" which helped individuals think more efficiently and effectively, to now being used as a tool for interaction and embeddedness in the global social context in which we live and work. This dramatic shift in the power of technology has direct implications for us as business educators. When used effectively, technology creates a context for online learning and networking which facilitates peers working together inside and outside the classroom to construct knowledge in a collaborative and personally meaningful way (Jonassen, Mayes, & MacAleese, 1993; Lankshear & Knobel, 2003).

To make a meaningful impact on student learning, it is important that we as business faculty understand net generation students' changing values, needs, behaviors, and the way they learn. This cultural change facilitated by the Internet has led to a very different pattern of behavior and approaches to learning within the younger generation when compared to students from the baby boomer generation (Rettie, 2002). This new generation of students has shaped a culture of learning shifting from a teaching centered focus to student centered learning design which demands greater student engagement (Hartman, Dziuban, & Brophy-Ellison, 2007). As part of the course design, business faculty can start by identifying the specific ways that net generation students are different than students were even a decade ago. Faculty also need to remain up-to-date on how organizations are using technology and social media in order to teach students how to use their technology skills to make positive contributions to the organizations that they create (through entrepreneurship) or for whom they work (as leaders and employees).

PARADIGM OF NET GENERATION STUDENTS

Growing up immersed in the digital world, net generation students (persons who were born after 1980) have gained the interests of many researchers in that they are very different in their approaches to work, learning, collaborating, playing, shopping, and thinking when compared to previous generations (Tapscott, 2008). Primarily, exposure to Internet at a young age has given them a different set of skills and approaches when it comes to learning. Mainly, they are empowered by the digital age to voice and publish their opinions in the absence of any specific organizational context or physical structure. They are familiar with and understand how to Google information, to collaborate, and to share (peer-to-peer) any type of documents, from music to homework assignments via the Internet, without waiting for someone to tell them what to do or give them a specific assignment (Tapscott, 2008). Alch (2000) described the six core values of the net generation students. These core values include optimism, civic duty, confidence, achievement, morality, and diversity. The study further asserted that students from the net generation see the Internet as something they have control over.

While majority of the students we have seen arrive on our campuses with some degree of confidence using technology, it is incumbent on faculty to help students to learn how to use these tools to think critically and make important choices, rather than "believing everything they see and hear." Similar to the evolution that occurred with the advent of TV, baby boomers had to learn to think critically about the content and "messages" being broadcast to them rather than being passive, noncritical recipients of information and "entertainment." The same principles hold for web content which can be made to look as if it comes from expert sources based on substantive research. As faculty, we need to consciously incorporate learning assignments and discussions into courses that assist net generation students develop critical thinking skills to avoid becoming passive recipients of information and making faulty assumptions and decisions without having more rigorously analyzed the information they pull from the web.

One important value faculty often seek to nurture in students is the desire for lifelong learning and growth. While social networks have demonstrated its power to bring people together who have shared interests, knowledge and collaboration to achieve common goals (Mazman & Usluel, 2009), educators have yet to fully exploit its potential and impact on learning. Designing a social media oriented curriculum inside and outside the classroom can be a powerful tool to facilitate collaboration, knowledge sharing, and reflective thinking so that students are not only developing the passion for lifelong learning, but are honing their critical thinking skills in the process.

THE CULTURE OF NET GENERATION STUDENTS: IMPLICATIONS FOR COURSE DESIGN

Many scholars have written about the characteristics of net generation students (Brown, 2000; Oblinger, 2005; Skiba & Barton, 2006; Tapscott, 1998). In this section, we will focus on four broad themes that take the characteristics learned from their boomer parents to an entirely new level due to the development and wide dissemination of technologies that their boomer parents would have never imagined.

Multitasking, Multiprocessing Behavior

The net generation students seem to have a greater ability to divide their attention into fragments and pay attention to multiple inputs simultaneously. According to Tapscott (1998) as a result of the years of expo-

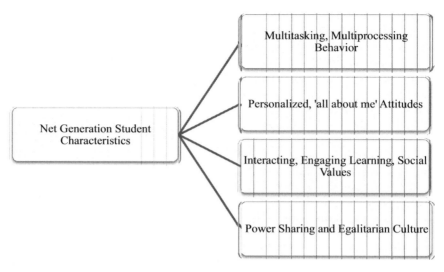

Figure 16.1.   Net generation characteristics.

sure to a wide range of technologies, net generation students have largely developed hypertext minds by playing, linking, cutting, and pasting information that they find to be interesting. Research has shown that these students are highly effective at multitasking and can juggle multiple tasks and electronic devices simultaneously (Brown, 2000). However, the impact of multitasking is not all positive. Ophira, Nass, and Wagner (2009) identified groups of students who multitasked continuously throughout the day and another group of students who rarely multitasked. The results of their study showed that in general, students who multitasked most often performed significantly more poorly on computer based tests (e.g. categorizing a random strings of words) when compared to students who rarely multitasked. The computer based tests that these students completed in this research were standard tests used by psychologists in a wide range of research contexts. For the students who score poorly on the tests used in this research, it is an indication of an inability to ignore less relevant contextual information and organize ideas and concepts. The question that needs to be answered regarding this research and its relationship to multitasking is whether those who multitask frequently had difficulties organizing and focusing before they began multitasking constantly throughout the day, or if the behavior of multitasking in some way had a negative impact on their ability to organize and focus on relevant information. Multitasking seems to habituate the brain to become more superficial and results in the individual having no or little memory about what they have done or learned (Ophira et al., 2009). Being more fragmented and less focused will clearly have a negative impact on the ability to be creative and think about more complex inter-relationships among concepts and issues.

The challenge for business faculty is to design course assignments and simulations that are integrated with the learning outcomes of the class and allow students to use the skills at multitasking in a manner that deepens their learning and understanding. To facilitate deep learning and retention, faculty are challenged to develop and use approaches and assignments which facilitate engagement in the learning process. To be effective in helping others learn, faculty need to continue to be creative in their approach to ensure relevance and meaning in both the concepts they are presenting and the processes they use to engage students. When students do not see or agree with the course relevance demonstrated to them, minimal learning occurs and faculty can even drive students out of the formal learning process. For example, a recent college drop out commented that, as a communications major, the classes he was taking were not relevant to him because the faculty focused mainly on using print, radio and television rather than learning about communications that are pervasive in the digital world ("The Ne(x)t," 2009).

For business faculty, the challenge when designing courses becomes how to ensure that the students' skills at multitasking actually result in a final and finish product that meets the expectations of a completed assignment. Presenting class material with a series of PowerPoint slides that sequentially defines the concepts to be learned in the class will more than likely completely disengage students. Lack of engagement, of course, results in students not understanding the concepts and how those concepts are relevant in organizations. A lack of engagement also can motivate students to start looking at their phones to see if anyone has written on their Facebook wall or respond to a new text message that just came in. Faculty can design each class to include multitasking through such approaches as using embedded video clips in their PowerPoint, integrating cases to apply concepts, and giving assignments in which students generate their own examples to explain how to apply the organizational concepts. Using these approaches in each class becomes important to facilitate and maintain student engagement and involvement in the learning process.

Self-Focused Attitudes

When describing the perspectives of students from the net generation, Tapscott (1999a) notes that they commonly thrive on collaboration, enjoy taking initiative, and many find the idea of having someone as a "boss" somewhat bizarre. Net generation students in general do not communicate effectively by traditional standards (written and oral), they prefer to use technology to retrieve and integrate information, and prefer working collaboratively (Feiertag & Berge, 2008). Net generation students tend to gravitate toward innovation and seek out fast and immediate results (Tapscott, 1999b). They can be perceived as having a sense of entitlement coming across with the attitude of "what can you do for me" (Generation Y, 2009). Students of the net generation can be both outspoken and informal. According to a longitudinal study conducted by Rowlands et al. (2008), people born after 1993 have demonstrated a greater reliance on search engines to obtain information rather than relying on traditional hard copy reading materials. One of the major concerns with the reliance on retrieving information from the web is that net generation students often do not possess the critical analytical skills to assess the accuracy of the information they are accessing on the net. This behavior pattern has clear implications for the design of assignments. As a result, we recommend that faculty spend more time showing students how to search for relevant information and make meaningful interpretations of the data they are getting when they do a Google search. In our experience, we have found that students do not consistently have a basic understanding of the difference between finding an empirical article from the online library and pulling information off Wikipedia to answer questions related to concepts presented in class. One of the authors teaching a senior level undergraduate class, recently had several students in that class ask her what it meant to find an empirical article through the online library and whether information from the *Denver Post* or *Newsweek* would be consider empirical sources. The students asking these questions were bright and engaged juniors and seniors. Despite the fact that they had already 2-3 years of college under their belt, they did not have a clear understanding of the difference between the "content" in peer reviewed journal articles as compared to *Wikipedia* entries (since the people who make Wikipedia entries are also "experts" and have experience in what they are writing about). This is a perfect example of how being dependent on using technology has had a negative impact on the development of critical thinking skills. This provides an opportunity for faculty to build exercises into their curriculum so that meaningful and continuous discussions occur about these types of topics. Similarly, we have also had students use quotes from blogs as if they were experts on the topics on which they were blogging rather than seeing the blogs entries as one person's opinion.

Business faculty need to consciously think through strategies to make these distinctions clear so that students understand the differences in the quality of information that they access from the web to think critically about its relevance and meaningfulness. As business students and future business professionals, it is essential that they understand how to gather information which can be used to draw valid inferences and make important decisions.

Learning and Social Values

According to Oblinger (2005), "When asked about their best learning experiences, net generation students use words like engagement, interaction visual, and active. (p 69)" A big part of social life for net generation students, it seems, is social activities and postings facilitated by the use of computer mediated technology. Rather than face-to-face meetings, they prefer to communicate and coordinate events via twitter and social networking sites (SNS). They are not afraid to publicly share homework assignments and projects via P2P platforms such as YouTube. They embrace the technology to collaborate to cocreate documents such as Google documents. They maintain friendships and meet new people online through social networking sites. They take pictures of daily events and share them instantly via smart phones. They enjoy the convenience of publishing their thoughts and the gratification of receiving instant feedback as others comment on their posts. Building assignments that engage the students' natural social desires will not only facilitate the learning process, but will be more fun for both the students and the faculty.

Power Sharing and Egalitarian Culture

Word of mouth marketing is a familiar concept to net generation students. Many grew up with the ability to engage others of the same interests in discussions and sharing of experiences (both good and bad) about products, companies, and professors (www.ratemyprofessors.com). In addition, practitioners and scholars believe that the students from the net generation have directly influenced the development of new trends, shaping a new culture, and changing the rules of marketing (Tapscott, 2007). For example, companies like Dell and Nike have used open source technology and discussion forums soliciting user feedback to better service customers. These user comments have led to critical product improvements and new product creations. For example, companies like Dell and Nike have used open sourced technology and discussion forums soliciting user feedback to better service customers. These user comments have led to critical product improvements and new product creations. Use of social media and technology reshaped the processes used in the political arena and played a critical role in helping President-elect Barack Obama win his victory in the Presidential election (Tapscott, 2008).

Leung (2004) conducted a survey of 976 net generation students between the ages of 16-24 to more deeply understand their interests, characteristics, and values. Results of this research showed that net generation students tend to be: (1) strongly principled and believe in fundamental rights to information, (2) openly express emotions and ideas on the net, (3) innovative and investigative, and (4) independent, confident, and preoccupied with maturity (Leung, 2004). It appears that this cohort of students tends to enjoy the power and freedom of being able to express themselves and are not afraid to ask for what they want. They want to be heard and to share power with older generations (Tapscott, 2008).

The characteristics of net generation students described above show the importance of redesigning and adjusting the processes faculty use to engage students in the learning process. These characteristics serve as a backdrop for understanding the norms (both implicit and explicit) that students have evolved and that directly impact their expectations of their business faculty. We have found it valuable to reflect on the norms listed in Table 16.1 along with the characteristics of net generation students that we just summarized as we develop course assignments and prepare the overall course curriculum to ensure student engagement and retention of the important concepts and principles that will make a positive impact on students' career development. There are many tactics and approaches that can be used in engage net generation students. At the end of this chapter, we will share some of the approaches that we have used in class and which have received excellent feedback from the net generation students we have had in our classes.

CURRICULUM (RE)DESIGN: IDEAS AND SUGGESTIONS FOR INTEGRATING SOCIAL MEDIA

When we talk with our faculty colleagues about the growing phenomenon of social media, their reactions are often mixed. While some are fasci-

Table 16.1. Net Generation Eight Norms

Net generation students behave very different than their boomer parents. Tapscott (1998) contends that they possess eight norms that distinguished them from their boomer parents. These can be broadly defined as follows.

1. They prize freedom and freedom of choice.
2. They want to customize things, make them their own.
3. They are natural collaborators, who enjoy a conversation, not a lecture.
4. They will scrutinize you and your organization.
5. They insist on integrity.

nated with the trend, many are unsure of the real advantages and the impact it will make in the classroom and the ability of students to learn. Engaging with students via social technologies will require instructors to always be "on" and may even require them to relinquish certain level of control over the course content being discussed by students. It is often a difficult and risky first step to take. Consequently, we suggest that instructors invest time into planning and defining the key objectives that are important to them before diving into a total integration of social empowered course design. The following objectives help illustrate and provide some ideas on how instructors can integrate social media and the use of social technology in their courses (both online and traditional classroom course delivery).

SKILL BUILDING, TEACHING, AND INSTRUCTING

What it takes to be successful in organizations today is different in terms of the types of tools and approaches used to engage customers and retain their "business" over time. This is true for all organization, public and private, for-profit and not-for-profit. At our college, we consistently emphasize the importance of students developing effective communication skills and abilities. Building skills in both written and oral communication has been a primary focus in all of our business classes. With the constant use of texting to communicate ideas and information, students' communication skills can be impacted in both positive and negative ways. Writing and speaking in full, complete, meaningful sentences are skills which still need to be developed and nurtured as part of the learning process and course assignments in business classes. The challenge for business faculty becomes how to help students develop and refine their communication skills through: (1) synthesizing a great amount of information (and being able to critically evaluate what is valid and what is opinion or conjecture), (2) ensure relevance and clarity in communications, and (3) ensure that everyone who receives the information has a shared understanding of what was communicated. The processes that can be used to develop these essential skills have changed significantly.

For example, consider the rapid growth and escalation in the use of Twitter.com since its inception in 2006. From a business perspective, Twitter.com has had both positive and negative impacts on communication between individuals and between individuals and organizations. As Twitter is currently used, it focuses on "where someone is and what they are doing (or just did)." Often meaningless information is shared and can fall in the domain of "who cares that you just ate a hamburger for lunch." The learning point that becomes salient for business students in particular is the power of using social media like Twitter to keep everyone in the organization informed about relevant decisions or actions that have been taken, and doing this in a timely manner. In this context, Twitter can be used as a powerful tool for keeping everyone in the loop about small, but significant changes and decisions. For example, Twitter has the capability of keeping everyone up to date by describing what is happening right now in the organization. Short tweets can be sent to employees and team members that a brief, timely, and relevant information. This is a very valuable communication tool that can harness the power of the technology that organizational leaders can use to keep everyone up to date and aware of what is happening. This takes us beyond the "need to know" mentality of the past in which most employees and managers were kept in the dark about decisions and actions that had an impact on them personally. Or the information is delivered in "weekly staff meetings" or in summary e-mails with large distribution lists. When information is delivered weekly or through mass e-mail distributions, it may no longer be timely or helpful for the people who need to use it to make other decisions based on that information.

Another new organizational trend that has been recently highlighted (CNN, April, 2010) is the use of Twitter to post job openings. As described by CNN, qualified applicants are encouraged to send tweets in response to job openings which they are interested in pursuing. Using this approach, human resources staff and hiring managers can quickly sort through applicants and determine which individuals to follow up with and invite for an interview (either face to face or on Skype). Rather than culling through thousands of resumes to find the optimal candidates, 140 character messages sent to the human resource director can be sorted and assessed to determine which applicants to invite for a job interview or further assessment of their "fit" for the position and the organization. Since this is a new trend, it is unclear how widespread this recruitment process will become. This does, however, provide business faculty with another avenue to use social media in a meaningful way to continue to develop students' communication skills and ability to position themselves for jobs that fit their career goals. For example, business faculty teaching classes such as organizational behavior and human resource management can develop assignments in which students practice developing crisp and succinct messages which articulate their skills and abilities. In this type of assignment, instructors can have students write a 140 character message to Tweet to an employer describing their skills and talents and how well they "fit" with the job posting. Students can then share their 140 character messages with each other and learn from their peers in class by providing feedback to each other as well as learning from those students who wrote particularly effective 140 character messages.

ENGAGING AND ENERGIZING COMMUNICATIONS

Most faculty have had to address the challenges of student's texting during class and phones ringing in the middle of class lectures, cases, and even exams. It has been said that net generation students are often addicted to their technology devices and want the feeling of always being in contact with their network of friends. As an example of this addiction, it is now being reported on Twitter.com (April, 2010) that over 25% of people under at 25 keep their phones near their beds and when they wake up in the middle of the night, they check new posts and update their Facebook walls with new information. This may partially explain why students are interested in where others are eating lunch and who is at the mall right now, it gives a feeling of involvement in a larger community, even if they do not know the people in their network, they feel "a part" of something bigger then themselves.

Social factors and the feeling of being a part of something outside oneself becomes an important value that is related to the continuous use of technology for net generation students. The importance of social networks and the impact of internalizing the norms of one's reference or peer group is a well established phenomenon in the social psychology literature (Cartwright & Zander, 1968; Douglas, 1983; Feldman, 1984; Steiner, 1972; Turner, 2000). Business faculty can reinforce these, very human, needs and values in students and incorporate them into the design of the class and learning experiences. For example, assignments which focus students on Tweeting every time they observe someone exhibiting a specific leadership behavior that was reviewed in an organizational behavior class can be a way to engage the students in the learning process and reinforcing the point that leadership behaviors are occurring everyday all around you. Leadership behaviors are not the exclusive domain of someone in a formal position of power. Reinforcing this learning point about leadership is also consistent with net generation students who tend to highly value a lower power distance in their relationships.

POWER SHARING AND COCREATING KNOWLEDGE

Using social media tools can also give faculty a sense of being closer to their student's learning and seeing through the eyes of their students. Faculty who involve their students in the process of developing the examples that illustrate the concepts presented in class, can also learn from their students and expand their own understanding of what is important and relevant to their students. In traditional course design, instructors would identify or develop the examples that demonstrate the course concepts or select the cases that business students will analyze to ensure the learning points are clear. But the question becomes, clear to whom? Did the students really understand the linkages that were made between the concepts and the case by the faculty member and his/her analysis? Social media provides the students with many more venues to find their own "cases" and create the linkages to the course concepts. This reduces the power distance between the faculty and the students and allows students to collaborate with each other and with the instructor to make the learning points clear. Using this approach in the course design also reinforces the collaborative learning and cocreation of knowledge that is a key strength inherent in the design of social media tools.

SUPPORTING, REFLECTING AND CREATING A RICH LEARNING EXPERIENCE

In the global business context we are working in today, it is essential that our students understand how to engage others through using social tools and can critically reflect on the content they are viewing in their searches. Not everything on the web is completely true and "accurate." Students should learn to understand how to sort through information and establish networks of people who can provide them with reliable and valid information in order to draw accurate and relevant inferences from the information that is posted on the web.

Organizations use the web to post information and maintain websites that help to reinforce their brand in the market to attract and retain long term customer relationships. In this same regard, student need to understand that what they post on social media websites reflects their personal image and brand. Students need to be savvy about the impact of their "posts" and understand that images and messages can be saved indefinitely by others. What students have chosen to post on their Facebook account as sophomores may be very different than what they would choose to post as graduating seniors who are looking for their first professional position. Students need to understand the impact of their decisions can be just as long lasting as the impact of leaders/role models (think about Tiger Woods) on their "brand" and how customers perceive them. Students' personal brand is impacted by the choices they make when they post on their MySpace about how much they hate their professor of operations and blog about how they think their manager at the ice cream store they work at is a flaming #!$%#.

Learning about the importance of their personal brand through classroom discussions and through carefully designed assignments will help students develop their organizational savvy and professionalism. These skills can be developed through both formal classroom learning (e.g. assignments and reflections) as well as informal learning that occurs spontaneously in an unplanned way (e.g., students who find YouTube clips and send them to each other because they are funny and are related to the points that were discussed in class).

The use of social networking tools creates a rich learning experience for the students when faculty nurture and reinforce spontaneous informal learning that occurs (just by searching YouTube for examples). Consciously integrating informal learning opportunities as well as taking advantage of them when they emerge reinforces the importance of seeing the concepts being discussed in class "all around us." This is particularly relevant in a business context where we have seen many examples of new markets emerging based on customer requests and idea sharing (e.g., iPod that led to iphone and ipad; as well as the marketing of Window 7 as the product designed by users in the "this was my idea" commercial).

This process is related to Rogers (2003) theory of diffusion of innovation. In this theory, Rogers (2003) asserts that innovations are driven via communications among individuals in which they influence each other's perceptions. This is the process that faculty are looking to create in business classes to influence the perceptions of students to help them think critically and understand processes and systems that contribute to business effectiveness and ongoing innovation. In this case, social media serves as a tool that is used to influence how others in their network perceive information and form perceptions. Faculty who use social media will engage students in critically evaluating and understanding the tremendous power they have to impact others and learn from others through their social media interactions.

In addition, business faculty can spend time with their students and consistently reinforce the importance of how to use these social media to facilitate their opportunities and not limit their ability to be considered as a viable candidate for positions they are seeking. A simple, but highly relevant example that we often discuss in our classes is helping students understand that what they consider fun and entertaining posts (showing students partying with alcohol, drugs, and exhibiting behaviors that show poor taste/judgment), may be seen as a demonstration of poor judgment by hiring managers. Thinking through the need to set "privacy settings" high so that access is limited and overcoming the narcissistic need to "show your peers how cool you are" is essential for students to think through what pictures they post and what information they share for everyone to see. Thinking about the long term implications of choices and actions when posting to social media becomes significant in a business context since images can be stored and brought up later (without one's knowledge that this has happened). This is analogous to organizational leaders who spend significant amounts of time and money to carefully sculpt their images and select what is posted on their websites so that the reputation of the organization and its mission and values are congruent. Students need to learn the importance of these decisions in their personal use of social media. These broader issues become significant to help students understand how their own image and "brand" is impacted by each of these small choices and decisions that they may take for granted when they are using social media.

In summary, Table 16.2 provides a brief summary and examples of social media applications for different teaching purposes. The authors suggest that faculty members incorporate some level of social media component to meet the specific needs of their students.

Table 16.2.   Ideas for Incorporating Social Media in the Classroom

Faculty Objective	Social Media Applications	Success Measure
Skill building, teaching and instructing	Enable digital content for course material. Podcasts, instructional videos	Informing and instructing by providing real time information. Avoid miscommunications and allow students have access to the necessary course information and content.
Engaging, reinforcing and energizing	Research user generated content reflecting concepts and theories	Highlight topics from textbook. Increase awareness and understanding of concepts and foster teamwork. By researching upon current social communities, the process will help students understand the power of aggregated voices and collective intelligence.
Sharing and cocreating knowledge	Blogs, Wikis, online discussion forums, communities, and chats	Open, two-way conversations for effective collaboration and knowledge building. Deepen understanding of concepts allowing students to share opinions peer to peer. Increase conversations. Foster multiple avenues to communicate.
Supporting and Reflecting	Wikis, RSS feeds, social networks (e.g. Facebook, LinkedIn, YouTube, hi5, twitter)	Increase efficiency in answering to student questions, support the overall learning environment. Enrich learning experience. Foster two way communications.

INTEGRATING SOCIAL MEDIA TO FACILITATE LEARNING

There are many social media tools that can be integrated into the course assignments. Faculty can choose to integrate as many social media technologies as they are comfortable with. Social media approaches can be used to cover different learning outcomes. It can be used as a research tool to highlight topics from textbooks, to facilitate class discussion and to guide student thinking, or to expand upon theories and to create knowledge collaboratively. In this section, some examples are provided which describe how social media tools can be integrated into the curriculum to enhance student learning experience and retention of the concepts.

Example 1: Social Media Application in a Management Course

The authors of this chapter have designed a class assignment which serves as an example of an in-class project that requires collaborative work using social media content in an undergraduate organizational behavior class. The assignment given to the students was to identify a key motivation concept in the text (e.g. equity theory, needs theory, expectancy theory, etc.), and find a video clip on YouTube (or other media) that illustrates the motivation theory their team selected. Working in teams, the students created a one page summary which: (1) defined the theory their team selected on motivation, (2) discussed how the video clip was illustrative of that theory of motivation, and (3) described why the theory of motivation they selected was important to understand in order to motivate people in an organizational context. Each team presented their analysis to the class and then the all the students voted for the team's presentation that they felt was the clearest articulation of the motivational theory. This process reinforced collaborative learning and the cocreation of meaningful presentations on the concepts of motivation. The students had a great time doing the assignment and did not have to be subjected to a "boring" lecture on motivation. Even more important, their presentations and one-page summaries clearly showed that the students understood the concepts! What more could a faculty member want in a class, full engagement, and clear demonstration that the students understood the concepts, and everyone was laughing and having fun in the process.

Example 2: Use of Weblog in Reflective Learning Assignments in a Marketing Course

While YouTube is very useful for students to search for information through videos and rich media, Weblog is an excellent way to build content collaboratively. The purpose of this assignment is to help students understand some of the more difficult concepts and theories in a Consumer Behavior course. The assignment given to the students was to create a weekly online journal to reflect upon what they have learned and to expand upon the theories that have discussed in class. The students were expected to keep a weekly online journal that included: (1) what did they learn that was interesting and useful (pick a theory that was discussed in class or from the textbook), (2) explain why they find the theory interesting, (3) how can they apply the theory in the work place or in their personal lives, (4) suggest possible topics and factors that might influence the theory (it is recommended for students to link any related readings or web content to this topic), and (5) other comments and observations. These journals were visible and subscribed to by all the students. Each student was expected to contribute original content, read blogs written by their classmates, and provide feedback to further each other's critical thoughts.

Example 3: Blog Sites and SNS Used to Understand Branding

Another assignment encourages students to seek out brand impression formation from popular blog sites and social networking sites. The objective of this exercise is to help students understand how social media is an important phenomenon that has changed the traditional way of building public relations. It is also important to note that online conversations are becoming a powerful source of information for consumers; it requires companies to carefully monitor and shape conversations in order to satisfy their customers and maintain a consistent brand image online and offline. Students are to work in teams and prepare a one-page summary of reporting based on their research. The report included: (1) a reporting of impressions about the brand through various and popular online communities and social networks, (2) an analysis of brand congruency with the image that brand is attempting to communicate, (3) propose an action plan based on customer feedback and online communications, and (4) provide references to all the sites, online communities, and social networks that were visited.

The examples above have been provided to demonstrate how social media technology can be successfully incorporated into management and marketing courses. While the discussion has been on management and marketing courses, we believed that these learning activities are applicable to a wide range of business courses.

CONCLUSION

The evolution in student values and the importance of technology and being a part of a social network indicate the need for business faculty to make adjustments to redesign traditional curriculum to enhance engagement in the learning process (Feiertag & Berge, 2008; Greenhow, Robelia, & Hughes, 2009). At the beginning of this chapter, we shared a brief vignette about our student "David" and his need to respond to the blinking light on his iphone. We have all had "Davids" in our classes and have been frustrated in our attempts to keep their attention. Using strategies to harness students' desire to use their technology and respond immediately to the red blinking lights can be an opportunity for us as business educators. The challenge is how do we as educators take the energy that net generation students have for their technology and focus it into the learning process.

As with all professionals, it is crucial for business educators to continuously integrate innovative teaching methods and adopt new learning tools to facilitate engagement and reinforce the desire for lifelong learning in our students. The evolution of social media has grown to such an extent that it provides faculty with unique opportunities to support student learning and engagement. In the global business context, it is essential that students learn how to use social media to expand their approaches to solving problems and making decisions in collaborative ways, often without having face-to-face communication with their peers and others involved in the process (Minocha, 2009). Understanding the changing needs required to be effective in a wide range of organizations allows faculty to maintain their edge and provide their students with the learning opportunities that directly contribute to their long term effectiveness.

REFERENCES

Alch, M. (2000). The echo-boom generation: A growing force in American society. *Futurist, 34*(4), 42-46.

Brown, J. S. (2000). Growing up digital: How the web changes work, education, and the ways people learn. *Change,* 10-20.

Cartwright, D., & Zander, A. (1968). *Group dynamics: Research and theory.* New York, NY: Harper & Row.

Douglas, T. (1983). *Groups: Understanding people gathered together.* New York, NY: Tavistock Publications.

Feiertag, J., & Berge, Z.L. (2008). Training generation N: How educators should approach the net generation. *Education & Training, 50*(6), 457-464.

Feldman, D. C. (1984). The development and enforcement of group norms. *Academy of Management Review, 9*, 48-53.

Generation Y goes to work: Management. (2009). *The Economist, 390*(8612), 47-48.

Goodfellow, R., & Hewling, A. (2005). Reconceptualizing culture in virtual learning environments: From an "essentialist" to a "negotiated" perspective. *E-learning, 2(4)*, 356-368.

Greenhow, C., Robelia, B., & Hughes, J.E. (2009). Web 2.0 and classroom research: What path should we take now? *Educational Researcher, 38*(4), 246-259.

Hartman, J. L., Dziuban, C. & Brophy-Ellison, J. (2007). Faculty 2.0. *Educause Review, 42*(5), 62-76.

Jonassen, D., Mayes, T., & MacAleese, R. (1993). A manifesto for constructivist approaches to the use of technology in higher education. In T. M. Duffy, J. Lowyck, & D.H. Jonassen (Eds). *Design environments for constructive learning* (pp. 231-247). New York, NY: Springer Verlag.

Lankshear, C., & Knobel, M. (2003). *New literacies: Changing knowledge and classroom learning.* New York, NY: Open University Press.

Leung, L. (2004) Net-Generation attributes and seductive properties of the internet as predictors of online activities and internet addiction. *Cyber Psychology & Behavior. 7*(3), 333-348.

Mazman, S. G., & Usluel, Y. K. (2009). The usage of social networks in educational context. *International Journal of Behavioral, Cognitive, Educational, and Psychological Sciences, 1*(4), 224-228.

Minocha, S. (2009). Role of social software tools in education: A literature review. *Education & Training, 51*, 353-369.

The Ne(x)t generation. (2009). *Customer Relationship Management, 13*(1), 21.

Oblinger, D. G. (2005). Learners, learning, & technology. *Educause Review, 40*(5), 66-75.

Ophira, E., Nass, C., & Wagner, A.D. (2009). Cognitive control in media multitaskers. *Proceedings of the National Academy of Sciences, 106*, 33.

Rettie, R. (2002). Net generation culture. *Journal of Electronic Commerce Research, 3*(4), 254–264.

Rogers, E. (2003). *Diffusion of innovation.* New York: Free Press.

Rowlands, I., Nicholas, D., Williams, P., Huntington, P., Fieldhouse, M., Gunter, B., et al. (2008). The Google generation: The information behaviour of the researcher of the future. *Aslib Proceedings, 60*(4), 290-310.

Skiba, D. J., & Barton, A. J. (2006). Adapting your teaching to accommodate the net generation of learners. *The Online Journal of Issues in Nursing, 11*(2).

Steiner, I.D. (1972). *Group processes and productivity.* New York, NY: Academic Press.

Tapscott, D. (1998). *Growing up digital: The rise of the net generation.* New York: McGraw-Hill.

Tapscott, D. (1999a). Minds over matters. *Business 2.0*, 89-97.

Tapscott, D. (1999b). Educating the net generation. *Educational Leadership, 56*(5), 6-11.

Tapscott, D. (2007). Future web: The N-generation. *Index on Censorship, 4*, 51.

Tapscott, D.   (2008). The net generation takes the lead. *Business Week*, 21.

Turner, M. E. (2000). *Groups at work: Theory and research.* Mahwah, NJ: Erlbaum.

ABOUT THE AUTHORS

Geoff Archer is an associate professor on the Faculty of Management and the director of the Eric C. Douglass Centre for Entrepreneurial Studies at Royal Roads University in Victoria, British Columbia. Geoff has taught introductory business, entrepreneurship and environmental entrepreneurship to more than 2,000 students at Duke University's Nicholas School of the Environment, the Oregon Executive MBA program, the University of Virginia's McIntire School of Commerce and Oregon State University. His research interests include entrepreneurial opportunity, environmental entrepreneurship, microfinance, microfranchising, green microfinance, and cleantech venture capital.

Jo Axe is the associate dean in the Faculty of Management at Royal Roads University in Victoria, British Columbia. Bringing over 20 years business experience to the classroom, Jo has taught accounting and finance courses in the face-to-face, blended, and distance learning environments at both the undergraduate and graduate level. Her research interests include learning community development, student engagement in the online environment, and aboriginal postsecondary education.

Domen Bajde is an assistant professor of marketing at the Faculty of Economics, University of Ljubljana (FELU). He earned his PhD at FELU in 2006, after undergoing doctoral training at Lancaster University Management School (United Kingdom) and additional training in consumer culture research in Denmark (University of Southern Denmark) and Turkey (Bilkent University). He has lectured on marketing and consumer behavior at FELU (in Slovenia and Macedonia) and at the Vienna University of

337

Economics and Business (Austria). As a member of the European Commission project called COUNTER, he has recently investigated the cultural, economic and legal aspects of user-generated content in social media contexts (i.e., YouTube).

Vladlena Benson is a senior lecturer at the Faculty of Business and Law, Kingston University, United Kingdom. Vladlena's research interests include information management, e-learning and web technologies, including social networking. She has published a number of papers, books, and invited chapters in the area of information technology. Vladlena teaches managing information, information systems development and information security on postgraduate and undergraduate programs.

Thomas Bryer is assistant professor in the Department of Public Administration at the University of Central Florida. His research and teaching focuses on public participation, cross-sector collaboration and consensus building, and bureaucratic responsiveness. His work has been published in *Public Administration Review, Journal of Public Administration Research and Theory, Public Administration and Praxis, American Review of Public Administration, Public Performance and Management Review, International Journal of Public Participation*, and the *International Journal of Organization Theory and Behavior*. He has also published award winning teaching cases and simulations on the topics of public participation and collaboration. Dr. Bryer also serves as president of the Central Florida chapter of the American Society for Public Administration.

Guido Caicedo is a professor at ESPAE—Graduate School of Management and at the Electrical and Computer Engineering Department at Escuela Superior Politécnica del Litoral (ESPOL). He has worked on artificial intelligence and human computer interaction. He led the team that implemented an online coursework tool used at ESPOL. Recently he has been working on entrepreneurship and led the Entrepreneurship Center at ESPOL for several years. Ongoing research is focused on entrepreneurial competences and entrepreneurship education.

Baiyun Chen is an instructional designer at the University of Central Florida (UCF). She has worked with professors in diverse disciplines on integrating technologies into curriculum. Baiyun completed her PhD in education with an emphasis on instructional technology at UCF in 2007. Her research interests focus on using instructional strategies in online instruction, professional development for teaching online, and application of emerging technologies in teaching and learning.

Charlie C. Chen is an associate professor in the Department of Computer Information Systems at Appalachian State University. He received his PhD in management information systems from Claremont Graduate University in 2003. He has authored more than 50 referred articles and proceedings, presented at many professional conferences and venues. Dr. Chen has published in journals such as *Communications of Association for Information Systems, Behaviour and Information Technology, Journal of Knowledge Management Research Practice*, and *Journal of Information Systems Education*. Dr. Chen is also a project management professional (PMP) certified by the Project Management Institute. Dr. Chen likes to view the field of management information systems from infrastructural, managerial and operational perspectives. He is working on improving information system solutions in each of these three areas. His current main research areas are online learning, knowledge management, and supply chain technology.

Irvine Clarke III is a professor of marketing and the associate dean of academic affairs in the College of Business. He received his BSBA in marketing from the University of Richmond and his MBA and PhD from Old Dominion University. He currently teaches international marketing and marketing management to undergraduate and MBA students. Prior to joining JMU, he held the Freede Endowed Professorship of Teaching Excellence at Oklahoma City University. Dr. Clarke was recently named a JMU Madison Scholar and has received numerous research awards. He has taught at locations in Belgium, Canada, England, France, Germany, Malaysia, Mexico, Singapore, and the People's Republic of China and has 15 years of public and private sector organizational experience in various marketing areas. He also served as the faculty-member-in-residence for the JMU Study Abroad Program in Antwerp, Belgium. In 2009, Dr. Clarke was awarded the JMU Provost Award for Excellence in International Education. He currently serves on the editorial review boards of *Academy of Marketing Science Review, Industrial Marketing Management, International Marketing Review, Journal of Marketing Education, Health Marketing Quarterly*; also serving as section editor for *Marketing Education Review*.

Gary Coombs is an associate professor in the Management Systems Department of Ohio University's College of Business. Former director of the MBA program from 2002 to 2005, he has been actively engaged in innovations in curriculum development at both the undergraduate and graduate levels, including as a founding member of the development team that created Ohio University's award winning Integrated Business Cluster. He currently serves as the cluster coordinator. He has published and presented extensively in the area of management pedagogy, with a particular focus on problem-based learning methodologies. He served as an associate editor of the *Journal of Management Education* and also co-edited a special issue on problem-based learning. A second-time board member of OBTS: The Teaching Society for Management Educators, he is serving as chair of the communications committee and continues his long service as the administrator of the online discussion list, OBTS-L. He also serves on the business editorial board of the Multimedia Educational Resource for Learning and On-line Teaching.

Fragkiskos Filippaios is the international MBA course director at the Faculty of Business and Law, Kingston University, United Kingdom. He holds the responsibility for all international MBA programs offered by Kingston University London, in Russia, Greece, Cyprus, and India. The academic year 2007/2008 he was the Ministry of Economy and Finance Senior Research Fellow at the London School of Economics, where he still is a visiting fellow. He was awarded his PhD in 2004 by the Department of International and European Economic Studies, Athens University of Economics and Business.

Theresa B. Flaherty (University of Kentucky) is a professor of marketing and was recently named a Madison Scholar for excellence in scholarly achievement at James Madison University. She is a past recipient of the Kenneth Bartee Innovation in Teaching Award from the College of Business where she teaches principles of marketing, strategic internet marketing, integrated marketing communications, and information security ethics and policy. Prior to her work at JMU, she was a member of the marketing and e-commerce faculty at Old Dominion University. Dr. Flaherty has industry experience at the Rossborough Inn, JBI Customized Computer Solutions, California University of Pennsylvania's Entrepreneurial Assistance Center and Mon Valley Renaissance Program, IBM, and Service Corporation International. Dr. Flaherty is coeditor of the book entitled *Advances in Electronic Marketing* and her research has appeared in numerous journals. Dr. Flaherty is the Web Manager for *Marketing Education Review*, business portal editor for *MERLOT*, editor of the *Academy of Marketing Science Quarterly*, and serves on the review boards of various marketing journals. She also serves as a member of the Global Academic Panel for the Google Online Marketing Challenge. At JMU Dr. Flaherty is the faculty coadvisor for the March of Dimes Collegiate Council, a member of the Honor Council, and a member of the Judicial Council.

Caroline Flammer is assistant professor of management at Kean University. She holds a PhD in economics from the University of St. Gallen and was a visiting scholar at the Economics Department of New York University. Her research focuses on corporate social responsibility and the economics of education. She recently published a book on the sustainable financing of education in developing countries.

Walkyria Goode is a professor at ESPAE—Graduate School of Management at Escuela Superior Politécnica del Litoral. Her work is on human computer interaction and cognitive psychology. Recent projects include the use of online discussion forums in education, the effects of information displays on decision making and the influence of textual visualization on social impression management. Ongoing research is focused on the use of digital technology within a classroom setting for both primary and higher education and within teams.

Aditi Grover is an assistant professor at Plymouth State University, New Hampshire since 2008. She received her PhD in marketing from the Marshall School of Business, University of Southern California in 2008. She previously received her MBA in 1995 and has also spent a few years in the industry. Dr. Grover's research focus is on the adoption of new behaviors, and in understanding the role of emotions in advertising. Her current research aims to understand smokers' attitudes toward their own smoking and the likelihood of their quitting the habit. She has presented her work in various conferences, both in oral and written formats.

Hamid Kazeroony is the faculty development and quality control specialist at Walden College of Social and Behavioral Sciences. Walden is consistently ranked top-25 online graduate programs in the United States. Since 1999, he has taught various online Management graduate and undergraduate courses at University of Phoenix, South University, Piccolo International University, and developed online courses for Argosy DBA program, Piccolo graduate program, and Human Resource certification for William Penn University. Dr. Kazeroony regularly presents variety of multi-media tools for effective classroom facilitation and effective teaching and learning at academic conferences.

Allen H. Kupetz is the executive-in-residence at the Crummer Graduate School of Business, Rollins College in Winter Park, Florida. He teaches international business, entrepreneurship, and technology management courses. Crummer MBA students have twice voted him professor of the year. Kupetz is also a recognized thought leader on the present and future impact of technology on individuals and corporations. He regularly speaks to multimillion dollar firms in a wide variety of vertical markets about how they could use emerging technologies to enhance intracompany communications and customer dialog. He holds an MA in international relations from the University of Texas at Austin.

Jeanny Liu completed her doctoral research and received her PhD in marketing at the University of Turin, Italy. Currently, Dr. Liu is an assistant professor of marketing at University of La Verne. She is also the faculty adviser to the American Marketing Association La Verne Chapter and the faculty adviser to the Associated Student Government at the University of La Verne.

B. Dawn Medlin is the chairperson and associate professor of computer information systems in the John A. Walker College of Business at Appalachian State University. Her teaching, research, and consulting activities have primarily been in the areas of security, health care information systems, webpage development and design, and the interaction between computers and people. Dr. Medlin is very active in research activities and she has published her research in journals such as the *Journal of Computer Information Systems, International Journal of Information Security and Privacy, Journal of Information Technology Research, Journal of Information Privacy and Security, Information Systems Security: the (ISC)2 Journal,* as well as other national and international publications. Additionally, she had completed several funded research projects and served in several capabilities of leadership to many professional organizations.

Alanah Mitchell is an assistant professor of computer information systems in the John A. Walker College of Business at Appalachian State University. Her PhD is from the University of Nebraska at Omaha. Professor Mitchell's research focuses on collaboration through the use of technology and best practices for managing and using collaboration technologies in virtual and face-to-face teams. She has published in such journals as *Journal of the Association for Information Systems, Communications of the Association for Information Systems, Data Base for Advances in Information Systems,* and *American Journal of Business* as well as others.

Stephanie Morgan is the deputy head of Department, Leadership, HRM and Organisation, Faculty of Business and Law, Kingston University, United Kingdom. She is also the course director for the MSc in business and occupational psychology. She has a background in IT management, is a chartered psychologist, and has research interests in technology change, blended learning, and outsourcing.

Deborah Olson completed her masters and PhD in organizational psychology at Wayne State University. Dr. Olson is an assistant professor of management at the University of La Verne. She teaches classes in management and leadership for both graduate and undergraduate students. She has worked on course redesign to incorporate media and experiential learning in class assignments and led international travel study classes for both graduate and undergraduate students.

Eva Ossiansson is focusing on branding and communication in the consumption society and new media environments in her research and teaching. She is responsible for a master course in interactive market development in the marketing and consumption program. In this course students are responsible for managing virtual companies in a simulated environment (Simbiz). This course has been acknowledged both by Gothenburg University and the media for its innovative use of new technology in a pedagogical setting. She is also responsible for a new master course in Branding & Consumption Power 2.0 at the same master program, where branding and social media are interlinked. Facebook is used as the means of communication in this master course.

David W. Stewart is the dean of the A. Gary Anderson Graduate School of Management at the University of California, Riverside. Prior to assuming his responsibilities as dean in July of 2007 he was a member of the faculty of the Marshall School of Business at the University of Southern California where he held the Robert E. Brooker Chair in Marketing and served as deputy dean of the school for 5 years. Dr. Stewart is a past editor of both the *Journal of Marketing* and the *Journal of the Academy of Marketing Science*. Dr. Stewart has authored or coauthored more than 200 publications and seven books. His most recent book, *Marketing Champions* (Wiley 2006), focuses on how the marketing function can increase its influence and business impact. Dr. Stewart's research has examined a wide range of issues including marketing strategy, the analysis of markets, consumer information search and decision making, effectiveness of marketing communications, public policy issues related to marketing and methodological approaches to the analysis of marketing data. His research and commentary are frequently featured in the business and popular press. A native of Baton Rouge, Louisiana, Professor Stewart received his BA from the Northeast Louisiana University (now the University of Louisiana at Monroe) and his MA and PhD in psychology from Baylor University. In 2007, Dr. Stewart was award the Elsevier Distinguished Marketing Scholar Award by the Society for Marketing Advances and in 2006, Dr. Stewart was honored by the Academy of Marketing Science with the Cutco/Vector Distinguished Educator Award for lifetime contributions to marketing. In 2005, he received the Omicron Delta Kappa Men of Merit Award from his alma mater, Baylor University.

Charles Wankel is an associate professor of management at St. John's University, New York. He received his doctorate from New York University. Dr. Wankel has authored and edited many books including the best-selling *Management*, 3rd ed. (Prentice-Hall, 1986), *Rethinking Management Education for the 21st Century* (IAP, 2002), *Educating Managers with Tomorrow's Technologies* (IAP, 2003), *The Cutting Edge of International Management Education* (IAP, 2004), *Educating Managers through Real World Projects* (IAP, 2005), New *Visions of Graduate Management Education* (IAP, 2006), the *Handbook of 21st Century Management* (SAGE, 2008), and *Being and Becoming a Management Education Scholar* (IAP, 2008). He is the leading founder and director of scholarly virtual communities for management professors, currently directing eight with thousands of participants in more than seventy nations. He has taught in Lithuania at the Kaunas University of Technology (Fulbright Fellowship) and the University of Vilnius, (United Nations Development Program and Soros Foundation funding). Invited lectures include 2005 Distinguished Speaker at the E-ducation without Border Conference, Abu Dhabi and 2004 Keynote speaker at the Nippon Academy of Management, Tokyo. Corporate management development program development clients include McDonald's Corporation's Hamburger University and IBM Learning Services. Pro bono consulting assignments include reengineering and total quality management programs for the Lithuanian National Postal Service.

Natalie T. Wood earned her PhD from Auburn University and is now an associate professor of marketing, Erivan K. Haub School of Business, Saint Joseph's University. Professor Wood has published in journals such as *The Journal of Consumer Behaviour, Marketing Education Review, The International Journal of Internet Marketing and Advertising* and *The Journal of Website Promotion*. She is the coeditor of *Virtual Social Identity and Consumer Behavior* published by M.E. Sharpe and is the author of the *Marketing in Virtual Worlds* published by Prentice Hall. She is also an advisory editor for the *Journal of Virtual Worlds Research*.

Xiaolong Yang is currently an executive MBA student at Kean University. He has extensive consulting experience including 8 years of experience in e-learning platform training and consulting.

Suling Zhang is an assistant professor at Kean University in New Jersey. She received her PhD in information systems from New Jersey Institute of Technology. Her research areas are global teams and virtual team leadership. She is expanding her research portfolio to include social media. She has been publishing in several IS journals and presented at various IS conferences.